Sanjay Goel · Paulo Roberto Nunes de Souza
Editors

Digital Forensics and Cyber Crime

14th EAI International Conference, ICDF2C 2023
New York City, NY, USA, November 30, 2023
Proceedings, Part II

Editors
Sanjay Goel (ID)
University of Albany
Albany, GA, USA

Paulo Roberto Nunes de Souza (ID)
Universidade Federal do Espírito Santo
Alegre, Brazil

ISSN 1867-8211   ISSN 1867-822X (electronic)
Lecture Notes of the Institute for Computer Sciences, Social Informatics
and Telecommunications Engineering
ISBN 978-3-031-56582-3   ISBN 978-3-031-56583-0 (eBook)
https://doi.org/10.1007/978-3-031-56583-0

This Springer imprint is published by the registered company Springer Nature Switzerland AG
The registered company address is: Gewerbestrasse 11, 6330 Cham, Switzerland

Paper in this product is recyclable.

Preface

We are delighted to introduce the proceedings of the fourteenth edition of the European Alliance for Innovation (EAI) International Conference on Digital Forensics & Cyber Crime (ICDF2C), held in New York in 2023. This conference brought together researchers, developers, and practitioners from around the world who are exploring, producing, and applying scientific knowledge to the broad area of Digital Forensics and Cyber Crime. This year's conference focused on emerging topics, including the use of Artificial Intelligence and Machine Learning in Digital Forensics and Cyber Security.

The technical program of ICDF2C 2023 consisted of 34 full papers covering a selection of aspects of the field. The conference sessions were grouped according to the main topics being discussed: crime profile analysis and fact-checking; cybersecurity and forensics; information hiding; machine learning; password, authentication, and cryptography; and vulnerabilities. Apart from the high-quality technical paper presentations, the technical program also featured the keynote speech by Sanjay Goel from the University at Albany. In his keynote speech, Sanjay Goel teased the audience by wondering about the current and future possibilities and, also, threats to the use of artificial intelligence in digital forensics and cybercrime.

Coordination with the steering chairs, Imrich Chlamtac, Sanjay Goel, and Pavel Gladyshev, was essential for the success of the conference. We sincerely appreciate their constant support and guidance. It was also a great pleasure to work with such an excellent organizing committee team for their hard work in organizing and supporting the conference. In particular, the Technical Program Committee, led by our TPC Co-Chairs, Pavel Gladyshev, Daryl Johnson, and Nikolay Albayev, completed the peer-review process of technical papers and made a high-quality technical program. We are also grateful to the Conference Manager, Radka Vasileiadis, for her support and to all the authors who submitted their papers to the ICDF2C conference.

We strongly believe that the ICDF2C conference provides a good forum for all researchers, developers, and practitioners to discuss all science and technology aspects relevant to digital forensics and cybercrime, as indicated by the contributions presented in this volume.

Sanjay Goel
Paulo Roberto Nunes de Souza

Organization

Steering Committee

Sanjay Goel	University at Albany, SUNY, USA
Pavel Gladyshev	University College Dublin, Ireland

Organizing Committee

General Chair

Sanjay Goel	University at Albany, SUNY, USA

General Co-chair

Paulo Nunes	Universidade Federal do Espírito Santo, Brazil

TPC Chairs and Co-chairs

Pavel Gladyshev	University College Dublin, Ireland
Daryl Johnson	Rochester Institute of Technology, USA
Nikolay Akatyev	Horangi, Singapore

Publications Chair

Paulo Nunes	Universidade Federal do Espírito Santo, Brazil

Technical Program Committee

Ahmed Shosha	Microsoft, UK
Akib Shahriyar	Rochester Institute of Technology, USA
Anca Delia Jurcut	University College Dublin, Ireland
Andreas Wespi	IBM Zurich Research Laboratory, Switzerland
Aniello Castiglione	University of Naples Parthenope, Italy
Babak Habibnia	University College Dublin, Ireland
Bill Stackpole	Rochester Institute of Technology, USA

Zhenyu Na   Dalian Maritime University, China
Mu Zhou   Brunel University London, China
Zichuan Yi   University of Electronic Science and Technology
                     of China, China
Yuanquan Hong   Shaoguan University, China
Mingxiang Guan   Shenzhen Institute of Information Technology,
                     China
Jingdan Zhang   Shenzhen Institute of Information Technology,
                     China

Contents – Part II

Cybersecurity and Forensics

Contents – Part I

Machine Learning

Password, Authentication and Cryptography

A Quantum Physics Approach for Enabling Information-Theoretic Secure Communication Channels

Ivan Cvitić[(⊠)] [iD] and Dragan Peraković [iD]

Faculty of Traffic and Transport Sciences, University of Zagreb, Vukelićeva 4, 10000 Zagreb, Croatia
{ivan.cvitic,dragan.perakovic}@fpz.unizg.hr

Abstract. Quantum communication, a field of applied quantum physics, is closely tied to quantum teleportation and quantum information processing, with a primary focus on leveraging the laws of quantum mechanics to secure communication systems. An intriguing application within this field is the protection of information channels from unauthorized eavesdropping through the implementation of quantum cryptography. Quantum key distribution (QKD) represents the most advanced and well-known application of quantum cryptography. QKD utilizes quantum mechanical effects for cryptographic tasks and breaking cryptographic systems. This study aims to explore the potential of employing quantum mechanics laws to enhance the security of communication systems. The QKD system operates on a simple principle, where two parties, Alice (the sender) and Bob (the receiver), utilize individual photons randomly polarized to represent bits 0 and 1, respectively. These photons are used to transmit a series of random numbers, serving as cryptographic keys. The parties are connected via classical and quantum channels, with Alice generating a random stream of qubits transmitted through the quantum channel. By performing classical operations over the classical channel, Alice and Bob verify if any eavesdropping attempts have occurred during qubit transfer. The presence of an eavesdropper is identified through the imperfect correlation between the two sets of bits obtained after qubit transmission. A vital aspect of robust encryption schemes is the utilization of true randomness, which can be easily generated using quantum optics. Quantum communication holds promising applications in diverse sectors, including banking, government, industry, and military domains. This research seeks to investigate the possibilities of leveraging quantum mechanics laws to fortify communication systems' security.

Keywords: Quantum Communication · Quantum Cryptography · Quantum Key Distribution (QKD) · Eavesdropping Prevention · Secure Communication Systems

1 Introduction

In today's interconnected world, where information is the lifeblood of communication, ensuring its secure transmission has become a paramount concern. Traditional methods of data encryption and transmission, based on classical algorithms, are susceptible to

S. Goel and P. R. Nunes de Souza (Eds.): ICDF2C 2023, LNICST 571, pp. 3–22, 2024.
https://doi.org/10.1007/978-3-031-56583-0_1

various security threats and vulnerabilities. To address these limitations, researchers and scientists have turned to the remarkable principles of quantum mechanics, seeking to leverage its inherent properties to enable information-theoretic security.

The fundamental laws of quantum mechanics govern the behavior of particles at the microscopic level, providing a unique framework for encoding, transmitting, and decrypting information in a highly secure manner. Quantum communication and quantum cryptography have emerged as promising fields, aiming to exploit quantum phenomena to guarantee the confidentiality and integrity of transmitted data.

This scientific paper investigates the utilization of a quantum mechanics approach for enabling information-theoretic security. The objective is to explore the potential of harnessing quantum properties, such as superposition and entanglement, to develop robust cryptographic protocols and communication systems resistant to eavesdropping and cyber attacks.

The focus of this research is on analyzing the possibilities of utilizing the principles of quantum physics to enhance the security of information transmission and enabling Information-theoretical secure communication channel. The study will delve into the theoretical foundations of quantum communication, including quantum key distribution and quantum teleportation, while also examining practical implementations and ongoing research in the field.

By leveraging the unique properties of quantum mechanics, this research aims to pave the way for a new era of secure communication systems, revolutionizing the landscape of information exchange and ensuring confidentiality in an increasingly interconnected world.

2   Related Research

In recent years, significant research efforts have been devoted to exploring various aspects of quantum cryptography and its practical implementation. This section discusses key findings and advancements from a selection of relevant scientific papers, shedding light on the asymptotic analysis of quantum cryptographic protocols, public key distribution, practical challenges in quantum key distribution (QKD), dynamic routing for QKD networks, and the challenges and future research issues in quantum key distribution networks.

In the research [1] the authors perform an asymptotic analysis of a three-state quantum cryptographic protocol. The research focuses on understanding the protocol's behavior in terms of key rates and security limits as the system parameters scale. However, the paper does not delve into practical considerations or the impact of implementation constraints on the protocol's performance.

Paper [2] explores the fundamentals of quantum cryptography, with a specific focus on public key distribution and coin tossing protocols. It provides insights into the security guarantees offered by quantum cryptography schemes and compares them to classical cryptographic methods. However, the study primarily addresses theoretical aspects and lacks an in-depth analysis of practical challenges and potential vulnerabilities in real-world scenarios.

Addressing practical challenges, research [3] investigates various factors impacting the implementation of QKD systems. The study highlights issues such as detector inefficiencies, noise sources, and channel losses, which can significantly affect the performance and security of QKD systems. Nonetheless, the paper does not extensively discuss potential mitigation strategies or alternative solutions to overcome these challenges.

Paper [4] focuses on the design and optimization of routing protocols for QKD networks. It explores dynamic routing strategies that adapt to changing network conditions and aims to improve the efficiency and security of quantum key distribution. However, the paper does not address specific practical considerations, scalability challenges, or the potential impact of routing decisions on overall network performance.

Research [5] examines the challenges and future research issues in quantum key distribution networks from a security perspective. It discusses topics such as key management, authentication, and the integration of QKD with classical cryptographic systems. However, the paper lacks a comprehensive analysis of practical implementation challenges and the potential impact on network scalability and performance.

While these papers contribute valuable insights into various aspects of quantum cryptography and key distribution networks, they often focus on theoretical analyses or specific aspects of the protocols. Further research is needed to address practical challenges, scalability issues, and real-world limitations in order to pave the way for the broader adoption and deployment of quantum key distribution systems.

3 Overview of Quantum Communication Prerequisites

Quantum communication, rooted in applied quantum physics and closely tied to quantum information processing and quantum teleportation, presents significant applications, notably in quantum cryptography for safeguarding information channels against eavesdropping [1]. Quantum Key Distribution (QKD) stands as a prominent application. Quantum communication harnesses the principles of quantum physics to protect data, with particles like photons assuming superposition states, representing multiple 1 and 0 combinations simultaneously, referred to as qubits [2]. Both classical and quantum channels link the sender (Alice) and receiver (Bob), with the remarkable feature being the traceable interference by unauthorized observers (Eve) without altering the fragile quantum state of qubits. Quantum communication integrates classical and quantum information theory, utilizing mathematical tools from group theory, probability theory, and quantum statistical physics. While parallels with classical information theory exist, quantum information theory unveils unique consequences due to its connection between information and physics, enabling the study of communication limitations through quantum channels [3, 4].

Quantum information refers to information stored in very small structures called qubits. Qubits can be constructed from any quantum system that possesses two states. The central idea is to replace the classical bit, which can take one of two values, 0 or 1, with a quantum two-level system described in terms of two orthonormal state vectors, $|0>$ and $|1>$, which span a two-dimensional Hilbert space that encompasses all possible linear combinations, $a|0> + b|1>$, where $a, b \in C$ and $|a|^2 + |b|^2 = 1$ [5].

Every operation on quantum information, whether storage or transmission, can be represented as a quantum channel: a completely positive map that preserves trace-transforming states (density matrices) at the sender's end into states at the receiver's end. Often, the desired channel "S" that Alice and Bob (the sender and receiver) would like to implement is not readily available, usually due to the detrimental effects of noise, limited technology, or insufficient funding. They may attempt to simulate the channel "S" with another available channel "T". The capacity of the quantum channel can be denoted as Q (T, S). It quantifies how well this simulation can be performed, in terms of the limitation of long input sequences, so that Alice and Bob can exploit shared advantage before and after processing. Higher capacities may result if Alice and Bob are allowed to utilize additional resources in the process, such as classical side channels or ensembles of maximally entangled pairs shared between them [6].

A quantum channel transforms input systems described by Hilbert space H1 into output systems described by Hilbert space H2. Typically, H2 is assumed to be identical to H1. Mathematically, it is represented by a completely positive, unitary map "T" acting on a density operator ρ as:

$$T(\rho) = \sum_{j=1}^{n} E_j \rho E_j^{\dagger} \tag{1}$$

Here, E_j represents the Kraus operators, which satisfy:

$$\sum_j E_j^{\dagger} E_j < II \tag{2}$$

The capacity of a channel quantifies the number of qubits that can be reliably transmitted. For an ideal channel, we have $T = I$, the identity operation. The channel capacities of quantum channels are fully understood only for special cases. For instance, the Holevo-Schumacher-Westmoreland (HSW) theorem provides the capacity of the channel when only input product states are used [7].

3.1 Quantum Entanglement

Quantum communication centers on qubits, quantum counterparts of classical bits, which can exist as '0' and '1' superpositions. Quantum networks aim to entangle qubits across devices, serving various applications, notably encryption. Entangled entities' correlated measurements allow secret code generation through observed qubit states [8]. Classical networks transmit data, while quantum networks generate entanglement, often utilizing Bell states [9]. Particles can entangle to show instantaneous opposing states despite distance, but predicting states pre-measurement is impossible, necessitating a classical channel for communication via entanglement. Quantum teleportation, including classical data exchange, is exemplified by the Ekert (E91) protocol. Quantum entanglement shows interconnection between particles even across vast distances, crucial for quantum communication and computing [10].

Quantum physics dictates that an unobserved photon simultaneously occupies all possible states, collapsing to a single state upon measurement. Entanglement occurs when particles, like photons, physically interact, often produced via a crystal-split laser beam. These entangled photon pairs can span vast distances. The EPR paradox, formulated by Einstein, Podolsky, and Rosen in 1935, aimed to expose incongruities in quantum mechanics. It involves two entangled particles whose simultaneous measurement implies faster-than-light communication, challenging relativity. The paradox illustrates the tension between quantum mechanics and established laws, highlighting a need for additional variables to supplement the theory [11].

3.2 Concept of Bell States

The term "Bell states" or "EPR pairs" effectively delineates one of the four entangled quantum states of a qubit pair, collectively recognized as the four "Bell states". Two Bell states engender an identical superposition, wherein both qubits conclude in the same state upon measurement, with a 50% probability of both assuming either the $|0\rangle$ or $|1\rangle$ state. The other two Bell pairs likewise yield an equivalent superposition, causing both qubits to culminate in opposing states upon measurement. Consequently, when the first qubit is measured in the $|0\rangle$ state, the second qubit will be measured in the $|1\rangle$ state, and vice versa [11].

Table 1. Representation of the Bell state symbol and its associated mathematical notation [12]

Bell states symbol	Mathematical notation
$|\Phi^+\rangle$	$\dfrac{|00\rangle+|11\rangle}{\sqrt{2}}$
$|\Phi^-\rangle$	$\dfrac{|00\rangle-|11\rangle}{\sqrt{2}}$
$|\Psi^+\rangle$	$\dfrac{|01\rangle+|10\rangle}{\sqrt{2}}$
$|\Psi^-\rangle$	$\dfrac{|01\rangle-|10\rangle}{\sqrt{2}}$

In each of the Bell pairs, upon measuring one of the two qubits, we immediately ascertain the state of the other qubit upon measurement. If we consider one of the $|\Phi+\rangle$ or $|\Phi-\rangle$ states, as depicted in Table 1, it can be deduced that these are two Bell pairs in which both qubits must conclude in the same state upon measurement. When the first qubit is measured in the state $|0\rangle$, it is evident that the second qubit must also be in the same state, regardless of whether the qubits are separated by an infinite distance or measured in immediate succession. In either case, both qubits must be in the $|0\rangle$ state [12].

Bell states represent a rather straightforward example of entanglement; nevertheless, they find widespread application in both theoretical and experimental domains. Despite their simplicity, considering potential generalizations of Bell states is valuable for numerous applications. A significant body of work in this direction is focused on exploring entanglement among multiple qubits, as this approach is particularly suited for certain applications such as quantum computing [13].

3.3 Concept of Quantum Teleportation

Quantum teleportation, presented in Fig. 1, has a significant role within the realm of quantum communication research. Quantum teleportation represents a technique for transmitting quantum information from a source to a destination by utilizing entangled states [14].

Quantum teleportationn entails a method by which the state of one qubit is effectively replaced by the state of another. Its nomenclature, seemingly transcendent, derives from the fact that the state is "transferred" through the establishment of an entangled state space involving three qubits, followed by the disentanglement of two qubits (via measurement). Owing to the conservation of information through these measurements, said "information" (i.e., state) becomes localized within the final third qubit at the destination. Notably, this transference transpires without direct interaction between the source (initial) and destination (third) qubits. Interaction is facilitated through entanglement [14].

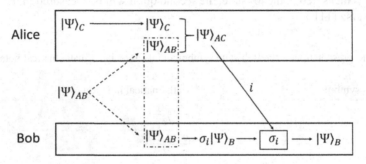

Fig. 1. Schematic of quantum teleportation algorithm [15]

As presented in Fig. 1, entangled state AB is split so that particle A goes to Alice and B to Bob. Alice then entangles A and C, disentangling B and sending Bob the information he needs to recover the state of C on the other end [15].

4   Application of Quantum Mechanics for Cryptographic Key Distribution

Cryptography is the process of encrypting and safeguarding data in such a manner that only an individual possessing the correct secret key can decrypt it. Quantum cryptography diverges from conventional cryptographic systems by relying on physics rather than mathematics as a central facet of its security framework. Quantum cryptography is grounded in the phenomena of quantum physics, enabling secure transmission of data between sender and receiver. It constitutes a revolutionary advancement in the realm of network security. It is a contemporary and advanced branch of cryptography, rooted in two quintessential quantum tenets: Heisenberg's Uncertainty Principle and the principle of photon polarization [16].

Quantum cryptography likely represents the fastest-growing domain within quantum information science. Novel theoretical protocols are routinely devised, security proofs continuously refined, and experiments progressively evolve from laboratory demonstrations of newfound capabilities to field implementations and technological prototypes [17].

It represents an encryption method harnessing the inherent properties of quantum mechanics to ensure the transmission of data impervious to hacking. It is a system that is utterly secure against compromise without the sender's or receiver's knowledge. In other words, copying or viewing data encoded in a quantum state is impossible without alerting the sender or recipient. Quantum cryptography is also expected to remain resilient against adversaries wielding quantum computing. It employs individual light particles or photons to transmit data via optical fibers. Photons represent binary bits. System security is contingent upon quantum mechanics, encompassing the following secure attributes:

- Particles can exist in more than one place or state simultaneously.
- Quantum properties cannot be observed without altering or disturbing them. Entire particles cannot be duplicated.
- These attributes prevent the measurement of a quantum state of any system without perturbing it.

Photons are chosen for quantum cryptography due to their provision of requisite qualities: their behavior is well understood, and they serve as information carriers in optical fiber cables. One of the most notable instances of quantum cryptography is QKD, furnishing a secure means of exchanging keys, elucidated in detail in the subsequent chapter [16].

Quantum cryptography can also prove valuable in safeguarding private information while facilitating public decision-making. A classical instance of such discrete decision-making is the "dating problem", where two individuals seek to arrange a date if and only if they each like the other, without disclosing further information. For instance, if Bob likes Alice but Alice does not reciprocate the sentiment, the date should be canceled without Alice discovering Bob's interest (conversely, it is logical that Bob will discern that Alice is not interested, as the date would ultimately be canceled) [18].

4.1 Overview of Differences Between the Classical and Quantum Cryptography

The primary distinction between quantum cryptography and classical cryptography resides in the fact that Quantum Key Distribution Protocols (QKDPs) employ quantum mechanics for session key distribution and public discussions to verify eavesdropping attempts and validate the correctness of the session key. In the case of public discussions, additional communication rounds are requisite between sender and receiver, whereas classical cryptographic approaches employ more efficient techniques for key verification and user authentication.

Classical cryptography involves mathematically encoding data to ensure that only individuals possessing the appropriate key can decipher it. Modern cryptography is rooted in principles of data integrity, authentication, non-repudiation, and confidentiality. This cryptographic approach finds applications in crucial domains like e-commerce, ATMs, computer passwords, and various other contexts. Traditional cryptography encompasses symmetric and asymmetric key distribution. Symmetric key algorithms use a single key for both encryption and decryption, while asymmetric cryptography employs a pair of keys—one public for encryption and one private for decryption [18].

Table 2. Representation of the Bell state symbol and its associated mathematical notation [16]

Classical Cryptography	Quantum Cryptography
Relies on logic based on digital logic	Relies on quantum theory
Transmits digital signals using bits	Transmits data using particles or photons
Range is not dependent on infrastructure	Range depends on infrastructure
Encryption is based on mathematical algorithms	Encryption is based on quantum properties

The security of traditional cryptographic methods is attributed to the impractical timeframes classical computers would require to generate the complex public and private keys [18].

Classical cryptography essentially involves converting plain text into encoded text through various machine learning algorithms. Keys used for data decryption are shared between sender and receiver to enable message encryption or decryption [16]. As depicted in Table 2, in contrast to traditional cryptography which is founded upon mathematical principles, quantum cryptography is rooted in the laws of quantum mechanics. While traditional cryptography relies on mathematical computation, quantum cryptography is significantly more challenging to decipher due to even the minutest act of observing the involved photons altering their anticipated outcomes, rendering both the sender and the receiver aware of the presence of eavesdroppers. Quantum cryptography also typically necessitates an interconnected infrastructure, as the process involves optical cables and repeaters at specific intervals to amplify the signal [16].

4.2 Quantum Cryptography Key Distribution

Key distribution is a critical process of sharing encrypted keys between parties, typically achieved through in-person or remote methods. The conventional approach involves secure in-person exchanges or remote mechanisms like RSA, Diffie-Hellman, and ciphers. However, these methods face vulnerabilities due to simplistic mathematical computations, potential third-party access, and the imminent impact of quantum computing on their security. QKD presents a robust alternative, utilizing quantum physics principles to exchange cryptographic keys securely, ensuring verification and confidentiality. QKD enables parties to generate and share keys for encryption and decryption, establishing Information-theoretic Secure (ITS) communication channels. A QKD system comprises classical and quantum channels, where the former mirrors conventional networks, and the latter, a lossy optical path, serves for probabilistic qubit transmission and necessitates transparency. Quantum computing advancements render traditional public-key encryption strategies insecure and outdated [16, 18]. QKD operates on a level significantly distinct from conventional key distribution in that it leverages a quantum system, relying on fundamental laws of physics for data protection, rather than mathematics. For instance, the No-Cloning Theorem stipulates that it is impossible to create identical copies of an unknown quantum state, preventing attackers from simply copying data in the same way network traffic can be copied today. Furthermore, if an attacker interferes with or observes the system, it will alter in a way that the interested parties will detect. This process is resistant to increased processing power [19]. QKD provides a means to distribute and share secret keys required for cryptographic protocols. Ensuring that these keys remain private, i.e., between communicating parties, is pivotal. To achieve this, reliance is placed on what was once deemed a problem of quantum systems; if you "observe" or disturb them in any way, you "break" their quantum characteristics. Typically, information is encoded on individual photons, as illustrated in Fig. 2. Alice can choose to encode them into a "sequence of bits" using one of two states, such as vertical (V) or horizontal (H) polarization and can also opt to encode in two different states: here, two combinations of these states denoted as +45° and −45°.

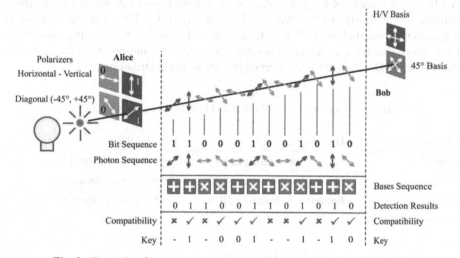

Fig. 2. Example of exchanging a cryptographic material using QKD [19]

Bob then selects measurement in one of two bases—what we term measurements H, V, or measurements +45°, −45°. If he measures in a base different from the one Alice used for preparation, his response will be random and discarded. However, if they choose the same, their results will be perfectly correlated; Alice sends H, and Bob reveals H, preserving these. This final step necessitates Alice and Bob communicating about which base was used but not revealing information about the outcome, which now becomes the secret key. This is just one method, but now there exist numerous variations.

4.3 Overview of QKD Approaches

In the realm of QKD, two fundamental methodologies emerge, each capitalizing on distinct attributes of quantum information carriers. The first, Discrete Variable QKD

(DV-QKD), revolves around particles as the vehicles of information. In this paradigm, quantum bits, or qubits, are encoded using the discrete quantum states of individual photons. The inherent properties of these photons, such as polarization or photon number, serve as the basis for encoding information. DV-QKD exploits the peculiarities of quantum mechanics, like superposition and entanglement, to securely transmit cryptographic keys. Notably, the no-cloning theorem guarantees that unauthorized parties cannot replicate these quantum states without altering their integrity, providing a robust foundation for secure communication. The entangled nature of qubits also enables the detection of eavesdroppers, ensuring a high level of security.

Continuous Variable QKD (CV-QKD) operates within the wave domain, harnessing the continuous nature of light waves to encode and transmit information. In this approach, the amplitude and phase quadratures of light waves are manipulated to carry information. CV-QKD systems leverage coherent states of light, typically produced by lasers, and modulate the amplitude and phase of these states to encode data. The continuous nature of the signal allows for high information rates and efficient transmission. Moreover, CV-QKD systems can be integrated into existing optical communication infrastructure, enabling compatibility with conventional optical networks. This approach introduces unique challenges, such as dealing with the effects of noise and maintaining the security of continuous-variable protocols. However, the flexibility and potential for high data rates make CV-QKD an attractive avenue for secure key distribution.

Table 3. Comparison of DV-QKD and CV-QKD characteristics [20]

Characteristics	DV-QKD	CV-QKD
Source	Single photons/dimmed laser	Weakly modulated laser
Detector	Single photon detector (SPD)	Homodin's detectors
Protocol	Bennett and Brassard (BB84)	Silberhorn, Grangier
ITS enabled	yes	no

In summary, the dual paradigms of DV-QKD and CV-QKD showcase the diverse ways in which quantum properties can be harnessed for secure key distribution, which is shown in Table 3. While DV-QKD exploits the particle-like attributes of photons, CV-QKD delves into the continuous wave nature of light to facilitate secure communication. Both approaches contribute to the ongoing advancement of quantum cryptography, paving the way for more secure and efficient communication protocols in the quantum era.

4.4 Comparison of Currently Used QKD Protocols

The majority of QKD protocols exhibit a similar fundamental structure, as illustrated in Fig. 3. The subsequent steps occur over a classical channel—a conventional public communication channel that is assumed to be susceptible to eavesdropping but not message insertion or alteration [21].

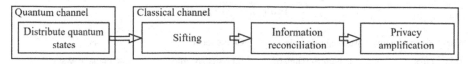

Fig. 3. Generic structure of QKD system [21]

Hence, it is ensured that the protocol's security endures perpetually, rather than being contingent upon the emergence of an exceptionally potent decryption mechanism. This enduring security foundation rests upon the unassailable tenets of physics, particularly the principles of quantum mechanics, rather than being confined to pragmatic limitations inherent in real-world implementations.

As a result, the protocol's imperviousness to breach remains indefinitely, guided by the unalterable precepts of quantum mechanics. In effect, the protocol's resilience prevails until such time as any potential contradictions or revisions within the realm of quantum mechanics are conclusively established. This underlines the protocol's overarching security, decoupled from transient factors, ensuring the continued confidentiality of communicated information [22]. Table 4 provides a comparison of QKD protocols based on their key attributes.

Table 4. Comparison of QKD protocols [22]

Year	Protocol name	Working principle	Characteristics	Authors
1984	BB84	Heisenberg's Uncertainty Principle	Utilizes the state of photon polarization for information transmission. Encompasses four polarization states (0°, 45°, 90°, 135°)	C:H.Bennet i G. Brassard
1991	E91	Quantum Entanglement	Utilizes entangled photon pairs	Ekert A.K
1992	BB92	Heisenberg's Uncertainty Principle	The sole distinction from BB84 lies in the requirement of only two states instead of four polarization states, i.e., (0°, 45°)	C.H. Bennett
1999	SSP	Heisenberg's Uncertainty Principle	This is the BB84 protocol with an extended basis, encompassing six states: $\pm x$, $\pm y$, $\pm z$ on the Poincaré sphere	Bechmann-Pasquinucci.H i Gisin.N

(continued)

Table 4. (*continued*)

Year	Protocol name	Working principle	Characteristics	Authors
2003	DPS	Quantum Entanglement	It boasts specific advantages, including a straightforward configuration, efficient utilization of the temporal domain, and resilience against Photon Number Splitting (PNS) attacks	K.Inoue, E.Waks i Y.Yamanoto
2004	SARG04	Heisenberg's Uncertainty Principle	It is equivalent to BB84 but exhibits increased robustness when employing dimmed laser pulses in lieu of single-photon sources. The Quantum Bit Error Rate (QBER) of SARG04 is twice that of BB84, rendering it more susceptible to losses. Nonetheless, it offers enhanced security compared to BB84 in the presence of PNS attacks	Scarani.V, A.Acin, Ribordy G i Gisin.N
2004	COW	Quantum Entanglement	Designed for operation with weak coherent pulses at high bit rates, this configuration is experimentally straightforward and exhibits tolerance to reduced PNS attacks, thereby mitigating information loss	Gisin N, Ribordy G, Zbinden H, Stucki D, Brunner N i Scarani V

5   Overview of Current Quantum Communication Projects and Initiatives

One of the most significant quantum technology development programs in Europe is the "Quantum Flagship". Launched in 2018, it stands as one of the largest and most ambitious research initiatives of the European Union. With a budget of at least one billion euros and a ten-year duration, this leading project brings together research institutions, academia, industry, businesses, and policymakers in a collaborative initiative of unprecedented scale. The objective is to consolidate and expand European scientific leadership and excellence in this research domain, drive competitive European quantum technology industries, and position Europe as a dynamic and attractive region for innovative research, business, and investment in this field. The long-term vision is the "quantum network":

interconnecting quantum computers, simulators, and sensors via quantum networks that distribute information and quantum resources such as coherence and entanglement [23].

During the period 2021–2027, quantum technologies is supported by the Digital Europe Program, which aims to develop and strengthen European strategic digital capabilities, as well as the Horizon Europe program by the Commission, which will contribute to research applications [23].

The rapid progress in both the theory and experimentation of QKD techniques is reflected in a series of successful demonstrations in recent years. Many groups worldwide have presented QKD setups operating in a point-to-point fashion, thereby achieving what is termed QKD links [24].

5.1 European Quantum Technology Roadmap

The progress in quantum computing illustrates three essential factors that are necessary to bring Quantum Technologies (QT) out of the laboratory: relevant use cases with significant market potential, professional large-scale engineering, and substantial research efforts to overcome current scientific and technological limitations. Many European Union (EU) member states have recognized this situation and have strongly invested in national QT programs or centers in the past. The European Commission (EC) has funded QT research over the last two decades with substantial financial resources, primarily through the Future and Emerging Technologies (FET) program for collaborative efforts, the European Research Council (ERC) for individual researchers, and Marie Skłodowska-Curie actions for researcher mobility and training. The European Quantum Technology Roadmap is a result of these activities, ultimately leading to the establishment of the Quantum Flagship initiative [25].

Within the past two decades, Quantum Technologies (QT) have achieved tremendous progress, transitioning from experiments in quantum physics, which were awarded the Nobel Prize, to an interdisciplinary field of applied research. Now, technologies are being developed that explicitly deal with individual quantum states and utilize the "strange" quantum properties such as superposition and entanglement.

The field consists of four domains [25]:

- Quantum communication, where individual or entangled photons are used to transmit data in a provably secure manner.
- Quantum simulation, where well-controlled quantum systems are used to replicate the behavior of other, less accessible quantum systems.
- Quantum computing, which leverages quantum effects for dramatically accelerating certain computations, such as factoring large numbers.
- Quantum sensing and measurement, which exploits the high sensitivity of coherent quantum systems to external disturbances to enhance the efficiency of measuring physical quantities.

One contributing factor to the rapid advancement of QT is a well-coordinated global research community with a shared understanding of challenges and objectives. In Europe, this community has benefited from several EC-funded coordination projects that have, among other things, facilitated the creation of the QT Roadmap. It is important to note that while the QT Roadmap is rooted in European coordination efforts and all its authors are from Europe, the scientific and technological status, challenges, and necessary advancements described therein are not perceived as specific to Europe but rather as applicable to global QT field development. Based on these assessments, the priorities of the European Quantum Flagship project have been developed [25].

5.2 The SECOQC Quantum Key Distribution Network

The SECOQC Quantum Key Distribution (QKD) Network was conceived and implemented by the European SEcure COmmunication based on Quantum Cryptography (SECOQC) project (2004–2008). This initiative brought together the collaborative efforts of 41 research and industrial organizations from the European Union, Switzerland, and Russia. The primary objective was to decisively promote and pave the way for the practical application of QKD technology, often referred to as "quantum cryptography". QKD had evolved progressively from its initial theoretical construct to its first experimental implementations and a wide range of different QKD technologies, leading to the development of initial commercial products, as exemplified by the ID Quantique facility. These products are now utilized by governments, businesses, industrial clients, as well as academic research laboratories in over 60 countries across all continents [26].

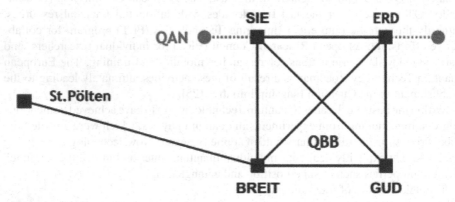

Fig. 4. The universal rectangular building block for QKD [27]

The fundamental idea of this project was to establish a network for the distribution of secrets through individual QKD links from point to point. The corresponding QKD link endpoints (i.e., QKD devices) are located within network nodes. These nodes are secure locations containing one or more QKD devices along with a central node module dedicated to processing, storage, and communication. These node modules are network agents that take full control over classical communication channels (in the SECOQC approach), managing generated secret keys and their information-theoretically secure transmission from node to node in a hop-by-hop manner. They handle tasks such as pathfinding to remote nodes and synchronizing the provision of secret keys to applications consuming keys throughout the network.

In order to showcase and demonstrate new network functionalities and exhibit various advantages over individual links, a universal rectangular building block (Fig. 4) consisting of four stations in Vienna (SIE, ERD, GUD, BREIT) was implemented. This building block was extended by one node in the nearby city of St. Polten. All QBB (Quantum Building Block) links were implemented, including two diagonals and two short QKD links to end users [27].

5.3 Inter-European Quantum Network

Quantum Key Distribution (QKD), introduced by Bennett and Brassard in 1984, is a protocol leveraging quantum physics to provide unconditionally secure data communication. QKD has matured from theoretical constructs to various technological implementations, including optical fiber links and satellites, enabling secure communication across cities and countries. However, a unified global quantum network faces practical challenges due to differing infrastructures and operators [28].

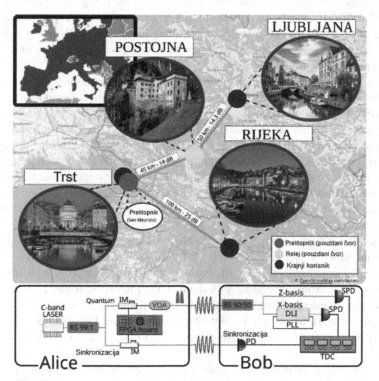

Fig. 5. Topology and architecture of QKD inter-European network [28]

The European Quantum Communication Infrastructure (EuroQCI) project seeks to address these challenges. EuroQCI has initiated a project connecting Italy, Slovenia, and Croatia through a quantum fiber network (Fig. 5), employing the BB84 protocol for secure communication. The implemented network features transmitters (Alice) and receivers (Bob) connected by optical fibers for both quantum and service signals [28].

5.4   QKD Development in Other European Countries

In addition to the aforementioned projects, quantum network initiatives are also underway in other European countries such as the United Kingdom, Germany, France, Portugal, and others. Substantial investments in recent years have sparked a desire to develop quantum networks across Europe. The following section provides an overview of the state of quantum networks in select European countries.

The United Kingdom, through a combination of government and industry funding, has committed over £1 billion over a ten-year period to a coordinated quantum technology program. Five years into this initiative, the UK's National Quantum Technology Programme (NQTP) has brought about a significant transformation in the nation's capabilities to establish a new sector in future quantum information technologies.

The precondition for a substantial increase in government support for quantum technology in the United Kingdom depended on the demonstrated strength of quantum science. Prompted by the efforts of numerous individuals, the UK government announced the NQTP in 2013 to steer quantum information science in the country toward quantum technology that would provide a new world-leading information processing technology and seed a technological sector opening up new business opportunities and creating economic prospects for the UK [29].

The European Commission has granted the PTQCI consortium, composed of Portuguese companies, the first segment of the European Quantum Communication Infrastructure (PTQCI) project in Portugal. The initiative aims to establish a national ultra-secure quantum communication infrastructure, utilizing terrestrial and potential satellite connections via technologies like QKD [30]. Building on the "Discretion" project initiated in 2021, which focuses on quantum communication for Portuguese defense entities, the PTQCI project integrates and expands upon Discretion's optical fiber infrastructure implementation in the Lisbon metropolitan area, connecting public bodies, academia, and testbed networks. A QKD node from the "Discretion" project will be integrated into the PTQCI network [30, 31].

Initiated in 2006, the Madrid Quantum Network has evolved. In 2013, a prototype for quantum network sharing was built at Telefónica. It was redesigned in 2014 to show entanglement distribution. A milestone was achieved in 2018 with installation at Telefónica's facilities. Operating as a metropolitan network, it has 12 nodes across research centers, companies, and universities (shown in Fig. 6). Photonics qubits traverse optical fibers as quantum channels. Notably, it's a Software Defined Network (SDN), seamlessly integrating quantum communication due to SDN's adaptable, programmable nature [32].

Currently, 26 European countries under EuroQCI are conducting national projects of implementation of terrestrial quantum communication infrastructure (QCI) segment with final goal of developing unique European quantum secure communication infrastructure. The EuroQCI's first implementation phase started in January 2023 with the support of the Commission's Digital Europe Programme, with a focus on the following areas [33]:

- A set of industrial projects to develop and mature the key technological building blocks for the EuroQCI, with the aim of developing Europe's quantum communication ecosystem and industry.

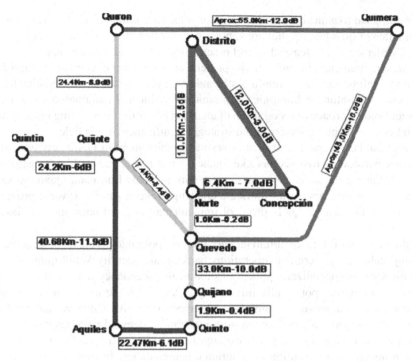

Fig. 6. Madrid QKD network [32]

- National projects allowing Member States to design and build the national quantum communication networks that will form the basis of the terrestrial segment, testing different technologies and protocols and adapting them to the specific needs of each country.
- A coordination and support action, PETRUS, to act as a link between all projects, facilitate collaboration, and identify standardisation needs.
- These first Digital Europe projects will together make it possible to take the first steps towards services offering operational quantum key distribution (QKD), a highly secure way of delivering encryption key material.

6   Conclusion

In conclusion, the intricate realm of quantum physics empowers us to grasp and exploit unique quantum phenomena, transcending classical paradigms. Leveraging these principles, we can engineer advanced sensors for precision measurements, computational systems simulating complex physical processes, and secure communication networks interlinking these innovations, offering fertile grounds for scientific exploration.

Evidenced by substantial expectations and investments, quantum technology is poised to reshape critical communication systems in the foreseeable future. While its direct impact may not be pervasive in everyday scenarios, sectors such as government entities, financial institutions, and military establishments, where data integrity is paramount, stand to gain significantly from quantum technological strides. The successful validation of quantum applications, both in controlled environments and real-world settings, underscores the feasibility and practicality of these advancements.

However, financial considerations present an imposing challenge. Establishing autonomous infrastructure remains a costly endeavor; yet, capitalizing on existing frameworks renders quantum technologies economically viable and sustainable. Notably, the European Union's proactive recognition of quantum potential, manifesting in substantial financial commitment, underscores the strategic significance of this field.

The global landscape already witnesses the establishment of QKD networks, serving diverse purposes across sectors like finance, governance, and healthcare. Mirroring this trend, Europe advances towards constructing a robust European Quantum Communication Network, navigating intricate challenges encompassing diverse providers, variant standards, diverse QKD protocol implementations, and harmonizing classical infrastructure.

In the imminent future, quantum technologies are poised to permeate diverse realms, spanning healthcare, government operations, banking, and security. While quantum communication serves specialized applications today, its ascendancy in technology augurs a wider incorporation, potentially integrating as a cornerstone in global communication networks. To achieve this ambitious prospect, extensive software and hardware engineering, coupled with intricate system integration, demand rigorous collaboration between academia and industry. As we approach the horizon of 2027, prospects are ripe for transformative evolution in quantum communication, technology, and network paradigms.

Acknowledgments. Financial support for this study was provided by a grant 101091513 Croatian Quantum Communication Infrastructure – CroQCI Digital Europe Programme (DIGITAL) (230247).

References

1. Krawec, W.O.: Asymptotic analysis of a three state quantum cryptographic protocol (2016)
2. Bennett, C.H., Brassard, G.: Quantum cryptography: public key distribution and coin tossing (2020). https://doi.org/10.1016/j.tcs.2014.05.025
3. Diamanti, E., Lo, H.-K., Qi, B., Yuan, Z.: Practical challenges in quantum key distribution. Npj Quantum Inf. **2**, 16025 (2016). https://doi.org/10.1038/npjqi.2016.25
4. Amer, O., Krawec, W.O., Manfredi, V.U., Wang, B.: Dynamic routing for quantum key distribution networks (2022)
5. Tsai, C.-W., Yang, C.-W., Lin, J., Chang, Y.-C., Chang, R.-S.: Quantum key distribution networks: challenges and future research issues in security. Appl. Sci. **11**, 3767 (2021). https://doi.org/10.3390/app11093767
6. Chitambar, E., George, I., Doolittle, B., Junge, M.: The communication value of a quantum channel. IEEE Trans. Inf. Theory **69**(3), 1660–1679 (2023). https://doi.org/10.1109/TIT.2022.3218540
7. Jones, J.A., Jaksch, D.: Quantum Information, Computation and Communication. Cambridge University Press, Cambridge (2012). https://doi.org/10.1017/CBO9781139028509

8. Castelvecchi, D.: Quantum network is step towards ultrasecure internet. Nature **590**(7847), 540–541 (2021). https://doi.org/10.1038/d41586-021-00420-5

9. Hasan, M.A., Calderin, L., Lata, T., Lucas, P., Runge, K., Deymier, P.A.: The sound of Bell states. Commun. Phys. **2**(1), 106 (2019). https://doi.org/10.1038/s42005-019-0203-z

10. Luo, Y.-H., et al.: Quantum teleportation in high dimensions. Phys. Rev. Lett. **123**(7), 070505 (2019). https://doi.org/10.1103/PhysRevLett.123.070505

11. Huang, W., Wen, Q.-Y., Liu, B., Gao, F., Sun, Y.: Quantum key agreement with EPR pairs and single-particle measurements. Quantum Inf. Process. **13**(3), 649–663 (2014). https://doi.org/10.1007/s11128-013-0680-z

12. Oliveira, P.A., Sanz, L.: Bell states and entanglement dynamics on two coupled quantum molecules. Ann. Phys. **356**, 244–254 (2015). https://doi.org/10.1016/j.aop.2015.02.036

13. Sych, D., Leuchs, G.: A complete basis of generalized Bell states. New J. Phys. **11**(1), 013006 (2009). https://doi.org/10.1088/1367-2630/11/1/013006

14. Djordjevic, I.: Quantum Information Processing and Quantum Error Correction. Elsevier, Amsterdam (2012). https://doi.org/10.1016/C2010-0-66917-3

15. Pirandola, S., Braunstein, S.L.: Physics: unite to build a quantum internet. Nature **532**(7598), 169–171 (2016). https://doi.org/10.1038/532169a

16. Pirandola, S., et al.: Advances in quantum cryptography. Adv. Opt. Photon. **12**(4), 1012 (2020). https://doi.org/10.1364/AOP.361502

17. Bennett, C.H., Brassard, G., Mermin, N.D.: Quantum cryptography without Bell's theorem. Phys. Rev. Lett. **68**(5), 557–559 (1992). https://doi.org/10.1103/PhysRevLett.68.557

18. Muruganantham, B., Shamili, P., Kumar, S.G., Murugan, A.: Quantum cryptography for secured communication networks. Int. J. Electr. Comput. Eng. (IJECE) **10**(1), 407 (2020). https://doi.org/10.11591/ijece.v10i1.pp407-414

19. Mavroeidis, V., Vishi, K., Zych, D.M., Jøsang, A.: The impact of quantum computing on present cryptography. Int. J. Adv. Comput. Sci. Appl. **9**(3) (2018). https://doi.org/10.14569/IJACSA.2018.090354

20. Trizna, A., Ozols, A.: An overview of quantum key distribution protocols. Inf. Technol. Manage. Sci. **21**, 37–44 (2018). https://doi.org/10.7250/itms-2018-0005

21. Wolf, R.: Quantum Key Distribution Protocols, pp. 91–116 (2021). https://doi.org/10.1007/978-3-030-73991-1_4

22. Nandal, A., Nandal, R., Joshi, K., Rathee, A.: Comparison of some of the most prominent QKD protocols: a review. IUP J. Telecommun. **13**(2), 19–62 (2021)

23. European Commission. New quantum project aims for ultra-secure communication in Europe (2019). https://digital-strategy.ec.europa.eu/en/news/new-quantum-project-aims-ultra-secure-communication-europe

24. Poppe, A., Peev, M., Maurhart, O.: Outline of the SECOQC quantum-key-distribution network in Vienna (2018). https://doi.org/10.1142/S0219749908003529

25. CEN-CENELEC Focus Group on Quantum Technologies (FGQT). Standardization Roadmap on Quantum Technologies (2023)

26. Peev, M., et al.: The SECOQC quantum key distribution network in Vienna. New J. Phys. **11**(7), 075001 (2009). https://doi.org/10.1088/1367-2630/11/7/075001

27. Riedel, M., Kovacs, M., Zoller, P., Mlynek, J., Calarco, T.: Europe's quantum flagship initiative. Quantum Sci. Technol. **4**(2), 020501 (2019). https://doi.org/10.1088/2058-9565/ab042d

28. Ribezzo, D., et al.: Deploying an inter-European quantum network (2022). https://doi.org/10.1002/qute.202200061

29. Knight, P., Walmsley, I.: UK national quantum technology programme. Quantum Sci. Technol. **4**(4), 040502 (2019). https://doi.org/10.1088/2058-9565/ab4346

30. Pinto, A., et al.: Hardware security modules enabled by QKD: a field experiment in Portugal (2020). https://az659834.vo.msecnd.net/eventsairwesteuprod/production-abbey-public/ea3b9ccfa8cf4eeaa018769b17e58bdd

31. DEIMOS Engenharia. DISCRETION – Quantum communication networks for Defence (2022).   https://www.spacequip.eu/2022/01/12/discretion-quantum-communication-networks-for-defence/

32. García Cid, M.I., Ortiz Martín, L., Martín Ayuso, V.: Madrid quantum network. In: The 16th International Conference on Availability, Reliability and Security, pp. 1–7 (2021). https://doi.org/10.1145/3465481.3470056

33. European Commission. The European Quantum Communication Infrastructure (EuroQCI) Initiative. The European Quantum Communication Infrastructure (EuroQCI) Initiative (2023)

Learning Framework for Guessing Alphanumeric Passwords on Mobile Phones Based on User Context and Fragment Semantics

Lilian Noronha Nassif[1,2]([⊠]) and Jonny Silva de Oliveira[1]

[1] Public Ministry of Minas Gerais State, Av. Álvares Cabral, 1690, Belo Horizonte, Brazil
{liliannassif,jsoliveira.plansul}@mpmg.mp.br
[2] Pontifical Catholic University of Minas Gerais, Av. Dom José Gaspar, 500, Belo Horizonte, Brazil

Abstract. When conducting a criminal investigation, accessing mobile phone data is crucial for law enforcement. However, encryption mechanisms and user locks are becoming increasingly complex and more challenging for forensic examiners. Although there are tools that can perform brute-force attacks to crack passwords on mobile phones, it becomes difficult when faced with alphanumeric passwords. The challenge is not only the algorithm but also the use of a customized dictionary. It is impractical to use a complete dictionary with all possible combinations as the attack conditions are very restrictive, and the time it takes to crack the password becomes too long depending on its length. In this article, we present a learning framework based on a set of dictionaries, variation rules, and fragment permutations. Dictionaries are organized from different perspectives of personal data, open sources, and groups of contexts. The naming and ordering of the dictionary help digital forensics examiners strategize and improve their chances of success in cracking alphanumeric passwords.

Keywords: Digital Forensics · Password Guessing · Mobile Forensics

1 Introduction

The branch of forensic science that deals with mobile devices, known as mobile forensics, has become increasingly relevant for criminal investigations. With the widespread use of digital devices for daily activities, as well as the advancements in computational power, storage, and memory, there is a vast amount of data that can be recorded [1]. However, there are also technologies in place to protect information privacy, such as encryption and access blocking.

One of the main obstacles that forensic examiners face when dealing with a locked mobile phone is confirming that it is secured with an alphanumeric password. The digital forensics industry has already managed to overcome the challenge of breaking codes for mobile phones locked with numeric passwords or pattern codes by utilizing a brute force technique. This involves making exhaustive attempts to try out all possible combinations,

S. Goel and P. R. Nunes de Souza (Eds.): ICDF2C 2023, LNICST 571, pp. 23–30, 2024.
https://doi.org/10.1007/978-3-031-56583-0_2

with the expectation of obtaining the correct password within a timeframe ranging from a few hours to a maximum of one year.

However, when it comes to alphanumeric passwords, a single dictionary is often not sufficient and the password length is unknown. The challenge in this scenario is not with the algorithm or device access, but in constructing a comprehensive dictionary of potential passwords.

In this work, we introduce a framework that enables the creation of dictionaries from various data sources. The framework involves applying modification rules and rearranging fragment positions. The data sources used in this approach include intelligence activities, digital forensics expertise, and research of generic and specific wordlists. Additionally, the framework allows for the incorporation of machine learning techniques.

The structure of this paper is as follows: Sect. 2 provides information on related works. Section 3 lays out the structured phases for creating and enhancing cracking dictionaries. Section 4 covers the implementation of the framework. Finally, Sect. 5 concludes the paper.

2 Related Works

In the literature, two main approaches are used to gain insight into how users create their own passwords. The first approach involves analyzing leaked password databases to present statistics on password length, data type correlation, and semantic analysis. The second approach involves conducting surveys with volunteer groups to ask about their password creation strategies.

In their study, Kanta et al. [2] examined the HIBP_v5 database which contained 3.9 billion accounts. The analysis examined usage statistics and identified the most common patterns in passwords, including fragments based on their semantic meaning.

According to the findings of Brown et al. [3], two-thirds of people create passwords using their personal data. The remaining one-third mostly uses personal data of their relatives, friends, or significant others. The most commonly used information for passwords is first names and birthdays. Shockingly, almost all respondents reuse passwords on different sites or devices. Additionally, about two-thirds of passwords are duplicates.

The work of Hunt [4], reveals that 14% of passwords derive from a first name and most people add numbers after words, usually 2 or 4 numbers, suggesting they are fragments of birthday dates. Hunt also describes that 8% of the analyzed passwords use place names. Dictionary words appeared in 25% of the analyzed passwords. He also identified that 14% of passwords are purely numerical, not having any other type of character. The length of purely numeric passwords were identified as follows: 4-digit passwords (8%); 6-digit passwords (48%); 8-digit pass-words (27%); other length passwords (17%). It is possible to realized that even password lengths are more frequent than odd passwords lengths. Hunt also analyzed that 2.7% of passwords repeated words, such as: "lovelove"; another 2.6% use email login as their password. It was also detected that 1.3% of the passwords use short phrases, such as "Iloveyou"; and 0.3% use keyboard patterns such as "qwerty". The remaining 31% of the analyzed passwords were not related to any pattern.

3 Structured Phases of Guessing Passwords

3.1 Data Sources for Customized Dictionaries

Various methods can be used to gather data sources for creating dictionaries for password attacks. These include investigation, research in open sources, digital forensics examination of devices belonging to the target, selecting wordlists based on themes, and using password generation programs.

Table 1 provides a taxonomy that categorizes data sources based on their origin, and includes examples of information and the corresponding dictionary name (DICX.Y) created from that source. The X refers to group identification and Y refers to group subset.

Table 1. Taxonomy of data sources for customizing dictionaries

Data sources	Category	Examples	Dictionary
Case investigators	Personal data	Name, date of birth, name of relatives and friends	DIC1
Digital evidence to attack (extraction BFU – Before First Unlock)	Digital forensics	e-mail, user name	DIC2
Other digital evidence of the same person or online credentials	Digital forensics	Words used in communications	DIC3
OSINT (Internet)	Open sources	Cities and places visited, friends, important dates, musical preferences, political preferences	DIC4
Generic searches of ready-made dictionaries (Internet)	Related word groups	People name dictionaries, animal name dictionaries, city name dictionaries, football team name dictionaries	DIC5.Y
Developed by the authors	Password generation program	Numbers, letters and special characters 4, 5, 6, 7, 8, 9	DIC6.Y
Leaked password dictionaries (Internet)	Hacker community	Rockyou, HIBP (Have I Been Pwned?), MySpace	DIC7.Y
Researched/elaborated by the authors	Short sentences	Short and common phrases: "IloveYou", "goodblessyou", "verygood"	DIC8
Researched/elaborated by the authors	Long sentences	Song initials, use of popular long phrase initials	DIC9

The dictionary named DIC1 is created from information provided by the investigator to the forensic examiner. This dictionary is based on the high likelihood of the target using personal information when creating passwords. Table 1 organizes dictionaries in order of personal to generic data and from simple to complex passwords.

The BFU data source, used to compile the DIC2 dictionary, extracts data from mobile phones before the first unlock. This includes information from the operating system, as well as mobile phone username, email [5], and cloud data access credentials login accounts. Researchers can explore this data in open data sources (OSINT), facilitated by various applications listed in Bielska's document [6]. DIC4 is a dictionary created from OSINT data sources which reveal target's habits, tastes, and relationships, such as preferences for sports teams, political and religious affiliations, and hobbies [7]. DIC5 contains specific groups related to hobbies, such as motorcycling, with subgroups containing all words, slang, brands, and models of motorcycles. Quick & Choo [8] refer to this correlation between OSINT and intelligence in digital forensics as DFINT.

Another strategy to guess passwords is to examine other electronic devices seized from the same target, such as notebooks with less complex passwords. This strategy can generate DIC3, a dictionary containing a wordlist ordered by the most frequent words and a profile analysis of the target's habits. Bang et al. [9] found that 80% of users keep their passwords, 16% use a password already used on another site, and only 4% change their password completely when creating a new one.

Thus, the data sources that form DIC1 to DIC5 dictionaries have interrelationships, as shown in Fig. 1. Analysis of DIC1 to DIC4 can be used to create DIC5 wordlists associated with hobbies, trips, favorite sports, and more.

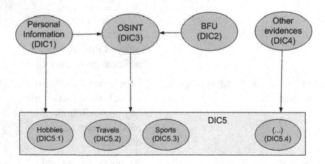

Fig. 1. Intercorrelation among dictionaries DIC1 to DIC5.

The dictionaries DIC6, DIC7, DIC8, and DIC9 listed in Table 1 are created using generic sources and do not contain any information specific to the target. DIC6 includes all possible word constructions, making it appear to be the most straightforward method to crack passwords by trying all combinations of letters, numbers, and special characters for all password lengths. However, as we will explain in Sect. 3.3, brute force attacks on locked mobile phones would only be effective for passwords up to 4 characters long.

3.2 Time to Crack Alphanumeric Passwords on Mobile Phones

Digital forensics tools often install agents with dictionary size limitations for cracking passwords on mobile phones. For Android phones, attacks are limited to files of 200 MB, while for iPhones, it is 15 MB. This means that every time a dictionary is exhausted, the device must be reconnected and the dictionary changed.

Studies have shown that internet passwords can be cracked within 8 h, but this is not the case for agents installed on locked mobile phones with alphanumeric passwords [10]. The processing power and conditions are much more restricted, leading to slower attacks with only a few thousand attempts per minute. Additionally, the forensic examiner must manually disconnect and change the dictionary every time it is exhausted.

For instance, if using DIC5 with 4 characters in Table 1, 3 files are used for Androids and 33 files are used for iPhones. This means that the forensic examiner would have to wait for each dictionary to be exhausted before selecting another one and reconnecting cables up to 33 times in the worst-case scenario. If the password length is 5 characters (with 26 letters, 10 numbers, and 7 special characters), this becomes even more impractical, requiring 3611 manual dictionary changes for iPhones. Therefore, brute-force methods become impractical for passwords with 5 digits and above, which is why this paper presents mechanisms to improve password guessing.

3.3 Variations in the Dictionary

Based on the data sources provided in Sect. 3.1, it is still possible to alter the dictionary by making mutations using special characters, modifying the position of capital letters, adding numbers, and utilizing acronyms.

These variations are typical human behaviors when creating passwords, such as adding a digit at the end, capitalizing the first letter, and replacing letters with similar symbols (@ for "a", 3 for "E", and 1 for "i").

Table 2. Variations in dictionaries according to predictable human behavior.

Variation Name	Description	Variation ID
Special character replacement	Replace "E" with "3", "i" with "1", "a" with "@", "o" with "0"	VAR1
Changing the position of the capital letter	Change capitalization in all positions where there are letters	VAR2
Addition of numbers	Add 2 to 4 numbers	VAR3
Use initial letters of words	Compose words using sentence and full names initials	VAR4

3.4 Personal Data Decomposition and Fragment Permutation

Creating a strong password can be made easier by breaking down personal data into separate parts. All personal information, including that of a person's relatives, friends and romantic partners, is important. Here are some examples of how to break down personal data: 1) For each birthday, it is important to separate the day, month, year, and full year in reverse order (dD, mM, yY, and yyYY); 2) For a full name, consider each word separately, including the initials; 3) For documents with numbers, separate them into groups of 3 and 4 numbers, as well as the complete number. This breakdown of personal data is also discussed in [11], which classifies birth dates, usernames, telephone numbers, emails, and other personal data as a semantic category of the password.

In addition to breaking down personal data, it is also important to identify common groups of fragments when creating a password. Typically, people start a sentence with a capital letter and end it with a punctuation mark. Therefore, a stronger password could be composed of three fragments: Fragment1 - a word or initials with the first letter capitalized (using words from dictionaries such as DIC5, 7, 8, 9); Fragment2 - numbers associated with dates or personal documents (Dd, Mm, Yy) or (dD, mM, yY) or (DdMm) or (YYYY); Fragment3 - special characters (&, *, $, #, @, %, !, ?) with variations of combination or repetition of the same special character (Fig. 2).

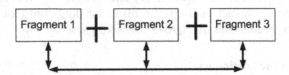

Fig. 2. Semantics of passwords by fragments.

Although the proposed fragment order (Fragment 1 + Fragment 2 + Fragment 3) are the most common rule, it is also important permutate each fragment position to create more password guessing possibilities.

Although the recommended order for fragments is usually Fragment 1 + Fragment 2 + Fragment 3, it is crucial to permute the position of each fragment to increase the number of possible password guesses.

4   Implementation of the Framework Model

The framework model was implemented through a series of steps outlined in Sect. 3. The authors developed a program to execute each step, which are summarized below:

1. Researching the data source
2. Breaking down personal data into each piece of information for the target and their relationships
3. Creating dictionaries for each data source (DIC1 to DIC9 in Table 1)
4. Creating variations for each dictionary (VAR1 to VAR4 in Table 2)
5. Changing the position of fragments for each DICx-y-VARx
6. Analyzing the semantics of cracked passwords and improving dictionaries through machine learning.

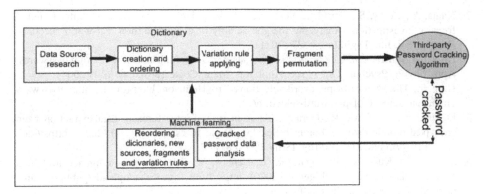

Fig. 3. Learning framework for guessing alphanumeric passwords

These steps were all successfully implemented, resulting in a comprehensive and efficient framework model.

Figure 3 presents the full framework of our solution. The creation of effective dictionaries for use in a third-party password cracking algorithm involves well-defined stages. The framework's mechanisms can be refined and customized through machine learning with additional real-world examples.

5 Conclusion

Cracking alphanumeric passwords on mobile devices during investigations has proven to be a challenging task for law enforcement. While a brute force attack can crack a password up to 9 characters in a few weeks, the scenario is different when it comes to cracking alphanumeric passwords on mobile phones. Digital forensics solutions install an agent on the device, which limits the dictionary size and processor performance. This size limitation requires forensic examiners to manually make changes to the dictionary, wasting precious time. Therefore, brute force is not feasible when the number of changes is large, that is, over or equal to 5 alphanumeric character combinations.

To overcome this challenge, this article presents the best dictionary assembly strategies that carefully select words and numbers related to the user's context. The article also includes necessary variations on the assembled dictionaries and permutations of fragment positions.

The learning framework for cracking alphanumeric passwords was able to organize the work within the forensic laboratory. This demonstrated the limitations of brute force and included intelligence in the dictionary's assembly. All dictionaries were named and organized to establish the correct preparations and sequence of use for each new mobile phone with an alphanumeric password to be cracked in the digital forensic laboratory.

References

1. Sathe, S.C., Dongre, N.M.: Data acquisition techniques in mobile forensics. In: 2018 2nd International Conference on Inventive Systems and Control (ICISC), Coimbatore, India, pp. 280–286 (2018). https://doi.org/10.1109/ICISC.2018.8399079

2. Kanta, A., Coray, S., Coisel, I., Scanlon, M.: How viable is password cracking in digital forensic investigation? Analyzing the guessability of over 3.9 billion real-world accounts. Forensic Sci. Int.: Digit. Invest. **37** (2021)
3. Brown, A.S., Bracken, E., Zoccoli, S., Douglas, K.: Generating and remembering passwords. Appl. Cognit. Psychol.: Off. J. Soc. Appl. Res. Mem. Cogn. **18**(6), 641–651 (2004)
4. Hunt, T.: The science of password selections. TroyHunt.com blog (2011). https://www.tro yhunt.com/science-of-password-selection/
5. Fukami, A., Stoykova, R., Geradts, Z.: A new model for forensic data extraction from encrypted mobile devices. Forensic Sci. Int.: Digit. Invest. **38**, 301169 (2021). https://doi. org/10.1016/j.fsidi.2021.301169. ISSN 2666-2817
6. Bielska, A., Kurs, N., Baumgartner, Y., Benetis, V.: OpenSource intelligence tools and resources handbook. I-Intelligence (2020). https://i-intelligence.eu/uploads/public-docume nts/OSINT_Handbook_2020.pdf
7. Kanta, A., Coisel, I., Scanlon, M.: A survey exploring open source intelligence for smarter password cracking. Forensic Sci. Int.: Digit. Invest. **35**, 301075 (2020). https://doi.org/10. 1016/j.fsidi.2020.301075
8. Quick, D., Choo, K.: Digital forensic intelligence: data subsets and open source intelligence (DFINT+OSINT): a timely and cohesive mix. Future Gener. Comput. Syst. **78**(Part 2), 558–567 (2018). https://doi.org/10.1016/j.future.2016.12.032. ISSN 0167-739X
9. Bang, Y., Lee, D., Bae, Y., Ahn, J.: Improving information security management: an analysis of ID–password usage and a new login vulnerability measure. Int. J. Inf. Manage. **32**(5), 409–418 (2012). https://doi.org/10.1016/j.ijinfomgt.2012.01.001. ISSN 0268-4012
10. Vo, N.: How long does it take to crack a password? A brief explanation. Locker (2022). https:// locker.io/blog/time-to-crack-a-password
11. Jiang, X., Sun, X., Liu, Q.: Password guessing attack based on probabilistic context free algorithm. In: 2022 IEEE 8th International Conference on Computer and Communications (ICCC), Chengdu, China, pp. 1234–1238 (2022). https://doi.org/10.1109/ICCC56324.2022. 10065766

Password Managers and Vault Application Security and Forensics: Research Challenges and Future Opportunities

Aleck Nash and Kim-Kwang Raymond Choo(✉) ⓘ

University of Texas at San Antonio, San Antonio, TX 78249, USA
Aleck.Nash@my.utsa.edu, raymond.choo@fulbrightmail.org

Abstract. Password manager and vault applications can be used by users to select strong passwords as well as storing user credentials locally or in the cloud. Such apps have been studied by various security researchers, for example in identifying potential vulnerabilities and bugs, as well as proposing techniques to forensically recover artifacts of interest/relevance to an investigation, which is also the focus of this paper. Specifically, we review the extant literature on the security and forensics of password manager and vault applications with the objective of identifying existing limitations and challenges.

Keywords: Password Manager · Vault Application · Forensic Analysis

1 Introduction

Passwords continue to be the dominant method for online authentication, say in e-commerce or many other electronic services. It is generally recommended to choose long and complex passwords (e.g., combination of numbers, letters, and special characters) to minimize the risk of password guessing and brute-force attacks (Fei Yu & Hao Yin 2021). However, passwords that are efficiently long and random are often difficult to remember by most users. In addition, in our increasingly digitalized society, it is not realistic to expect users to have different long and complex passwords for each account. Even if such passwords are used, they are still vulnerable to phishing and harvesting attacks (Rui Zhao & Chuan Yue & Kun Sun 2013a, b). Due to our limited capacities for remembering large sets of long and complex passwords, a typical user would tend to re-use the same passwords across their different accounts web applications (Ben Stock & Martin Johns 2014).

Users can use password manager (PM) applications (apps) to help them select strong passwords, store passwords for different accounts locally on their device or in the cloud, and/or be entered into password-matching dialogs (Ben Stock & Martin Johns 2014). There are many available open-source and commercial PM apps for desktops, as browser plug-ins (e.g., built-in feature), and for mobile devices (e.g., mobile apps). (Rui Zhao & Chuan Yue & Kun Sun 2013a, b). Table 1 provides a summary of several popular PM apps and their features.

© ICST Institute for Computer Sciences, Social Informatics and Telecommunications Engineering 2024
Published by Springer Nature Switzerland AG 2024. All Rights Reserved
S. Goel and P. R. Nunes de Souza (Eds.): ICDF2C 2023, LNICST 571, pp. 31–53, 2024.
https://doi.org/10.1007/978-3-031-56583-0_3

Table 1. Summary of most popular apps, based on Google Play Store

Password manager	Number of downloads, if applicable (as of 12/30/2022)	Open-Source	Features		
			2FA	Auto-fill	Zero Knowledge
Keeper	10M+	X	x	x	x
LastPass	10M+	X	x		x
Bitwarden	1M+	X	x	x	x
KeePass	1M+	X		x	
Dashlane	5M+		x	x	x
RoboForm	500K+		x	x	x
1Password	100K+		x	x	x
Passbolt	5K+	X	x	x	
PassPack	NA		x	x	
Encryptr	NA				x
Padlock	NA	x			

While there are many benefits in using such apps, the latter is also a single source/point of attack and any vulnerability in these apps (or their implementation) could have a cascading consequence. For example, the compromise of the master password for the app could reveal all passwords for many different accounts stored in the app (Chaudhary et al., 2019). The master password is generally 'transformed' into a key with many iterations of OBKDF2 key-generating algorithms, and the key is recomputed whenever the master password is entered. Another commonly used key generation approach is PassPack, which uses its own custom key generation algorithm that involves taking every other byte of a SHA-256 hash and doing several rounds of salted hashing. The master key is used to encrypt the account data to be stored. Most password managers use AES-256 to encrypt the vault, and others such as MSecure use Blowfish-256 (Elizabeth Walkup, 2016).

Vault apps (VAs) are mobile apps that store and hide sensitive files such as documents, photos, and other apps on the user's phone. The increased use of mobile devices that carry sensitive data reinforces the importance of protecting such data by saving them in the VA. However, studies such as those of (Gilbert & C. Seigfried-Spellar (2022), suggested that about over 30% Android vault apps stored passwords in cleartext, while others did not encrypt the photos. Such apps can also be used to store incriminating data such as terrorism and child abuse materials. In other words, both PM and vault apps are an invaluable source of evidence in digital investigations.

Hence, in this paper, we will review the extant review on password managers and vault applications, specifically focusing on the security and forensics aspects.

2 Research Methodology

In our literature review, we searched for and located articles using Google Scholar and other academic databases (e.g., IEEEXplore, ACM Digital Library, ScienceDirect and SpringerLink) using keywords and operators such as forensics AND "password managers", forensics AND "password vault", and vulnerability AND ("authentication app" OR "password manager").

Although during the initial search we located hundreds of papers, a closer read suggested that many of these papers are not relevant and subsequently excluded from our review. In the second pass, a total of 100 papers were downloaded and scanned more closely for relevance to our study. This yielded a total of 33 papers selected for the literature review. We then decided to expand the scope of the review by including articles related to user behavior and secure app development, of which we found 7 of them in the initially downloaded papers. This yielded a final total of 40 papers selected for our review.

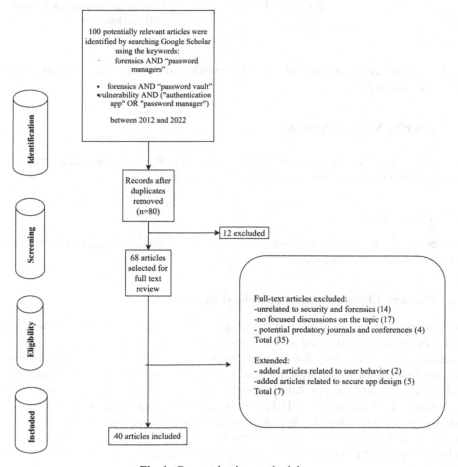

Fig. 1. Paper selection methodology

We also located one other literature review paper with overlapping focuses. Chaudhary et al., (2019) conducted a systematic literature review of 32 articles that dealt with security and usability problems related to PMs. The goal of the review is to provide guidance for PM developers, focusing specifically on the (in)security aspects. In our paper, however, we focus not only on the security of PM and vault apps, but also on the forensics aspects of these apps (Fig. 1 and Table 2).

Table 2. Summary of literature review articles

Study	Number of Papers	Scope
Chaudhary et al., (2019)	32 papers published between 2006 and 2015	A systematic review of the security and usability issues of PMs, specifically targeting PM developers
Our study	40 papers published between 2012 and 2022	A literature review of the security and forensics aspects of PMs and vault apps

In the next section, we will introduce the review of the security literature relating to PMs and vault apps.

3   Security Vulnerabilities

Here, we will discuss the existing literature relating to the potential attack types, the varying level of attacker expertise, and the adoption barriers.

3.1   Attack Types

A summary of the attack types is presented in Table 3, followed by detailed discussions in the subsections that follow.

3.2   Phishing, Clipboard Attack, and Keylogging Attacks

To examine the security of password managers, it is important to study the functionalities of these applications as well as their security policies. Silver et al., (2014), for example, conducted a study that examined ten browser built-in, third-party, and mobile password managers. These password managers include Chrome, Safari, LastPass, 1Passowrd, KeePass, and Keeper. All examined password managers offer either automatic or manual autofill functionality. The former functionality (automatic autofill) populates the username and password fields without requiring user interaction, and manual autofill requires user interaction prior to auto-filling by requiring the user to click the username field for example. In addition, all examined password managers allow password autofill pages within the same domain as pages from which the password was initially saved.

Table 3. Summary of attack types

Attack Types	Potential Attack Methods	Key vulnerability(ies)
Phishing	Sweep attacks Illegitimate/fake app Read-write Trojan-horse	Attackers' ability to access stored information utilizing the auto-fill functionality
Clipboard	Extracting data from the clipboard	
Cross-scripting	Cross-site scripting against the browser	
Key-logging	Clipboard and login page key logging	The ability of the attacker to capture keystrokes or information input by the user. While this seems to contradict the above observation, implementing the auto-fill functionality may prevent such an attack
Offline Brute Force	• Brute-force the master password • Automated brute-force against the master password • Brute force against authentication pin	The ability of the attacker to try different password combinations against locally stored password
Local decryption	• Monitoring HTTPS requests • Calling decryption functions	• Storing credentials without encryption • Transmitting in plain-text
Sensitive data extraction	• Extracting saved passwords from password managers using automated tools along with web crawlers	• Not implementing SSL • exposing secure login forms on HTTPS pages

This feature can be exploited by an attacker to target the password manager on the least secured page within the domain. Additionally, all password managers except Chrome are found to be vulnerable to iFrame sweep attacks, where a hotspot landing page contains invisible iFrames that point to random pages at various target sites. The attacker controlling the router (e.g., man-in-the-middle attacker) can inject a login form and JavaScript into each iFrame loaded by the browser. As each iFrame loads, the password manager will automatically populate the corresponding field with the user's password, which allows the injected JavaScript in each iFrame to steal these credentials. Another type of this sweep attack is called the Window sweep attack, in which windows are utilized to trick the user into disabling the popup blocker. Consequently, such an attack allows the landing page to open all of the victim pages each in a separate window. The JavaScript injected in each page will steal the passwords and hide the pages' content to make them appear as blank windows to the user as well as closing them immediately once the passwords are stolen. The authors found that nearly all the automatic autofill password managers they examined, with the exception of LastPass, are vulnerable to window-based attacks. They also uncovered vulnerabilities that allow a public wi-fi network attacker to leverage the policies of password managers to steal stored passwords without the user's awareness.

Carr and Shahandashti, (2020) analyzed the security of five popular commercial password managers (i.e., LastPass, Dashlane, Keeper, 1Password, and RoboForm), where they found both 1Passwore and LastPass to be vulnerable to a phishing attack as a result of weak matching criteria used to determine which saved credentials to recommend for autofill. This allows a malicious program to masquerade as a lawful one by using the same package name. The authors developed a malicious app with the package com.google and a login page that looks like the official login screen. When this malicious program is started, LastPass offers to autofill the login page with Google credentials stored in the user's vault, because LastPass' matching criteria are based solely on the application package name. When the autofill feature fails, password managers frequently provide the option to copy credentials to the clipboard. Apart for 1Password, the authors discovered that the evaluated PMs do not provide sufficient security while copying sensitive things to the clipboard. Although locking the system would reduce such risk, Windows 10 permits access to the clipboard of a locked machine, which allows an adversary with physical access to the machine or an application running on the machine to paste the value of the clipboard in plaintext. Even if the attacker is unaware of the account linked with the stolen password, they can test the credentials against a pre-compiled list of websites where autofill is known to fail.

Similarly, Aonzo et al., (2018) analyzed the auto-fill mechanism of Android password managers. Their strategy was to install a genuine Facebook app and enter the credentials into a password manager. Then, they removed the real app, deleted the legitimate app, and installed malicious software with the same package name as the legitimate Facebook app. The purpose of that is to check whether the auto-fill mechanism of the PM would suggest the credentials of the legitimate app. Then, if susceptible, they built a mechanism to exploit the vulnerability of a certain mapping implementation. The approach was successful for a number of PMs such as Keeper, Dashlane, LastPass, and 1Password.

Luevanos et al., (2017) were able to perform an attack that enabled them to capture a live copy of the user's session, which allowed them to edit coding lines and simulate the login screen as if it was real. This gives a potential for a phishing attack that allows the attacker to steal the master password of the user. The authors performed a custom user-script attack by hiding malicious code in a program that a user can install to get additional website functionalities. Because users rarely read all of the code, dangerous code lines might be hidden in the script of such a program. A good way to carry out this attack is to conceal a decent user script in an extension that injects JavaScript into the page. Some PMs, like Passbolt, contain a mechanism that prevents the extension from being edited by detecting any modifications and disabling the app if any modifications are found. However, installing a phony extension would bypass such feature because open-source extensions are easy to mimic. They authors also discovered that Passbolt is difficult to use and has no published security audits. Additionally, several major features seen in other password managers are missing from this program. The design of Passbolt makes it highly vulnerable to attacks on the main administrator. Encryptr was found to be particularly vulnerable to clipboard attacks since copying is the most convenient way to send data from the app to any form. The authors wrote a script that can reset any user account with a click of a button, which would subsequently delete all saved data such as passwords and other sensitive information. Padlock was also found to be vulnerable to clipboard attacks since it uses the clipboard without an autofill feature. Encryptr and Pablo were also found to be vulnerable to keyloggers when typing the master password and copying a password from the app to a form.

Gasti and Rasmussen, (2012) analyzed the storage formats used by 13 popular password managers by creating two adversaries, one which has read access to the password database, and another that has read-write access. The analysis of the selected password managers revealed that all of the examined PMs with the exception of PasswordSafe V3 are vulnerable to read-write attackers. Although PasswordSafe V3 was found to be secure in the authors' adversary and system mode, it had some interesting design flows. Li et al. (2014) conducted a comprehensive security analysis of five popular PMs (LastPass, RoboForm, My1login, PasswordBox, needMyPassword) and found them vulnerable to a threat model that allows the attacker, who controls one or several web servers and DNS domains, to trick the user into visiting the domains controlled by the attacker. Similarly, Zhao & Yue, (2013a, b) analyzed the vulnerabilities of existing browser-based Password Managers. The basic threat model they used allows the attacker to download malware, such as Trojan horses, temporarily on the victim's machine. Such malware can help the attacker collect the login information stored by the PM. The analysis of the source code of the examined PMs revealed that Firefox and Opera encrypt user passwords with three key triple-DES algorithms. The encrypted credentials are then saved into a database file and The triple-DES keys are saved into a binary file. The authors were able to verify that the attacker can simply decrypt the credentials by stealing both files.

3.3 Cross-Site Scripting Attacks

Stock & Johns (2014) assessed the potential threat of cross-site scripting attacks against browsers' PMs by analyzing the current features of password generation and password fields available in popular websites (Google Chrome version 31, Mozilla Firefox version 25, Opera version 18, Safari version 7, Internet Explorer version 11, and the Maxthon Cloud Browser version3). They discovered that among all of the examined web browsers, only Internet Explorer fills forms on any area of the same web application while the application bounds are controlled by the same Origin Policy. The Maxthon Cloud Browser only populates credentials when the same second-level domain is accessed, which bypasses the protocol and the port resources and allows the attacker to steal passwords from its storage. With respect to matching criteria, most browsers were found to be very relaxed. All examined browsers with the exception of Internet Explorer fill in the passwords only if they match the origins, while Maxthon Cloud Browser only considers the second-level domain. In such cases, the attacker can design a simple form to deceive the PMs into revealing the stored password from sites where two input fields are used for the login dialogue.

Oesch and Gautam and Ruoti (2021) evaluated the mobile autofill frameworks of iOS and Android devices by examining their capability of achieving significant improvements over desktop frameworks. The authors selected 14 mobile PMs for framework evaluation, and the three frameworks are iOS password autofill, iOS app extensions, and Android autofill service. The authors found that all frameworks require user involvement prior to autofill, and that iOS password autofill feature completely secures the autofill process for native UI app elements. Nevertheless, all mobile password manager frameworks fail to validate credential mapping accurately, and none of them successfully secure filled credentials, which makes them less secure than the weakest desktop password managers in many cases.

3.4 Brute Force and Local Decryption Attacks

Because the master password is so crucial in the concept, it must be strong in order to safeguard users' sensitive information including other passwords, files, and notes. Yu and Yin (2021); Zhao and Yue and Sun (2013a, b); examined the authentication mechanisms of well-known commercial PMs such as 1password, LastPass, and KeePass. They found that the authentication mechanisms of 1password, LastPass, and KeePass all use the same model that includes the master password or username as well as some database properties such as the KDF parameters. Yu and Yin (2021) used the brute force approach to crack the master password on the PMs, using a GPU platform (Graphic Processor Unit) due to its high parallelism and low energy consumption. They discovered that cracking the master password is far more difficult than cracking a basic hash like mdf($password). 1password, LastPass, and KeePass were found to have the same security level (Yu and Yin, 2021). However, LastPass's master password mechanism has serious security flaws. For example, the user is automatically authenticated when LastPass is re-used. This is because the master password is saved into an SQLite database table named LastPass-SavedLogins2. Regardless of encryption, locally stored master passwords are subject to local decryption attacks, which can be carried out by external attackers who have advanced computational and/or client-side stealing capabilities. Even if Lastpass does not store the master password locally, it is still vulnerable to brute-force attacks by external attackers. Internal attackers who are capable of server-side monitoring can also launch brute-force attacks on the master password (Zhao & Yue & Sun, 2013a, b). Similarly, Keeper, 1Password, and Dashlane are vulnerable to UI-driven brute force attacks. There was no defense mechanism in place to stop the authentication process after 10 failed login attempts, which implies that a dictionary attack on a user's account is feasible (Carr & Shahandashti, 2020).

The techniques utilized by PMs to implement autosave, autologin, and autofill functions vary greatly. Although the terms imply automated activity, these functions frequently require user participation. After a login submission, PMs usually autosave credentials by prompting the user after a login submission. In some applications, such as 1Password, Norton, and Blur, this functionality can be activated or removed via the settings. Other applications such as Passbolt, do not have an autosave function. Some PMs save credentials automatically when the login page loads, while others require user involvement like clicking a button. An in-between approach is utilized by Keeper where the user is asked to manually decide on whether credentials should be auto-filled (Huamanc et al., 2021). Some PMs allow the user to establish a four-digit PIN to ease authentication to Android applications, which eliminates the need to input a complex and lengthy master password when entering the vault. RoboForm and Dash-lane Android applications do not implement a permanent counter on the number of times an invalid PIN can be entered to access the app. Both applications (RoboForm and Dashlane) employ a four-digit long PIN and thus have 10,000 combinations. The manual testing of these applications reveals that a randomly selected pin can be cracked in less than three hours (Carr and Shahandashti, 2020). When the master password is not used, RoboForm provides no security to local storage. The user's website credential is not encrypted, but rather encoded without the usage of a cryptographic key. Therefore, external attackers with client-side stealing capabilities can obtain the file containing the website credentials of users who do not use master passwords. The attackers can then call the function RfUngarbleStringW() to retrieve the website's credentials entirely. Additionally, external attackers can still launch brute force attacks when the master password is used. Furthermore, RoboForm does not encrypt source code and traffic, instead, they are transmitted in plain text through HTTPS communication. Although HTTPS encrypts client-server communication to prevent MiTM attacks, inside attackers can get all credentials by monitoring incoming HTTPS requests and waiting for them to be decrypted on the server side. (Zhao and Yue and Sun, 2013a, b).

Oesch and Ruoti, (2020) evaluated the security improvements of thirteen popular password managers compared to their security prior to 2020, taking into account the three stages of the password manager lifecycle, password generation, autofill, and storage. They found extension and application-based password managers had improved since they were analyzed in previous years. They have addressed specific vulnerabilities related to securing metadata stored in password vaults as well as preventing password harvesting attacks by limiting auto-filling capabilities. In terms of security and functionality, browser-based PMs were found to lag behind extension and application-based PMs. Users must still verify that app and extension and application-based PMs are correctly configured, as neither LastPas nor Dashlane require user participation before auto-filling website passwords. Chatterjee et al., (2015) examined the development of vault applications that can prevent offline cracking attempts. The purpose of their "Kamofulage" system was to force the attacker to try login with a password from each of the vaults to identify the actual one. The authors aimed to discover a vulnerability in this approach and developed an attack to exploit it. They developed an ML-based cracking attack and used a number of datasets to train and test the model. They primarily used three large-scale password leaks which are Rock.You, Myspace, and Yahoo. They also simulated Kamouflage and found two vulnerabilities and their attack and exploited them. They were able to demonstrate how conventional techniques for cracking-resistant vaults actually weaken security through the attacks. The main strategy of Kamouflage, which is to store a list of cipher texts with one genuine vault buried amid several decoys created as a function of the real master password, offers attackers with an offline speedup.

3.5 Crawling, and Sensitive Data Extraction

Gonzalez & Chen and Jackson, (2013) presented a tool named Lupin that automatically saves passwords in password managers without the contest of the user. A network adversary can use the tool to extract credentials if the login form is on a non-HTTPS website. The authors used a web crawler that surveyed 45000 popular websites from Alexa's top website list. They found that more than 25% of these sites are vulnerable to such attacks. Examples of these vulnerable sites include Facebook, LinkedIn, and Twitter. It was also observed that about 12% of surveyed websites implemented SSL and about 27% exposed secure login forms on HTTPS pages. Stock and Johns (2014) performed a crawl of the top 4000 sites from Alexa. They discovered that less than 300 of the 2,143 examined domains do not utilize autocomplete characteristics, which prevents password managers from saving the credentials in the password manager's store.

3.6 Attacker's Level of Expertise

Ruffin et al., (2022) performed an empirical analysis of 20 popular vault applications to identify the vulnerabilities and expertise level required to exploit them. The expertise level consists of three categories, novice, intermediate, and expert. The beginner level reflects an attacker with little to no technical understanding of Android systems, which can only help in determining whether a vault program is installed on the mobile device. The intermediate level reflects an attacker who is familiar with the Android system and can access secret files saved by an app. The expert level reflects an attacker which advanced knowledge of Android systems, which allows the attacker to effectively use adp (Android Debug Bridge) to retrieve files and decompile apks (file format or distribution and installation used in Android). The authors determined that the majority of the tested vault applications may be located using noise level analysis by evaluating the program names and icons and matching them with other apps in the app library. They also found that an adversary with an elementary knowledge of Android systems can recover private files from 15 out of the 20 apps easily without rooting the mobile device. They also discovered that an attacker with a novice level may readily recover private files from about 75% of the apps without rooting the mobile device. It was also discovered that 5 apps' files cannot be recovered without root. Advanced-level adversaries can root the victim's mobile device and retrieve the data for two of the applications since these applications simply hide the contents by altering the file extension and adjusting the header bytes. Additionally, only 5 out of the 20 apps were found to have some encryption methods to protect the stored files. One of the common approaches is storing the files in a hidden folder. The authors, however, believe that this strategy is not safe since attackers may simply enable the option to view hidden files.

3.7 Adoption Barriers

The potential risk of losing all passwords is a significant barrier to using password managers. Some users are concerned that service providers would be able to access their passwords. A comparison of security and privacy issues reveals that security-related concerns outweigh privacy-related concerns in terms of adoption. The adoption of password managers can also be predicted while observing the dissatisfaction with the way passwords are handled without the use of PMs. This dissatisfaction mainly stems from the expense of having to memorize or save these credentials on notebooks or smartphones, which means that users need to look up the password every time they need to log in. Users' opinions of the benefits of PMs compared suggest a willingness to adopt this technology. Thus, it is critical to stress the benefits of using PMs in order to influence their adoption. Furthermore, the perception of the efficiency of PMs in protecting users' credentials also influences the adoption of this technology (Alkaldi & Renaud, 2022). The majority of issues in existing PMs relate to some features and functionalities such as optional auto-fill, and weak master passwords, while other issues can be resolved easily if the developers remain cautious and perform tests and trials with the established security methods, algorithms, and principles to correctly implement them. Additional unresolved challenges related to users' suspicion of PM software include the gap between the user and the developer, and improper web design practices, all of which are time-consuming and difficult to overcome. (Chaudhary et al., 2019).

Oesch et al., (2022) interviewed users of over 20 different Password Managers to identify how they practically utilize their password manager and to investigate underused capabilities and unexpected consumption behavior. They discovered that experts frequently use multiple password managers, which includes using browser-based managers such as Chrome in addition to an external manager such as LastPass. This practice was inspired by three important considerations. The first was a concern about losing passwords saved in the external manager, thus the user browser's manager was utilized as a backup. The second is that users are used to clicking through dialogue presented by the browsers, and the third is that participants utilized both managers such that if one failed to autofill a certain webpage, the other could. Although an unwillingness to use password generation was observed, there are two primary reasons behind that. The first is that participants often find generated passwords to be difficult to input if not auto-filled by a password manager, and the second is that participants worry that their manager fails to locate the generated password and subsequently locks out their accounts. While some users are more concerned about convenience than security, most users find breach notifications helpful and that they are willing to update their breached accounts' passwords. Participants favored Chrome's account breach notifications over those offered by external managers. Participants in the study, on the other hand, disliked the credential audit service offered by many external managers. It was also observed that some PMs fail to identify login forms and modify credentials or save them. Participants indicated that such issues are widespread. Additionally, mobile PMs usability is a big barrier to their use and adoption in the real world.

Michael Fagan et al., (2017) performed an online survey of 137 users and 111 non-users to evaluate differences between PM users and non-users, which included questions on emotion given its psychological significance when making decisions. The authors found that users of PMs are likely to have greater computer skills, better password managers, and better computer security in general. To these users, password managers are useful and convenient. Non-Users, on the other hand, are likely to rate their computer professionally and have fewer accounts. These non-users do not view PMs as an effective way to protect their accounts. While convenience was found to be important for many users, security concerns are the primary reasons why non-users do not utilize PMs. A combination of both quantitative and qualitative results suggests that non-users do not generally regard PMs as secure, which is not a true generalization considering that some PMs do provide good security if used properly.

4   Forensic Analysis

(See Table 4).

Table 4. Summary of artifacts across different apps

Source of evidence	Type of artifacts that could potentially be recovered	Reasons
Device-level (Main Memory)	Credentials (stored password's hash value and pin)	Credentials stored in plain-text Screen lock leaves the pin in the memory
Device-level (Login Screen)	Accessible files once the login screen protection is bypassed such as photos, videos, notes, and logged-in accounts	The ability of the investigator to make unauthorized changes to security settings such as Disabling the Screenshot prevention mechanism disabling password field visibility protection Bypassing login security
App-Level (Database)	Recovery of Photo, video, and timestamps that provide an indication of various app-related activities such as installation and uninstallation	The key used for encrypting these files was hard-coded in the source code
Server-level (Cloud server)	Credentials (clear text passwords, authentication tokens, and pin)	TLS is not implemented, which allows credential discovery when performing MiTM attack

4.1   Memory Forensics

Sabev and Petrov conducted a series of studies on two popular Android PMs (Keeper and Bitwarden). In 2021, they Analyzed the runtime behavior of two popular Android Password managers/vault applications (Keeper and Bitwarden) from a security and forensics perspective. The authors conclude that Keeper gives a large time frame for possible attackers to acquire the user's Master Password and data through inspecting Keeper's main memory. Moreover, Keeper retains any entrusted data in cleartext in main memory for the duration of its process. Unlike Keeper, Bitwarden's Master Password was only discovered in its _MD2. Additionally, Bitwarden only loads a tiny part of the data entrusted to it in clear text into the main memory. Based on this, Bitwarden is believed to take stronger security measures to restrict data exposure in main memory verses Keeper (Sabev and Petrov, 2021a, b).

Barten (2019) used File system-based and memory-based for client-side attacks on the LastPass extension for the Chrome browser. Because both file system and memory-based attacks take advantage of the local storage of the encrypted vault, the vault may be quickly decrypted if the password is memorized. Thus, disabling the offline access is arguably the best practice for the user. However, disabling offline access can only be achieved if a form of multi-factor authentication is enabled and cannot be disabled independently. The authors suggest that offline access is a security flaw since it enhances the opportunity to steal credentials through client-side attacks. The vault key, which is needed to open the vault in both file system and memory-based attacks, may be obtained through the Chrome developer tools. As a result, instead of inspecting the memory dump, an attacker may utilize the Chrome developer tools to retrieve the key. Today, the vault key is always available in memory and may be requested at any moment to decrypt the vault. Even when deleted, the key must be generated from the master password. As a result, the users may be repeatedly prompted for their master password in order to produce the key, which degrades the user experience. (Derk Barten, 2019).

Apostolopoulos et al., (2013) investigated the possibility of detecting authentication credentials stored in the volatile memory of Android mobile devices, using existing tools. They used a Dalvik Debug Monitor Server (DDMS), which is a graphical debugging tool used to examine the running process. They were able to recover their credentials in most of the examined applications because the credentials were stored in plaintext. They were also able to retrieve the passwords of five apps of major Greek banks and the username of four of these apps. In another set of experiments, the authors discovered a unique pattern indicating where the password is saved. For instance, they found the string "password " in the memory dump, which means that a forensic investigator or a malicious actor can look for such patterns to find passwords and usernames in the device. Most Android apps seem to be vulnerable to credential discovery. What is more disturbing is learning that web banking apps were also found to be vulnerable to credential discovery, which leaves their customers' credentials at risk. Similarly, Christoforos Ntantogian et al., (2014) conducted an experimental analysis to investigate the possibility of discovering authentication credentials from the volatile memory of 13 Android mobile devices, using open source tools such as Linux memory exactor (LiME) software, a loadable kernel module that allows recovering volatile memory from Linux and Linux-based devices. The authors were able to recover their own credentials in most of the examined applications as they were found in plaintext.

Gray and Franqueiraand and Yu, (2016) analyzed three popular password managers: KeePass (v2.28) Password Safe (b3.35.1) and RoboForm (v7.912). Their investigation showed that KeePass master password is saved in the hard drive within the page files when the computer capacity is low, which allows the identification of the password in plain text using keyword search. For Password Safe, the keyword search showed that a copied entry (the password for instance) could be found unencrypted and saved in pagefile (C\fpagefile.sys). As for RoboForm, it was observed that it stores crucial information on the pagefile, which includes name, address, pin number, email, and credit card number. Lee & Chen & Wallach, (2019) selected 11 Android apps (including 4 password managers) to study the password retention problem. The study involved performing a full physical memory dump and per-process dump. The authors found that all tested apps are vulnerable to credential discovery as they successfully received passwords in plain text for all apps. The lock screen system also retains the PIN password inside the memory. Although Android spends a significant effort to protect the PIN password, however, the retention of the PIN password in the memory defeats the purpose of the added security measure completely.

Martini and Do & Choo, (2015) analyzed Universal Password Manager and other apps to determine what kind of sensitive information can be obtained. The authors were able to discover crypto classes instances of UPM extension, which allowed them to locate the 8-character salt used by the app to encrypt and decrypt the database that contains the user's data. Additionally, they were able to find an instance of the java class that contains the user's password in plaintext inside the memory. Because UPM does not directly interact with a server, the only ways to access data from its database are brute-force techniques or other means of acquiring the user's password.

4.2 Investigation of Current Encryption and Security Approaches

Fahl et al., (2013) analyzed 13 free and 8 non-free Android password managers. They found that ost analyzed PMs use Advanced Encryption Standards (AES) within several key lengths. Seven applications improve the security of encrypted credentials by deriving the symmetric encryption key from the user's master secret using a specific key derivation mechanism. Passwords with fewer than 16 characters get appended to strengthen the password. The Android standard browser does not provide encryption for passwords, but rather protects against unauthorized access. The mechanism of Android's Account Manager enables a centralized way to store credentials and provides protection from unauthorized access. Nevertheless, the accounts.db database lacks an additional layer of encryption, making the password vulnerable to forensic investigation. Furthermore, an attacker can discover the services for which a victim has accounts and which services use the same login credentials. This is because certain PMs store databases on the SD card, which is globally accessible without permission on all Android 4.0 and earlier devices. Additionally, the authors discovered that many app developers do not properly implement TLS, leaving their apps vulnerable to MiTM attacks. Although RoboForm and Secure-Safe implement TLS, they failed to authenticate the cloud server's TLS certificates, and accept all certificates instead. But this has no security implication for SecureSafe because it implements a session-specific symmetric key during the SRP login to ensure end-to-end encryption for passwords.

Zhang & Baggili & Breitinger, (2017) analyzed 18 Android vault applications and investigated the forensic artifacts they generate. They discovered that the majority of developers used obfuscation and native libraries to safeguard their code. While this method disturbed the process of reverse engineering the apps, examiners can still exploit these applications. The authors found that photos and videos entrusted in these applications may be undecrypted, encrypted, or deconstructed. While the photos and videos in about a third of the total anlyzed applications were changed or renamed, the examiner can easily recover such files since the data of the media files were not modified. On the other hand, a similar portion of the applications stored deconstructed files by erasing data from the header. Although about a third of the analyzed applications encrypt the photos, the encryption method was insecure because the information used for generating the key was hard coded in the source code. Furthermore, around one-third of the applications saved the password in cleartext on the Android device, while about one-half of the examined applications store the password hash value, allowing the authors to perform brute force and similar password-cracking attacks. Keeper used a salute password hashing function, while Coverme saved the hash value of the key generated by the password rather than the hash value of the password itself. Therefore, the authors regarded these two applications as more secure since they offered a more complicated password system or used a more robust hashing technique. The authors were able to easily recover hidden contents from all vaults with the exception of Keeper and Coverme, and concluded that Coverme offeres a higher chance for brute force attack because it limits the password length to 16 digits.

Sabev & Petrov (2021b) were able to remove password field visibility protection by modifying the security settings in keeper and increasing the auto-lock time. Furthermore, they manipulated the application record by altering the value of link between the fields. They were successful in making Bitwarden's vault constantly open and fully available by switching the vault time from 15 min to "Never". In a different study, Sabev & Petrov (2021a) used the SEC, which is "an extensive body of knowledge about software security that is widely accepted security recommendations and guidelines for building secure software", to evaluate LastPass, Bitwarden, and Dashlane based on public information about their security that is available in the official documentation. They found Bitwarden to provide the highest security among these applications. On the other hand, Laspass appeared to be the least secure app, while Keeper and Dashlane were found to be equal in terms of security. Btiwarden was found to provide better trustworthiness and transparency compared to the other applications. However, the results may change significantly if advanced analysis and debugging techniques were performed.

4.3   Content Hiding App Identification

Although content-hiding applications are considered a good approach for securely storing users data, yet, it can also be a perfect tool for bad actors to hide their illegal data. Peng et al., (2021) created a system that uses deep learning to detect content-hiding applications that can discover and retrieve targeted data from Android devices. The authors deployed a crawler to collect GooglePlay Store apps in order to acquire information about probable content-hiding applications. Their system was able to recognize every vault app that was active on a rooted device in addition to extracting data such as pictures, videos, and text. Although the system successfully recognized all vault apps for all third-party programs in the unrooted device, the extraction of the hidden data was only successful in one of the vault applications.

Gokila Dorai et al., (2020) developed a fast way of identifying vault apps using common keyword search based on Machine Learning-based binary classification to assess whether an app is indeed a vault application. They developed a system that can automatically extract hidden contents from each potential target. This system is called VIDE and is designed for iOS devices. Although existing data extraction tools are capable of extracting all data from smartphones, yet they frequently necessitate the user to categorize and filter the data. Thus, the proposed system can make the process easier for the investigator as it automatically identifies and extracts data from the set of vault applications. Similarly, Gilbert & Seigfried-Spellar, (2022) Conducted a forensic analysis on 5 iOS photo vaults (KeepSafe, Photo Vault, Calculator+, Secret Safe, and Purple photo vault). The authors found that each vault left evidence and images for the investigator and each of the forensic toolkits used in the investigation generated different scan findings. The forensic tools used are UFED Cellebrite (v.7.3), Magnet Axiom (v.3.8.0), and Black Bag Mobilyze 2019 R1. Mobilyze found the least amount of information from the vault applications and was only able to identify 3 out of 5 vault apps, which implies the importance of using more than one forensic software to provide the most correct evidence. Axiom was not able to locate every picture in the vault apps' camera roll, while Cellebrite did. Amongst the three applications, Cellebrite produced the most results and was the only tool to discover one of the passcodes from the "Photo Vault" of photos.

5   Design of Secure Password Managers and Vaults

Decades after inventing them, PMs are still subject to many attacks including online guessing (brute force), offline dictionary, and shoulder surfing. Some of these attacks rely on issues with the nature of the password itself, such as memorability. Users tend to pick unsophisticated passwords that are easy to remember, which carries the risk of easier attack, whereas safe random passwords expose alternative attack venues owing to memorability difficulties where users write such passwords down or store them electronically. Online password managers provide a solution for these problems by encrypting web accounts passwords and storing them in the cloud (Shirvanian et al, 2021). But this carries its own risks as these credentials stored in the cloud or locally are subject to massive password breaches. To mitigate the risk of storing passwords locally or in the cloud, Shirvanian et al., (2021) proposed a cloud-based password manager named HIPPO that does not memorize or save accounts or master passwords. The proposed application relies on the device-enhanced password key exchange cryptographic principle, which has been shown to be resistant to dictionary and online guessing attacks. When HIPPO receives the user's master password, it immediately produces a strong, random account password for each website without saving it. The randomized account password is generated using an obvious-pseud random function (OPRF) protocol, which is a crucial component of the master password. The user (the client) starts the authentication process with the master password, and the cloud-based password manager stores a different key for every service that needs authentication. By using this protocol (OPRF), the password manager is prevented from learning or storing the randomized account password or any passwords that are derived from them. The security of the proposed app is derived from the formal framework and security proofs of the Device Enhanced Password Authenticated Key

Exchange (DE-PAKE) protocol which offers many security benefits such as resilience to both online and offline attacks, and resistance to attacks upon compromised servers. A limitation of this approach is that it may be a target for guessing attempts to log in to the web server because it is implemented as an online service without requiring a user authentication. Y. Li et al., (2017) addressed the same issues by proposing a password manager named BluePass that stores the vault (all encrypted site passwords) locally in mobile devices and the decryption key to the vault on the user's computer BluePass separates the password for a decryption key from the password for the password vault, allowing the password vault to be kept locally while the decryption key is kept on the BluePass server. When the user needs to log in to a website account, the computer will automatically request the password associated with the website account from the mobile device. The computer will then utilize the local decryption key to decode the site password that was received through Bluetooth and automatically fill out the user's online forms. BluePass uses two-factor authentication as its model, requiring a master password and a mobile device to decrypt and retrieve site credentials. Given today's computing power and the weak password selection on the user side, the master password database can almost certainly be cracked by offline attacks. But since BluePass does not store passwords on the server, it provides security against massive data breaches, which can reveal both hashed master passwords and password vaults. However, since this model utilizes the auto-fill feature, all of the security issues related to auto-fill vulnerabilities discussed in the previous sections apply to this model. Additionally, severe security issues can occur when the user fails to capture the correct mental model.

Stobert & Biddle, (2014) Proposed a prototype for a password manager called Versipass that incorporates cued graphical passwords to address the issue of password memorability. According to psychological findings known as the "picture superiority effect", people are more likely to recall pictures than texts. Graphical passwords leverage this result by cueing graphical passwords for more memorable passwords. Verispass does not retain passwords; instead, it remembers picture clues for graphical passwords, which makes it function more like a password cue manager. The app only stores the password cues and enables users to securely create passwords and send them to websites. The password system sends a cue to the user, which helps the user to memorize the original password. This model does not only cue graphical passwords, but more generally, the cue may be visual or audio with the goal of cueing memory and providing context to the user. This approach eliminates the risk imposed by an attacker that can access the user account when accessing Versipass because the passwords are not stored in the app. However, such an attacker can still access personal information such as lists of sites and usernames, which can cause significant disruption for the user if the attacker deletes information or change the category password. Thus, despite the benefits of not remembering passwords, the app is still vulnerable to fishing, guessing, and capture attacks.

AlMuhanna and AlFaadhel and Ara, (2022) presented a system that provides resilience against brute-force attacks by implementing honey encryption (HE) in the password manager. In this system, the password manager hashes the user's inputted password to produce a group of Honey words that closely resemble the original password. These honey phrases serve as a warning system to catch intruders. OTP encryption, which encrypts all application credentials, adds an extra degree of protection to websites and other application passwords stored in this password manager. The password manager will give the user three attempts to input their credentials before granting access if the provided hashed master password matches the one that is already saved. When an attacker types the incorrect key, the Honey encryption algorithm creates a genuine-looking false message while securely hiding the real message. In a way, the system analyzes the attackers' activity to identify and deceive them. When a collection of automatically created honey words is used to identify brute-force attacks, the system blocks access to the account if one of the words matches the master password that was input. The attacker will be directed to a phony account with fictitious passwords. One of the biggest problems with this method is that it might mistakenly identify a genuine user as an attacker if they make a typo that matches one of the honeywords. To address the same issue, Yuchen & Rui, & Wenchang, (2016) proposed an approach based on hardware trusted platform module (TPM) in order to improve the security of browser password managers. This method employs the master password as the authorization credential for permitted access to TPM and encrypts the user's passwords using keys generated by TM. The experiments performed by the authors show that this system can successfully protect against brute force and password-stealing attacks. One of the limitations of this approach is its inability to prevent keyboard recording attacks from stealing user-entered passwords (Table 5).

Table 5. Summary of design principles

Study	Characteristics	Benefits	Problem addressed	Limitations
Shirvanian et al., (2021)	OPRF: derived from the formal framework and security proofs of the Device Enhanced Password Authenticated Key Exchange	Proven to resist online guessing and dictionary attacks Does not store passwords	Massive password breaches of passwords stored in the cloud or locally by PMs	Susceptible to guessing attack against the web server
Y. Li et al., (2017)	Stores password vault locally while the decryption key is stored in the server of PM	Does not store passwords on the server	Massive data breaches which can leak both password vaults and hashed master passwords	Security issues related auto-fill may also apply to this model User can fail to capture the correct mental model
Stobert and Biddle, (2014)	incorporates cued graphical passwords as well as visual or audio with the purpose of cueing memory and providing context to the user	Remembers image cues for graphical passwords instead of remembering passwords Eliminates the risk of attackers accessing the user account	Password memorability and associating passwords with accounts	Susceptible to fishing, guessing, and capture attacks

(continued)

Table 5. (*continued*)

Study	Characteristics	Benefits	Problem addressed	Limitations
AlMuhanna and AlFaadhel and Ara, (2022)	Implements honey encryption in the password manager which hashes the password and creates a set of Honey words that mimic the real password	Provides resilience against brute-force attacks Detects brute force attempts Misleads the attacker by analyzing their behavior	Brute Force attack	Incapable of distinguishing between a brute force attempt and a typographical error by a legitimate user
Yuchen and Rui, and Wenchang (2016)	based on hardware trusted platform module (TPM) that encrypts the user's passwords with keys generated by TM which uses the master password as the credential for authorized access to TPM	Defends against password stealing and brute force attacks	Brute Force attack	Incapable of protecting against key loggers

6 Discussion and Future Research Directions

Username and password are still, by large, the predominant method of authentication. Although password managers provide many benefits to the user by generating sophisticated random passwords and storing user passwords locally or in the cloud, there are important barriers to the adoption of these applications. In this research, we observe that security concerns are important barriers to the adoption as not all users view password managers as a secure method of storing their credentials. Many users have concerns about the security of these credentials stored in the cloud or in the application's server. These concerns can be confirmed by existing research that finds many security problems with PMs. Most of the problems in existing PMs are related to features and functionalities of PMs such as weak passwords and auto-fill that allow attackers to perform a variety of attacks including phishing, brute-force, cross-site scripting, and local decryption. In this research, we observed how critical the autofill feature is for password managers. In addition to the convenience it provides for the user, some researchers found that PMs that use clipboard without implementing auto-fill can be vulnerable to key loggers and clipboard attacks (Carlos Luevanos1 et al., 2017). On the other hand, the autofill feature can allow fishing, clipboard, iFrame sweep, and cross-site scripting attacks (Silver et al, 2014); (Carr and Shahandashti, 2020); (Aonzo et al, 2018); (Stock and Johns, 2014); (Oesch and Gautam and Ruoti, 2021). One of the ways Password managers can prevent that is by never auto-filling under certain conditions, and requiring user interaction through some form of trusted browser UI that cannot be affected by untrusted JavaScript. Password managers should also provide an option to clear the clipboard after a set amount of time (Carr and Shahandashti, 2020). It was observed that there was no strict enforcement of a strong master password in a number of PMs (Luevanos et al., 2017).

On the forensics side, the remanence of sensitive data such as passwords, in the main memory is still an issue, as a number of researchers were able to obtain authentication credentials from the volatile memory. Others were able to find the master password and other passwords in plain text. Additionally, most PMs and VAs do not protect the password with an extra encryption layer from forensic analysis. Many developers use obfuscation and implement native libraries to protect their code. Although that hindered reverse engineering these applications, it did not protect them from other types of exploitation performed by the examiners.

With respect to the secure design of password managers, the approaches we observed can be valuable in protecting against brute-force and credential-stealing attacks. The major theme among these studies is to solve the problem of storing passwords locally, on the app server, or in the cloud which can lead to massive data breaches. However, these approaches do not address other common vulnerabilities such as those related to auto-fill, clipboard, and keylogging.

It was observed that researchers make their selection of password managers/vault applications for security analysis based on popularity which is determined by the number of downloads from google play, and the vast majority of them are open-source. Although being an open source allowed people to find vanuralites, not everyone reports the vulnerabilities they discover. Thus, attackers can choose to keep these vulnerability secrets and exploit them in the future. In addition, a number of these open-source password managers lack many features that closed-source password managers have. Since such features strengthen the security of the applications, more effort is needed to investigate other closed-source password managers.

Some studies such as Christoforos Ntantogian et al., (2014) did not mention the apps they investigated. As a result, we were unable to verify the relevance of their results to the popular PMs often investigated in other studies. We also make similar observation to that of Chaudhary et al., (2019) as they mentioned that their selected papers often focused on the engineering perspective of PM design. They also mention that their study was not able to establish any particular importance of the security features and usability described, due to the different approaches of the password managers reviewed such as cloud-based and wallet based.

A limitation of this study is that the majority of the reviewed papers were conducted prior to 2018, which means that some of the vulnerabilities might have been patched in the newer versions of the PMs. Although Oesch & Ruoti, (2020) suggest that app-based and extension-based password managers have improved since the time they were analyzed in previous years, we did not find a comprehensive comparative analysis that covers all of the improvements in all of the analyzed apps over the years. But Oesch & Ruoti, (2020) also mentioned some remaining issues related to autofill in which the client is vulnerable to password harvesting attacks, which suggests that some security issues remain unresolved.

7   Conclusions

In this paper, we conducted a comprehensive literature review on password managers and vault apps, focusing on both security and forensics. We highlighted key security issues related to these applications based on the existing literature. We also reviewed studies that discussed user behavior towards these applications and the existing approaches for designing secure password managers. We hope that this work will inform future design of password manager and vault apps.

References

Alkaldi, N., Renaud, K.: MIGRANT: modeling smartphone password manager adoption using migration theory. ACM SIGMIS Database: DATABASE Adv. Inf. Syst. **53**(2), 63–95 (2022)

AlMuhanna, A., AlFaadhel, A., Ara, A.: Enhanced system for securing password manager using honey encryption. In: 2022 Fifth International Conference of Women in Data Science at Prince Sultan University (WiDS PSU). IEEE (2022)

Aonzo, S., et al.: Phishing attacks on modern android. In: Proceedings of the 2018 ACM SIGSAC Conference on Computer and Communications Security (2018)

Apostolopoulos, D., Marinakis, G., Ntantogian, C., Xenakis, C.: Discovering authentication credentials in volatile memory of android mobile devices. In: Douligeris, C., Polemi, N., Karantjias, A., Lamersdorf, W. (eds.) I3E 2013. IFIP Advances in Information and Communication Technology, vol. 399, pp. 178–185. Springer, Heidelberg (2013). https://doi.org/10.1007/978-3-642-37437-1_15

Barten, D.: Client-side attacks on the LastPass browser extension (2019)

Carr, M., Shahandashti, S.F.: Revisiting security vulnerabilities in commercial password managers. In: Hölbl, M., Rannenberg, K., Welzer, T. (eds.) SEC 2020. IFIP Advances in Information and Communication Technology, vol. 580, pp. 265–279. Springer, Cham (2020). https://doi.org/10.1007/978-3-030-58201-2_18

Chatterjee, R., et al.: Cracking-resistant password vaults using natural language encoders. In: 2015 IEEE Symposium on Security and Privacy. IEEE (2015)

Chaudhary, S., et al.: Usability, security and trust in password managers: a quest for user-centric properties and features. Comput. Sci. Rev. **33**, 69–90 (2019)

Dorai, G., et al.: Vide-vault app identification and extraction system for iOS devices. Forensic Sci. Int.: Digit. Invest. **33**, 301007 (2020)

Fagan, M., et al.: An investigation into users' considerations towards using password managers. Hum.-Cent. Comput. Inf. Sci. **7**(1), 1–20 (2017)

Fahl, S., Harbach, M., Oltrogge, M., Muders, T., Smith, M.: Hey, you, get off of my clipboard. In: Sadeghi, A.R. (ed.) FC 2013. Lecture Notes in Computer Science, vol. 7859, pp. 144–161. Springer, Heidelberg (2013). https://doi.org/10.1007/978-3-642-39884-1_12

Gasti, P., Rasmussen, K.B.: On the security of password manager database formats. In: Foresti, S., Yung, M., Martinelli, F. (eds.) ESORICS 2012. LNCS, vol. 7459, pp. 770–787. Springer, Berlin, Heidelberg (2012). https://doi.org/10.1007/978-3-642-33167-1_44

Gilbert, A., Seigfried-Spellar, K.C., Gilbert, A.K.: Forensic discoverability of iOS vault applications. J. Digit. Forensics Secur. Law **17**(1), 1 (2022)

Gonzalez, R., Chen, E.Y., Jackson, C.: Automated password extraction attack on modern password managers. arXiv preprint arXiv:1309.1416 (2013)

Gray, J., Franqueira, V.N.L., Yu, Y.: Forensically-sound analysis of security risks of using local password managers. In: 2016 IEEE 24th International Requirements Engineering Conference Workshops (REW). IEEE (2016)

He, Y., Wang, R., Shi, W.: Implementation of a TPM-based security enhanced browser password manager. Wuhan Univ. J. Nat. Sci. **21**(1), 56–62 (2016)

Huaman, N., et al.: They would do better if they worked together: the case of interaction problems between password managers and websites. In: 2021 IEEE Symposium on Security and Privacy (SP). IEEE (2021)

Li, Z., et al.: The {Emperor's} new password manager: security analysis of web-based password managers. In: 23rd USENIX Security Symposium (USENIX Security 2014) (2014)

Li, Y., Wang, H., Sun, K.: Bluepass: a secure hand-free password manager. In: Lin, X., Ghorbani, A., Ren, K., Zhu, S., Zhang, A. (eds.) SecureComm 2017. Lecture Notes of the Institute for Computer Sciences, Social Informatics and Telecommunications Engineering, vol. 238, pp. 185–205. Springer, Cham (2017). https://doi.org/10.1007/978-3-319-78813-5_10

Luevanos, C., et al.: Analysis on the security and use of password managers. In: 2017 18th International Conference on Parallel and Distributed Computing, Applications and Technologies (PDCAT). IEEE (2017)

Martini, B., Do, Q., Choo, K.-K.R.: Mobile cloud forensics: an analysis of seven popular Android apps. arXiv preprint arXiv:1506.05533 (2015)

Ntantogian, C., et al.: Evaluating the privacy of Android mobile applications under forensic analysis. Comput. Secur. **42**, 66–76 (2014)

Oesch, S., et al.: "It basically started using me": an observational study of password manager usage. In: CHI Conference on Human Factors in Computing Systems (2022)

Oesch, S., Gautam, A., Ruoti, S.: The emperor's new autofill framework: a security analysis of autofill on iOS and Android. In: Annual Computer Security Applications Conference (2021)

Oesch, S., Ruoti, S.: That was then, this is now: a security evaluation of password generation, storage, and autofill in browser-based password managers. In: Proceedings of the 29th USENIX Conference on Security Symposium (2020)

Peng, M., et al.: DECADE-deep learning based content-hiding application detection system for Android. In: 2021 IEEE International Conference on Big Data (Big Data). IEEE (2021)

Sabev, P., Petrov, M.: Android password managers and vault applications: data storage security issues identification. J. Inf. Secur. Appl. **67**, 103152 (2022)

Sabev, P., Petrov, M.: Android password managers and vault applications: an investigation on data remanence in main memory (2021a)

Ruffin, M., et al.: Casing the vault: security analysis of vault applications. In: Proceedings of the 21st Workshop on Privacy in the Electronic Society (2022)

Sabev, P., Petrov, M.: Android password managers and vault applications: comparative security analysis. In: 2021 International Conference Automatics and Informatics (ICAI). IEEE (2021b)

Shirvanian, M., et al.: A hidden-password online password manager. In: Proceedings of the 36th Annual ACM Symposium on Applied Computing (2021)

Silver, D., et al.: Password managers: attacks and defenses. In: 23rd USENIX Security Symposium (USENIX Security 2014) (2014)

Stobert, E., Biddle, R.: A password manager that doesn't remember passwords. In: Proceedings of the 2014 New Security Paradigms Workshop (2014)

Stock, B., Johns, M.: Protecting users against XSS-based password manager abuse. In: Proceedings of the 9th ACM Symposium on Information, Computer and Communications security (2014)

Walkup, E.: The password problem. No. SAND2016-5208T. Sandia National Lab. (SNL-NM), Albuquerque, NM (United States) (2016)

Yu, F., Yin, H.: A security analysis of the authentication mechanism of password managers. In: 2021 IEEE 21st International Conference on Communication Technology (ICCT). IEEE (20210

Zhang, X., Baggili, I., Breitinger, F.: Breaking into the vault: privacy, security and forensic analysis of Android vault applications. Comput. Secur. **70**, 516–531 (2017)

Zhao, R., Yue, C., Sun, K.: A security analysis of two commercial browser and cloud based password managers. In: 2013 International Conference on Social Computing. IEEE (2013)
Zhao, R., Yue, C.: All your browser-saved passwords could belong to us: a security analysis and a cloud-based new design. In: Proceedings of the third ACM Conference on Data and Application Security and Privacy (2013)
Zhao, R., Yue, C., Sun, K.: Vulnerability and risk analysis of two commercial browser and cloud based password managers. ASE Sci. J. 1(4), 1–15 (2013)

Lattice-Based Secret Sharing Scheme (Chinese Remainder Theorem)

Songshou Dong[1,2,3], Yanqing Yao[1,2,3(✉)], Yihua Zhou[4,5], and Yuguang Yang[4,5]

[1] State Key Laboratory of Software Development Environment, Beihang University,
Beijing 100191, China
yaoyq@buaa.edu.cn
[2] State Key Laboratory of Cryptology, Beijing 100878, China
[3] Key Laboratory of Aerospace Network Security, Ministry of Industry and Information
Technology, School of Cyber Science and Technology, Beihang University, Beijing 100191,
China
[4] Faculty of Information Technology, Beijing University of Technology, Bejing 100124, China
{zhouyh,yangyang7357}@bjut.edu.cn
[5] Beijing Key Laboratory of Trusted Computing, Beijing 100124, China

Abstract. Secret sharing schemes are used as a tool in many cryptographic protocols including revocable electronic cash, electronic voting, cloud computing and key management in sensor networks. But the existing post-quantum secret sharing schemes are all based on Shamir's (t, n) threshold scheme, there is currently no post-quantum secret sharing scheme based on the Chinese Remainder Theorem (CRT), so we construct a verifiable lattice-based secret sharing scheme using some number theory methods and interaction methods. Furthermore, we prove our scheme is safe in the post-quantum era. Finally, we compare our scheme with other schemes. And the comparison shows that our scheme is more efficient and occupies less memory.

Keywords: Chinese remainder theorem · secret sharing · lattice · post-quantum · verifiable

1 Introduction

Secret sharing is an important means in information security and data confidentiality. In 1979, its concept was first proposed by Shamir [1] and Beimel [2]. It refers to dividing the secret s into several shares and distributing them among a group of participants $P = \{P_1, P_1, \cdots, P_n\}$, so that each participant gets a secret share about the secret s, and only P's some specific subsets (called qualified subsets or authorized subsets) can effectively recover s, while other subsets of P (non-qualified subsets) cannot effectively recover s, or even get any useful information about the secret s.

A secret sharing system, consists of secret distributors, participant set P, access structure Γ, secret space S, share space T, distribution algorithm, recovery algorithm, and so on. The secret space gives the value range of the secret: the set of participants

S. Goel and P. R. Nunes de Souza (Eds.): ICDF2C 2023, LNICST 571, pp. 54–62, 2024.
https://doi.org/10.1007/978-3-031-56583-0_4

gives the members who participate in the secret sharing; the access structure Γ points out which participants can recover the secret together, and Γ has properties: if $A \in \Gamma$ and $A \subset B$, then $B \in \Gamma$; the share space gives the value range of the secret share; the distribution algorithm gives the probability polynomial time algorithm for generating the secret share from the secret; the recovery algorithm is deterministic. The subset of P in the access structure is called a qualified subset. According to the containment relationship, the minimal element in Γ is called the minimum qualified subset, and Γ is uniquely determined by its minimal element set Γ_0, and Γ_0 is called the basis of Γ. A secret-sharing scheme is said to be complete if all non-qualified subsets do not have any information about the secret s. We call $\rho = \log|T|/\log|S|$ the information rate of a secret sharing scheme. A secret sharing scheme is said to be ideal if its information rate is 1.

The threshold method is the most common in secret sharing systems. There are many threshold systems proposed, among which Shamir's Lagrange interpolation polynomial method [1], Blakley's vector method [3], Asmuth et al.'s congruence class method [4, 5], and Karnin's matrix method [6] are the main representatives, and these have been widely used. There are two main problems [7–25] in the usual secret sharing scheme: one is that it cannot resist the sharer's cheating well, that is, some sharers will provide false shares when recovering the secret, so some members of the qualified subset cannot recover the correct share. Second, it cannot effectively prevent distributors from cheating, that is, distributors may distribute false shares to some sharers when distributing secret shares. To solve these problems, Chor et al. [7] proposed the concept of verifiable secret sharing. The verifiable secret sharing scheme is composed of an additional verification algorithm based on the usual secret sharing scheme. A verifiable secret sharing scheme is a basic tool for designing multi-party security protocols. It has been widely used in many aspects such as multi-party secure computing, group-oriented cryptosystem, key escrow system, and electronic commerce. In the verifiable secret sharing scheme, the sharer can check whether the secret share he receives is valid (whether it is compatible with other shares) through the verification algorithm. Let $P_1, P_2, \ldots, P_n$ be the sharers, s is the secret to be shared, and the access structure is Γ, then the verification algorithm satisfies

$$\exists u \forall A \in \Gamma : (\forall P_i \in A : Verify(s_i = 1) \rightarrow Rcover(\{s_i; P_i \in A\}) = u$$

When the distributor is honest, $u = s$. If there is no need to exchange information between sharers or between sharer and distributor when running the verification algorithm, the corresponding verifiable secret sharing scheme is called non-interactive. The first verifiable secret sharing scheme is interactive, and Benloh [26] gave the first non-interactive verifiable secret sharing scheme, but this scheme has a trusted center. Afterwards, Feldman [12], Pedersen [13] and others successively proposed some non-interactive verifiable secret sharing schemes that do not require the trusted center. Lin et al. [10] proposed a verifiable multiple secret sharing scheme. In the usual verifiable secret sharing scheme, only the sharer himself can verify the validity of the shares he gets, which limits the verifiability greatly. To solve this problem, Stadler [23] further proposed the concept of publicly verifiable secret sharing. In a publicly verifiable secret sharing scheme, the verifier can verify the correctness of the distribution of the secret share, and the sharer can verify the validity of the shares held by himself. Stadler [23] gave two publicly verifiable secret sharing schemes, Fuiisaki et al. [24] gave a practical provably secure publicly verifiable secret sharing scheme and its application. In these schemes, the verification algorithm relies on tools such as public key encryption and zero-knowledge proof, and the structure is relatively complex, so the efficiency is not ideal.

According to Ref. [17], a verifiable secret sharing scheme must satisfy the following two security properties:

1) If the distributor is honest, the share distribution process will always succeed, and the attacker (including the malicious sharer) will not get any information about the shared secret during the share distribution process. During the recovery process, no matter how the attacker behaves, the honest sharer can always recover the shared secret correctly.
2) If the distributor is colluded by the attacker (distributor is malicious), then either the malicious behavior of the distributor is discovered by the honest sharers, causing all honest sharers to withdraw from the share distribution process; or the distribution process is accepted by the honest sharer, as a result of the distribution process, a certain secret is uniquely fixed by the information held by the honest sharer, and during the recovery process, the honest sharer is able to reconstruct the secret.

The present secret sharing scheme based on classical number theory problem is threatened by quantum computer. Lattice structure is considered to be resistant to attacks by quantum computers. In recent years, some sharing schemes based on lattice secrets have been put forward [27–36]. In 2015, Pilaram et al. [34] proposed a lattice based (t, n) threshold multi-stage secret sharing (MSSS) scheme according to Ajtai's construction for one-way functions. The principle of his scheme is based on Shamir's secret sharing method. In 2022, Yang et al. [35] pointed out that there were loopholes in Pilaram et al. [34]'s scheme and proposed a filling method. In the same year, Kiamari et al. [36] proposed a non-interactive verifiable LWE-based multi secret sharing scheme. It is the first LWE based threshold multi secret sharing scheme that has formal security in the standard model.

But none of them are constructed based on the Chinese remainder theorem (CRT), and there are some security and efficiency issues. Therefore, we construct a verifiable secret sharing scheme based on the CRT that is secure in the post-quantum era. Our contributions are as follows:

1) We use number theory knowledge and interaction method to propose a post-quantum secure verifiable secret sharing scheme based on the CRT, which makes the post-quantum secret sharing scheme based on the CRT one more alternative;
2) We analyzed the security of our scheme and compared it with other schemes;

2 Preliminaries

2.1 Notations

Table 1 describes some system parameter notations needed by our scheme.

Table 1. System parameter notations

Notation	Description
n	Total number of people
$p_1, p_2, \cdots, p_n$	n primes which satisfied $p_1 < p_2 < \cdots < p_n$
ϕ	Empty set
$\Lambda, \Lambda_1, \Lambda_2, \cdots, \Lambda_n$	Lattice $\Lambda_1 = p_1 Z^n$, $\Lambda_2 = p_2 Z^n$, $\cdots$, $\Lambda_n = p_n Z^n$, $p_1 Z^n \cap p_2 Z^n \cap \cdots \cap p_n Z^n = p_1 p_2 \cdots p_n Z^n \neq \varnothing$
t	Threshold size
s	Secret value
m	The size of matrix
ϕ	Empty set
σ	Gaussian parameter
$D_{\Lambda, \sigma, v}(\cdot)$	Discrete Gaussian distribution
$\| \cdot \|$	l_2 norm
log	The logarithm based on 2
O and ω	the growth of functions

2.2 Algorithm Model and Security Model

1) Secret Sharing

A secret sharing scheme is a method of sharing secrets among a set of parties called participants. A trusted third party, called a dealer, assigns a private value (called a share), to each participant. Only the authorized subset of the participant can recover the secret by running a pre-specified algorithm. The set of all authorization subsets is called the access structure. In general, the access structure is a subset of the power set of participants.

A concrete instance of a general access structure is the threshold structure. A (t, n) threshold secret sharing scheme is called perfect if less than t participants cannot obtain information about the secret. A secret sharing scheme is said to be ideal when the entropy of each share is equal to the entropy of the secret.

A secret sharing scheme usually consists of two phases:

(1) Share distribution: In this phase, the dealer computes the shares using a prespecified algorithm and sends them securely to the participants.
(2) Secret reconstruction: In this phase, the authorized subsets of participants send their shares to a combiner to recover the secret by running the algorithm.

2) Security Requirements

Each secret can only be recovered by any t or more participants who receive shares, and fewer than t participants cannot get any information about the secret.

2.3 Lattice

Lattice [37]: $b_1, b_2, \cdots, b_n$ are n linearly independent vectors in R^n, let $B = [b_1, b_2, \cdots, b_n]$, $\Lambda(B) = \{Bc = \sum_{i=1}^{n} b_i c_i | c \in Z^n\}$ represent the n-dimensional lattice Λ generated by the basis B, where B is a basis of the lattice $\Lambda^{\perp}(B)$. The orthogonal lattice $\Lambda^{\perp}(B) = \{e \in \mathrm{R}^m | Be = 0 \bmod q, B \in \mathrm{R}_q^{n \times m}\}$.

Discrete Gaussian Distribution [37]: For any $\sigma > 0$ and $x \in \mathrm{R}^m$, the discrete Gaussian distribution with σ as the parameter and $v \in \mathrm{R}^m$ as the center is defined as $\rho_{v,\sigma}(x) = \exp(-\pi \|x - v\|^2/\sigma^2)$.

The discrete Gaussian distribution on lattice $\Lambda \subseteq Z^m$ is defined as $\forall x \in \Lambda$, $D_{\Lambda,\sigma,v}(x) = \rho_{\sigma,v}(x)/\rho_{\sigma,v}(\Lambda)$, where $\rho_{\sigma,v}(\Lambda) = \sum_{z \in \Lambda} \rho_{\sigma,v}(z)$.

In particular, when representing a Gaussian distribution centered at 0, we often omit 0.

Intersection Method [38]: Λ_1 and Λ_2 are two lattices such that $\Lambda_1 + \Lambda_2 = Z^m$ and $\Lambda_1 \cap \Lambda_2 \neq \phi$; here, the addition is elementwise. For $v_1, v_2 \in Z^m$, which provide two co-sets Λ_1 and Λ_2, a vector $e \in Z^m$ exists such that $e = v_1 \bmod \Lambda_1$ and $e = v_2 \bmod \Lambda_2$. This result can be generalized from two lattices to multiple lattices.

About more than two lattices, [39] can be viewed an example.

3 Our Scheme

3.1 Proposed Algorithm

1) Setup

In terms of $n \geq 2$, let $\Lambda_1 = p_1 Z^n$, $\Lambda_2 = p_2 Z^n, \cdots, \Lambda_n = p_n Z^n$ with n primes $p_1, p_2, \cdots, p_n (p_1 < p_2 < \cdots < p_n)$. Because $p_1, p_2, \cdots, p_k$ are different primes, $p_1 Z^n + p_2 Z^n + \cdots + p_n Z^n = Z^n$ and $p_1 Z^n \cap p_2 Z^n \cap \cdots \cap p_n Z^n = p_1 p_2 \cdots p_n Z^n \neq \varnothing$. Let $v = [\underbrace{1, 1, \cdots 1}_{n}]^T$, $N = p_1 \times p_2 \times \cdots \times p_t$, $M = p_{n-t+2} \times p_{n-t+3} \times \cdots \times p_n$. Secret s satisfies $N > s > M$. Let $H : \{0,1\}^* \to \{0,1\}^*$ is a collision-resistant hash function.

2) Share distribution

For secrets s, the trusted center computing
$$\begin{cases} s_1 v \equiv sv(mod \ \Lambda_1) \\ \vdots \\ s_n v \equiv sv(mod \ \Lambda_n) \end{cases}.$$

Then the sub-secret of secret s is (Λ_i, s_i) $(i \in [n])$.

The trusted center sends the sub-secret (Λ_i, s_i) to participants P_i and publish $h_i = H(s_i v)$ $(i \in [n])$

3) Verification

Upon receiving the sharing, the participant P_i verifies whether the hash value of his share is the same as that on the bulletin board, i.e., $H(s_i v)? = h_i$

4) Secret reconstruction

Aggregators randomly select t sub-secrets from n participants, $(\Lambda_1, s_1), (\Lambda_2, s_2), \cdots, (\Lambda_t, s_t)$, use the intersection method to calculate the solution sv of $\begin{cases} sv \equiv s_1 v \pmod{\Lambda_1} \\ \quad \vdots \\ sv \equiv s_t v \pmod{\Lambda_t} \end{cases}$, and

recover the secret $s \equiv s(\mathrm{mod} N_1)$, $N_1 = p_1 p_2 \cdots p_t$.

3.2   Correctness and Security

1) Correctness

In our scheme, according to the ordinary secret sharing scheme based on the CRT, a secret is divided into n parts, so that at least t of n parts can obtain the secret s.

For any t sub-secrets:

$$(s_1, p_1), (s_2, p_2), \cdots , (s_t, p_t)$$

Calculate $s \equiv s(\mathrm{mod} N_1)$, $N_1 = p_1 p_2 \cdots p_t$, since $N_1 \geq N > s > M$, then the secret s can be determined.

And the same goes for expanding into the scheme based on lattice.

2) Security

Theorem 1. In the proposed scheme, any less than t participants cannot recover the undisclosed secret s.

Proof. In our scheme, according to the ordinary secret sharing scheme based on the CRT, a secret is divided into n parts, so that at least t parts can obtain the secret s.

For any $t - 1$ sub-secrets:

$$(s_1, p_1), (s_2, p_2), \cdots , (s_{t-1}, p_{t-1})$$

Calculate $s \equiv s(\mathrm{mod} M_1)$, $M_1 = p_1 p_2 \cdots p_{t-1}$, since $N_1 \geq N > s > M \geq M_1$, then there is not enough information to determine s.

And the same goes for expanding into the scheme based on lattice.

Theorem 2. The scheme which we proposed is post-quantum safe.

Proof. The security of our scheme depends on the intersection method. The intersection method [38] is post-quantum safe, so our scheme is also post-quantum safe.

4   Cost Analysis

In this section, we mainly compare the memory cost and time cost of our scheme with other schemes. The comparison is shown in Table 2.

Table 2. Cost requirements for different schemes

Schemes	Size of shares	Time of share distribution	Time of secret reconstruction
Our scheme	$O(1)$	$O(n)$	$O(t\log t)$
Pilaram et al. [34]	$O(n)$	$O(n^3)$	$O(t^3)$
Kiamari et al. [36]	$O(1)$	$O(nt)$	$O(t\log t)$

5 Conclusion

In this paper, we construct a verifiable lattice-based secret sharing scheme using some number theory methods and interaction method. Our scheme is safe in the post-quantum era. Furthermore, we analyse the security of our scheme. Finally, we compared our scheme with other schemes, and the comparison shows that our scheme is more efficient and occupies less memory.

Acknowledgement. This work is supported by the National Natural Science Foundation of China (grant no. 62072023), the Open Project Fund of the State Key Laboratory of Cryptology (grant no. MMKFKT202120), Beijing Municipal Natural Science Foundation, the Exploratory Optional Project Fund of the State Key Laboratory of Software Development Environment, and the Fundamental Research Funds of Beihang University (grant nos. YWF-20-BJ-J-1040, YWF-21-BJ-J-1041, etc.).

References

1. Shamir, A.: How to share a secret. Commun. ACM **22**(11), 612–613 (1979)
2. Beimel, A., Chor, B.: Secret sharing with public reconstruction. IEEE Trans. Inf. Theory **44**(5), 1887–1896 (1998)
3. Blakley, G.R.: Safeguarding cryptographic keys. In: International Workshop on Managing Requirements Knowledge, p. 313. IEEE Computer Society (1979)
4. Asmuth, C.A., Blakley, G.R.: Pooling, splitting, and restituting information to overcome total failure of some channels of communication. In: 1982 IEEE Symposium on Security and Privacy, p. 156. IEEE (1982)
5. Asmuth, C., Bloom, J.: A modular approach to key safeguarding. IEEE Trans. Inf. Theory **29**(2), 208–210 (1983)
6. Jackson, W.A., Martin, K.M.: Perfect secret sharing schemes on five participants. Des. Codes Crypt. **9**, 267–286 (1996)
7. Chor, B., Goldwasser, S., Micali, S., et al.: Verifiable secret sharing and achieving simultaneity in the presence of faults. In: 26th Annual Symposium on Foundations of Computer Science (SFCS 1985), pp. 383–395. IEEE (1985)
8. Shieh, S.P., Sun, H.M.: On constructing secret sharing schemes. In: Infocom 94 Networking for Global Communications. IEEE (1994)
9. Sun, H.M., Shieh, S.P.: On dynamic threshold schemes. Inf. Process. Lett. **52**(4), 201–206 (1994)
10. Lin, T.Y., Wu, T.C.: (t, n) threshold verifiable multisecret sharing scheme based on the factorisation intractability and discrete logarithm modulo a composite problem. IEE Proc.-Comput. Digit. Tech. **146**(5), 264–268 (1999)

11. Wu, T.C., Wu, T.S.: Cheating detection and cheater identification in secret sharing schemes. IEE Proc.-Comput. Digit. Tech. **142**(5), 367–369 (1995)
12. Feldman, P.: A practical scheme for non-interactive verifiable secret sharing. In: 28th Annual Symposium on Foundations of Computer Science (SFCS 1987), pp. 427–438. IEEE (1987)
13. Pedersen, T.P.: Non-interactive and information-theoretic secure verifiable secret sharing. In: Feigenbaum, J. (ed.) CRYPTO 1991. LNCS, vol. 576, pp. 129–140. Springer, Heidelberg (2001). https://doi.org/10.1007/3-540-46766-1_9
14. Cramer, R., Damgård, I., Maurer, U.: General secure multi-party computation from any linear secret-sharing scheme. In: Preneel, B. (ed.) EUROCRYPT 2000. LNCS, vol. 1807, pp. 316–334. Springer, Heidelberg (2000). https://doi.org/10.1007/3-540-45539-6_22
15. Cramer R: Introduction to secure computation. In: Damgård, I.B. (ed.) Lectures on Data Security. EEF School 1998. LNCS, vol. 1561, pp. 16–62. Springer, Heidelberg (1999). https://doi.org/10.1007/3-540-48969-X_2
16. Gennaro, R., Micali, S.: Verifiable secret sharing as secure computation. In: Guillou, L.C., Quisquater, J.J. (eds.) EUROCRYPT 1995. LNCS, vol. 921, pp. 168–182. Springer, Heidelberg (1995). https://doi.org/10.1007/3-540-49264-X_14
17. Gennaro, R.: Theory and practice of verifiable secret sharing. Massachusetts Institute of Technology (1996)
18. Rabin, T., Ben-Or, M.: Verifiable secret sharing and multiparty protocols with honest majority. In: Proceedings of the Twenty-First Annual ACM Symposium on Theory of Computing, pp. 73–85. ACM, New York (1989)
19. Goldreich, O., Micali, S., Wigderson, A.: How to play any mental game, or a completeness theorem for protocols with honest majority. In: Providing Sound Foundations for Cryptography: On the Work of Shafi Goldwasser and Silvio Micali, pp. 307–328. ACM, New York (2019)
20. Gennaro, R., Jarecki, S., Krawczyk, H., Rabin, T.: Robust threshold DSS signatures. In: Maurer, U. (ed.) EUROCRYPT 1996. LNCS, vol. 1070, pp. 354–371. Springer, Heidelberg (1996). https://doi.org/10.1007/3-540-68339-9_31
21. Gennaro, R., Jarecki, S., Krawczyk, H., et al.: Secure distributed key generation for discrete-log based cryptosystems. In: Stern, J. (ed.) EUROCRYPT 1999. LNCS, vol. 1592, pp. 295–310. Springer, Heidelberg (1999). https://doi.org/10.1007/3-540-48910-x_21
22. Gennaro, R., Rabin, M.O., Rabin, T.: Simplified VSS and fast-track multiparty computations with applications to threshold cryptography. In: Proceedings of the Seventeenth Annual ACM Symposium on Principles of Distributed Computing, pp. 101–111. ACM, Puerto Vallarta (1998)
23. Stadler, M.: Publicly verifiable secret sharing. In: Maurer, U. (ed.) EUROCRYPT 1996. LNCS, vol. 1070, pp. 190–199. Springer, Heidelberg (1996). https://doi.org/10.1007/3-540-68339-9_17
24. Fujisaki, E., Okamoto, T.: A practical and provably secure scheme for publicly verifiable secret sharing and its applications. In: Nyberg, K. (ed.) EUROCRYPT 1998. LNCS, vol. 1403, pp. 32–46. Springer, Heidelberg (1998). https://doi.org/10.1007/BFb0054115
25. Schoenmakers, B.: A simple publicly verifiable secret sharing scheme and its application to electronic voting. In: Wiener, M. (ed.) CRYPTO 1999. LNCS, vol. 1666, pp. 148–164. Springer, Heidelberg (1999). https://doi.org/10.1007/3-540-48405-1_10
26. Benaloh, J.C.: Secret sharing homomorphisms: keeping shares of a secret secret. In: Odlyzko, A.M. (ed.) CRYPTO 1986. LNCS, vol. 263, pp. 251–260. Springer, Heidelberg (2000). https://doi.org/10.1007/3-540-47721-7_19
27. Georgescu A: A LWE-based secret sharing scheme. Netw. Secur. Cryptogr. (2011)
28. El Bansarkhani, R., Meziani, M.: An efficient lattice-based secret sharing construction. In: Askoxylakis, I., Pöhls, H.C., Posegga, J. (eds.) WISTP 2012. Lecture Notes in Computer

Science, vol. 7322, pp. 160–168. Springer, Heidelberg (2012). https://doi.org/10.1007/978-3-642-30955-7_14

29. Khorasgani, H.A., Asaad, S., Eghlidos, T., et al.: A lattice-based threshold secret sharing scheme. In: 2014 11th International ISC Conference on Information Security and Cryptology, pp. 173–179. IEEE, Tehran (2014)

30. Asaad, S., Khorasgani, H.A., Eghlidos, T., et al.: Sharing secret using lattice construction. In: 7th International Symposium on Telecommunications (IST 2014), pp. 901–906. IEEE, Tehran (2014)

31. Babai, L.: On Lovász'lattice reduction and the nearest lattice point problem. Combinatorica **6**, 1–13 (1986)

32. Bendlin, R., Damgård, I.: Threshold decryption and zero-knowledge proofs for lattice-based cryptosystems. In: Micciancio, D. (ed.) TCC 2010. LNCS, vol. 5978, pp. 201–218. Springer, Heidelberg (2010). https://doi.org/10.1007/978-3-642-11799-2_13

33. Bendlin, R., Krehbiel, S., Peikert, C.: How to share a lattice trapdoor: threshold protocols for signatures and (H) IBE. In: Jacobson, M., Locasto, M., Mohassel, P., Safavi-Naini, R. (eds.) ACNS 2013. LNCS, vol. 7954, pp. 218–236. Springer, Heidelberg (2013). https://doi.org/10.1007/978-3-642-38980-1_14

34. Pilaram, H., Eghlidos, T.: An efficient lattice based multi-stage secret sharing scheme. IEEE Trans. Dependable Secure Comput. **14**(1), 2–8 (2015)

35. Yang, Z., He, D., Qu, L., et al.: On the security of a lattice-based multi-stage secret sharing scheme. IEEE Trans. Dependable Secure Comput. (2022)

36. Kiamari, N., Hadian, M., Mashhadi, S.: Non-interactive verifiable LWE-based multi secret sharing scheme. Multimed. Tools Appl. 1–13 (2022)

37. Ajtai, M.: Generating hard instances of the short basis problem. In: Wiedermann, J., van Emde Boas, P., Nielsen, M. (eds.) ICALP 1999. LNCS, vol. 1644, pp. 1–9. Springer, Heidelberg (1999). https://doi.org/10.1007/3-540-48523-6_1

38. Boneh, D., Freeman, D.M.: Homomorphic signatures for polynomial functions. In: Paterson, K.G. (ed.) EUROCRYPT 2011. LNCS, vol. 6632, pp. 149–168. Springer, Heidelberg (2011). https://doi.org/10.1007/978-3-642-20465-4_10

39. Lu, X., Yin, W., Wen, Q., et al.: A lattice-based unordered aggregate signature scheme based on the intersection method. IEEE Access **6**, 33986–33994 (2018)

A PUF Based Audio Fingerprint Based for Device Authentication and Tamper Location

Zhi Lu[1], Haochen Dou[1], Songfeng Lu[1,2], Xueming Tang[1(✉)], Junjun Wu[1], and Samir Mohammed Umran[1]

[1] Hubei Key Laboratory of Distributed System Security, Hubei Engineering Research Center on Big Data Security, School of Cyber Science and Engineering, Huazhong University of Science and Technology, Wuhan 430074, China
xmtang@hust.edu.cn
[2] Shenzhen Huazhong University of Science and Technology Research Institute, Shenzhen 518063, China

Abstract. As bioinformation authentication gains prominence, the significance of audio data in industries such as speech recognition intensifies, with audio storage becoming a pivotal concern for data protection. Existing audio tampering solutions fail to identify the producing device. This paper introduces an innovative method employing physical unclonable function (PUF) and audio features for identifying recording equipment and detecting tampered areas in judicial authentication within the Industrial Internet-of-Things (IIoT). The method comprises two components: the recording device, which generates an audio fingerprint using audio features and a PUF-determined random number seed, and the server, which registers, analyzes, and verifies the fingerprint. The unique, tamper-resistant PUF response is generated only when a server-provided challenge is initiated. The proposed audio fingerprint, evaluated using the Carioca 1 database and NXP LPC54S018-EVK-provided PUF functionality, enables varying tamper area identification accuracy and achieves 100% original device identification, resisting replay, cloning, and brute force attacks.

Keywords: Physical Unclonable Function · Voice Recoder Identification · Digital Audio Forensics · Landmark

1 Introduction

As information technology progresses incessantly, multimedia evidence has emerged as a crucial component in criminal prosecution. Audio, one of the most

This work is supported by the Major Research Plan of Hubei Province under Grant/Award No. 2023BAA027 and the Key Research & Development Plan of Hubei Province of China under Grant No. 2021BAA038 and the project of Science, Technology and Innovation Commission of Shenzhen Municipality of China under Grant No. JCYJ20210324120002006 and JSGG20210802153009028.

S. Goel and P. R. Nunes de Souza (Eds.): ICDF2C 2023, LNICST 571, pp. 63–78, 2024.
https://doi.org/10.1007/978-3-031-56583-0_5

fundamental biological characteristics of humans, plays a vital role in court proceedings and other contexts. Over the past decade, recording devices have frequently served as vital evidence in verifying the authenticity and falsehood of particular crimes. The ongoing development of big data and the Internet of Things (IoT) has facilitated large-scale storage and utilization of audio data. However, the low cost of audio data acquisition has also increased the prevalence of audio-based attacks. Additionally, high-quality audio recording has contributed to the decreasing costs associated with audio tampering and theft. With the aid of manual technology, audio can be falsified and distorted, leading to miscarriages of justice in court. Consequently, audio tamper detection and recording equipment authentication are of utmost importance in the forthcoming digital era. In other words, it is essential to securely store audio data and ensure its protection, verification, and detection throughout its usage. At present, several studies have addressed image tamper detection and camera source recognition [6,13,20], but to the best of our knowledge, no work has effectively detected audio tampering while simultaneously identifying recording devices.

This paper proposes the utilization of audio features for identifying recording equipment and tampered regions in forensic authentication. The main contributions of our work include:

1. The proposed audio fingerprint can uniquely identify recording devices, enabling registration with a server. The server can link the audio requiring authentication and perform forgery detection. PUF-based SRAM is employed to generate the response of specific devices. The counter signifies the frequency of audio authentication, utilized for the projection transformation of audio landmark features to obtain audio fingerprints.
2. The generation of the audio fingerprint proposed in this paper depends on the number of authentications, audio data, and recording equipment, significantly enhancing the system's security. This method streamlines the recognition of individual recording devices, improving recognition speed and accuracy.
3. This work addresses the issue of impersonating original recording equipment in existing audio forensics. As the proposed audio fingerprint is device-dependent, authentication is undeniable. By authenticating the tagged audio, forgery attacks and re-defense attacks of recording equipment are eliminated.
4. The proposed method can dynamically adjust the effective detection region of tampering by modifying the threshold G and differentiate between malicious tampering and content-saving operations.

The remainder of this article is organized as follows: Sect. 2 discusses existing related work. Section 3 provides background information on Landmark and PUF in Shazam. Section 4 details the security model, system architecture, audio fingerprint generation, and server utilization for audio tamper detection and source recording device identification. Section 5 outlines the experimental setup and results, including data used, experiment preparation, testing, and security analysis. Section 6 provides a summary of the entire paper.

2   Related Work

In early audio forensics, the focus centered on analog tape recordings, gauging integrity via magnetic head switching transients, mechanical joints, overlapping recording signatures, and analog recorder fingerprints. Yet, contemporary audio data has largely shifted to digital format [2,11,12], posing challenges in verifying digital audio authenticity, establishing device-to-record links, spotting copies, and sequencing recorded events [8]. In recent times, diverse methods emerged to counter digital audio forgery, with [18] categorizing these detection techniques into three main groups:

1. ENF-based methods [1,2,7,12]: Electric network frequency (ENF) serves as a naturally embedded signature, which has emerged as a crucial development in audio evidence authentication. Owing to the natural regularity of ENF, audio clip insertions or deletions can create discontinuities in instantaneous phase information and produce abnormal changes in the registered ENF [12].
2. Post-processing distortion-based methods: [8,16] typically utilize Mel frequency cepstral coefficients or the statistical properties of modified DCT coefficients to identify traces of double compression left by operations.
3. Acoustic environment-based methods: By extracting inconsistencies in acoustic environment features from audio files, [10] detect tampered positions and splicing. Researchers have verified audio recordings by examining audio reverb introduced during recording due to sound persistence after the sound source's termination.

These methods are considered passive audio forgery detection techniques [14]. In contrast, active detection mechanisms involve inserting or attaching additional information to ensure security and integrity when creating target digital audio. Active audio forgery detection methods are primarily divided into two categories:

1. Watermark-based methods: These methods enhance audio integrity and security by embedding watermarks, which can be extracted from the audio after network transmission. An intact watermark in the audio content signifies its origin from an authenticated source, distinguishing it from recordings or playback devices [4].
2. Digital signature-based methods: Employing the user's private key, digital signatures encrypt information. The recipient decrypts the received content using the sender's public key, maintaining integrity and authenticity during transmission over insecure public channels [3].

3 Preliminaries

3.1 Landmark

We use the 'Landmark' audio fingerprint generated by Shazam's hashing process, consisting of three modules [15]:

1. **Robust Constellations:** Shazam identifies spectral maxima indicating points where a time-frequency region's value surpasses neighbors. A density criterion ensures robustness by evenly distributing selected maxima, simplifying the spectral graph into sparse coordinates.
2. **Fast Combinatorial Hashing:** Shazam swiftly indexes constellations by hashing two time-frequency points. Anchor points, tied to target zones, are sequentially combined with target area points, yielding two frequencies and a time difference. Each fingerprint, stored as an INT, includes the time difference from the file's start to the anchor point, excluding absolute time.
3. **Searching and Scoring:** Extracted hashes match database hashes, creating time pairs for each match. These pairs form a scatter plot. When test audio matches database audio, similar time pairs form a diagonal line: $t'_k = t_k + offset$, where t'_k is the source audio's matched hash time, and t_k is the test audio's matched hash time.

3.2 Physical Unclonable Function

A Physical Unclonable Function (PUF) is a unique hardware response/challenge function [9] that exploits inherent random variations introduced by manufacturing processes to form secret keys on-the-fly, analogous to a unique fingerprint [5]. PUFs can be utilized with minimal hardware investment and are unclonable due to their unpredictable challenge-response behavior. This study uses Static Random-Access Memory (SRAM) PUF as the response generator, which is based on the behavior of SRAM cells in memory. Each cell's state after power-up is determined by random differences in threshold voltages, yielding a unique binary pattern. The response of SRAM PUF depends on the threshold voltage error, making it challenging to clone the PUF's challenge-response behavior.

4   Proposed Approach

4.1   Security Model

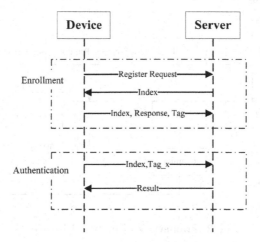

Fig. 1. Framework of proposed authentication process between server and device.

We assume that during the enrollment phase, communication between parties is secure, relying on existing security protocols such as SSL and TLS. Each audio enrollment request receives a unique index, and the server obtains a device response. In the authentication phase, the channel between the device and server is unreliable, allowing adversaries to manipulate, eavesdrop, and replay messages. Adversaries can request authentication from the server using past or predicted messages and attempt to impersonate the original device using a sham device with enrolled original audio. The original device can also submit tampered audio to the server. Upon receiving tags, the server verifies their correctness, integrity, time sequence, and origin. Consequently, our scheme ensures verifiability and resists replay and cloning attacks.

4.2 System Architecture

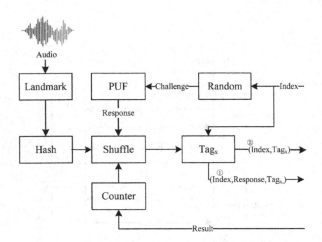

Fig. 2. Framework of proposed Device.

Figure 1 illustrates a system involving two entities: the client authentication device and the server. When a device enrolls audio, it sends an enrollment request to the server, which returns a unique index. The device generates a Tag and a PUF Response for reshuffling, sends the index, Tag, and Response to the server, which securely stores them in a database. To verify audio legitimacy, the device sends the index and Tag to the server for integrity and identity authenticity checks. The server sends the result to the device and increments the Counter, ensuring distinct tags each time. The client-side authentication device framework in Fig. 2 includes an SRAM PUF, adding device-specific "genes" to the generated audio fingerprint. The device uses the server-provided index as a Random seed, projecting the index onto PUF's required mapping space. The PUF receives the challenge and outputs the corresponding Response. The device owner extracts audio landmarks, hashes them, and shuffles the hash with the PUF's Response and a Counter representing authentication requests. During enrollment, the device outputs the index, Response, and Tag_x (Fig. 2's ①); for authentication, it outputs the index and Tag_x (Fig. 2's ②). The device retrieves the result and increments the Counter. Figure 2 shows the device shuffling the landmark hash list into a Tag using the Response and Counter of authentication requests.

We adapted the Knuth shuffle for our framework (Algorithm 1). The shuffle function appends the Counter to the hash list's tail and sets x to the Counter's number. First, it XORs every hash in the list, incrementing x. The XOR hash key is generated by a Random function with the input of the x_{th} response item. Second, it swaps hash items with k generated by the Random function. As the

Response is a PUF output, adversaries cannot imitate this shuffle process, which also acts as symmetric encryption. The Response, stored in the server during enrollment, serves as the encryption key, ensuring resistance to replay attacks.

Algorithm 1. Shuffle

Input: $H = h_0, ..., h_{n-1}$, $Response = r_0, ..., r_{m-1}$, $Counter$
Output: Tag
 1: **function** SHUFFLE($H, Response, Counter$)
 2: $\quad i \leftarrow 0$
 3: $\quad H \leftarrow$ append $Counter$ to the end of the H
 4: $\quad x \leftarrow Counter$
 5: $\quad$ **for** $i \leftarrow 0$ to n **do**
 6: $\quad\quad Random.seed(Response[x \bmod m])$
 7: $\quad\quad b \leftarrow Random$
 8: $\quad\quad H[i] \leftarrow H[i]$ XOR b
 9: $\quad\quad x \leftarrow x + 1 \bmod m$
10: $\quad$ **end for**
11: $\quad$ **for** $i \leftarrow 0$ to n **do**
12: $\quad\quad Random.seed(Response[x \bmod m])$
13: $\quad\quad k \leftarrow random$
14: $\quad\quad swap(H[i], H[k])$
15: $\quad\quad x \leftarrow x + 1 \bmod m$
16: $\quad$ **end for**
17: $\quad$ Tag $= H$
18: $\quad$ **return** Tag
19: **end function**

The server, a secure service provider, generates an index for each device and performs information authentication. As shown in Fig. 3, upon enrollment request, the server generates a unique index, sends it to the client, and stores the hash, Response, index, Counter, and times in the database. The hash is reshuffled from the audio Tag, and the Counter represents authenticated audio requests and consecutive failed requests. In the authentication phase, the server receives the index and unverified Tag, reshuffles the tags using the stored Response and Counter, and obtains unverified hash and Counter. Comparing the two counters, if they differ, the request is deemed tampered or a replay attack, failing authentication. If the Counter values match, the server uses Shazam's Searching and Scoring to compare the hashes and identify tampered audio sections. A threshold value G controls the tampered area, as landmark values near the tampered area change. The tampered area is always smaller than the detected area. A limit G bounds the largest detected area; if exceeded, tamper location detection fails. The limit area, given t_o as the stored audio time and t_t as the time of the audio awaiting authentication, is:

$$log_{10}^{\frac{3}{32}G^2 + \frac{5}{8}} min(t_0, t_t) + log_2^{\frac{10}{G}} |t_0 - t_t| \tag{1}$$

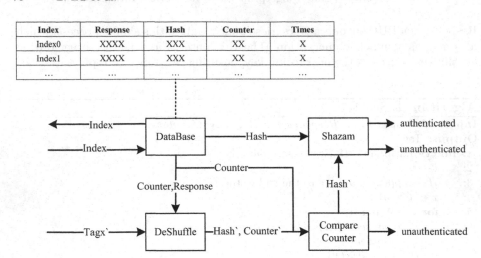

Index	Response	Hash	Counter	Times
Index0	XXXX	XXX	XX	X
Index1	XXXX	XXX	XX	X
...	...	...	...	...

Fig. 3. Framework of proposed Server.

On the server-side, the server makes reshuffle to get the landmark hash and the Counter to be authenticated with the input of Tag, Response, and the Counter stored in the server's database. The reshuffle function's process is the inverse of shuffle. It should be considered that the initial x is not Counter but Counter plus $2n - 1$, n representing the length of Tag.

5   Experiments and Results

5.1   Database

In this section, we utilize the publicly available Carioca 1 database [17] as the test database, allowing for direct comparisons with methods from [1,2,7,11], and [12]. The Carioca 1 database contains 100 original audio files, 50 from female speakers and 50 from male speakers. Additionally, there are 100 tampered versions of these audio files, with 50 containing inserted audio clips and 50 featuring deleted audio clips, distributed evenly between male and female speakers. Each audio file undergoes a single cut or insertion. The timings (sample indices) and extents of each edit are carefully documented. Edits are performed in sound-inactive portions of the signal. Upon analyzing the Carioca 1 audio files, the Signal-to-Noise Ratio (SNR) distribution in the active voice areas ranges from 16 dB to 30 dB, with an average of 22.3 dB.

5.2   Experimental Setup

In our experiments, during the landmark extraction process, we set the parameters as follows: $N_{FFT} = 512$, $N_{HOP} = 256$. We limit the maximum number of local maxima per frame to 5 and restrict the number of pairs derived from each peak to less than 3. The density of landmarks found is represented by $density = 20$, and the spectrogram enhancement has an $HPF\ POLE = 0.98$. We set the target sampling rate at 44.1 kHz, matching the sampling rate of the audio files in the Carioca 1 database. To reduce the framing effect, we extract the hash value from two shifted waveforms $(shifts = 2)$. The hash is generated from the Landmark feature and has the following form: $landmark = (time, bin1, bin2, \Delta time)$. We perform fast combinatorial hashing on the landmark, combining two time-frequency points to form a fingerprint $hash = [time, h_o]$, where $h_o = h_1 | h_2 | h_3$.

$$h_1 = (bin1 \& 255) \ll 12$$
$$h_2 = (bin2 - bin1) \& 63) \ll 6 \qquad (2)$$
$$h_3 = \Delta time \& 63$$

Then, we combine the $time$ and h_o together by: $H = time \ll 32 + h_o$. By doing the inverse operation to the H, we can get $time = H \gg 32, h_o = H \& ((1 \ll 32) - 1)$. The 32-bit hash, H, is derived from the 256-bit PUF Response, which is divided into 32 groups, each containing 8 bits. The PUF is provided by the LPC54S018-EVK, an NXP Development Board with LPC54S0xx MCU as shown in Fig. 4. This MCU utilizes dedicated SRAM to generate a PUF root key.

Fig. 4. NXP LPC54S018-EVK Development Board.

The proposed edit detection method's performance, measured in tamper detection rate (TDR), is evaluated under four conditions: original audio recordings from the database; compressed database audio; amplitude clipping applied to database audio; and additional noise added to the database audio. It is important to note that edit detection is divided into two situations: detecting whether the audio has been tampered with and determining the location of the tampering. These situations are controlled by the parameter G, a threshold determining the accuracy of tampered location detection. Smaller values of G yield more accurate tamper localization. At its maximum value, G allows the proposed method to function as an edit detector. The performance of the proposed identification method is assessed under three conditions, with each condition selecting one audio, device, or challenge as the independent variable. Concurrently, the analysis of the audio database reveals that the signal-to-noise ratio of the original audio background noise estimation does not exceed 30 dB.

5.3   Tamper Location Detection Test

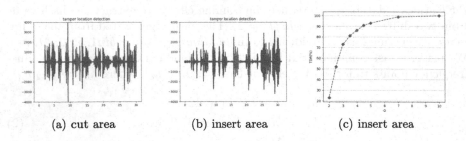

(a) cut area   (b) insert area   (c) insert area

Fig. 5. Sample of original audio tamper detection

Original Recording of Audio. Figure 5(a) and (b) showcase samples identifying the cut area and insert area. Contaminated areas are in red and normal areas are in blue Fig. 5(c) depicts a line chart of TDR with different values of G. As G decreases, TDR declines. When $G = 10$, the method serves as a tamper detector; when $G = 2$, the method succeeds only if the tampered area size is nearly equal to the allowed detection area size. Given that the server possesses audio information, a G value of 10 consistently detects tampering. We prefer $G = 4.5$, as it achieves over 90% accuracy, and the tampered area size is roughly half the allowed detection area size.

Compression of Database Audio. We employ the same method as [12] to test our proposed method's performance under MP3 compressed audio signals. To assess the robustness of our method under compression, we converted the Carioca 1 database audio files to MP3 format and recoded the entire database at a sample rate of 2250 Hz and a set of $Br = [16, 32, 64, 128]$ kbps, similar to [12], to compress the bit rate.

Table 1 demonstrates that accuracy decreases with decreasing G or BR values. When $G = 10$, the tamper detection rate is 100%, and compression does not impact performance. Our proposed method's performance is only greater than 93% when $G \geq 7$, permitting an allowed detection area nearly larger than half the audio. When $G = 4.5$, the TDR is reduced by 1%–8%.

Table 1. TDR of Compress tests with different kpbs and G

G	16BR	32BR	64BR	128BR
10	100%	100%	100%	100%
7	93%	97%	97%	98%
5	83%	87%	89%	90%
4.5	76%	80%	86%	87%
4	66%	72%	79%	80%
3.5	59%	61%	66%	69%
3	40%	54%	56%	58%
2.5	21%	28%	30%	30%
2	8%	11%	12%	12%

Apply Amplitude Clipping. To achieve amplitude clipping of the database signal, we use the same VAD method employed in [12]. The saturation level (SL) represents the percentage of active speech samples clipped to a maximum, corresponding to a specified number. The set of specified $SL = [0, 0.2, 0.5, 1, 2, 4]\%$ is the same as in [12].

Table 2. TDR of Amplitude tests with different SL and G

G	0.2SL	0.5SL	1SL	2SL	4SL
10	100%	100%	100%	100%	100%
7	98%	97%	97%	97%	96%
5	91%	91%	89%	87%	80%
4.5	89%	87%	83%	80%	71%
4	79%	73%	71%	69%	64%
3.5	66%	64%	59%	58%	52%
3	58%	52%	48%	43%	38%
2.5	33%	27%	24%	21%	19%
2	13%	12%	10%	6%	7%

Table 2 demonstrates that accuracy decreases with the decrease of G or BR values. When $G = 10$, the tamper detection rate is 100%, and the compression operation does not affect the performance. The performance of our proposed method is only greater than 96% when $G \geq 7$, allowing for a detection area nearly larger than half the audio. When $G = 4.5$, the TDR is affected and decreased by 2%–20%. The performance of tamper location detection decreases significantly when the amplitude clipping is at $4SL$.

Additional Noise. To calculate the audio signal's power P_s and the power of generating noise P_{n1} (assuming the signal length is both N):

$$P_s = \frac{\sum_{i=1}^{N}(x_i)^2}{N}, P_{n1} = \frac{\sum_{i=1}^{N}(n_i)^2}{N} \tag{3}$$

It is important to note that the noise we currently generate, which is the SNR with an audio signal, does not match the $SNR\ dB$ we require. In other words, we need to multiply all the noise data by a number k, ensuring its power meets our requirements. Where P_n is the power of noise we ultimately need:

$$SNRdB = 10 \cdot log_{10}\frac{P_s}{P_n} \tag{4}$$

By deducing and sorting out Eqs. (3) and (4):

$$k = \frac{P_s}{10^{\frac{SNR}{10}} \cdot P_{n1}} \tag{5}$$

Table 3 displays the results of our proposed method's performance. The performance of $G = 4.5$ has decreased by 6%–23%.

Table 3. TDR of Noisy tests withe different SNR and G

G	5SNR	10SNR	15SNR	20SNR	25SNR	30SNR
10	100%	100%	100%	100%	100%	100%
7	96%	96%	96%	96%	96%	97%
5	72%	80%	84%	86%	87%	87%
4.5	68%	73%	78%	82%	83%	84%
4	52%	63%	70%	72%	75%	75%
3.5	41%	51%	58%	63%	64%	64%
3	26%	37%	46%	49%	52%	55%
2.5	13%	18%	22%	26%	29%	30%
2	4%	4%	8%	10%	10%	11%

5.4   Source Audio Identification

Our proposed method ensures that the Tag to be validated can only be reshuffled successfully by the device that generated the audio. The feature unique to the original device is mixed into registration information. The server has the ability to detect whether the device that sent the audio for detection is the device that produced the audio. On this basis, it can also detect tampering and tampering location, which has been tested above. There are three independent variables: device, audio, and challenge. We perform three tests to verify the identification ability, similar to [19].

Test 1: The degree of differentiation of the Tag generated by using different PUF challenges with the same audio and the same device.
Test 2: The degree of differentiation of PUF responses generated by the same PUF challenge input into different devices.
Test 3: The degree to which the PUF response generated by the same PUF challenge input to the same device is distinguishable from the Tag generated by the combination of different audio frequencies.

We use two LPC54S018-EVK development boards, 100 authentic audio files belonging to the Carioca 1 database, and 100 indexes that represent the device challenges. The devices are labeled as d_1 and d_2, the audio files are labeled as a1 to a100, and the challenges are labeled as 1 to 100. For each test, there are a total of $2 \times 100 \times 100 = 20,000$ test data points.

Table 4. EAR of Source audio Identification with three independent variables

EAR	challenge	device	audio
condition1	0%	0%	0%
condition2	0%	0%	0%

Here we chose the Tag generated by d_1 and index $= 1$ to be the enrollment information. The landmark of the audio, Response of PUF, and the Counter of times the audio has been authentic generate the Tag. We assume two conditions: 1. Each time the test audio is authenticated, the Counter defaults to be 1, and the Counter of the audio is known to the attacker. 2. The Counter increases with time, which means that the Counter ranges from 1 to 100. Meanwhile, the adversary does not know the value of the count. Table 4 shows the error acceptance rate (EAR) of Test 1, Test 2, and Test 3. The result of the challenge test is 0. This is because the Response of the PUF does not have a collision. The Response here is 256 bits, and the space of Response is 2^{256}. The equation for the probability of a collision is:

$$1 - e^{\frac{-k(k-1)}{2N}} \approx 0, N = 2^{256}, k = 20000$$

The result of the device test is 0. This is because of the PUF's feature, which ensures the device's unique unclonability. The result of the audio test is 0. This is due to the feature of the landmark. As the length of the feature depends on the peaks and length of the audio, it means that two audios rarely have the exact same landmark unless they are the same audio.

5.5   Comparison

Our proposed method is compared with the existing audio tamper detection methods in recent years. The comparison methods all use the same database,

Carioca 1. The comparison is carried out from the following four aspects: robustness, tamper detection, tamper location detection, and device authentication, as shown in Table 5. For robustness, as different methods have a significant difference between their theories, the methods of [2,7,12] use ENF variations with different technology. Meanwhile, [12] uses SVM and [7] uses an autoregressive model. Tables 1, 2, 3 show the compress, amplitude, and noise, respectively. One significant difference between our approach and theirs is that our method is built with known basic audio information, and it can determine whether the device verifying the audio is the original device.

Table 5. Comparison with existing methods

Method	Robustness			Tamper		Authentication
	Compress	Noisy	Amplitude	Detection	Location	
[12]	YES	YES	YES	YES	YES	NO
[7]	YES	YES	NO	YES	NO	NO
[2]	NO	YES	YES	YES	YES	NO
proposed method	**YES**	**YES**	**YES**	**YES**	**YES**	**YES**

5.6 Security Analysis

In this section, we describe details about how the proposed system defends against the adversary's attacks mentioned above.

The **replay attack** in our scenario is that during the authentication, the adversary could monitor the communication channel and get the index and tags. Then, the adversary could impersonate the client to perform the authentication. In order to defend against the replay attack, we incorporate a counter in our design. During the shuffle process, the input of the mask code is the counter value, making the mask code one-time use. After accepting the tags, the server reshuffles the tags with the stored counter and updates it. Thus, the tags captured by the adversary are useless and cannot be verified the next time.

The **cloning attack** in our scenario refers to the duplication of another device that gets the same input as the claimed device in order to generate the same Response. After capturing the index in the authentication process and assuming the adversary has the ability to count the authentication times, typically, if we adopt a one-way hash function like SHA, the Response is absolutely the same with the same input. What is worse, the attacker could generate the same tags and index itself and complete the authentication process. However, PUF makes such an attack infeasible even with the same input. Because of the physical characteristics, the whole manufacturing process is uncontrollable, which is entirely different from cryptography methods applied in hash algorithms. That is, our system can link each registered audio to the specified device due to the application of PUF.

The **brute force attack** in our scenario occurs during the authentication phase. Assume the adversary has the past or predicted Tag of this audio. The time in the server's database provides an additional layer of security against opponents who use random input to brute force a break on the server. When the number of authentication failures is greater than a threshold value, the server rejects the request for this index until the administrator resets it.

6 Conclusion

The method we proposed is the first of its kind to utilize PUF as a device gene for generating audio fingerprints. The generated audio fingerprints enable tamper detection and tamper location under conditions of anti-compression, shearing, and noise. The detection of the original audio device can be achieved to prevent device cloning and counterfeiting. Additionally, defenses against possible brute force and replay attacks are implemented. This is achieved by using landmarks as the audio feature, which, in conjunction with PUF and Counter, generates audio fingerprints. Due to PUF's unclonability and unpredictability, it is virtually impossible for an attacker to predict the correct audio fingerprint. This innovative approach offers a robust and secure method for verifying the integrity and authenticity of audio files, as well as identifying the devices responsible for their creation, effectively protecting against various types of attacks.

References

1. Esquef, P.A.A., Apolinário, J.A., Biscainho, L.W.P.: Improved edit detection in speech via ENF patterns. In: 2015 IEEE International Workshop on Information Forensics and Security (WIFS), pp. 1–6 (2015). https://doi.org/10.1109/WIFS.2015.7368585
2. Esquef, P.A.A., Apolinário, J.A., Biscainho, L.W.P.: Edit detection in speech recordings via instantaneous electric network frequency variations. IEEE Trans. Inf. Forensics Secur. 9(12), 2314–2326 (2014). https://doi.org/10.1109/TIFS.2014.2363524
3. Forouzan, B.: Cryptography and Network Security. McGraw-Hill, New York (2007)
4. Garlapati, B.M., Kakkirala, K.R.: Malicious audio source detection using audio watermarking. In: 2015 Asia Pacific Conference on Multimedia and Broadcasting, pp. 1–5 (2015). https://doi.org/10.1109/APMediaCast.2015.7210288
5. Herder, C., Ren, L., van Dijk, M., Yu, M.D., Devadas, S.: Trapdoor computational fuzzy extractors and stateless cryptographically-secure physical unclonable functions. IEEE Trans. Dependable Secure Comput. 14(1), 65–82 (2017). https://doi.org/10.1109/TDSC.2016.2536609
6. Hu, W., Chang, C.H., Sengupta, A., Bhunia, S., Kastner, R., Li, H.: An overview of hardware security and trust: threats, countermeasures, and design tools. IEEE Trans. Comput. Aided Des. Integr. Circuits Syst. 40(6), 1010–1038 (2021). https://doi.org/10.1109/TCAD.2020.3047976
7. Lin, X., Kang, X.: Supervised audio tampering detection using an autoregressive model. In: 2017 IEEE International Conference on Acoustics, Speech and Signal Processing (ICASSP), pp. 2142–2146 (2017). https://doi.org/10.1109/ICASSP.2017.7952535

8. Liu, Q., Sung, A.H., Qiao, M.: Detection of double MP3 compression. Cogn. Comput. **2**, 291–296 (2010). https://doi.org/10.1007/s12559-010-9045-4
9. Maes, R.: Physically Unclonable Functions: Constructions, Properties and Applications. Springer, Heidelberg (2013). https://doi.org/10.1007/978-3-642-41395-7
10. Malik, H.: Acoustic environment identification and its applications to audio forensics. IEEE Trans. Inf. Forensics Secur. **8**(11), 1827–1837 (2013). https://doi.org/10.1109/TIFS.2013.2280888
11. Nicolalde Rodriguez, D.P., Apolinario, J.A., Biscainho, L.W.P.: Audio authenticity: detecting ENF discontinuity with high precision phase analysis. IEEE Trans. Inf. Forensics Secur. **5**(3), 534–543 (2010). https://doi.org/10.1109/TIFS.2010.2051270
12. Reis, P.M.G.I., Lustosa da Costa, J.P.C., Miranda, R.K., Del Galdo, G.: ESPRIT-Hilbert-based audio tampering detection with SVM classifier for forensic analysis via electrical network frequency. IEEE Trans. Inf. Forensics Secur. **12**(4), 853–864 (2017). https://doi.org/10.1109/TIFS.2016.2636095
13. Shi, J., Wang, G., Su, M., Liu, X.: Effective medical image copy-move forgery localization based on texture descriptor. In: Goel, S., Gladyshev, P., Johnson, D., Pourzandi, M., Majumdar, S. (eds.) ICDF2C 2020. LNICST, vol. 351, pp. 62–77. Springer, Cham (2021). https://doi.org/10.1007/978-3-030-68734-2_4
14. Teerakanok, S., Uehara, T.: Digital media tampering detection techniques: an overview. In: 2017 IEEE 41st Annual Computer Software and Applications Conference (COMPSAC), vol. 2, pp. 170–174 (2017). https://doi.org/10.1109/COMPSAC.2017.109
15. Wang, A.L.: An industrial-strength audio search algorithm. In: Choudhury, S., Manus, S. (eds.) 4th Symposium Conference on Music Information Retrieval, ISMIR 2003, pp. 7–13. The International Society for Music Information Retrieval (2003). http://www.ismir.net. http://www.ee.columbia.edu/~dpwe/papers/Wang03-shazam.pdf
16. Yang, R., Shi, Y.Q., Huang, J.: Detecting double compression of audio signal. In: Memon, N.D., Dittmann, J., Alattar, A.M., Delp, E.J., III. (eds.) Media Forensics and Security II, vol. 7541, pp. 200–209. International Society for Optics and Photonics, SPIE (2010). https://doi.org/10.1117/12.838695
17. Zeng, J., et al.: Audio recorder forensic identification in 21 audio recorders. In: 2015 IEEE International Conference on Progress in Informatics and Computing (PIC), pp. 153–157 (2015). https://doi.org/10.1109/PIC.2015.7489828
18. Zhao, H., Chen, Y., Wang, R., Malik, H.: Anti-forensics of environmental-signature-based audio splicing detection and its countermeasure via rich-features classification. IEEE Trans. Inf. Forensics Secur. **11**(7), 1603–1617 (2016). https://doi.org/10.1109/TIFS.2016.2543205
19. Zheng, Y., Cao, Y., Chang, C.H.: A PUF-based data-device hash for tampered image detection and source camera identification. IEEE Trans. Inf. Forensics Secur. **15**, 620–634 (2020). https://doi.org/10.1109/TIFS.2019.2926777
20. Zuo, H., Li, Q., Zheng, H., Yang, Y., Zhao, X.: An optically-reconfigurable PUF based on logarithmic photoreceptor of CMOS dynamic vision sensors. IEEE Trans. Electron Devices **69**(9), 5395–5398 (2022). https://doi.org/10.1109/TED.2022.3191628

SHIELD: A Specialized Dataset for Hybrid Blind Forensics of World Leaders

Qingran Lin🆔, Xiang Li🆔, Beilin Chu🆔, Renying Wang🆔, Xianhao Chen🆔,
Yuzhe Mao🆔, Zhen Yang🆔, Linna Zhou, and Weike You(✉)🆔

Beijing University of Posts and Telecommunications, Beijing, China
{linqingran,xli,chuchad1998,wangry017,chenxianhao,
maoyuzhe,yangzhenyz,zhoulinna,ywk}@bupt.edu.cn

Abstract. The speech videos of public figures, such as movie celebrities and world leaders, have an extensive influence on the Internet. However, the authenticity of these videos is often difficult to ascertain. These videos may have been carefully imitated by comedians or manipulated using Deepfake methods, which creates significant obstacles for the video forensics of specific characters. Moreover, the vast amount of data on social networking platforms renders manual screening impractical. To specifically address this issue, we present SHIELD, which stands for **S**pecialized dataset for **H**ybrid bl**I**nd for**E**nsics of wor**L**d lea**D**ers. Unlike most previous public Deepfake datasets that only contain Deepfake samples, this dataset exquisitely includes a collection that can quickly test this issue, encompassing both impersonator and Deepfake videos. We provide a detailed dataset production process and conduct an elaborate experiment under the hybrid blind detection scenario. Our findings reveal the limitations of existing methods, demonstrate the potential of identity-based models, and illustrate the increased challenges posed by SHIELD.

Keywords: Video forensics · Deepfake detection · Dataset

1 Introduction

Compared to videos of ordinary people, videos of specific characters (such as world leaders and famous actors/actresses) may significantly impact political activities and public opinion. With the popularity and development of AI manipulation technology, Deepfake videos of specific characters are more likely to be maliciously exploited and lead to severe consequences [5,10]. Additionally, some specific characters have many impersonators who mimic their facial expressions and gestures for entertainment or other purposes [2,3]. An impersonation performance is costly for a given character due to its more realistic visual effects, but it may exert a more substantial deceptive impact.

Under the combined effect of the above two factors, the mass of online videos can become misleading for viewers. Therefore, in the realistic scenario, the video forensics

---

Q. Lin and X. Li—Equal contribution.

ⓒ ICST Institute for Computer Sciences, Social Informatics and Telecommunications Engineering 2024
Published by Springer Nature Switzerland AG 2024. All Rights Reserved
S. Goel and P. R. Nunes de Souza (Eds.): ICDF2C 2023, LNICST 571, pp. 79–91, 2024.
https://doi.org/10.1007/978-3-031-56583-0_6

task of specific characters can be regarded as a hybrid detection of both the Deepfake and impersonator videos (Fig. 1).

Fig. 1. SHIELD contains real and faked videos of four world leaders and provides a dataset dedicated to character-specific video forensics models. Shown from top to bottom are example frames of clips from the original, FaceSwap [36], Wav2Lip [29], FOMM [32], and impersonator videos.

Current methods for this task mainly focus on one kind of forgery data: the Deepfake detection methods (used to classify Deepfake videos) [6,13,25] or the face recognition methods (used to identify imitators) [1,4]. One mainstream idea of Deepfake detection pays attention to the inconsistencies between faces generated by Deepfake and natural faces [17,26,28], which can effectively detect deepfake videos and meet the expectations. As for face recognition models, they can obtain excellent results when identifying impersonators. However, in the hybrid blind detection scenario where the manipulation methods are unknown, this type of Deepfake detection models cannot achieve the ideal results on videos with real faces because they ignore the videos' identity information. As some Deepfake generation methods [29,32] do not change the identity information of the source video, face recognition models misjudge the samples. Therefore, these methods alone may not be effective for addressing the complexities of the hybrid blind detection scenario.

The absence of public dataset for studies on hybrid blind detection of specific characters prompted us to develop the dataset for specialized forensics of world leaders (SHIELD), which specifically addresses the challenges of detecting Deepfakes and impersonators in online videos featuring public figures with significant societal impact, such as celebrities and leaders. Differing from most public Deepfake datasets, SHIELD targets the protection of people with broad influence on society, such as movie celebrities and leaders. The dataset is primarily used for fine-tuning the data on individual characters, and its lightweight scale makes it easier for the model to conduct experiments.

Our contributions are as follows: (1) We propose a specialized dataset for hybrid blind forensics of world leaders (SHIELD), which is a public dataset with impersonator and Deepfake videos, addressing video forensics techniques for specific characters. (2) We conduct a systematic experiment to evaluate the performance of proper methods for video forensics on the SHIELD and offer open issues for future research in the video forensics of specific individuals. (3) Our experimental results indicate that the identity-based model performs well on our dataset, thereby highlighting their potential in the hybrid blind detection task.

2   Related Works

The generation of Deepfake forensics methods requires specific supervised datasets, which gives rise to the need for suitable, well-crafted datasets. The early appearing datasets like UADFV [37] and DeepFakeTIMIT [22] dataset have laid the foundation for deepfake detection models. After that, many outstanding public Deepfake detection datasets have emerged in recent years [16,20,21,23,24,27,31,38], which have given a significant boost to the development of this field. Here are some representative datasets.

In 2019, the FaceForensics++ dataset [31] was presented by Rössler et al. Until now, it is still one of the most popular and influential Deepfake video datasets. It introduced an automated benchmark and a large-scale dataset where the original real dataset contains 1000 real videos and 509,914 images. FaceSwap [36], DeepFakes [36], Face2Face [35], and NeuralTextures [34] are used to generate Deepfake videos. Because of its huge scale and the diversity of manipulation methods, FF++ has become a baseline dataset for many Deepfake detections.

The DFDC dataset [16] was published in a competition and is widely used in numerous works. It is a large dataset with 48,190 videos and over 25TB of raw data, the videos were mostly filmed at the resolution of 1080p. The dataset contains videos of real-world scenarios, individuals were filmed indoors and outdoors. In addition to image tampering, audio swapping was performed on partial clips.

In 2020, Li et al. introduced the Celeb-DF dataset [27], which was specifically designed for deepfake detection and comprises 590 authentic videos and 5,639 Deepfake videos. The dataset includes videos of 59 celebrities delivering speeches, which were sourced from YouTube, as well as Deepfake videos generated using an enhanced face-swapping technique. Notably, the Celeb-DF dataset features significant improvements in visual quality, such as higher resolution and the application of color conversion. Despite these advancements, the dataset remains a difficult challenge for deepfake detection models, and it continues to serve as a benchmark for evaluating the efficacy of various detection techniques.

In 2019, Agarwal *et al.* presented the World Leaders dataset (WLDR) [8], which marks a significant advancement in the field of protecting specific individuals from both deepfake and impersonator videos. This dataset introduces a forensics technique that is customized for specific characters, utilizing biometric features unique to each individual. The WLDR dataset includes authentic videos of five U.S. political figures and their corresponding impersonator videos and deepfake videos generated by applying face-swap deepfake methods. After that, the clips were extracted by sliding a window across the segment five frames at a time. The proposed technique is tailored to address the challenges posed by deepfake and impersonator videos, thereby enabling the effective detection of these malicious videos.

Our study draws inspiration from the WLDR and is motivated by the need to develop a more "omnipotent" approach for detecting forged videos. Our lightweight dataset contains sufficient video hours with more comprehensive data, where every character has its corresponding authentic and forged videos. Specifically, we adopted a rigorous evaluation using both Deepfake detection methods and face recognition methods in a systematic manner. SHIELD utilized updated forgery methods to generate Deepfake videos, which enriched the amount of data. In order to enhance the diversity and complexity of our dataset, the 10-second clips are partitioned from the videos directly, making it more suitable for fine-tuning and evaluating the advanced forensics algorithms.

3   SHIELD Dataset

This section specifies the specific production process and information about the dataset.

SHIELD, proposed by us, is a dataset specified for protecting specific characters' videos, consisting of real and forgery data of four world leaders (Barak Obama, Donald Trump, Hillary Clinton, and Joe Biden). It is a lightweight and diverse dataset, where four leaders of different skin colors and genders are selected. The dataset contains 255 Deepfake videos of four leaders, 297 real videos, and 40 impersonator videos. The Deepfake videos are generated with three different and typical synthesis models. We introduce the forgery methods and detailed production process in the following subsections (Table 1).

Table 1. Specific information of SHIELD dataset.

Video Type		Leaders - video duration (hours)/count of clips			
		Barak Obama	Donald Trump	Hillary Clinton	Joe Biden
Authentic Videos		7.25 h/2,647	7.66 h/3,188	5.19 h/2,028	4.79 h/1,956
Deepfake Videos	FaceSwap	10.02 h/3,696	13.44 h/4,993	13.12 h/4,885	11.10 h/4,124
	Wav2Lip	4.08 h/1,205	2.69 h/807	4.15 h/1.247	2.87 h/860
	FOMM	3.34 h/1,209	3.35 h/1,216	3.35 h/1,212	3.34 h/1,213
Impersonator Videos		0.71 h/256	1.71 h/620	1.33 h/487	1.12 h/406

3.1   Real Data

We first gather the videos of four world leaders delivering speeches on official occasions, like press conferences, public debates, and television broadcasts. All the source videos were downloaded from public sources online, which are highly trusted. Besides, these videos are carefully selected in which the leaders constantly talk and face straight toward the camera most of the time. Lastly, qualified videos are cut into non-overlapping 10-second clips for standardization.

3.2   Forgery Data

Forgery data consists of videos forged by Deepfake methods and videos of impersonators. The details of data collection and processing are shown as follows.

Impersonator Videos. We collect and download the videos of impersonators from YouTube. In these videos, comedians imitate our target world leaders' physical appearance, facial expression, and postures. Unlike Deepfake videos, these videos contain genuine footage of real individuals whose expressions and movements exhibit natural features. Also, they do not contain any artifacts that may indicate a synthetic source.

Deepfake Videos. To generate manipulation videos with diversity, we adapted three state-of-the-art Deepfake techniques (Fig. 2).

FaceSwap. FaceSwap [36] is one of the most popular methods in graphical Deepfake forgery. It generates Deepfake videos by transferring the face area from a source video to a target one. The model first extracts the landmarks of the face area, encodes the source and target images into the same latent space, and the two decoders are used to reconstruct different facial features.

We employ the use of FaceSwap software to facilitate the automatic detection and extraction of the facial area belonging to a specific leader from the collected videos. This process involves the replacement of the identified leader's face with the faces of three other leaders. The resulting sequences of both the processed face images and the original videos serve as input data for the subsequent face-swapping operation.

Wav2Lip. Wav2Lip [29] is a way of tampering through audio-driven video. It manipulates the movements of one's mouth area according to the content of the source audio, resulting in the alteration of the original video content. The quality of the corresponding audio plays a vital role in this type of tampering method. In the meantime, audios from VOA were selected for forgery to avoid possible artifacts.

Therefore, two components are necessary for the Wav2Lip approach. In our implementation, we use the videos of world leaders giving speeches, while the audio comes from the TED-LIUM 3 dataset [19].

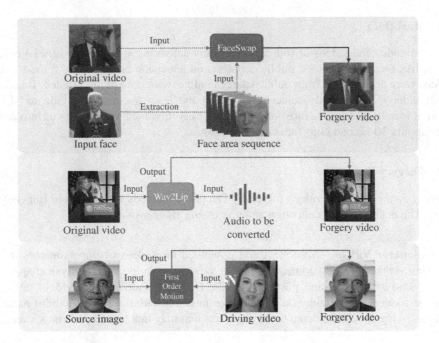

Fig. 2. Process illustration of the three deepfake methods.

FOMM. First order motion model [32] is a self-supervised network that transfers a series of motions from a driving video to a target image. Both the video and the image should contain objects of the same category. The model decouples appearance and motion by modeling the movement around the key points using affine transformations in a self-supervised manner. We use this method to represent the face-reenactment strategy.

A source image and a driving video are needed when generating a FOMM Deepfake video. In order to ensure the quality of the tampered video and reduce artifacts as much as possible, we chose the videos of the news anchor as driving videos, in which their head basically facing towards the camera with a slight angle of rotations during continuous talking.

3.3 Postprocessing

The postprocessing phase of our dataset creation comprises three key steps: segmentation, quality assurance, and audio track retention. First, all videos are sliced into non-overlapping 10-second segments to facilitate downstream usage. Next, to ensure the integrity and fidelity of the forged videos, manual quality checks are performed by qualified personnel. Videos deemed to be of low quality or containing significant artifacts are subsequently excluded from the dataset. Notably, as the FaceSwap and FOMM deepfake techniques do not involve audio manipulation, we opt to retain the original audio tracks of the source videos.

4   Evaluation

The objective of this performance evaluation is to demonstrate that although a relatively adequate amount of data is available for a particular world leader, the Deepfake detection models fail to accurately differentiate between genuine videos and those created by impersonators. Additionally, face recognition models are incapable of identifying the individuals appearing in the Deepfake videos. Thus, a hybrid blind detection approach is required to effectively identify the authenticity of these videos. In this section, we present our experimental setups, including detailed training procedures, and conduct an elaborate evaluation of various state-of-the-art Deepfake detection and face recognition models using our dataset. We analyze the obtained results and highlight their respective limitations.

4.1   Preprocessing of Evaluation

To implement frame-level evaluation, we first preprocess our dataset. We cut the video clips to be evaluated into frames and used RetinaFace [15] to extract the face area within them. Finally, we pass the crops of faces to the detection model as input. In order to make an independent analysis of different world leaders, we repeat the above steps and store their outputs separately.

4.2   Deepfake Detection Methods

With the development of Deepfake technology and the rise of comedic impersonator videos, ensuring massive online videos' authenticity has become challenging. To solve this task, most of the literature deals with Deepfake videos and focuses on various features of the video, such as learned features and identity-based features [12]. To achieve improvement, one category of works utilizes learned features in the video for detection, which involves constructing the novel network architecture [6], designing the data augmentation method [13], proposing new loss fuction [25], etc. The other category of works emphasizes the high-level semantics that exhibits impressive performance in terms of generalizability, such as biometrical features [7] and identity. Nowadays, some identity-based models have come to light. ID-Reveal [12] is a method that only requires real videos for training but exhibits high generalizability. In the detection method proposed by Dong *et al.* [17], photos of known identities are brought in as a reference set, which improves the detection effect to a certain extent. Boháček *et al* [9]. constructed a model leveraging Zelenskyy's distinctive features of facial and gestural behaviors.

In order to ensure the diversity of evaluation, we choose different Deepfake detection models to evaluate our dataset, and the categories are as follows (Table 2).

Learned Features

XceptionNet. The XceptionNet [11] has been the baseline model by many well-known Deepfake datasets, such as FF++ [31], DF-TIMIT [22], Deepfake MNIST+ [20], etc. The model has achieved high accuracy in detecting deepfake videos: 99.26% on FF++

Table 2. Detection accuracy of selected models evaluated on SHIELD. Bolded are the best results on each forgery method of different world leaders.

Methods	Leaders	Evaluating Indicator (%)			
		Impersonator	FaceSwap	Wav2Lip	FOMM
XceptionNet-c40 [11] (w/ finetune)	Joe Biden	69.34	**97.68**	93.30	**97.12**
	Hillary Clinton	63.01	**98.82**	93.20	80.23
	Barak Obama	71.65	88.86	**92.19**	87.89
	Donald Trump	63.77	86.66	72.55	79.98
F^3-Net [30] (w/ finetune)	Joe Biden	69.14	92.60	88.84	92.99
	Hillary Clinton	69.63	94.73	**94.49**	90.71
	Barak Obama	64.43	**90.01**	70.18	73.34
	Donald Trump	67.30	87.33	78.29	69.04
EfficientNet-B3 [33] (w/ finetune)	Joe Biden	**77.44**	94.77	**94.27**	93.67
	Hillary Clinton	67.60	91.20	90.87	**93.75**
	Barak Obama	**72.92**	89.27	90.69	**88.28**
	Donald Trump	74.75	**87.50**	**87.33**	**86.40**

(a) Detection accuracy of Deepfake detectors based on learned features.

ICT-Ref [17] (w/o finetune)	Joe Biden	65.47	91.77	51.01	61.77
	Hillary Clinton	**73.43**	93.61	60.50	64.25
	Barak Obama	63.22	88.35	66.78	53.91
	Donald Trump	**78.19**	87.26	50.22	68.16

(b) Detection accuracy of Deepfake detectors based on identity features

Methods	Leaders	Evaluating Indicator (%)			
		Impersonator	FaceSwap	Wav2Lip	FOMM
ArcFace [14] + ResNet50 [18] (w/ finetune)	Joe Biden	84.68	69.37	41.36	64.14
	Hillary Clinton	88.17	59.03	58.49	59.49
	Barak Obama	87.50	57.56	33.50	45.42
	Donald Trump	69.58	66.50	54.95	56.53

(c) Detection accuracy of face recognition model

(RAW), 99.91% on DF-TIMIT(HQ), and 92.38% on Deepfake MNIST+(Raw). It is an image-level method for Deepfake detection, which is a CNN model inspired by Inception. In our evaluation, we used the XceptionNet-c40 model pertained on ImageNet.

F^3-*Net* F^3-Net [30] is a novel face forgery detection method, which takes advantage of two frequency-aware clues, 1) frequency-aware decomposed image components and 2) local frequency statistics. Two clues are mixed in a two-stream collaborative learning framework, realizing Deepfake detection in the frequency domain.

EfficientNet. EfficientNet [33] is a convolutional neural network architecture and scaling method that uses a compound coefficient to scale all depth, width, and resolution dimensions uniformly. Considering the promising results of the EfficientNet in DFDC public competition, we use EfficientNet-B3 as a convolutional extractor for processing the input faces.

Identity-Based Features

Identity Consistency Transformer. ICT [17] achieves the state-of-the-art performance over many benchmark datasets. It is a novel face forgery detection method that focuses on using high-level semantics: identity information. It detects suspicious faces by finding identity inconsistencies between the inner and outer face regions. Particularly, ICT-Ref leverages the real face available to build a reference set. Due to the addition of general identity information for enhancement and the availability of authentic videos, it is well suited for video forensics scenarios of world leaders.

4.3 Face Recognition Methods

Unlike most Deepfake datasets, SHIELD contains videos of impersonators of the four leaders. However, the actors imitate the leaders by their appearance and mannerisms. Rather than crafted employing Deepfake techniques, such videos are usually obtained by direct filming. Under this circumstance, facial recognition technology is selected to identify the face in the video. Accordingly, out of the above considerations, we add a face recognition model to evaluate our dataset.

Arcface. ArcFace [14] is a widely adopted loss function due to its easiness in implementation and state-of-the-art performance on a number of benchmarks. It improves the conventional softmax loss by optimizing the feature embedding on a hypersphere manifold where the learned face representation is more discriminative. We use ResNet-50 [18] pretrained on CASIA Webface as the backbone network.

4.4 Experimental Settings

There are four world leaders in SHIELD where leader $p \in \mathcal{P} = \{BarakObama, DonaldTrump, JoeBiden, HillaryClinton\}$. Videos in SHIELD can be divided into three categories: authentic videos $a_p \in \mathcal{A}_p$, Deepfake videos $f_p \in \mathcal{F}_p$, impersonator videos $i_p \in \mathcal{I}_p$. In that way, SHIELD dataset can be described as $\mathcal{D}_p = \{(v_p, l_p)\}$, where $v_p \in \mathcal{V}_p$ and $l_p \in \mathcal{L}_p = \{0, 1\}$. All the video samples in SHIELD can be formulated as $\mathcal{V}_p = \{\mathcal{A}_p, \mathcal{F}_p, \mathcal{I}_p\}$. In most of the Deepfake detection tasks, the positive samples are $\mathcal{A}_p$, while the negative samples are $\mathcal{F}_p$. However, in the hybrid blind detection task, $\mathcal{F}_p$ and $\mathcal{I}_p$ are negative samples of p. The label of real videos is $l_p = 0$, and the label of forged videos is $l_p = 1$. What we want is that there exist classification models f, which can map the video space to the class space: $f : \mathcal{V}_p \rightarrow \mathcal{L}_p$. To achieve this, the classification error of f can be minimized on training set $\mathcal{T}_p$:

$$\arg \min_{\theta} \mathbb{E}_{(v_p, l_p) \in \mathcal{T}_p} l(f(v_p), l_p), \tag{1}$$

where l is the loss function and θ is the parameters of model f for training.

We conduct two different comparison experiments on each leader separately. In the first experiment, we use the training set $\mathcal{T}_p = \{\mathcal{A}_p, \mathcal{F}_p\}$ of a specific leader p to train the detection models, which are then used to discriminate all the forgery videos $\{\mathcal{F}_p, \mathcal{I}_p\}$ of this very leader. We also use faces from $\mathcal{A}_p$ to train the face recognition model. Results of the first experiment are shown in Table 2.

In the second experiment, to see how Deepfake detection models perform when dealing with the type of forgery data outside the training set, we compared the detection results of $\mathcal{I}_p$ where detectors are respectively trained on $\mathcal{I}_p$ and $\{\mathcal{I}_p, \mathcal{F}_p\}$.

We construct our training set with balanced real and fake samples. All the models are initialized by their pretrained weights and trained using cross-entropy loss and Adam optimizer with batch size 64. We set the initial learning rate at 0.0001 and trained for 10,000 iterations. The model with the best test accuracy was chosen as the final model.

Table 3. Detection accuracy of detectors trained on impersonators videos $\mathcal{I}_p$ or mixed data $\{\mathcal{I}_p, \mathcal{F}_p\}$.

Methods	Evaluating Indicator (%)			
	Joe Biden	Hillary Clinton	Barak Obama	Donald Trump
XceptionNet-c40 [11]	81.74/**90.14**	87.02/**90.01**	76.22/**84.55**	76.94/**79.65**
F^3-Net [30]	**78.32**/76.07	69.50 / **82.74**	73.78/**80.56**	**71.03**/68.92
EfficientNet-B3 [33]	90.62/**92.87**	75.20/**80.03**	84.67/**88.99**	76.90 / **77.80**

4.5 Results and Analysis

The ultimate goal of SHIELD would be to help develop effective forensics techniques that take full advantage of the identity information in the hybrid blind detection task of face forgery.

To evaluate the performance of each detection method on four world leaders person-specifically, we employ frame-level accuracy rate as the performance metric. As presented in Table 2a, our experimental results demonstrate that all three models based on learned features exhibit satisfactory performance in detecting Deepfake videos. Notably, the detection accuracy rates are slightly higher with the FaceSwap method, ranging from 86.66% to 98.82%. This phenomenon could be attributed to the widespread use of the FaceSwap method in the pretraining dataset. Furthermore, a notable variance in detection accuracy is observed across the four leaders. In particular, the detection accuracy rate of Biden and Trump on Wav2Lip using the XceptionNet model demonstrates a 20.75% difference.

There is a noticeable drop in accuracy rate when using the Deepfake classifier to detect impersonator videos. After training on the data of specific characters, the Deep-Fake classifier cannot reach the ideal result. In contrast, the identity-based model, such as ICT-Ref shown in Table 2b, exhibits similar levels of accuracy in detecting impersonator videos as the other models, despite not having undergone fine-tuning on our dataset.

The notable difference in performance could potentially be attributed to the potential for further enhancement through additional identity information in the reference set.

In the case of detecting impersonator videos, the face recognition model produces satisfactory results as in Table 2c but is unable to accurately detect all three categories of Deepfake videos. While the aforementioned deepfake detection methods can detect some forged samples, there remains considerable room for improvement in their results.

As presented in Table 2, the performance of classifiers in detecting impersonator videos exhibits a noticeable improvement after adding Deepfake videos to the training data. This outcome suggests that the inclusion of identity information can enhance the model's ability to portray specific characters comprehensively and capture more features in the forensic task.

In conclusion, despite having adequate data on a specific world leader, the Deepfake detection model falls short in discriminating the videos of impersonators, while face recognition models cannot identify the person appearing in the Deepfake videos. The face recognition model can achieve satisfying results in detecting impersonator videos but cannot deal with hybrid blind scenarios in Deepfake detection. From the results of the identity-based model, the inclusion of identity information can improve the performance of classifiers when detecting impersonator videos, indicating that the identity information in Deepfake videos should not be ignored. The study suggests that incorporating identity information can enhance the model's ability to depict specific characters from multiple dimensions well-roundedly in the hybrid blind detection task of video forensics.

5 Conclusion

In this study, we introduce a compact hybrid dataset named SHIELD for video forensics of specific characters, which expands the current literature by addressing the challenging hybrid blind detection task. Our experimental results highlight the potential for further improvements in this area, particularly in leveraging identity information for enhanced classification performance. Furthermore, we emphasize the importance of considering the identity information present in deepfake videos when developing detection methods. While our dataset has some limitations, we believe that SHIELD can provide a valuable foundation for future research in this field.

Acknowledgments. Research was supported by the National Natural Science Foundation of China (No. 62172053), the National Key Research and Development Program of China (No. 2021YFC3340700, No. 2022YFC3303300, No. 2021YFC3340600, No. 2022YFC3300800), and the Fundamental Research Funds for the Central Universities (No. 2023RC30).

References

1. Amazon rekognition: Automate your image and video analysis with machine learning. https://aws.amazon.com/cn/rekognition/. Accessed 11 Oct 2022
2. Hillary Clinton impersonator teresa barnwell on vibe with sinbad. https://www.youtube.com/watch?v=r-1KbeOg0ro. Accessed 11 Oct 2022

3. Life as donald trump, hillary clinton impersonators. https://www.youtube.com/watch?v=bBl67bYAJm8&t=113s. Accessed 11 Oct 2022
4. Microsoft azure cognitive services: an AI service that analyzes content in images and video. https://azure.microsoft.com/en-us/products/cognitive-services/computer-vision/#overview. Accessed 11 Oct 2022
5. A nixon deepfake, a 'moon disaster' speech and an information ecosystem at risk. https://www.scientificamerican.com/article/a-nixon-deepfake-a-moon-disaster-speech-and-an-information-ecosystem-at-risk1/. Accessed 11 Oct 2022
6. Afchar, D., Nozick, V., Yamagishi, J., Echizen, I.: Mesonet: a compact facial video forgery detection network. In: WIFS, pp. 1–7. IEEE (2018)
7. Agarwal, S., Farid, H., El-Gaaly, T., Lim, S.: Detecting deep-fake videos from appearance and behavior. In: WIFS, pp. 1–6. IEEE (2020)
8. Agarwal, S., Farid, H., Gu, Y., He, M., Nagano, K., Li, H.: Protecting world leaders against deep fakes. In: CVPR Workshops, pp. 38–45. Computer Vision Foundation/IEEE (2019)
9. Boháček, M., Farid, H.: Protecting president zelenskyy against deep fakes. CoRR abs/2206.12043 (2022)
10. Castillo, M.: Fake video news is coming, and this clip of Obama 'insulting' Trump shows how dangerous it could be. https://www.cnbc.com/2018/04/17/jordan-peele-buzzfeed-psa-edits-obama-saying-things-he-never-said.html. Accessed 11 Oct 2022
11. Chollet, F.: Xception: deep learning with depthwise separable convolutions. In: CVPR, pp. 1800–1807. IEEE Computer Society (2017)
12. Cozzolino, D., Rössler, A., Thies, J., Nießner, M., Verdoliva, L.: Id-reveal: identity-aware deepfake video detection. In: ICCV, pp. 15088–15097. IEEE (2021)
13. Das, S., Seferbekov, S.S., Datta, A., Islam, M.S., Amin, M.R.: Towards solving the deepfake problem : an analysis on improving deepfake detection using dynamic face augmentation. In: ICCVW, pp. 3769–3778. IEEE (2021)
14. Deng, J., Guo, J., Xue, N., Zafeiriou, S.: Arcface: additive angular margin loss for deep face recognition. In: CVPR, pp. 4690–4699. Computer Vision Foundation/IEEE (2019)
15. Deng, J., Guo, J., Zhou, Y., Yu, J., Kotsia, I., Zafeiriou, S.: Retinaface: Single-stage dense face localisation in the wild. CoRR abs/1905.00641 (2019)
16. Dolhansky, B., Howes, R., Pflaum, B., Baram, N., Canton-Ferrer, C.: The deepfake detection challenge (DFDC) preview dataset. CoRR abs/1910.08854 (2019)
17. Dong, X., et al.: Protecting celebrities from deepfake with identity consistency transformer. In: CVPR, pp. 9458–9468. IEEE (2022)
18. He, K., Zhang, X., Ren, S., Sun, J.: Deep residual learning for image recognition. In: CVPR, pp. 770–778. IEEE Computer Society (2016)
19. Hernandez, F., Nguyen, V., Ghannay, S., Tomashenko, N., Estève, Y.: TED-LIUM 3: twice as much data and corpus repartition for experiments on speaker adaptation. In: Karpov, A., Jokisch, O., Potapova, R. (eds.) SPECOM 2018. LNCS (LNAI), vol. 11096, pp. 198–208. Springer, Cham (2018). https://doi.org/10.1007/978-3-319-99579-3_21
20. Huang, J., Wang, X., Du, B., Du, P., Xu, C.: Deepfake MNIST+: a deepfake facial animation dataset. In: ICCVW, pp. 1973–1982. IEEE (2021)
21. Khalid, H., Tariq, S., Kim, M., Woo, S.S.: Fakeavceleb: a novel audio-video multimodal deepfake dataset. In: NeurIPS Datasets and Benchmarks (2021)
22. Korshunov, P., Marcel, S.: Deepfakes: a new threat to face recognition? assessment and detection. CoRR abs/1812.08685 (2018)
23. Kwon, P., You, J., Nam, G., Park, S., Chae, G.: Kodf: a large-scale korean deepfake detection dataset. In: ICCV, pp. 10724–10733. IEEE (2021)
24. Le, T., Nguyen, H.H., Yamagishi, J., Echizen, I.: Openforensics: large-scale challenging dataset for multi-face forgery detection and segmentation in-the-wild. In: ICCV, pp. 10097–10107. IEEE (2021)

25. Li, J., Xie, H., Li, J., Wang, Z., Zhang, Y.: Frequency-aware discriminative feature learning supervised by single-center loss for face forgery detection. In: CVPR, pp. 6458–6467, Computer Vision Foundation/IEEE (2021)
26. Li, Y., Chang, M., Lyu, S.: In ictu oculi: exposing AI generated fake face videos by detecting eye blinking. CoRR abs/1806.02877 (2018)
27. Li, Y., Yang, X., Sun, P., Qi, H., Lyu, S.: Celeb-df: a large-scale challenging dataset for deepfake forensics. In: CVPR, pp. 3204–3213. Computer Vision Foundation/IEEE (2020)
28. Matern, F., Riess, C., Stamminger, M.: Exploiting visual artifacts to expose deepfakes and face manipulations. In: WACV Workshops, pp. 83–92. IEEE (2019)
29. Prajwal, K.R., Mukhopadhyay, R., Namboodiri, V.P., Jawahar, C.V.: A lip sync expert is all you need for speech to lip generation in the wild. In: ACM Multimedia, pp. 484–492. ACM (2020)
30. Qian, Y., Yin, G., Sheng, L., Chen, Z., Shao, J.: Thinking in frequency: face forgery detection by mining frequency-aware clues. In: Vedaldi, A., Bischof, H., Brox, T., Frahm, J.-M. (eds.) ECCV 2020. LNCS, vol. 12357, pp. 86–103. Springer, Cham (2020). https://doi.org/10.1007/978-3-030-58610-2_6
31. Rössler, A., Cozzolino, D., Verdoliva, L., Riess, C., Thies, J., Nießner, M.: Faceforensics++: learning to detect manipulated facial images. In: ICCV, pp. 1–11. IEEE (2019)
32. Siarohin, A., Lathuilière, S., Tulyakov, S., Ricci, E., Sebe, N.: First order motion model for image animation. In: NeurIPS, pp. 7135–7145 (2019)
33. Tan, M., Le, Q.V.: Efficientnet: rethinking model scaling for convolutional neural networks. In: ICML. Proceedings of Machine Learning Research, vol. 97, pp. 6105–6114. PMLR (2019)
34. Thies, J., Zollhöfer, M., Nießner, M.: Deferred neural rendering: image synthesis using neural textures. ACM Trans. Graph. 38(4), 66:1–66:12 (2019)
35. Thies, J., Zollhöfer, M., Stamminger, M., Theobalt, C., Nießner, M.: Face2face: real-time face capture and reenactment of RGB videos. Commun. ACM 62(1), 96–104 (2019)
36. torzdf: Faceswap. https://github.com/deepfakes/faceswap. Accessed 11 Oct 2022
37. Yang, X., Li, Y., Lyu, S.: Exposing deep fakes using inconsistent head poses. In: ICASSP, pp. 8261–8265. IEEE (2019)
38. Zi, B., Chang, M., Chen, J., Ma, X., Jiang, Y.: Wilddeepfake: a challenging real-world dataset for deepfake detection. In: ACM Multimedia, pp. 2382–2390. ACM (2020)

Vulnerabilities

Optir-SBERT: Cross-Architecture Binary Code Similarity Detection Based on Optimized LLVM IR

Yintong Yan, Lu Yu, Taiyan Wang, Yuwei Li, and Zulie Pan[✉]

College of Electronic Engineering, National University of Defense Technology, Hefei 230037, China
{yanyintong.edu,yulu,wangty,liyuwei,panzulie17}@nudt.edu.cn

Abstract. Cross-architecture binary code similarity detection plays an important role in different security domains. In view of the low accuracy and poor scalability of existing cross-architecture detection technologies, we propose Optir-SBERT, which is the first technology to detect cross-architecture binary code similarity based on optimized LLVM IR. At the same time, we design a new data set BinaryIR, which is more diverse and provides a benchmark data set for subsequent research work based on LLVM IR. In terms of cross-architecture binary code similarity detection, the accuracy of Optir-SBERT reaches 94.38%, and the contribution of optimization is 3.99%. In terms of vulnerability detection, the average accuracy of Optir-SBERT reach 93.9%, and the contribution of optimization is 7%. The results are better than existing state-of-the-art (SOTA) cross-architecture detection technologies. In order to improve the efficiency of vulnerability detection in realistic scenarios, we introduced a file-level vulnerability identification mechanism on the basis of Optir-SBERT. The new model Optir-SBERT-F saved 45.36% of the detection time on the premise of a slight decrease in detection F value, which greatly improves the efficiency of vulnerability detection.

Keywords: Binary code similarity detection · Cross-architecture · Optimized LLVM IR · SBERT · File-level vulnerability identification mechanism

1 Introduction

Binary code similarity detection (BCSD) takes binary representation of a pair of functions as input and output as a value, which can reflect the degree of similarity between two functions. It is mainly used to find similar or homologous binary functions. This technology plays a vital role in different security research fields, including known vulnerability detection [3,12,20,47], malware analysis [2,37], patch analysis [15,38,43] and software supply chain analysis [14,44]. However, many software programs, especially IoT firmware applications, are often compiled into binary files with different instruction set architectures, which brings

© ICST Institute for Computer Sciences, Social Informatics and Telecommunications Engineering 2024
Published by Springer Nature Switzerland AG 2024. All Rights Reserved
S. Goel and P. R. Nunes de Souza (Eds.): ICDF2C 2023, LNICST 571, pp. 95–113, 2024.
https://doi.org/10.1007/978-3-031-56583-0_7

great challenges to binary code similarity detection. Therefore, cross-architecture binary code similarity detection technology continues to emerge and gradually becomes a research hotspot.

With the development and application of machine learning, most of the state-of-the-art cross-architecture binary code similarity detection technology are based on machine learning [42]. In general, these detection techniques characterize binary functions in different architectures as vectors and calculate the similarity of the functions in vector space. Cross-architecture binary code similarity detection technology can be divided into code-based embedding [25,32,34] and graph-based embedding [10,12,19,46] according to the representation form. These technologies have realized binary code similarity detection under different architectures, but there are still some limitations and large room for improvement.

First, the existing cross-architecture similarity detection technologies rarely consider binary differences caused by compilers. The same source code under different compilation architectures, with different compilers, optimization options, and obfuscation strategies, will generate different binaries, and these binaries will vary significantly. Most of the existing cross-architecture binary code similarity detection technologies deal with these codes by constructing more complex models, larger thesaurus, or transforming binary function comparison into graph comparison problems. Such approach do not fundamentally solve the problem of binary differences caused by compilers, and the technologies used in the existing cross-architecture methods are not perfect, which makes the accuracy of binary code similarity detection and vulnerability detection low.

Second, the scalability of existing cross-architecture binary code similarity detection technologies is poor. Most of the cross-architecture binary code similarity detection technologies based on code embedding are established based on BERT. Such a model can only convert a binary function into a representation vector in a single operation, which will lead to huge computational overhead in the case of large detection samples. In addition, assembly instructions differ greatly under different architectures, and cross-architecture binary code similarity detection requires word segmentation representation of assembly instructions under all architectures. The increase of thesaural will lead to a large increase in the computational amount and time required for training models. What's more, the trained models have poor scalability, and they can only be used under the trained architectures.

Third, the existing evaluation data sets for cross-architecture binary code similarity detection are not diverse enough. Different detection technologies typically target different detection targets, and each technical solution trains and tests the model with its own data set and represents the results with different evaluation metrics (ROC curve area, MRR10, or Recall@5). However, binary code similarity detection technologies in the real world have a wider application range and needs to deal with more diverse and complex data sets. There is a big gap between the test results of existing detection technologies in small data sets and those in practical applications, which is not convincing enough.

Therefore, we propose Optir-SBERT and construct dataset BinaryIR to solve the above problems. Optir-SBERT is developed based on SEBRT network architecture. The SBERT network architecture contains two BERT. On this basis, the representation vector with binary function semantic information is generated by the twin neural network. The two binary functions can be converted into representation vectors by a single run, which is more suitable for similarity comparison [35]. At the same time, Optir-SBERT performs binary code similarity detection based on optimized LLVM IR. That is, the model firstly lift the binary code under different architectures to the LLVM IR, then optimizes the LLVM IR to eliminate binary differences caused by different compilers, and then realizes cross-architecture binary code similarity detection based on optimized LLVM IR.

Part of the existing work [22] uses IR to detect binary code similarity and achieved good results. We further optimize the LLVM IR and use the optimized LLVM IR to perform binary code similarity detection. As far as we know, Optir-SBERT is the first technique for cross-architecture binary code similarity detection based on optimized LLVM IR.

Optir-SBERT is evaluated on the dataset BinaryIR. BinaryIR contains a total of 2,025 binary projects under multiple architectures such as X86_32, X86_64, ARM32, ARM64, MIPS32, and PowerPC. The data sets are typical and diverse, and the evaluation results are more convincing. Experimental results show that the accuracy of Optir-SBERT in cross-architecture binary code similarity detection can reach 94.38%, which is significantly better than Genius [10], Gemini [46] and VulSeeker [12], with the accuracy increased by 46.58%, 52.18% and 20.17%, respectively. In terms of vulnerability detection, Optir-SBERT's average vulnerability identification accuracy rate reach 93.9%, well ahead of Gemini's 41.6%. In addition, we also conduct ablation experiments to explore the effect of the optimization on Optir-SBERT, and the results show that the optimization have a positive effect on the model. In conclusion, our research has the following contributions:

- We proposed Optir-SBERT, which solves the problem of binary code differences caused by compilers through optimization, and greatly improves the accuracy of cross-architecture binary code similarity detection and vulnerability detection. On this basis, Optir-SBERT-F is designed to greatly improve the detection efficiency by sacrificing the F value slightly.
- Optir-SBERT has strong scalability. When detecting binary functions under the new architecture, it is no need to retrain the model, but only need to lift the binary code under the architecture to the LLVM IR and optimize it for similarity detection or vulnerability detection, which greatly improves the universality of the model.
- We designed a more diversified dataset BinaryIR, which contains binary files under various architectures, IR files corresponding to binary files, and four kinds of optimized IR files (O0, O1, O2, O3), providing reference data sets for subsequent research on cross-architecture binary code similarity detection based on LLVM IR.

2   Related Work

Traditional binary code similarity detection technologies are mainly based on manually extracting binary function features [4,7,11,27,29] or using CG/CFG graph [9,33] for similarity comparison. The binary function information obtained in this way is often not comprehensive enough and the detection accuracy is low. With the development of machine learning technology, especially inspired by natural language processing, binary code similarity detection has made great progress. Binary code similarity detection technologies based on learning can be divided into single-architecture detection and cross-architecture detection.

2.1   Single-Architecture Binary Code Similarity Detection

The single-architecture detection technologies [15,42] can only detect binary code similarity in a specific architecture. When binary codes come from different compilation architectures, the detection effect will be very unsatisfactory, which is related to the fact that its model is only trained in a specific architecture. In the learning-based single-architecture binary code similarity detection technologies, Bingold [1] extracted semantic information of binary functions based on control flow graphs and data flow graphs, and then synthesized them into semantic flow graphs to represent binary functions. BinSim [28] proposed the system call slice equivalence checking, which is a hybrid method used to identify fine-grained semantic similarities or differences between two execution tracks. BinSign [29] provides an accurate and scalable solution for binary code fingerprinting by calculating and matching structure and syntax code profiles for disassembly. Asm2Vec [5] uses PV-DM, a natural language processing model, to learn assembly instructions and generate representations. Each assembly instruction is treated as a sentence, and operands and opcodes are separated into token units, which is more granular than migrating Word2Vec directly.

In general, single-architecture binary code similarity detection technologies have achieved high detection accuracy and have been applied in some network security fields [3,6,15,20,21]. With the increasing number of cross-architecture binary code similarity detection scenarios, single-architecture detection methods can no longer meet the actual detection requirements [31].

2.2   Cross-Architecture Binary Code Similarity Detection

With the application and popularity of IoT firmware applications, cross-architecture binary code similarity detection becomes more practical, but it is also more difficult to implement. Existing cross-architecture detection methods are generally based on code embedding or graph embedding.

The cross-architecture detection technologies based on code embedding [25,34,36,51] map binary functions under different instruction set architectures to the same vector space, and then calculates similarity. Most of these cross-architecture detection technologies are based on BERT, such as OrderMatters [48], Trex [32], PalmTree [18]. BERT is the best pre-trained representation model for natural language processing based on Transformer [40]. Cross-architecture detection technologies based on code embedding often need to build larger corpora [50] to support binary function similarity identification of models under different architectures. Therefore, the construction of such models are complicated and its scalability are poor.

The detection technologies based on graph embedding [8,10,12,19,45,46] are more widely used in cross-architecture detection, which is related to the small change of graph structure information of binary function under different architectures [13,30]. This kind of technologies firstly extract the control flow graph, data flow graph, abstract syntax tree and other graph structure information in binary function, and then use graph neural network to characterize the graph structure information, and then carry out similarity detection, such as VulSeeker [12], Asteria [47] and CodeCMR [49]. QBindiff [26] also solves the matching problem between two binary functions according to the similarity of function content and call graph. GMN [19] is a graph structure similarity detection technology based on graph neural network proposed in recent years. After large-scale experimental evaluation [23], it is found that its detection effect is most prominent. However, when considering the structure information of binary function graphs, the cross-architecture detection technologies based on graph embedding ignore the relationship between basic block instructions, so that the captured binary function information is not comprehensive enough [24,42,48].

3   Methodology

3.1   Overview

In order to solve the shortcomings of existing cross-architecture binary code similarity detection technologies, we propose Optir-SBERT, which is based on SBERT network structure design and performs similarity detection for optimized LLVM IR. The new design idea enables Optir-SBERT to effectively solve the challenges encountered by the existing cross-architecture binary code similarity detection technologies.

Firstly, Optir-SBERT is designed based on the SBERT network structure, which uses twin neural networks to generate embedding vectors with semantic information, and pools the output results to generate fixed-length representation vectors. In the pooling operation, MEAN strategy is used to calculate the embedding vector of binary functions, and experiments show that this strategy has the highest accuracy in obtaining results [35,39]. Meanwhile, the training methods of Optir-SBERT include next instruction prediction (NSP) and mask language model (MLM).

Secondly, binary files under different compilation architectures can be lifted to the same LLVM IR. Therefore, binary code similarity detection based on LLVM IR has natural advantages in cross-architecture detection, and has better scalability. On this basis, we optimize the LLVM IR to eliminate the binary code differences caused by different compilers, so as to obtain higher quality initial input data of the model, and then carry out binary code similarity detection and vulnerability detection based on the optimized LLVM IR.

Thirdly, in terms of vulnerability detection, Optir-SBERT-F, a model that can detect vulnerabilities faster, is proposed based on practical application scenarios. Compared with Optir-SBERT, this model introduces a file-level vulnerability identification mechanism, which determines whether the binary file to be detected has any vulnerability through the traditional way. If there is no vulnerability, lifting and a series of subsequent operations are not required. If there are vulnerabilities, lifting is carried out and specific vulnerability functions in the file are located and judged, thus saving a lot of detection time.

Finally, we design a new dataset, BinaryIR, which is more diverse, including many typical binary projects and a large amount of IoT firmware, to match real-world application scenarios. We lift all binary files in BinaryIR to obtain the corresponding LLVM IR files, and optimized the LLVM IR files in four ways (O0, O1, O2, O3). These data are incorporated into BinaryIR to provide a benchmark data set for subsequent researchers. The overall design of Optir-SBERT is shown in Fig. 1.

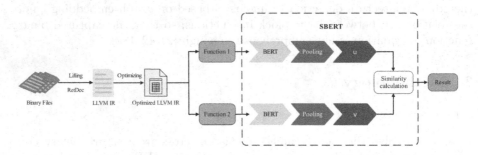

Fig. 1. The overall design of Optir-SBERT.

3.2 Optimized LLVM IR

LLVM IR is the internal representation generated by the compiler after scanning the source program. All stages of the compiler analyze or optimize the transformation on the LLVM IR [17,41], so it has a great impact on the overall structure, efficiency and robustness of the compiler. LLVM IR has m compiler design for front-end compiler languages (C, C++, Go, Rust, Toy, etc.) and n compiler designs for back-end platforms (X86, MIPS, ARM, PowerPC, etc.), which reduces the number of m*n compilers designed for m languages and n platforms, greatly improving compilation efficiency. LLVM structure design is shown in Fig. 2.

The binary files compiled by the same source program are very different. The fundamental reason for these differences are that the source program goes through different compilation architectures, compilers, optimization options, and obfuscation strategies when it is compiled into binary. Therefore, by lifting binary

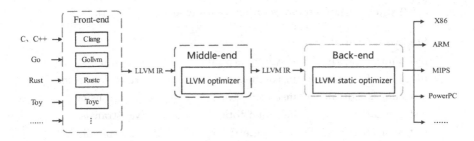

Fig. 2. LLVM structure design.

files to LLVM IR, assembly languages under different architectures can be unified into one LLVM IR, and the model based on this LLVM IR can perform cross-architecture binary code similarity detection. At the same time, in order to eliminate binary differences caused by the compiler, we optimize the LLVM IR to obtain higher quality initial input data. The Optir-SBERT trained based on this data will have higher detection accuracy.

The lifting tool we use is RetDec, which is based on the LLVM design and supports binary files lifting in various architectures (X86, ARM, MIPS32 and PowerPC, etc.). It is the best open source lifting tool known. RetDec can directly decompile the binary file to the source code. In this process, bin2llvmir is called to convert the binary file into LLVM IR.

3.3   File-Level Vulnerability Identification Mechanism

In the actual vulnerability detection scenario, the model often needs to detect a large number of binary files, which puts forward a high requirement for the detection efficiency of the model. Optir-SBERT we designed needs to lift binary files, which will take up lots of time and greatly affect the detection efficiency. To this end, we design Optir-SBERT-F. This model adds a file-level vulnerability identification mechanism on the basis of Optir-SBERT, which can improve the vulnerability detection efficiency of binary files in practical applications.

The file-level vulnerability identification mechanism first needs to build the binary file vulnerability library. The specific method is to collect the binary files containing the vulnerability and make statistics on its assembly instruction information, so as to obtain the assembly instruction characteristics of the binary files containing a certain vulnerability. Through analysis and experiment, we decide to make statistics on 28 typical assembly instruction characteristics of binary files, and build the binary file vulnerability library. Instruction features vary from architecture to architecture. The 28 instruction features we screened are available in common architectures (X86, ARM and MIPS32). The specific characteristics of binary file assembly instructions are shown in Table 1.

Mark the detected binary files as $F = \{f_1, f_2, \ldots, f_i, \ldots, f_m\}$. Mark the binary files in the vulnerability library as $G = \{g_1, g_2, \ldots, g_j, \ldots, g_n\}$. Mark the characteristics of assembly instructions as $C = \{c_1, c_2, \ldots, c_k, \ldots, c_{28}\}$. The

Table 1. Characteristics of binary file assembly instructions

Statistical Characteristics		
inst_num_abs_arith	inst_num_grp_jump	inst_avg_cmp
inst_num_abs_ctransfer	inst_num_grp_ret	inst_avg_cndctransfer
inst_num_abs_dtransfer	inst_num_logic	inst_avg_ctransfer
inst_num_arith	inst_num_total	inst_avg_dtransfer
inst_num_bitflag	inst_avg_abs_arith	inst_avg_grp_call
inst_num_cmp	inst_avg_abs_ctransfer	inst_avg_grp_jump
inst_num_cndctransfer	inst_avg_abs_dtransfer	inst_avg_grp_ret
inst_num_ctransfer	inst_avg_arith	inst_avg_logic
inst_num_dtransfer	inst_avg_bitflag	inst_avg_total
inst_num_grp_call		
Total	**28**	

lower bound of G is Low, the upper bound is $High$, and the evaluation function is E. In the actual vulnerability detection process, as long as formula (5) is satisfied, binary file f_i is considered suspicious. Then, it is necessary to lift binary file f_i to LLVM IR and conduct subsequent function-level vulnerability detection. Otherwise, the assembly instructions characteristics of next binary file $f_{(i+1)}$ are matched until all binary files F are detected. The calculation formulas are:

$$Low_{jk} = g_j(c_k) \times 0.9, j \in [1, n], k \in [1, 28] \tag{1}$$

$$High_{jk} = g_j(c_k) \times 1.1, j \in [1, n], k \in [1, 28] \tag{2}$$

$$q_{ik} = f_i(c_k), i \in [1, m], k \in [1, 28] \tag{3}$$

$$E_j(k) = \begin{cases} 0, q_{ik} \notin [Low_{jk}, High_{jk}] \\ 1, q_{ik} \in [Low_{jk}, High_{jk}] \end{cases} \tag{4}$$

$$\forall \sum_{k=1}^{28} E_j(k) \geq 14, f_i = g_j, i \in [1, m], j \in [1, n] \tag{5}$$

By introducing the file-level vulnerability identification mechanism, the efficiency of Optir-SBERT-F in actual vulnerability detection is greatly improved. The overall design of this model is shown in Fig. 3.

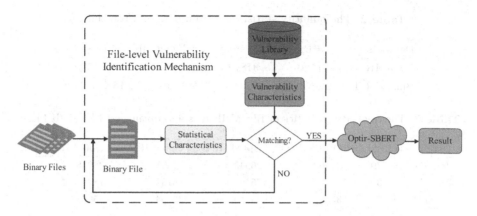

Fig. 3. The overall design of Optir-SBERT-F.

4 Experimental Setup

4.1 Experimental Environment

The environment of this experiment is Ubuntu 20.04 system under Linux 64-bit. The main configuration of the server is Intel Xeon Gold 6230R@104x 4 GHz processor, 256 GB memory and RTX3090 graphics card.

4.2 The BinaryIR Dataset

The existing binary code similarity detection technologies can only be detected for some specific data sets, which is divorced from the actual application scenarios in the real world. Therefore, we built a more diversified dataset, BinaryIR, and conduct training and testing Opti-SBERT on this dataset, so as to obtain more realistic detection results.

BinaryIR is built based on the dataset BinKit [16], BinaryCorp [42], and our collection of binary projects, IoT firmware, and vulnerability function library, including 2,025 projects, 41,172 binary files, and 388,2046 binary functions. The size of the binary files ranges from 14K to 27M. At the same time, we lift all binary files to obtain their corresponding LLVM IR files, and optimized the LLVM IR using four optimizations (O0, O1, O2, and O3), all of which are included in BinaryIR. The quantity statistics of specific train data and test data are shown in Table 2.

The process of lifting binary files to the LLVM IR files is relatively smooth, but errors may be reported during the optimization of the LLVM IR files, resulting in a failure to generate the optimized LLVM IR files. Therefore, the number of optimized LLVM IR files is less than the number of the binary files. Table 3 shows the actual number of LLVM IR files and the optimized LLVM IR files.

Table 2. The quantity statistics of train data and test data

DataSets	#Projects	#Binaries	#Functions	#File size
BinaryIR Train	1520	31879	2981536	14K–27M
BinaryIR Test	505	9293	900510	15K–19M

Table 3. The quantity statistics of LLVM IR files and optimized LLVM IR files

DataSets	LLVM IR	Opted IR(O0)	Opted IR(O1)	Opted IR(O2)	Opted IR(O3)
Train	31879	27463	26943	27591	28038
Test	9293	7842	7506	7613	7837
Total	41172	35305	34449	35204	35875

4.3 Evaluation Metrics

In order to evaluate the performance of Optir-SBERT in cross-architecture binary code similarity detection and vulnerability detection, a unified evaluation index needs to be established. Mark the function to be detected as $S = \{s_1, s_2, \ldots, s_i, \ldots, s_n\}$. Mark the recall rate of the function as $Recall@k$. The evaluation function is T. Then, the formulas of calculating the recall rate of the function can be expressed as:

$$T(x) = \begin{cases} 0, x = False \\ 1, x = True \end{cases} \tag{6}$$

$$Recall@k = \frac{1}{|S|} \sum_{i=1}^{n} T(Rank_{s_i} \leq k) \tag{7}$$

In specific experiments, the evaluation index used by Optir-SBERT in cross-architecture binary code similarity detection is $Recall@1$. The evaluation index used for vulnerability detection is $Recall@5$.

5 Evaluation

Our evaluation aims to answer the following questions.

- Question 1: How does the optimization affect and contribute to Optir-SBERT?
- Question 2: With the increase of the functions to be detected, how does the detection accuracy of Optir-SBERT change?
- Question 3: The accuracy of Optir-SBERT in cross-architecture binary code similarity detection?
- Question 4: How does the vulnerability detection effect of Optir-SBERT?
- Question 5: What are the advantages and disadvantages of Optir-SBERT-F compared to Optir-SBERT?

5.1 Binary Code Similarity Detection

The Contribution of Optimization to Optir-SBERT. To explore the contribution of optimization to Optir-SBERT, an ablation experiment is conducted. Firstly, a cross-architecture detection model Ir-SBERT based on LLVM IR is designed. The input data of this model is LLVM IR, and other structures are the same as Optir-SBERT. In order to explore the influence of different optimization options on Optir-SBERT, four optimization methods (O0, O1, O2, O3) are evaluated experimentally under different architectures. All experiments carry out in this paper are based on BinaryIR dataset. In order to simulate the application effect of Optir-SBERT in actual scenarios, a function pool is designed in this experiment. The construction method of the function pool is as follows: 10 binary files were randomly selected from data set BinaryIR, and 5 binary functions were randomly selected from each binary file to form a function pool containing 50 binary functions. Optir-SBERT and Ir-SBERT are tested in the constructed function pool. The results of the two experiments are shown in Table 4.

Table 4. The contribution of optimization to Optir-SBERT

	X86_32, ARM32	X86_32, MIPS32	X86_64, ARM64	X86_64, MIPS32	ARM32, MIPS32	ARM64, MIPS32	Average
Ir-SBERT	0.9158	0.9352	0.9071	0.9091	0.8755	0.9077	0.9084
Optir-SBERT (O0)	0.9301	0.9044	0.9542	0.9454	0.9226	0.9290	0.9310
Optir-SBERT (O1)	0.9507	0.9560	0.9640	0.9270	0.9531	**0.9521**	0.9505
Optir-SBERT (O2)	**0.9525**	**0.9607**	**0.9676**	**0.9464**	0.9497	0.9416	**0.9531**
Optir-SBERT (O3)	0.9249	0.9511	0.9219	0.9335	**0.9537**	0.9403	0.9376

As can be seen from Table 4, in the cross-architecture binary code similarity detection, the average detection accuracy of Optir-SBERT under the four optimization is higher than that of Ir-SBERT, indicating that the optimization has a positive contribution to Optir-SBERT, and the contribution rate is up to 4.47%. Among the four optimization methods, O2 optimization option has the best effect to obtain optimized LLVM IR, and the average accuracy of Optir-SBERT obtained by optimized LLVM IR training based on this method can reach 95.31%. The Optir-SBERT used in the following experiments are all based on the O2 optimization option training.

With the increasing number of binary functions to be detected, the accuracy of the existing binary code similarity detection techniques will decrease. Through experiments, we detect the variation of the accuracy of Optir-SBERT under different number of function pools, and compared it with the existing SOTA large-scale detection tool jTrans [42]. The specific changes are shown in Fig. 4. Let the number of binary functions in the function pool to be detected be Q, the horizontal coordinate be $log_{10}Q$, and the vertical coordinate be the detection accuracy.

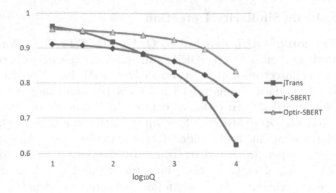

Fig. 4. The variation of models detection accuracy under different number of binary functions.

According to Fig. 4, with the increasing number of binary functions to be detected, the detection accuracy of the three models all declined, while the decline of Ir-SBERT and Optir-SBERT is smaller. When the number of binary functions to be detected reaches 10,000, the accuracy of jTrans decreases by 35.03%, while that of Ir-SBERT decreases by 15.96% and that of Optir-SBERT decreases by 12.62%. It shows that our propose Optir-SBERT can still maintain better performance in large-scale binary code similarity detection.

Performance of Optir-SBERT in Cross-Architecture Binary Code Similarity Detection. In order to explore the performance of Optir-SBERT in cross-architecture binary code similarity detection in real scenarios, the experiment is carred out under any compilation architecture. The function pool construction method designed in this experiment is as follows: 1000 binary files are randomly selected from data set BinaryIR, and 10 binary functions are randomly selected from each binary file to form a function pool P containing 10000 binary functions. Meanwhile, in order to make the experimental evaluation results of Optir-SBERT more convincing, we compare Optir-SBERT with Genius [10], Gemini [46] and VulSeeker [12], the three SOTA cross-architecture detection technologies. The experimental results are shown in Fig. 5.

As can be seen from Fig. 5, Optir-SBERT has the highest accuracy of 94.38% for similarity detection of binary functions under any architecture, and its accuracy is much higher than that of the existing SOTA cross-architecture detection technologies. The experiment results indicate that Optir-SBERT designed by us is more practical in real scenarios. In addition, the detection accuracy of Ir-SBERT is also high, which is 90.39%, second only to Optir-SBERT, indicating that the structure performance of SBERT network is better. Among them, the contribution of optimization to the improvement of Optir-SBERT accuracy is 3.99%. Genius and Gemini are excellent binary code similarity detection tools.

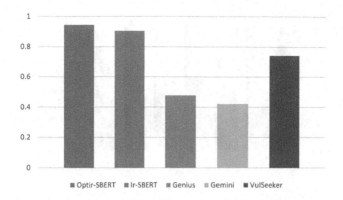

Fig. 5. Comparison of cross-architecture binary code similarity detection accuracy for models.

The reason for their low detection accuracy in this experiment may be that the number of functions in the function pool is too large and the sources of binary functions are more diverse.

5.2   Vulnerabilities Detection

Performance of Optir-SBERT in Real Vulnerability Detection. Vulnerability detection is one of the important research directions in the field of computer security. In order to evaluate the actual performance of Optir-SBERT in the task of vulnerability detection, we conduct this experiment.

Firstly, the vulnerability data set Busybox is collected in the experiment, and 7 vulnerability functions are extracted from the vulnerability data set to build the vulnerability function library. Secondly, the optimized LLVM IR corresponding to the vulnerability function is generated. After that, we mixed them into the optimized LLVM IR generated by the normal binary functions. Then, Optir-SBERT is used to match the vulnerability in the optimized LLVM IR. In this experiment, 2000 binary functions are randomly selected from the function pool P, and 7 vulnerability functions are mixed into them. What's more, the experimental evaluation index is $Recall@5$, and the experimental comparison model is Gemini [46] and Ir-SBERT. The results of vulnerability matching are shown in Fig. 6.

According to Fig. 6, the accuracy of Optir-SBERT is significantly higher than Gemini and Ir-SBERT in detecting vulnerability functions. For example, for CVE-2021-42385, the detection accuracy of Optir-SBERT is 100%, while that of Gemini is only 51%. In addition, the average vulnerability detection accuracy of Optir-SBERT is 93.9% and that of Ir-SBERT is 86.9%, indicating that the optimization improve the accuracy of Optir-SBERT by 7% in terms of vulnerabilities.

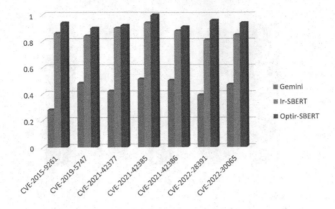

Fig. 6. Comparison of vulnerabilities detection results for models.

Comparison of Vulnerability Detection Effect Between Optir-SBERT and Optir-SBERT-F. In the real vulnerability detection scenario, the model often needs to detect binary files, which requires it to convert binary files into detectable binary codes or assembly instructions. The input of Optir-SBERT is optimized LLVM IR, which requires it to lift the binary file. However, lifting will occupy a lot of time, which seriously affects the vulnerability detection efficiency of Optir-SBERT. In addition, among a large number of binary files to be detected, only a few binary files have vulnerable functions. Based on this actual situation, we design Optir-SBERT-F.

Optir-SBERT-F is mainly applied to scenarios requiring rapid vulnerability detection. Compared with Optir-SBERT, Optir-SBERT-F introduces a file-level vulnerability identification mechanism, which improves the efficiency of vulnerability detection but sacrifices the F value of vulnerability detection.

The main performance changes of Optir-SBERT and Optir-SBERT-F are evaluated experimentally. In the experimental setting, 10 to 15 normal binary files and 1 to 5 vulnerable binary files are randomly selected to form a test data set. Then, the vulnerability detection F value and detection time of Optir-SBERT and Optir-SBERT-F are tested on this data set, and the average value of multiple tests is taken. The experimental results are shown in Table 5.

Table 5 shows that the average vulnerability detection F value of Optir-SBERT is 91.6% and the average detection time is 390.2 s. The average vulnerability detection F value of Optir-SBERT-F is 77.7%, 15.17% lower than Optir-SBERT, and the average detection time is 213.2 s, 45.36% lower than Optir-SBERT. It can be seen that Optir-SBERT-F saves 45.36% time at the expense of 15.17% F value, which greatly improves the efficiency of vulnerability detection on the premise that the F value is not significantly reducing.

Table 5. Comparison of vulnerability detection effect between Optir-SBERT and Optir-SBERT-F

CVE-	2015-9261	2019-5747	2021-42377	2021-42385	2022-28391	average
Optir-SBERT (F Value)	0.909	0.889	0.923	1	0.857	0.916
Optir-SBERT (Time-s)	337	273	446	339	556	390.2
Optir-SBERT-F (F Value)	0.8	0.667	0.833	0.857	0.727	0.777
Optir-SBERT-F (Time-s)	179	157	213	226	291	213.2

6   Conclusion

In this paper, we propose Optir-SBERT, which is the first technology for cross-architecture binary code similarity detection based on optimized LLVM IR, and has strong robustness and scalability. Optir-SBERT is mainly designed based on SBERT network structure, which can better understand and characterize the semantic information of optimized LLVM IR, and its twin network structure is more suitable for similarity detection. In addition, we built the dataset BinaryIR, which has a more diverse set of data including binary projects, IoT firmware, LLVM IR files, and four optimized (O0, O1, O2, O3) LLVM IR files.

The detection accuracy of Optir-SBERT is more stable. When the number of binary functions to be detected increases to 10,000, the detection accuracy decreases by only 12.62%. In terms of binary code similarity detection, the detection accuracy of Optir-SBERT can reach 94.38% under any compilation architecture, which is much higher than the existing SOTA cross-architecture detection technologies, in which the contribution of optimization is 3.99%. In terms of vulnerability detection, Optir-SBERT have an average vulnerability detection accuracy of 93.9%, of which the optimization contributed 7%. In addition, in order to detect binary file vulnerabilities more efficiently in real scenarios, we construct Optir-SBERT-F by introducing file-level vulnerability identification mechanism on the basis of Optir-SBERT. Optir-SBERT-F can save 45.36% of the time compared with Optir-SBERT, and greatly improves the efficiency of vulnerability detection without significantly reducing the F value.

However, the generation stage of the optimized LLVM IR files may make mistakes, mainly because the LLVM IR file contains characters that cannot be optimized, which has a certain impact on the universality of Optir-SBERT. At the same time, the file-level vulnerability identification mechanism of Optir-SBERT-F can be further improved to reduce the false positive rate and false negative rate. In the next work, we will try to improve the optimization method of LLVM IR files and optimize the file-level vulnerability identification mechanism, so as to make the model more practical and efficient in real scenarios.

Acknowledgment. We sincerely appreciate the anonymous reviewers for their valuable comments to improve our paper. This work is supported by NSFC under No. 62202484.

References

1. Alrabaee, S., Wang, L., Debbabi, M.: BinGold: towards robust binary analysis by extracting the semantics of binary code as semantic flow graphs (SFGs). Digit. Investig. **18**, S11–S22 (2016)
2. Darem, A., Abawajy, J., Makkar, A., Alhashmi, A., Alanazi, S.: Visualization and deep-learning-based malware variant detection using opcode-level features. Futur. Gener. Comput. Syst. **125**, 314–323 (2021)
3. David, Y., Partush, N., Yahav, E.: FirmUp: precise static detection of common vulnerabilities in firmware. ACM SIGPLAN Not. **53**(2), 392–404 (2018)
4. Ding, S.H., Fung, B.C., Charland, P.: Kam1n0: MapReduce-based assembly clone search for reverse engineering. In: Proceedings of the 22nd ACM SIGKDD International Conference on Knowledge Discovery and Data Mining, pp. 461–470 (2016)
5. Ding, S.H., Fung, B.C., Charland, P.: Asm2Vec: boosting static representation robustness for binary clone search against code obfuscation and compiler optimization. In: 2019 IEEE Symposium on Security and Privacy (SP), pp. 472–489. IEEE (2019)
6. Duan, Y., Li, X., Wang, J., Yin, H.: DeepBinDiff: learning program-wide code representations for binary diffing. In: Network and Distributed System Security Symposium (2020)
7. Dullien, T., Rolles, R.: Graph-based comparison of executable objects (English version). Sstic **5**(1), 3 (2005)
8. Eschweiler, S., Yakdan, K., Gerhards-Padilla, E., et al.: discovRE: efficient cross-architecture identification of bugs in binary code. In: NDSS, vol. 52, pp. 58–79 (2016)
9. Feng, Q., Wang, M., Zhang, M., Zhou, R., Henderson, A., Yin, H.: Extracting conditional formulas for cross-platform bug search. In: Proceedings of the 2017 ACM on Asia Conference on Computer and Communications Security, pp. 346–359 (2017)
10. Feng, Q., Zhou, R., Xu, C., Cheng, Y., Testa, B., Yin, H.: Scalable graph-based bug search for firmware images. In: Proceedings of the 2016 ACM SIGSAC Conference on Computer and Communications Security, pp. 480–491 (2016)
11. Gao, D., Reiter, M.K., Song, D.: BinHunt: automatically finding semantic differences in binary programs. In: Chen, L., Ryan, M.D., Wang, G. (eds.) ICICS 2008. LNCS, vol. 5308, pp. 238–255. Springer, Heidelberg (2008). https://doi.org/10.1007/978-3-540-88625-9_16
12. Gao, J., Yang, X., Fu, Y., Jiang, Y., Sun, J.: VulSeeker: a semantic learning based vulnerability seeker for cross-platform binary. In: Proceedings of the 33rd ACM/IEEE International Conference on Automated Software Engineering, pp. 896–899 (2018)
13. Haq, I.U., Caballero, J.: A survey of binary code similarity. ACM Comput. Surv. (CSUR) **54**(3), 1–38 (2021)
14. Hemel, A., Kalleberg, K.T., Vermaas, R., Dolstra, E.: Finding software license violations through binary code clone detection-a retrospective. ACM SIGSOFT Softw. Eng. Notes **46**(3), 24–25 (2021)
15. Huang, H., Youssef, A.M., Debbabi, M.: BinSequence: fast, accurate and scalable binary code reuse detection. In: Proceedings of the 2017 ACM on Asia Conference on Computer and Communications Security, pp. 155–166 (2017)
16. Kim, D., Kim, E., Cha, S.K., Son, S., Kim, Y.: Revisiting binary code similarity analysis using interpretable feature engineering and lessons learned. IEEE Trans. Softw. Eng. (2022)

17. Lattner, C.: LLVM and clang: next generation compiler technology. In: The BSD conference, vol. 5, pp. 1–20 (2008)
18. Li, X., Qu, Y., Yin, H.: PalmTree: learning an assembly language model for instruction embedding. In: Proceedings of the 2021 ACM SIGSAC Conference on Computer and Communications Security, pp. 3236–3251 (2021)
19. Li, Y., Gu, C., Dullien, T., Vinyals, O., Kohli, P.: Graph matching networks for learning the similarity of graph structured objects. In: International Conference on Machine Learning, pp. 3835–3845. PMLR (2019)
20. Lin, J., Wang, D., Chang, R., Wu, L., Zhou, Y., Ren, K.: EnBinDiff: identifying data-only patches for binaries. IEEE Trans. Dependable Secure Comput. (2021)
21. Luo, L., Ming, J., Wu, D., Liu, P., Zhu, S.: Semantics-based obfuscation-resilient binary code similarity comparison with applications to software and algorithm plagiarism detection. IEEE Trans. Software Eng. **43**(12), 1157–1177 (2017)
22. Luo, Z., Wang, B., Tang, Y., Xie, W.: Semantic-based representation binary clone detection for cross-architectures in the internet of things. Appl. Sci. **9**(16), 3283 (2019)
23. Marcelli, A., Graziano, M., Ugarte-Pedrero, X., Fratantonio, Y., Mansouri, M., Balzarotti, D.: How machine learning is solving the binary function similarity problem. In: 31st USENIX Security Symposium (USENIX Security 2022), pp. 2099–2116 (2022)
24. Massarelli, L., Di Luna, G.A., Petroni, F., Querzoni, L., Baldoni, R.: Investigating graph embedding neural networks with unsupervised features extraction for binary analysis. In: Proceedings of the 2nd Workshop on Binary Analysis Research (BAR), pp. 1–11 (2019)
25. Massarelli, L., Di Luna, G.A., Petroni, F., Baldoni, R., Querzoni, L.: SAFE: self-attentive function embeddings for binary similarity. In: Perdisci, R., Maurice, C., Giacinto, G., Almgren, M. (eds.) DIMVA 2019. LNCS, vol. 11543, pp. 309–329. Springer, Cham (2019). https://doi.org/10.1007/978-3-030-22038-9_15
26. Mengin, E., Rossi, F.: Binary diffing as a network alignment problem via belief propagation. In: 2021 36th IEEE/ACM International Conference on Automated Software Engineering (ASE), pp. 967–978. IEEE (2021)
27. Ming, J., Pan, M., Gao, D.: iBinHunt: binary hunting with inter-procedural control flow. In: Kwon, T., Lee, M.-K., Kwon, D. (eds.) ICISC 2012. LNCS, vol. 7839, pp. 92–109. Springer, Heidelberg (2013). https://doi.org/10.1007/978-3-642-37682-5_8
28. Ming, J., Xu, D., Jiang, Y., Wu, D.: BinSim: trace-based semantic binary diffing via system call sliced segment equivalence checking. In: Proceedings of the 26th USENIX Security Symposium (2017)
29. Nouh, L., Rahimian, A., Mouheb, D., Debbabi, M., Hanna, A.: BinSign: fingerprinting binary functions to support automated analysis of code executables. In: De Capitani di Vimercati, S., Martinelli, F. (eds.) SEC 2017. IAICT, vol. 502, pp. 341–355. Springer, Cham (2017). https://doi.org/10.1007/978-3-319-58469-0_23
30. Pan, Z., Wang, T., Yu, L., Yan, Y.: Position distribution matters: a graph-based binary function similarity analysis method. Electronics **11**(15), 2446 (2022)
31. Pan, Z., Yan, Y., Yu, L., Wang, T.: Identification of binary file compilation information. In: 2022 IEEE 5th Advanced Information Management, Communicates, Electronic and Automation Control Conference (IMCEC), vol. 5, pp. 1141–1150. IEEE (2022)
32. Pei, K., Xuan, Z., Yang, J., Jana, S., Ray, B.: TREX: learning execution semantics from micro-traces for binary similarity. arXiv preprint arXiv:2012.08680 (2020)

33. Pewny, J., Schuster, F., Bernhard, L., Holz, T., Rossow, C.: Leveraging semantic signatures for bug search in binary programs. In: Proceedings of the 30th Annual Computer Security Applications Conference, pp. 406–415 (2014)
34. Redmond, K., Luo, L., Zeng, Q.: A cross-architecture instruction embedding model for natural language processing-inspired binary code analysis. arXiv preprint arXiv:1812.09652 (2018)
35. Reimers, N., Gurevych, I.: Sentence-BERT: sentence embeddings using Siamese BERT-networks. arXiv preprint arXiv:1908.10084 (2019)
36. Shalev, N., Partush, N.: Binary similarity detection using machine learning. In: Proceedings of the 13th Workshop on Programming Languages and Analysis for Security, pp. 42–47 (2018)
37. Sriram, S., Vinayakumar, R., Sowmya, V., Alazab, M., Soman, K.: Multi-scale learning based malware variant detection using spatial pyramid pooling network. In: IEEE INFOCOM 2020-IEEE Conference on Computer Communications Workshops (INFOCOM WKSHPS), pp. 740–745. IEEE (2020)
38. Sun, P., Yan, Q., Zhou, H., Li, J.: Osprey: a fast and accurate patch presence test framework for binaries. Comput. Commun. **173**, 95–106 (2021)
39. Thakur, N., Reimers, N., Daxenberger, J., Gurevych, I.: Augmented sBERT: data augmentation method for improving bi-encoders for pairwise sentence scoring tasks. arXiv preprint arXiv:2010.08240 (2020)
40. Vaswani, A., et al.: Attention is all you need. In: Advances in Neural Information Processing Systems, vol. 30 (2017)
41. VenkataKeerthy, S., Aggarwal, R., Jain, S., Desarkar, M.S., Upadrasta, R., Srikant, Y.: IR2VEC: LLVM IR based scalable program embeddings. ACM Trans. Archit. Code Optim. (TACO) **17**(4), 1–27 (2020)
42. Wang, H., et al.: jTrans: jump-aware transformer for binary code similarity. arXiv preprint arXiv:2205.12713 (2022)
43. Wang, X., Wang, S., Sun, K., Batcheller, A., Jajodia, S.: A machine learning approach to classify security patches into vulnerability types. In: 2020 IEEE Conference on Communications and Network Security (CNS), pp. 1–9. IEEE (2020)
44. Wang, Y., Jia, P., Peng, X., Huang, C., Liu, J.: BinVulDet: detecting vulnerability in binary program via decompiled pseudo code and BiLSTM-attention. Comput. Secur. **125**, 103023 (2023)
45. Xiu, H., Yan, X., Wang, X., Cheng, J., Cao, L.: Hierarchical graph matching network for graph similarity computation. arXiv preprint arXiv:2006.16551 (2020)
46. Xu, X., Liu, C., Feng, Q., Yin, H., Song, L., Song, D.: Neural network-based graph embedding for cross-platform binary code similarity detection. In: Proceedings of the 2017 ACM SIGSAC Conference on Computer and Communications Security, pp. 363–376 (2017)
47. Yang, S., Cheng, L., Zeng, Y., Lang, Z., Zhu, H., Shi, Z.: Asteria: deep learning-based AST-encoding for cross-platform binary code similarity detection. In: 2021 51st Annual IEEE/IFIP International Conference on Dependable Systems and Networks (DSN), pp. 224–236. IEEE (2021)
48. Yu, Z., Cao, R., Tang, Q., Nie, S., Huang, J., Wu, S.: Order matters: semantic-aware neural networks for binary code similarity detection. In: Proceedings of the AAAI Conference on Artificial Intelligence, vol. 34, pp. 1145–1152 (2020)
49. Yu, Z., Zheng, W., Wang, J., Tang, Q., Nie, S., Wu, S.: CodeCMR: cross-modal retrieval for function-level binary source code matching. In: Advances in Neural Information Processing Systems, vol. 33, pp. 3872–3883 (2020)

50. Zhang, X., Sun, W., Pang, J., Liu, F., Ma, Z.: Similarity metric method for binary basic blocks of cross-instruction set architecture. In: Proceedings of the 2020 Workshop on Binary Analysis Research, vol. 10 (2020)
51. Zuo, F., Li, X., Young, P., Luo, L., Zeng, Q., Zhang, Z.: Neural machine translation inspired binary code similarity comparison beyond function pairs. arXiv preprint arXiv:1808.04706 (2018)

SdShield: Effectively Ensuring Heap Security via Shadow Page Table

Linong Shi, Chuanping Hu, Yan Zhuang$^{(\boxtimes)}$, and Yan Lu

Zhengzhou University, Zhengzhou, China
yan.zhuang@zzu.edu.cn

Abstract. Heap security has become a serious threat in recent years. To address the problem of heap vulnerabilities that are hard to detect and mitigate, this paper proposes a new heap protection scheme using shadow page tables. This scheme builds on the traditional idea of page permission and designs a novel shadow page table structure that stores the virtual address and random value of each object. This enables checking the boundaries and validity of heap objects, and effectively detects various types of heap-related attacks, such as heap overflow, use-after-free, invalid free, and double free. In addition, the scheme adopts a dynamic system call addition method, which is not dependent on specific runtime environments or kernel modifications, and has high scalability and portability. Experimental evaluation on various applications shows that our proposed scheme is effective in detecting many types of heap vulnerabilities, providing more comprehensive security with low performance overhead than comparable solutions.

Keywords: Heap vulnerabilities · Shadow page table · Page protection

1 Introduction

Heap-related memory corruption vulnerabilities have remained a serious threat and caused many catastrophic exploits in the past decades [5, 16]. The number of heap-related vulnerabilities has grown in recent years, out-of-bounds write bugs and use-after-free bugs were ranked first and seventh in the CWE top 25 of the most common and impactful issues in software [36]. Attacks that exploit these vulnerabilities not only affect the normal execution of programs, but may also lead to sensitive data leakage, control flow hijacking, arbitrary code execution, and other impacts.

So far, many studies have focused on solving heap security problems through memory allocators [1–5, 10, 17–21, 23]. Robertson et al. [20] proposed using canaries and checksums to detect possible buffer overflows. Gene et al. [2] provide probabilistic memory safety through the random layout of heap area and randomized object placement and reuse. Sam et al. [3] borrowed the idea of "freelist" from performance allocators and shadow memory technology, providing better performance than previous secure allocators. Liu et al. [4] employed an efficient fine-grained class indexing scheme and implemented a dynamic canary scheme, further increasing security. Such schemes achieve

S. Goel and P. R. Nunes de Souza (Eds.): ICDF2C 2023, LNICST 571, pp. 114–131, 2024.
https://doi.org/10.1007/978-3-031-56583-0_8

heap area protection by overriding the system's allocator, however, they change the system's default memory allocation strategy, which may result in overhead and compatibility problems.

On the other hand, other researchers have proposed various solutions that target a single vulnerability by combining some form of static analysis and runtime checking [6–9, 11, 28–33]. Nikiforakis et al. [7] prevent heap overflows by detecting the state of heap objects during the system calls. Tian et al. [33] monitor heap buffer overflows using multicore technology and concurrent monitoring algorithms. Lee et al. [8] prevent the use of dangling pointers by tracking the relationship between pointers and objects and invalidating the corresponding pointers when released. Dang et al. [14] and Gorter et al. [15] use the page protection scheme by creating a new virtual page (called a shadow virtual page) for each memory allocation to prevent use-after-free errors. However, most of these solutions either require a specific environment or are compiler-based and cannot handle compiled binaries.

In this paper, we introduce SdShield, an efficient, portable, and more comprehensive heap protection scheme that builds on the traditional idea of page permission. This scheme design a novel shadow page table structure that stores the canonical address and the random value of each object in the process shadow page table, which allows for higher security and quicker information access. We adds an interceptor between the target program and the memory allocator to intercept all memory allocation and deallocation requests from the program without needing the program source code. Specifically, we implement information transfer between user space and kernel space using dynamically added system calls that do not require a specific environment or kernel recompilation and can be easily adopted in desktop and server environments.

In brief, this paper makes the following contributions:

(1) A new heap protection scheme using shadow page tables, which utilizes page management to provide more comprehensive heap protection.
(2) A novel shadow page table structure design, which can conveniently store and access relevant information of heap objects.
(3) Using the cooperative scheme between user space and kernel space, dynamic management of program heap memory and page tables without program source code.
(4) Using NIST Juliet test suite and SPEC CPU 2006 benchmark, the security and performance of this scheme are studied in detail.

The rest of this paper is organized as follows. In Sect. 2 we introduce the background and present the threat model of SdShield. In Sects. 3 and 4 we respectively present the design and implementation details of SdShield, and then evaluate its security and performance consumption in Sect. 5. We finally discuss the current limitations of SdShield in Sect. 6 and conclude in Sect. 7.

2 Background

In this section, We detail the background of SdShield, including the common heap-related vulnerabilities and the page table structure. Then discuss the development of the methods that protect heap by page permissions, and point out their limitations that drive the design of SdShield. Finally, we present the threat model of SdShield.

2.1 Heap-Related Vulnerabilities

Spatial heap-based vulnerabilities include heap overflows and heap over-reads. Heap overflows occur when a program performs an out-of-binding write operation to a heap object due to an error or lack of proper boundary checks [4]. The less common heap underflow is when incorrect access to the heap buffer results in a write to memory before the buffer. Heap overflows overwrite memory space that does not belong to the object and may lead to many security issues. Similarly, if built-in boundary checks for memory accesses are lacking, over-reads will occur when accessing heap objects.

Temporal heap-based vulnerabilities include use-after-free (or dangling pointer), double free, and invalid free. Use-after-free is caused by the dereference of a heap-allocated object, because the pointer (now called a dangling pointer) to the freed object remains unchanged even though the memory location pointed to is no longer valid [15], so the freed memory can be forced to be used by the corresponding dangling pointer. Double free is considered a special case of use-after-free, which occurs when an object is freed twice [3]. Invalid free occurs when an application attempts to free a value that does not point to an object created by the memory allocator.

2.2 Page Table

Most modern operating systems use the paging mechanism, under which both virtual and physical memory is divided into fixed-size chunks called Pages. The mapping between virtual and physical pages is established through the Page Table, which are data structures maintained by the system and stored in the kernel space. The memory management unit (MMU) of the CPU uses them to obtain the mapping relationship between virtual memory and physical memory. Each process has a separate page table that describes the process address space, and the kernel has its own set of page tables that manage the kernel space. Some modern CPUs also have 5-level page tables, but most 64-bit architectures use 4-level page tables. In the remaining part of this paper, we assume a 4-level page table structure, which is commonly referred to as the Page Global Directory (PGD), the Page Upper Directory (PUD), the Page Middle Directory (PMD), and the page table (PT).

2.3 Page Permission Schemes

In early work, Perens et al. [23] proposed a debugging tool that uses the page protection mechanism to detect dangling pointer errors. The tool allocates a new virtual and physical page for each allocation of the program. However, this scheme means that even small allocations would occupy a whole page of actual physical memory. This would cause a drastic increase in the memory consumption of the application, making it impractical for real production environments. Following this idea, Dhurjati et al. [12] proposed a key improvement, where they mapped each allocation using a new virtual page to the same physical page as the original allocator to solve the physical memory consumption problem. And they used a compiler transformation called automatic pool allocation to mitigate the problem of virtual address space exhaustion.

In recent years, Dang et al. [14] demonstrated the theoretical basis for such schemes and argued that page permissions should be the ideal method in principle. Unlike Dhurjati's automatic pool allocation, Dang's design can unmap shadows immediately after object release. They also discussed compatibility with fork, which seems to be an unknown limitation in Dhurjati's scheme. Then Gorter et al. [15] provided a more efficient implementation that relies on direct page table access in ring 0. In addition, Gorter introduced a new garbage collection style recycling module, which can safely reuse the freed areas and address the key scalability issues that plague such solutions.

However, all existing solutions based on page permissions lack portability, need to run in a specific environment (such as KML), or require kernel editing. Furthermore, all such solutions currently focus only on mitigating the use-after-free bugs while ignoring the dangers of other vulnerabilities. In this paper, we show that these limitations are not fundamental and that an efficient, portable, and more comprehensive heap protection solution can be unlocked by using shadow virtual page tables.

2.4 Threat Model

It is well-known that security by obscurity is not a good practice, so we hypothesize that it is possible for the attacker to access the sources of SdShield. We assume a standard threat model [15], in which the host operating system (such as Linux) is trusted; and the attacker can perform any arbitrary operation on the heap area of the victim program (including allocation, free, read and write, such as), and try to achieve information leakage and privilege escalation through the vulnerabilities. We consider all vulnerabilities in the heap area, whether buffer overflow, use-after-free, or some other types of attack technique, and assume that the program has no other vulnerabilities (such as stack).

3 Overview

SdShield is a scheme based on page protection policies designed to detect and prevent heap vulnerabilities through the cooperation between user space and kernel space. The structure of SdShield is divided into two parts: the interceptor running in user space and the kernel module running in kernel space, and the interaction process is mainly divided into two phases: allocate and release. Figure 1 describes the main components of SdShield and their interaction process.

When the application requests memory allocation, the interceptor intercepts all such requests and sends them to the system allocator. The system allocator requests virtual and physical memory from the operating system and then returns the allocated heap area address, which we call the canonical virtual address of the object, to the interceptor. After receiving the allocated address, the interceptor passes the relevant data to the kernel module using a system call. The kernel module creates several shadow page table entries in the process page table, calculates an unused address in the shadow virtual space, and returns it to the interceptor. Finally, the interceptor transparently returns the corresponding shadow address to the user program, so that the user program can only use this address to reference the allocated object, without knowing that it is related to the shadow page table.

In the application memory release phase, when the interceptor intercepts a memory release request, it first uses a system call to pass the relevant data to the kernel module, and the kernel module modifies the valid bit in the process page table to invalidate its mapping. It then obtains the canonical virtual address of the object from the page table entry and returns it to the interceptor. Finally, the interceptor passes the canonical virtual address to the default allocator, so that its physical memory is released by the system allocator and can be reused.

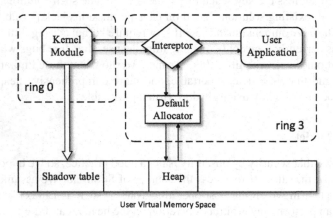

Fig. 1. Structure of SdShield's components

We provide SdShield's interceptor as a shared library for applications, so that SdShield can be used with only existing binaries, without scanning the program source code or modifying the default allocator, and is theoretically compatible with all allocators of modern operating systems as well as those described in the literature.

In addition, SdShield requires system calls for communication between the interceptor and the kernel module. However, modifying the operating system source code contradicts SdShield's philosophy of portability, so we dynamically add system calls by modifying the syscall_table array in the kernel without recompiling the kernel. If this method of modifying kernel instructions adversely affects some production environments or workloads, user program access to kernel space can be achieved by recompiling the kernel or using Kernel Module Linux [14, 15, 34].

3.1 Shadow Address for Object

The core idea of SdShield is the shadow virtual address [12, 14, 15]. Typically, virtual pages and physical pages are in one-to-one correspondence, while using shadow address allows mapping the same physical page frame to multiple virtual pages. Figure 2 illustrates the relationship between the shadow address, canonical address, and physical address of each object. We refer to the virtual address generated by SdShield as the shadow virtual address, and the address allocated by the system default allocator as the canonical virtual address of the object. SdShield places each object allocated by the program in a different shadow virtual page, but these shadow pages are all mapped to the same physical pages as the original allocator, and their offsets remain the same as the offsets of the actual physical pages. This allows each object to have an independent shadow page, to achieve the purpose of managing each object individually through page permissions. While multiple objects can be located on the same physical page, making the program physical memory consumption almost the same as the original.

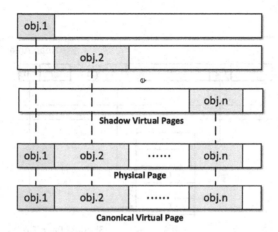

Fig. 2. The object in the virtual pages and physical pages

Generally, multiple small memory objects share a system page, but it is possible in process that there are large objects which occupy multiple pages. If an object spans multiple pages, SdShield will allocate the same number of shadow pages as the physical pages and keeps its in-page offset consistent with the original. When the application frees an object, we need the corresponding canonical virtual address to initiate the release process from the default allocator. For this purpose, we add a shadow page table entry for each object that stores the canonical virtual address. Note that placing a canonical virtual address as an entry into the page table requires a separate flag bit to locate it and that the page table entry should always be in the page-fault status.

3.2 Security Features

The security features implemented in SdShield are as follows: Add a random value at the end of each allocated heap object and check it at each malloc and free to prevent overflow. Create different shadow virtual pages for each heap object and prevent use-after-free by invalidating the mapping of its shadow page to the actual physical page as soon as the object is freed. Use unmapped protection pages at the end of each object, to prevent overflow, over-read and spray attacks, and free checks to prevent double free and invalid free, are detailed below.

Random Canary. SdShield borrows a common mechanism from the existing secure allocators to prevent potential buffer overflow errors: it adds an extra random value at the end of each allocated heap object, called canary [3, 4, 17]. SdShield generates a random value from the kernel entropy and places it at the end of each object—meaning that each malloc(n) call is changed to malloc(n + sizeof(void*)). Unlike the secure allocators, SdShield stores the random values in the kernel space, so it is not affected by the processes and attackers. Figure 3 shows the canary in the heap area and the shadow page table. Similar to the canonical virtual address, SdShield also saves the random value as a separate page table entry in the shadow page table, and keeps the entry always in a page-fault status.

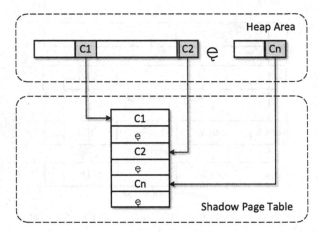

Fig. 3. Canary in heap area and shadow page table

For the most part, using canary to prevent data overflow of applications is effective. Although the timeliness is limited by the frequency of canary checks, we can always detect whether its canary has been modified when an object is freed. For each memory request or release in the program, SdShield checks all the random values in the same page table of that object, so the number of objects checked each time may be between 1 and 173 (the case where only one object in a single shadow page table and the case where a single shadow page table is full). If any canary is modified, SdShield reports information about the potential buffer overflow location and optionally stops the execution of the current program.

Shadow Page Permissions. The memory management unit (MMU) in most modern processors perform a runtime check for each memory access. One idea is to use the operating system page access and protection policy to detect and prevent use-after-free, but MMU can only manage access permissions at the granularity of page (typically 4096 bytes). Placing each object on a separate physical page would result in a significant memory over-head caused by fragmentation.

In SdShield, due to the shadow virtual pages, each object can have a separate page mapping, so the object granularity of mapping can be disabled through page permission management. SdShield prevents the use-after-free by deleting the application's access to the freed heap object. When the corresponding object is released, SdShield sets the valid bit of the shadow page to zero, and all subsequent accesses to this page will generate invalid access information and cause MMU to trigger an exception.

Guard Pages. Guard page is an unmapped virtual memory page that is placed before or after an allocated heap object. Guard pages can prevent heap overflow, over-read, and heap spraying attacks, as any access involving guard pages will immediately trigger a page fault. Since guard pages are not mapped to actual physical pages, they only consume the size of a page table entry (8B) instead of a whole page (4 KB). Normally they can only be placed with page granularity, so it is not possible to place guard pages before and after every allocated heap object.

In some secure allocator schemes [3, 4, 17], guard pages need to be explicitly placed by using the mprotect system call. While in SdShield the canonical virtual address entries and random value entries placed before and after each object in the shadow page table just serve the purpose of guard pages, so that protection pages can be easily set at object granularity and all accesses to them will result in exceptions.

Free Check. When the application performs free operations, SdShield prevents double and invalid releases by checking the status marker bits of each object's shaded page table entry. SdShield can easily detect the following exceptions: The pointer of the free operation points to a range outside the heap area; The shadow page table entry corresponding to the free pointer is in the unallocated status; The shadow page table entry corre-sponding to the free pointer is already in the freed status. For each allocation, SdShield marks its shadow page table entry as in use. When deallocating, SdShield first judges its status bits and confirms whether this release is valid.

4 Implementation

In the previous section, we introduced the design ideas of SdShield and the security features SdShield uses. In this section, we continue to cover the implementation details of SdShield, including the selection of the shadow area, the structure of the shadow page table, and the dynamic addition of system calls. In addition, this section discusses some optimizations to reduce the overhead of SdShield and to solve address space exhaustion and compatibility issues.

4.1 Shadow Page Table

To support the use of multiple processes, SdShield stores the shadow page mapping in the process page table. Each user process has an independent virtual address space, and its virtual pages to physical pages mapping are stored in its process page table, which is managed by the operating system kernel. Although the kernel module has direct access to system memory, such as page table data structures, the operating system is unaware of the module and may overwrite the mappings that SdShield changes in the user process page tables. Therefore, SdShield chooses an unused area in the user virtual address space as the shadow page table, and directly writes into the page table entries corresponding to that area via the kernel module, thus avoiding interference from the user process and the system kernel.

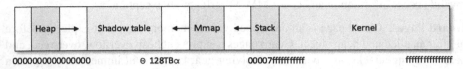

Fig. 4. Virtual memory space layout

Figure 4 shows a simplified layout of virtual memory space. Each user process has 2^{47} bits of virtual address space, while the actual physical space size of most machines is less than 1 TB, so the vast majority of the process's address area is unused. SdShield utilizes a part of these free address areas as the range of the shadow page table. Considering the VMA structure of the process and methods such as ASLR, SdShield chooses between entries 96 and 160 of the Page Global Directory (PGD) as the area of the shadow page table. This area can accommodate up to 20 TB of virtual alias space, corresponding to up to two billion concurrent 4K pages.

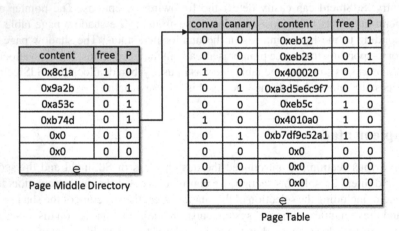

Fig. 5. PMD and PT in shadow page table

SdShield stores the status and attributes of the page table entries in the ignored bits of the shadow page table entries, thus avoiding extra memory overhead. Figure 5 shows a Page Middle Directory structure and a Page Table page structure, where the content column shows the actual content saved of each page table entry, the P flag bit indicates the presence bit, and the free flag bit indicates the release information of the page table entry. In addition, in the lowest-level page table, there are two additional flag bits (called conva and canary) used to distinguish canonical virtual address entries and random value entries from the page table. The right side of the figure describes a mixed situation of in-use objects (PT entries 1–4), freed objects (PT entries 5–7), and available entries (PT entries 8–10).

4.2 Free and Reuse

The main limitation of using shadow virtual pages is that the used shadow address can never be reused throughout the execution of the program, because it is impossible to determine whether the program still retains pointers to the freed address. SdShield is designed with as large as 20 TB of shadow space, but due to the non-reusability of shadow address, they will still be exhausted after excessive consumption. In fact, the following two problems were found in practice: (1) Each non-reusable shadow page table entry takes up a small amount of operating system resources (page table entries). (2) Long-running programs will eventually run out of shadow address space.

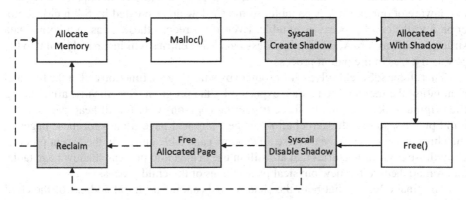

Fig. 6. The process of allocate and free memory

In order to solve the above problem, SdShield has designed the page table release and reclaim components. The main goal of the release component is to allow the safe release of page tables that are completely invalid. And the main goal of the reclaim component is to allow the safe reuse of shadow address that have already been freed. The whole process of memory allocation and release is shown in Fig. 6. Each time SdShield performs a release operation (when deleting a shadow), it determines whether the page on which the page table entry is located is releasable or not. If any one of the 512 entries of a shadow page table is in the valid status, the entire page table needs to be retained because SdShield may still need to access physical pages or obtain relevant information through it. However, when all entries in a shadow page table are free (unused or freed), retaining such page tables will waste a lot of memory space, so that the release component will run to set the release flag bit and free this page table.

In addition, in order to solve the problem that the limited shadow address space may be exhausted, SdShield's reclaim component starts when the shadow address space utilization reaches a critical point and reclaims all reusable shadow address. The reclaim is divided into two main phases: marking and scanning. In the marking phase, SdShield scans all memory of the program. For any data pointing to the shadow area, we will set a flag bit in the corresponding shadow page table entry that represents a still referenced one. If a piece of used shadow address does not find a pointer associated with it in memory, this area is considered safe for reuse. During the scan phase, SdShield traverses all shadow page tables and adds all freed and unmarked shadow address ranges to a reusable linked list. To improve memory utilization, SdShield reclaims only completely free shadow page tables, avoiding the situation where only a few active objects exist in some page tables.

4.3 Shadow Page Fork

When a process creates a child process using the fork system call, the parent and child process share some pages, and copies of these pages are only created using copy-on-write (CoW) by the operating system when modifying them. Unfortunately, since SdShield bypasses the kernel and modifies the process page table directly, the operating system is unaware of our shadow page table, so the shadow areas created by SdShield are not copied to the child process page table. Even if we record these areas in a kernel data structure such as VMA, the child process page table entries will incorrectly point to the physical pages in the parent process.

Therefore, SdShield solves this problem by wrapping the function call of the fork and simulating the memory semantics expected by the program. Specifically, after calling the original fork function, we force triggering copy-on-write for all heap pages in the child process, so that the kernel allocates new physical page frames for these pages of the child process. Next, we traverse all shadow page table entries in the parent process, copy those page table entries that are still in use to the child process shadow page table, and remap them to the new physical page frames of the child process.

The final effect is that both the shadow and canonical virtual address of the child process remains unchanged and valid, while their mapped physical pages are separated from the parent process. Throughout the algorithm, the parent process will remain in the waiting status until all shadow page table entries in child processes are copied and mapped to new physical page frames. Thus achieving a consistent memory status for the parent and child processes.

5 Evaluation

In this section, we evaluated the security features and performance characteristics of SdShield using different benchmarks. For the security performance evaluation of SdShield, we used the Juliet Test Suite [24], as well as some real-world bugs. For the performance evaluation of SdShield, we used the SPEC CPU2006 benchmark tests. For all reported values, the average of 3 runs was used to reduce the effect of noise.

5.1 Security Evaluation

In the previous sections, we introduced SdShield and provided descriptive arguments about the attacks it covers. In this section, we quantify the security of heap protection provided by SdShield using the NIST Juliet test suite. The test suite contains hundreds of test cases and is categorized by vulnerability type (CWE). We experimentally confirm that by running the NIST Juliet test suite v1.3 [24], SdShield can accurately detect and mitigate vulnerabilities in the heap. For heap buffer overflow errors (CWE-122) in the test suite, SdShield is always able to detect overflows to other objects' behavior when object free. For heap over-read errors (CWE-126), SdShield can detect those that cross pages. In addition, SdShield successfully detects all use-after-free (CWE-416), double free (CWE-415), and invalid free errors (CWE-590) in the test suite.

To verify the effectiveness of SdShield, we tested it on several different real-world vulnerabilities, as shown in Table 1. And, these vulnerabilities were also evaluated on other schemes, including the latest secure memory allocator (SlimGuard [4]) and the latest schemes using shadow virtual address (Dangzero [15]). We verified whether SdShield can prevent or detect potential errors in these applications. As in Guarder [17] and slimguard [4], we moved the target buffers of some of these programs from the stack to the heap. In Table 1, "reported" means that the error can be detected immediately, "delay-reported" means that the occurrence of the error cannot be detected in time, but it can be reported with a delay, "probable" means that the error is detected probabilistically, and "unreported" means that no such error is reported.

Table 1. Effectiveness evaluation on known vulnerabilities.

Application	Vulnerability	Reference	SlimGuard	Dangzero	SdShield
gzip-1.2.4	Overflow	Bugbench [25]	delay-reported	unreported	delay-reported
Libtiff-4.0.1	Overflow	CVE-2013-4243	delay-reported	unreported	delay-reported
Heartbleed	Over-read	CVE-2014-0160	probable	unreported	probable
PHP-5.3.6	Use-After-Free	CVE-2016-6290	probable	reported	reported
PHP 7.0.7	Use-After-Free	CVE-2016-5773	probable	reported	reported
Python 2.7	Use-After-Free	Issue-24613 [26]	probable	reported	reported
PHP-5.3.6	Double Free	CVE-2016-5772	reported	reported	reported
ed-1.14.1	Invalid Free	CVE-2017-5357	reported	unreported	reported

From the table, SlimGuard reports overflow, double free, and invalid free types of errors, but for use-after-free, SlimGuard can only probabilistically mitigate them through its delayed reuse and random allocation methods [4]. On the other hand, Dangzero only targets the use-after-free error but cannot detect buffer overflow and invalid free. On the contrary, SdShield can both eliminate the occurrence of use-after-free through the shadow pages and detect potential overflows through dynamic canary as well as guard pages.

5.2 Performance Evaluation

To quantify the performance overhead of SdShield in a real-world scenario, we ran the SPEC CPU2006 benchmark suite (for CPU and memory intensive real-world program mix) on the Intel (R) Core (TM) i5–7400 CPU @ 3.00 GHz configured machine using the Ubuntu 18.04 operating system with the Linux v4.04 kernel. We measured performance by comparing the overhead of each program between the protected version and the base version without any modifications. SdShield benchmark results in SPEC CPU2006 are shown below and compared to previous related work. To avoid interference, we also disable all optional CPU mitigation.

Runtime Overhead. Similar to SdShield, there are also schemes that use allocators to secure the comprehensive heap such as freeguard [3], guarder [17], and silmguard [4], but they do not provide evaluation results based on the SPEC CPU2006 benchmark, and we were not able to rerun them on SPEC CPU2006. Therefore, we compare SdShield with Oscar [14] and DangZero [15], which use the same core principle (shadow virtual page scheme) as SdShield.

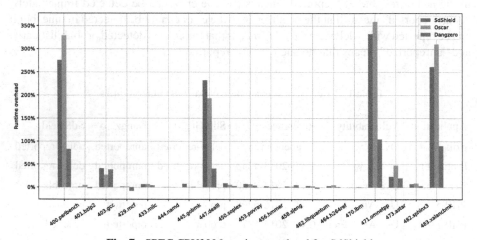

Fig. 7. SPEC CPU2006 runtime overhead for SdShield

Figure 7 compares the runtime overhead of SdShield with Oscar and Dangzero on the binary files of SPEC CPU2006. The results show that four of the 19 benchmarks incur exponential overhead due to the guard scheme. The Highly affected benchmarks, perlbench, dealII, omnetpp, and xalancbmk, are highly allocation-intensive programs, resulting in a large number of shadow page table creation and deletion operations. In addition, for some benchmark programs with few heap objects, such as bzip2, namd, hmmer, and lbm, the runtime overhead of SdShield, Oscar, and DangZero are both less than 1%, or even negligible. For the complete SPEC CPU2006 benchmark suite, the average SdShield runtime overhead was 64%. It should be noted that none of the test suites ran SdShield's reclaim component, because SPEC CPU2006 only contains short-term applications, and the virtual address space usage in the system did not reach the configuration limit of the reclaim component. Therefore, if we forced the reclaim component to run once at the end of each program it would increase the runtime overhead by approximately 2%.

Memory Overhead. SdShield requires additional space to store relevant information when applying for memory. For each memory allocation, the user-space interceptor allocates an object that is 8 bytes larger than the original request, which is used to store a random value for overflow detection, the kernel module needs at least three page table entries (typi-cally 24 bytes) to store information, including the canonical virtual address, the ran-dom value at the end of the object, and the physical page address that is actually mapped. Table 2 shows the relationship between the memory usage of each space and the number of heap objects in the process when SdShield does not use the release component. However, the system's memory overhead hardly reaches this upper val-ue in practice, because most objects will be freed after use, and the information stored by SdShield will also be cleaned up when the release component runs.

Table 2. Memory usage of SdShield without releasing components

Heap Objects	User Space	Kernel Space	Total
1	8 B	4120 B	4128 B
1000	8 KB	27 KB	35 KB
100,000	781 KB	2361 KB	3142 KB
10,000,000	76 MB	239 MB	315 MB

Because SdShield's shadow page table is created in the kernel space by the kernel module, we cannot represent all of SdShield's memory overhead by just the applica-tion's memory usage. Instead, we calculate the overall memory overhead by the sum of application's resident set size (RSS) and the maximum number of page tables in the application's shadow range. Figure 8 compares the maximum memory overhead of SdShield with Oscar and Dangzero on the binary files of SPEC CPU2006. Similar to the runtime statistics, all three generate multiple overheads in those highly allocation-intensive programs. Although SdShield needs to store additional information for heap overflow detection compared to Oscar and Dangzero, due to the unique release feature, SdShield consumes less system memory than Oscar and is close to Dangzero, which uses a compression method. For the complete SPEC CPU2006 benchmark suite, the average SdShield memory overhead is 59%.

5.3 Comparison to Other Systems

The previous article compared the performance overhead of SdShield with Oscar and Dangzero, but due to the different actual effects of the schemes, it is limited to evaluate the quality of the schemes based solely on performance. Therefore, we next conducted a comprehensive comparison of the time overhead, memory overhead, and defense capa-bilities of each scheme, as shown in Table 3. Among this table, "$\sqrt{}$" means that such vulnerabilities can be detected, "×" means that they cannot be detected, and we indicate the average running overhead impact of the tool on the program by percentage.

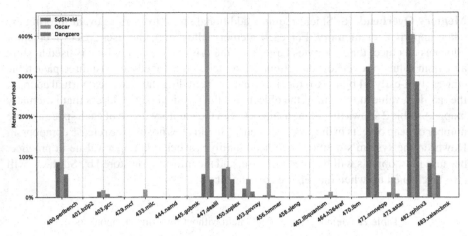

Fig. 8. SPEC CPU2006 memory overhead for SdShield

Table 3. General comparison between SdShield and Oscar and Dangzero

Feature	SdShield	Oscar	Dangzero
Runtime Overhead	64%	69%	20%
Memory Overhead	59%	98%	37%
Overflow	√	×	×
Use-After-Free	√	√	√
Double Free	√	√	√
Invalid Free	√	×	×
Over-read	√	×	×

Overall, on the complete CPU2006 benchmark suite, Oscar reported a geometric mean runtime overhead of 69% and memory overhead of 98%, Dangzero reported a geometric mean runtime and memory overhead of 20% and 37%, respectively, while SdShield's values were 64% and 59%. However, Dangzero requires running in a specific Kernel Mode Linux environment, and Oscar requires modifying the kernel source code. The generally shorter runtimes reported in Dangzero also seem to be a result of the Kernel Mode Linux environment. In contrast, although the overhead of SdShield is similar to the other two, SdShield demonstrates stronger portability and defense capabilities—it has no running environment restrictions, does not require compiling the kernel, and can defend against other types of heap vulnerabilities including heap overflows rather than just use-after-free, which proves the effectiveness of our design.

6 Limitations and Future Work

SdShield, as a solution that uses shadow virtual address, has similar limitations to other designs with the same principle [12, 14, 15]. All such designs currently target the system's default memory allocator, but applications may also rely on custom allocators [27]. In principle, our scheme can be applied to all applications by implement a separate interceptor for all custom allocators. Second, the current implementation of SdShield is not yet thread-safe, as competition between threads may lead to a confusing mapping of shadow pages. Future work could address the issue of thread competition through page table locking or by dividing a separate shadow area for each thread.

Besides that, while SdShield can prevent almost all use-after-free errors and report them as soon as it happens, for heap overflow we can only detect them when the program does an allocation or release operation. Although we can always check the canary of all objects in its page table when an object is free, we may not be able to detect it immediately when an overflow occurs. Future work could investigate checking the relevant canary when the process performs certain specific operations, such as dangerous system calls or memory write operations, rather than just memory allocation and release, as a way to improve the timeliness of heap overflow detection.

7 Conclusion

Using a page protection mechanism for process security is an old idea that was originally used for debugging. Although researchers have made optimizations based on shadow pages and solved the critical scalability costs in recent years, the state-of-the-art solutions still only support the detection of use-after-free errors and face portability issues. In this paper, we propose a new scheme based on shadow pages and page table permissions. We design a novel page table structure to secure the overall security of the heap area and not just for use-after-free only. We use a method that dynamically adds system calls to access and modify the process page table, enabling it to run on any Linux operating system without requiring a specific environment. Finally, our experimental evaluation demonstrates that our design significantly improves the security of the current page permission-based solutions.

References

1. Akritidis, P.: Cling: a memory allocator to mitigate dangling pointers. In: USENIX Security (2010)
2. Novark, G., Berger, E.D.: DieHarder: securing the heap. In: Proceedings of the 17th ACM Conference on Computer and Communications Security, pp. 573–584 (2010)
3. Silvestro, S., Liu, H., Crosser, C., Lin, Z., Liu, T.: FreeGuard: a faster secure heap allocator. In: Proceedings of the 2017 ACM SIGSAC Conference on Computer and Communications Security, pp. 2389–2403 (2017)
4. Liu, B., Olivier, P., Ravindran, B.: SlimGuard: a secure and memory-efficient heap allocator. In: Proceedings of the 20th International Middleware Conference (2019)
5. Ainsworth, S., Jones, T.M.: MarkUs: drop-in use-after-free prevention for low-level languages. In: IEEE Symposium on Security and Privacy, pp. 578–591 (2020)

6. Nagarakatte, S., Zhao, J., Martin, M.M.K., Zdancewic, S.: CETS: compiler enforced temporal safety for C. In: ISMM (2010)
7. Nikiforakis, N., Piessens, F., Joosen, W.: HeapSentry: kernel-assisted protection against heap overflows. In: Rieck, K., Stewin, P., Seifert, J.-P. (eds.) DIMVA 2013. LNCS, vol. 7967, pp. 177–196. Springer, Heidelberg (2013). https://doi.org/10.1007/978-3-642-39235-1_11
8. Lee, B., et al.: Preventing use-after-free with dangling pointers nullification. In: NDSS, pp. 1–15 (2015)
9. Kouwe, E.V.D., Nigade, V., Giuffrida, C.: DangSan: scalable use-after-free detection. In: EuroSys, pp. 405–419 (2017)
10. Erdős, M., Ainsworth, S., Jones ,T.M.: MineSweeper: a clean sweep for drop-in use-after-free prevention. In: ASPLOS, pp. 212–225 (2022)
11. He, L., Hu, H., Su, P., Cai, Y., Liang, Z.: FREEWILL: automatically diagnosing use-after-free bugs via reference miscounting detection on binaries. In: 31st USENIX Security Symposium (USENIX Security 2022), pp. 2497–2512 (2022)
12. Dhurjati, D., Adve, V.: Efficiently detecting all dangling pointer uses in production servers. In: DSN (2006)
13. Younan, Y.: FreeSentry: protecting against use-after-free vulnerabilities due to dangling pointers. In: NDSS, pp. 1–15 (2015)
14. Dang, T.H.Y., Maniatis, P., David Wagner, D.: Oscar: a practical page-permissions-based scheme for thwarting dangling pointers. In: USENIX Security, pp. 1–18 (2017)
15. Gorter, F., Koning, K., Bos, H., Giuffrida, C.: DangZero: efficient use-after-free detection via direct page table access. In: Proceedings of the 2022 ACM SIGSAC Conference on Computer and Communications Security, pp. 1–15 (2022)
16. Szekeres, L., Payer, M., Wei, T., Song, D.: SoK: eternal war in memory. In: Proceedings of the 2013 IEEE Symposium on Security and Privacy (2013)
17. Silvestro, S., Liu, H., Liu, T., Lin, Z., Liu, T.: Guarder: a tunable secure allocator. In: 27th USENIX Security Symposium, pp. 117–133 (2018)
18. Yun, I., Song, S.W., Min, S., Kim, T.: HardsHeap: a universal and extensible framework for evaluating secure allocators. In: Proceedings of the 2021 ACM SIGSAC Conference on Computer and Communications Security (2021)
19. Wickman, B., et al.: Preventing use-after-free attacks with fast forward allocation. In: USENIX Security (2021)
20. Robertson, W., Kruegel, C., Mutz, D., Valeur, F.: Run-time detection of heap-based overflows. In: Proceedings of the 17th USENIX Conference on System Administration (2003)
21. Younan, Y., Joosen, W., Piessens, F., Eynden, H.V.D.: Security of memory allocators for C and C++. Technical report (2005)
22. Shin, J., Kwon, D., Seo, J., Cho, Y., Paek, Y.: CRCount: pointer invalidation with reference counting to mitigate use-after-free in legacy C/C++. In: NDSS (2019)
23. Perens, B.: Electric fence malloc debugger. http://perens.com/FreeSoftware/ElectricFence/. Accessed 10 Apr 2023
24. Boland, F., Black, P.: The juliet 1.1 C/C++ and Java test suite. IEEE Comput. 45(10), 88–90 (2012)
25. Lu, S., Li, Z., Qin, F., Tan, L., Zhou, P.: BugBench: benchmarks for evaluating bug detection tools. In: Workshop on the Evaluation of Software Defect Detection Tools (2005)
26. Leitch, J.: Issue 24613. array.fromstring use after free. https://bugs.python.org/issue24613. Accessed 10 Apr 2023
27. Berger, E.D., Zorn, B.G., McKinley, K.S.: Reconsidering custom memory allocation. In: OOPSLA (2002)
28. Bernhard, L., Rodler, M., Holz, T., Davi, L.: xTag: mitigating use-after-free vulnerabilities via software-based pointer tagging on Intel x86-64. In: IEEE EuroS&P (2022)

29. Burow, N., McKee, D., Carr, S.A., Payer, M.: CUP: comprehensive user-space protection for C/C++. In: AsiaCCS, pp. 381–392 (2018)
30. Farkhani, R.M., Ahmadi, M., Lu, L.: PTAuth: temporal memory safety via robust points-to authentication. In: USENIX Security (2018)
31. Gui, B., Song, W., Huang, J.: UAFSan: an object-identifier-based dynamic approach for detecting use-after-free vulnerabilities. In: ISSTA (2021)
32. Microsoft: GFlags and PageHeap. https://docs.microsoft.com/en-us/windows-hardware/drivers/debugger/gflags-and-pageheap. Accessed 10 Mar 2023
33. Tian, D., Li, X., Chen, M., Hu, C.: ICruiser: an improved approach for concurrent heap buffer overflow monitoring. IEICE Trans. Inf. Syst. 97(3), 601–605 (2014)
34. Maeda, T., Yonezawa, A.: Kernel Mode Linux: toward an operating system protected by a type theory. In: Saraswat, V.A. (ed.) ASIAN 2003. LNCS, vol. 2896, pp. 3–17. Springer, Heidelberg (2003). https://doi.org/10.1007/978-3-540-40965-6_2
35. Boehm, H.J., Demers, A.J., Shenker, S.: Mostly parallel garbage collection. In: PLDI (1991)

Unraveling Network-Based Pivoting Maneuvers: Empirical Insights and Challenges

Martin Husák[1,2(✉)] ⓘ, Shanchieh Jay Yang[3] ⓘ, Joseph Khoury[2,4] ⓘ,
Đorđe Klisura[2,4] ⓘ, and Elias Bou-Harb[2,4] ⓘ

[1] Institute of Computer Science, Masaryk University, Brno, Czech Republic
husakm@ics.muni.cz
[2] The Cyber Center for Security and Analytics, The University of Texas
at San Antonio, San Antonio, TX, USA
[3] Department of Computer Engineering, Rochester Institute of Technology,
Rochester, NY, USA
jay.yang@rit.edu
[4] Division of Computer Science and Engineering, Louisiana State University,
Baton Rouge, LA, USA
{jkhour5,dklisu1,ebouharb}@lsu.edu

Abstract. Pivoting is a sophisticated strategy employed by modern malware and Advanced Persistent Threats (APT) to complicate attack tracing and attribution. Detecting pivoting activities is of utmost importance in order to counter these threats effectively. In this study, we examined the detection of pivoting by analyzing network traffic data collected over a period of *10* days in a campus network. Through Net-Flow monitoring, we initially identified potential pivoting candidates, which are traces in the network traffic that match known patterns. Subsequently, we conducted an in-depth analysis of these candidates and uncovered a significant number of false positives and benign pivoting-like patterns. To enhance investigation and understanding, we introduced a novel graph representation called a pivoting graph, which provides comprehensive visualization capabilities. Unfortunately, investigating pivoting candidates is highly dependent on the specific context and necessitates a strong understanding of the local environment. To address this challenge, we applied principal component analysis and clustering techniques to a diverse range of features. This allowed us to identify the most meaningful features for automated pivoting detection, eliminating the need for prior knowledge of the local environment.

Keywords: pivoting · lateral movement · monitoring · NetFlow

1 Introduction

Lateral movement has become a major research topic in network security [22]. Adversaries are always finding new ways of breaching systems and avoiding detection, often by moving laterally in the target network. The most valuable targets

---

The original version of the chapter has been revised. A correction to this chapter can be found at https://doi.org/10.1007/978-3-031-56583-0_23

ⓒ ICST Institute for Computer Sciences, Social Informatics and Telecommunications Engineering 2024,
corrected publication 2024
Published by Springer Nature Switzerland AG 2024. All Rights Reserved
S. Goel and P. R. Nunes de Souza (Eds.): ICDF2C 2023, LNICST 571, pp. 132–151, 2024.
https://doi.org/10.1007/978-3-031-56583-0_9

are often not accessible from the Internet, or the network is protected by intrusion detection systems (IDS) on the perimeter. The goal of the adversary in such cases is to get a foothold elsewhere in the network, such as on a common workstation exploited by social engineering attack (e.g., a phishing email) or a weakly secured IoT device. Creating a backdoor to such a device allows the adversary to use it as a *pivot* and connect to other targets in the network from within. The term *pivoting* [2,22] refers to such a scenario and can also be referred to as *island hopping* [23], *stepping stone attack* [33] or *command propagation* in the literature. Pivoting is no longer an advanced attack technique reserved for Advanced Persistent Threats (APT) and other advanced adversaries [9,22] but is more and more often seen adopted by novel malware [8,26].

Although pivoting or lateral movement detection, in general, has gained much attention in recent years [22], the state-of-the-art in the field is limited by several factors. First, the existing pivoting detection methods (e.g., [5,7,18]) are mostly host-based, meaning they can only detect the pivoting on (or with access to the data from) the machine that acts as a pivot. While such methods achieve high accuracy, their scope is limited to machines that have the necessary software equipment or those that can forward their logs elsewhere, which is often infeasible in large and heterogeneous networks. Moreover, the attacker may exploit a common workstation or IoT device as a pivot, where such devices would likely not be equipped with proper detection mechanisms. Thus, a network-based approach is vital and could play a key complementary role in such a context. Second, the related works mostly evaluated the detection capability using datasets or in environments with an insufficient amount of background traffic. Thus, existing approaches may achieve a high true positive rate but also a high false positive rate because it is not clear what false positive or benign events can be detected. Attempts to approach this problem were made [15] but needed to deliver long-term measurements or a detailed analysis of the false positives. We aim herein to fill this gap by detecting pivoting in real-world settings while differentiating between benign and suspicious events.

The contributions of this work to the state-of-the-art can be summarized as follows. First, we employ a modified state-of-the-art network-based pivoting detection algorithm [2] to detect pivoting and pivoting-like events in a campus network, focusing on SSH communication. Following the observations in related work [15], we employ a two-layer detection tactic starting with pivoting *candidate* detection with a high true positive rate followed by a second analytical phase aiming at false positive reduction leading to the selection of true positive candidates. The scope of this measurement vastly exceeds any experiments in related work. Second, we empirically analyze the measurement results, identify true and false positives, and investigate the benignity or maliciousness of the detected events. To this end, we (*i*) extract a list of heuristics based on knowledge of the local environment and convert them into rules for automatic annotation. Consequently, we (*ii*) devise a novel graph-based representation of pivoting activities, which provides comprehensive visualization and additional contextual features. Further, (*iii*) we study the evolution of pivoting-like events over time. Third, we perform principle component analysis and clustering in order to identify the most meaningful features and feature sets that would allow for the design and development of a (semi-)automated pivoting detection tool without relying on local knowledge.

The remainder of this work is structured as follows. Section 2 comprehensively summarizes the background and relevant related work. Section 3 inititally presents the scenario and experiment setup for pivoting detection in the campus network. Subsequently, the pivoting detection algorithm and measurement results are described. Section 4 presents a detailed analysis of the measurement results using three approaches, heuristic filtering, graph-based representation, and timing analysis. Section 5 presents the approaches taken toward for the automation of the analysis. Section 6 discusses the measurement findings and their implication towards in-practice, pragmatic usages. Section 7 concludes the paper and paves the way for future work.

2   Background and Related Work

In this section, we first define the pivoting maneuver and its characteristics. Then, we provide the necessary background on network measurements. We also provide an overview of the related work on pivoting detection.

2.1   Pivoting Maneuver and its Characteristics

Pivoting, also known as island hopping or stepping stone attack, is gaining more and more popularity among attackers. The documented cases of cyber attacks involving pivoting include the events of Operation Aurora [8], in which the attackers gained control over the system of large corporations and exfiltrated business secrets. In 2015, the Ukrainian power grid faced a complex attack involving pivoting [12]. Such an attack caused a blackout in hundreds of thousands of households. The MEDJACK attack [26] abused hospital equipment, such as X-ray scanners, to exfiltrate data on patients. The report by TrapX Security [28] comments on other pivoting-based attacks in the healthcare domain. SamSam is an example of ransomware leveraging pivoting activities [1], while the Archimedes tool [31] uses pivoting and forwards network traffic to fake websites to steal authentication credentials. In line with the strategic pivoting tactics, amid the Russo-Ukrainian conflict, an attacker laterally maneuvered within the trusted management network of KA-SAT which eventually allowed him to execute legitimate, targeted management commands on a large number of residential modems simultaneously [30].

Here, we define pivoting as a pair of network connections involving three actors. First, the *Source* initiates a connection to the *Pivot*. Subsequently, either immediately or up to ϵ seconds later, the *Pivot* initiates a connection to the *Target*. The *Target* is different from the *Source*. The scenario is depicted in Fig. 1.

A malicious case of pivoting may involve an attacker located anywhere on the Internet as the *Source*. The attacker aims at a *Target* that is behind a firewall or in a private network segment. Thus, the attacker exploits a *Pivot* first since

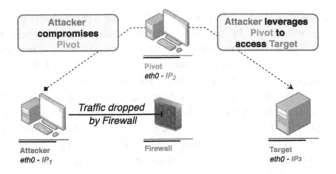

Fig. 1. An illustrative depiction of a pivoting maneuver through SSH.

it has both a public IP address and can reach the *Target*. However, pivoting can also be benign and even part of a typical daily workflow. For example, a user working from home connects to a publicly accessible SSH server in the employer's network and uses it to connect to another device in the network that is not directly accessible. This is essentially pivoting but conducted by a legitimate user and, thus, is benign unless it violates internal security policy that would, for example, prohibit connecting to SSH from outside of the network.

2.2 Related Work on Pivoting Detection

Despite the rising frequency of attacks involving pivoting, the research on detecting such events it is still scarce or limited in its applicability [22]. Earlier works [3,27] conceptualized pivoting attacks without proposing a detection method. Since pivoting and lateral movement is often a part of APT attacks as carefully studied by Gonzales et al. [13] according to the MITRE ATT&CK framework, it was mostly studied in terms of detecting and preventing APT [9,22]. The earliest works focused on alert correlation, not processing raw data. The foundational work by Valeur et al. [29] illustrates the correlation of alerts raised by IDS (Intrusion Detection Systems). However, the malicious activity may avoid being detected or would not trigger an alert, which complicates this approach [21].

The topic of lateral movement spans intrusion detection as well as forensics. Liu et al. [16] proposed Latte, a lateral movement detection system based on graphs with computers and users as nodes and connection and logon events as edges. Their approach is host-based and bridges forensic analysis and detection. Wilkens et al. [32] researched the reconstruction of lateral movement. Their contribution is a detection method where, using indicators of compromises, suggests the path of the attacker's lateral movement and narrows down the set of nodes to analyze to only 5% of all network hosts.

Host-based approaches are the most common in the proposed pivoting detection research. Here, Bai et al. [4,5] proposed an approach to detect lateral movement in RDP logs; the work is limited only to Windows-based hosts. Their approach utilizes an ML classifier which yielded high performance illustrated on several datasets while also being robust against adversarial attacks [5]. Bian et al. [7] further elaborated on the topic, scrutinizing graph-based features and conducting dimensionality reduction. However, the low quality of network flow data in the used dataset prevented the authors from including such data in their approach. Recent approaches to lateral movement detection do not rely solely on system logs but combine multiple data sources, including monitoring network traffic. APIVADS [18] is a privacy-preserving approach to pivoting detection that can be used in complex networks. The proposed approach relies on NetFlow data collected on the pivot and, thus, it is a de-facto host-based method, even though network-based data are used. Powell [20] proposed a role-based lateral movement detection using unsupervised learning, utilizing systems calls and network connections alike, leveraging earlier work on graph-based anomaly detection in authentication logs [19]. Smiliotopoulos et al. [24] propose a Sysmon log-based lateral movement detection technique encompassing the labelling and pre-processing of the data, as well as the classification through a supervised machine learning approach.

The first attempts at characterizing stepping stones dated back to 1995 [25] and detecting it to 2000 [33]. Even back then, the authors mention the vast false positive rates. Since then, the dynamics of network traffic and the threat landscape have fundamentally changed, and research has mostly focused on host-based methods. The work of Apruzzese et al. [2] is the state-of-the-art network-based pivoting detection algorithm. The authors proposed an algorithm that correlates NetFlow data [14] and is capable of detecting sequences of pivoting activity of arbitrary length. Such an approach is well suited to private networks with not much background traffic. However, Husák et al. [15] recently evaluated an algorithm by Apruzzese et al. [2] in operational settings and pinpointed the challenges related to that, given that they have achieved a high rate of false positive detections and too few true detections of pivoting activity involving relevant services (e.g., SSH, RDP, Telnet). The authors proposed Principal Component Analysis (PCA) to infer characteristics of true pivoting events to enable further development of ML-based detection. Another angle was considered by Dong et al. [10, 11] in which they identified lateral movement traces in enterprise network by performing behavior deviation measurement.

With respect to the state-of-the-art, the proposed work herein is scoped towards the detection of pivoting activities based on network traffic analysis (namely using NetFlow); hence it aims at detecting pivoting occurring anywhere in the network. Such a goal is highly ambitious and will require long-term empirical measurements and evaluation. In this vein, we start with the setup of the pivoting detection pipeline that would enable the latter. With the help of contextual information, heuristics, and machine learning, our goal is to devise an approach which reduces the false positive rate while distinguishing between benign and suspicious (or even malicious) pivoting activities.

3   Pivoting Candidate Detection

We describe in this section the experimental environment and the measurement setup (see Fig. 2) followed by the pivoting detection algorithm and the generated results. By pivoting candidates, we refer to the outputs of the detection algorithm as is, without any post-processing, which is discussed in the subsequent sections.

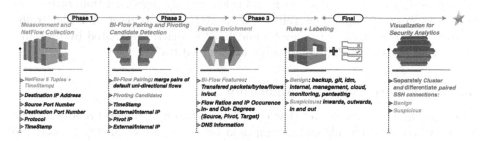

Fig. 2. Pivoting detection pipeline.

3.1   Environment and Experiment Setup

We executed a longitudinal measurement in March 2023 in the campus network of Masaryk University[1]. The campus network serves more than 30,000 students and 6,000 employees. Over 15,000 unique IPv4 addresses in the /16 IPv4 address range can be seen on a daily basis. The campus network is to be open and restrict only malicious network traffic and hazardous services rather than blocking everything and allowing only certain services. This makes the campus network an excellent environment to study benign pivoting-like activities.

The university operates a cybersecurity team CSIRT-MU[2] to manage cybersecurity in the network and operate a network monitoring infrastructure based on the NetFlow technology [14]. NetFlow monitoring enables the CSIRT-MU to perform intrusion detection and network forensics. The NetFlow probes are located at strategic locations to monitor network traffic flowing through major links in the campus network. No measurement is conducted on the routers or other active network devices. Two probes are located on the perimeter, monitoring any inbound and outbound traffic, and six are located inside the network, monitoring the most important internal links. The probes on the perimeter observe the highest traffic rates but do not have any visibility into internal network traffic, while the internal probes are capable of observing the majority of network connections within the campus network, including any connection inbound or outbound to the campus network. Thus, we chose to use only the data from the internal probes. As such, all the data from the probes are sent to two NetFlow collectors, where they are retained. Since the NetFlow measurement is primarily

---

[1] https://www.muni.cz/en.
[2] https://csirt.muni.cz/?lang=en.

used for security purposes, no traffic sampling is applied, even on high-speed links, to allow for precise monitoring. The active time-out is set to 30 s for the same reason, diverting from traditional settings of 5 min [14].

Notably, only SSH communication (i.e., identified by TCP destination port *22*) is considered during our measurement. The reasons are two-fold; *(i)* considering multiple protocols or protocol-agnostic detection would explode in complexity and would complicate the analysis (see the discussion); and *(ii)* SSH is widely used in the campus network and is less strictly regulated than other considerable protocols, including Telnet and/or RDP. The amount of Telnet traffic in the campus network is negligible, and RDP is strictly regulated by firewalls, which also leads to negligible amounts of observed traffic.

3.2   Candidate Detection Algorithm

The pivoting detection in NetFlow data follows two fundamental related works. First, we adapted the algorithm proposed by Apruzzese et al. [2]. Second, we enhanced the two-level approach proposed by Husák et al. [15], i.e., detecting candidates first and then using other approaches to classify the candidates as true and false positives (and benign and suspicious ones).

The algorithm by Apruzzese et al. [2] extracts the bi-flows (i.e., bi-directional network flows created by merging pairs of default uni-directional flows in opposite directions [14]) and then finds the paths of arbitrary lengths in which the next flow's source is the previous flow's destination. In addition, the new biflow has to start immediately or up to 30 s after the previous one. The algorithm is capable of detecting pivoting of arbitrary length.

We made several changes to the algorithm. First, we process data from multiple probes. Thus, all the biflows from all probes are merged into one list and sorted by timestamp. Duplicate biflows (e.g., connections observed by two or more probes) are removed. Second, we detect only simple pivoting consisting of two network connections (source to pivot, pivot to target). Pivoting over several pivots would still appear in the results as several candidates. Moreover, candidates of fixed form are easier to post-process. Finally, the time limit of 30 s was kept as a default but implemented as an optional parameter. The default time window is one day (midnight to midnight), but it is also subject to settings. The final form of the algorithm is summarized in pseudocode in Algorithm 1.

3.3   Results

The measurement and pivoting candidate detection spanned ten days. The results are summarized in Table 1. Processing the NetFlow data collected throughout the day by six probes took around 30 min on average on commodity hardware.

The pivoting detection algorithm has one parameter, namely, the time propagation delay (ϵ), i.e., a maximal time difference between the source-to-pivot and pivot-to-target communication [2]. We were interested in how various settings of ϵ influence the overall results. The values of 2, 10, 30 (default), and 60 s were

Algorithm 1. Pivoting candidate detection algorithm.

```
1: f ← list of flows on the input
2: ε ← 30
3: len ← size of f
4: for i in [0, len] do
5:     for j in [i+1, len] do
6:         if f_i.dstIP == f_2.srcIP then
7:             if f_1.ts < f_2.ts < f_1.ts + ε then
8:                 candidates ← (f_i, f_j)
9:             end if
10:        end if
11:    end for
12: end for
```

Table 1. Pivoting candidate detection.

Measurement Artifacts	Min	Max	Total
Biflows	3,416,328	6,412,670	39,399,832
Candidates	17,026	75,116	313,193
Unique Sources (S)	297	646	3,410
Unique Pivots (P)	64	112	238
Unique Targets (T)	76	227	468
Unique Triplets (S, P, T)	695	6,956	22,655
Pivoting Graph Components	12	21	14

considered. The higher the ϵ, the higher the number of detected candidates and unique actors, but also highly increased processing time (from several minutes at lowest ϵ to close to one hour with the highest ϵ). However, the increases were observed mostly in false positive detections (see the following section). The number of suspicious candidates (i.e., those we aim to detect, see the next section) changed only marginally with various ϵ. It is also worth noting that higher fragmentation of NetFlows in time due to active timeouts is an influential factor allowing the use of low ϵ values.

4   Manual Pivoting Candidate Analysis

The second phase of the experiment is the analysis of pivoting candidates, i.e., the output of the pivoting detection algorithm. The algorithm is relatively simple but provides a solid true positive detection rate. However, it is prone to a high false positive rate, which needs to be addressed. Thus, the second phase primarily addresses the false positive rate reduction manner. Three approaches were taken and are discussed in the sequel. First, we leverage the knowledge of the environment and manually classify the candidates. Second, we employ a novel approach based on graph-based visualization. Finally, we analyze the evolution of pivoting candidates over time.

4.1 Empirical Analysis and Heuristic Filtering

The empirical analysis of the results was conducted in collaboration with administrators of the campus network. The administrators have detailed knowledge of the environment and the roles of most of the deployed devices. The goal of this analysis was to either confirm that the detected candidate is some sort of pivoting-like activity or a false positive. Simultaneously, the empirical analysis served as a basis for the construction of a heuristic filter that can be used to filter the candidates, disregard false positives, and mark benign events. The empirical analysis was conducted manually. All the IP addresses were translated to domain names for increased comprehension. The analysts iterated the list starting with the most frequently appearing sources, pivots, targets, and their combinations. Several frequent patterns became apparent and a heuristic filter was filled with entries. A detailed breakdown of its results is displayed in Table 2.

Table 2. Rule-based annotation of pivoting candidates.

Class	Rule	Candidates
Benign and False Positives	Monitoring	288,161
	(Anonymized Services)	15,761
	Git & Backup	5,404
	Management & Cloud	1,288
	Pentesting	1,627
Unclassified and Suspicious	Internal	29
	Inwards	338
	Outwards	19
	In and Out	566
Total	-	313,193

First, a large number of candidates included one of the network measurement nodes. Tools like *Nagios* and *Icinga* deployed in the network use SSH to connect to or receive connections from other hosts in the network to update the status of the devices and services running on them. If the monitored nodes open another network connection, a candidate is detected. Either the monitored host received an SSH connection from elsewhere and then updated its status, or the monitoring node queried a monitored host, which then connected elsewhere. At one department, the administrators operate two monitoring hosts, one actively probing the devices and the second receiving updates. Simultaneous connections to and from both of them resulted in a number of pivoting candidates with the same source and target but different pivots. All the cases can be declared as false positives, and the following filtering rule was established: if a known network monitoring node is involved in pivoting-like activity, the candidate is marked as *monitoring* and dismissed. The list of monitoring hosts can be provided by network administrators. Alternatively, if a common naming scheme is used, a rule can be stated as: if the actor's domain name is *{monitor,icinga,nagios}*.domain*, then dismiss this candidate. A network-wide penetration test from a known dedicated host taking the role of a source was also observed and was marked as *pentesting*.

Second, a similar observation was made with hosts belonging to the cloud or network management infrastructure. However, in such cases, the behavior is rather true benign pivoting than false positive. For example, a cloud management device receives a command via SSH connection from a controller and propagates it to one or more hosts in the cloud. Other network infrastructures, such as centralized identity management systems or various APIs to services in the private network display similar behavior. Again, a rule can be set: if a pivot is one of the hosts providing pivoting-like service, it is marked as *management* and considered benign or dismissed. Again, the list of hosts is provided by network administrators or derived by its domain name (e.g., *cloud-management*.domain*).

Third, some candidates involved the IP address of the Git repository or a backup device as a target. Typically, a user connected to a server via SSH did some development work, and committed the code to the Git repository via SSH, thus generating a pivoting-like event. This is a benign scenario and could be filtered by a rule checking for a domain name of a target containing strings, such as **.github.com*, *gitlab*.domain*, or *backup*.domain*. One distributed system in the network used three hosts constantly updating each other via SSH, generating many pivoting-like events (without interacting with other hosts in the network). This was marked separately, and the rule contained three distinct domain names.

The heuristic filtering marked the vast majority of candidates as false positives or benign events. The remaining candidates (less than 1%) were sorted by the location of the actors. A small number of candidates had all three actors inside the network. Since no interaction with the Internet was observed, we may assume these candidates as benign.

Other unclassified candidates involved an actor outside the network, which was either the source (*inwards* scenario), target (*outwards* scenario), or source and target *in and out scenario*. In such scenarios, actors outside the network may pose a danger. Moreover, the vast majority of such actors and candidates were unique in the sense that they appeared only once during the measurement.

We were mostly interested in the *inwards* scenario since it corresponds the most to the attack model. A few detected candidates were attributed to users working from home and pivoting through their own SSH servers to internal services, which turned out to be the most problematic observed behavior (the use of VPN is recommended instead). Although no violation of security was observed, the few observed *inwards* candidates served as true positive samples.

Algorithm 2. Pivoting graph construction.

```
1:  G ← new empty directed graph
2:  for each candidate do
3:      for N in S, P, T do
4:          if N not in G then:
5:              insert node X
6:          end if
7:          if (S,P) not in G then:
8:              insert edge (S,P)
9:          end if
10:         if (P,T) not in G then:
11:             insert edge (P,T)
12:         end if
13:     end for
14: end for
```

The remaining candidates in the *in and out* and *outwards* scenarios were found to be associated with cloud computing, which was apparent from the domain names of the actors. The communication patterns involved hosts in cloud environments of the campus network, clouds of other institutions (collaborating universities), or public cloud service providers. Although we cannot tell what happened in those events (the cloud services are outside of our scope, and data sharing and distributed computing are expected there), we did not observe anything highly suspicious or clearly malicious. Setting a new location (*cloud*) should be considered for future work.

4.2 Visual Analysis via Pivoting Graph and Its Decomposition

In the second part of the manual analysis, we investigated an approach based on graph-based visualization. We composed the *pivoting graph* and subsequently decomposed it into components that are easier to evaluate than a list of candidates.

The pivoting graph is a directed graph that represents the network's hosts as nodes and the connections between them as edges. However, it is important to note that the construction of the pivoting graph is based solely on pivoting candidate events rather than capturing all network (or SSH) traffic within the network. The process of constructing the graph is outlined in Algorithm 2.

The pivoting graph contains all the network hosts that were detected to be involved in pivoting maneuvers at any role. The motivation for constructing the graph is correlating all the pivoting candidates that share some of the actors or (recalling the limitation to only one pivot per candidate) merging pivoting events with more pivots. Indeed, the pivoting graph represents various situations well. Moreover, it is also a graph with many unconnected components, which allows for approaching each component individually, which turned out to be highly valuable.

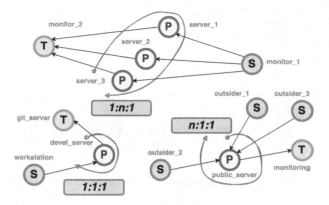

Fig. 3. An excerpt from the pivoting graph displaying the components of three different patterns.

The graph decomposition partitions the graph into components, precisely weakly connected components since the pivoting graph is directed. Standard decomposition algorithms from the NetworkX library [17] were used in this work. During the experiment, we found 12–21 components in the pivoting graph for every day of measurement and 14 components in the graph constructed from all the data. An excerpt from such a graph can be found in Fig. 3. Several patterns became imminent and are closely described next. For simplicity, we refer to the common component by the number of actors (sources, pivots, and targets) they contain, let the number be either 1 or n for 1 or more actors.

The $n : 1 : 1$ patterns represent a component with numerous sources but only one pivot and one target. Pivots in these components were typically Internet-facing SSH servers, which receive incoming connections all the time, while the target is a monitoring node, to which the pivot reports its status. Indeed, all of them were found to be related to monitoring in manual analysis. The $1 : n : 1$ was observed at one department due to the unique setting of their host monitoring infrastructure, as we discussed in the manual analysis. The $1 : 1 : n$ pattern with multiple targets usually indicates a cloud orchestration or host monitoring, which was confirmed in the manual analysis. Although it may seem that any pattern with n is benign, we are aware that an attacker may compromise one pivot and use it to exploit multiple targets. Thus, unless the pattern is labeled as benign by the local rules, it should be investigated.

The $1 : 1 : 1$ pattern was the most common; each component represented an isolated pivoting event involving actors not involved in other patterns. While some of these were evaluated as benign, it is rather a good indicator of suspicious activity that is worth investigating.

4.3   Pivoting over Time

Figure 4 shows the frequency of how often each pivot was detected throughout the measurement. Out of 238 unique pivots detected over 10 days, 120 were

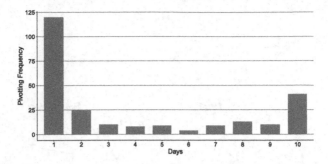

Fig. 4. Temporal analysis of pivot presence: observing candidate events across measurement days.

seen in only one day, while 41 were seen every day. It is not surprising that benign pivoting-like activities related to network management and monitoring are happening almost every day, while suspicious connections are more likely to happen in only one day.

Nevertheless, it would be a false assumption to automatically consider one-time events as suspicious and repeated as benign. We assume the attackers adopting the pivoting technique are also considerate of timing and, thus, perform "low and slow". With this in mind, a single event may not be significant, but a repeated, long-lasting activity involving unknown actors may be a sign of an advanced attacker, which we aim to expose.

5   Towards Automated Candidate Filtering

Herein, we present the third phase of our experiment. In the previous section, we presented the results of manual analysis, in which we outlined what frequent false positive and benign candidates were detected. Since the analysis was mostly based on the knowledge of the local environment, we could infer the contextual features of pivoting that could be leveraged for automated filtering of pivoting candidates.

5.1   Features

A total number of 39 features was selected for the experiment, along with the labeling provided by rule-based filtering. The first set of 18 features is derived from the NetFlow data and represents the duration and number of flows between the actors and the number of transferred packets and bytes in both directions. Moreover, the ratios of the features between the two communications are added. These features were already used in related work [15] and may signalize the similarity between the two flows.

The other features are contextual and describe the location of the actors and their relation to the remainder of the dataset. Three features designate the location of the actor: 0 for an external IP (anywhere on the Internet outside the campus network), 1 for public IP in the campus network, and 2 for an IP in a private address range. Subsequently, we assume seven features for each combination of the actors, i.e., Source (S), Pivot (P), Target (T), and their combinations (SP, PT, ST, SPT). These features designate how many times was the combination of actors observed in the candidate list. Four features are inspired by the degrees of a corresponding node in the pivoting graph, i.e., the out-degree of S, the in- and out-degrees of P, and the in-degree of T. The last seven features represent the timing. For each combination of actors, a feature indicates whether this combination was observed on the previous day or not. For practical reasons, we assume only the previous day. However, we can generalize this feature to indicate the number of occurrences in any number of previous days. It is worth noting that the candidates from the first day were excluded from this experiment since their history was not observed.

5.2   Analysis and Results

We used Principal Component Analyses (PCA) to find the relations between the 39 features and their labels. We limited the number of principal components to 2 so that we could plot them in the graph. This was done with different feature sets, with all features and with contextual features only. The results are presented in Fig. 5.

Unfortunately, the obtained results were inconclusive in providing a definitive answer to the questions we were most interested in. Specifically, we were unable to determine the most significant features or their combinations, as well as whether it is feasible to cluster the pivoting candidates in a manner that aligns with the given labels. Even though the true positive (i.e., suspicious) candidates can be found in certain small areas of the graph, they are still mixed with false positive and benign candidates. However, the enrichment of the pivoting candidate with additional contextual features seems to help. Employing only the NetFlow-based features is the least illustrative while using only the contextual features results in clearer clusters.

Despite making several attempts at clustering and visualization throughout the experiment, the ones presented here are considered the most compelling. However, the results are rather negative as they did not reveal any key features that could effectively differentiate between benign and suspicious pivoting activities.

6   Discussion

The discussion is structured in three areas. First, we list the limitations of our approach. Second, we comment on the security implications, such as avoiding detection. Finally, we put forward a few recommendations for pivoting detection using our approach in practice.

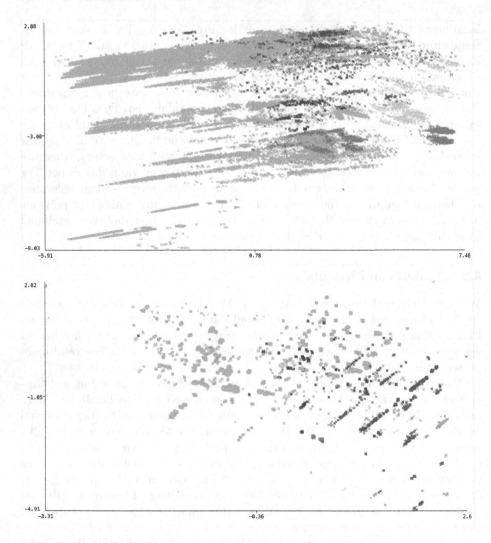

Fig. 5. Clustering analysis. The top figure shows clustering with all features, the bottom figure shows clustering with contextual features only. Colors are assigned as follows: blue for benign and false positive candidates, orange for in-and-out and outwards scenarios, red for inwards scenarios. (Color figure online)

6.1 Limitations

We are aware pivoting can be conducted using any suitable protocol, not only SSH. The other viable options would be RDP, Telnet, or even protocols associated with network printers (e.g., LPD, LPR, IPP). The attackers could even switch protocols and use one to access the pivot and another to contact the target. Nevertheless, it is not common in related work to use protocol-agnostic detections. At this stage of research, we have to first understand the command propagation before devising detection algorithms. Moreover, protocol-agnostic detections suffer from false positive detections far more and explode in complexity [15]. We estimate that if a measurement similar to this one is conducted with a focus on other protocols, we may gather enough insights to propose a detection method that would reduce the false positive rates across the protocols.

As for the second limitation of our work, we do not reflect the situation in which the pivot may use two different IP addresses (e.g., public and private). We have observed pivoting-like traffic from public to private IP address ranges and vice versa via single-interface pivots. However, pivoting through multi-interface pivots could have been missed and would be worth investigating, even though that would mean additional complexity.

The final limitation is the lack of ground truth and extreme imbalance given by the very few true positives. No attacks were observed nor confirmed, only a small number of suspicious behavior samples, which, compared to the tremendous amount of false positive and benign samples, look negligible. Indeed, it is extremely difficult to refine reasonable data mining outputs or machine learning models. On the contrary, we documented a number of pitfalls for pivoting detection in real-world network traffic that could not be observed in laboratory experiments or in the available datasets.

6.2 Security Implications

The fact that we did not observe any clearly malicious activity is good news, but the ground truth is missing. Thus, we had to label the suspicious events as true positives. We assume the attacker would gain a foothold in the network by exploiting unsecured network host, such as a common workstation or IoT device. Then, the attacker would use the exploited device to access services available only to hosts within the campus network. This corresponds to the *inwards* scenario. Subsequently, the attacker would instruct the pivot to access the internal resources and exfiltrate data. Then, it could also fit the *outwards* scenario.

We argue that a potential attacker would be detected using the proposed method. Malware or an attacker with no knowledge of the environment would explore the surrounding of the exploited device by network scanning and performing brute-force password attacks, which could be detected by common IDS, assuming it is deployed within the network and not only on the perimeter. Since perimeter protection is often a priority and IDS in the internal network can be costly, solely NetFlow-based detection might be key.

However, an advanced attacker, such as in the case of APT, would target specific services and remain unnoticed unless pivoting detection is in place. Considering we were able to detect benign pivoting conducted by personnel working from home, we assume the advanced attacker would be detected, too. They would have three options to hide:

1. switch protocols or port numbers to avoid detection, which is certainly possible but could be approached in the detection by further measurements, development, and combining with related work,

2. exploit hosts on the whitelist or move laterally in a way that avoids vantage points, but that would require excellent knowledge of the environment,
3. set large command propagation delays to disassociate connection to and from pivot; the attacker would then have to, for example, connect to pivot, instruct it to perform an action after 5 min, disconnect, wait for 10 min, and connect again to see the results.

6.3   Recommendation for Pivoting Detection in Practice

Unfortunately, fully automated precise network-based pivoting maneuver detection was not yet achieved. However, a semi-automated solution is achievable under these conditions.

First, the algorithm by Apruzzese et al. [2] is robust and efficient for the first stage of detection. The second stage may use the knowledge presented in this paper to filter the vast majority of unwanted results and comprehensively visualize the remaining ones, thus helping the users in the investigation of the detected patterns.

Second, while deploying the pivoting detector, the users should check for the monitoring and cloud management infrastructure and write up filtering rules, preferably with the detection running for several days to get more samples. Setting more *zones* or *locations* is advisable to filter benign events like pivoting within the network or across clouds of collaborating institutions.

Third, the filtered results should be presented in graphical form as components of the pivoting graph (preferably with domain names and with actors from different locations in different colors) so that the user may promptly comprehend what the actors are and if such traffic is benign or suspicious.

An important issue to mention is the number of results. Our experiment shows tens or hundreds of candidates per day with mostly tens of unique combinations of actors and a low number of pivoting graph components. After careful filtering, these numbers can be reduced to under 10, which is a fair number that could be processed even by analysts under a heavy workload. Additional filters may be used to highlight or alert pivoting candidates with interesting parameters, such as an unknown $1 : 1 : n$ pattern, *inwards* pivoting from an external IP address with low reputation [6], pivot or target is vulnerable or has been compromised recently, or pivoting involving valuable network assets, such as a part of critical infrastructure. Such events are not expected to be very rare and would definitely trigger further investigation, thus justifying the deployment of the presented pivoting detection procedures.

7   Conclusion

We presented an empirical study in pivoting maneuver detection in network traffic. Building upon a modified algorithm from related work [2], we performed experiments to identify real-world detection patterns. Although no clear malicious event was detected, our analysis yielded valuable insights into the network traffic landscape, revealing a significant number of false positives and benign pivoting-like events. The scope of the experiment exceeds previous works [15] and complements results achieved in laboratory settings [7] and host-based methods [18].

We discovered that distinguishing between benign and suspicious pivoting events heavily relies on contextual factors. Consequently, we explored several contextual features that enhance the understanding of automated detection outcomes, reduce false positive rates, and dismiss benign results. While achieving precise pivoting detection in real-world settings remains an open challenge, our study offers critical insights, paving the way for the development of an automated pivoting detection tool that minimizes the burden on human analysts. Implementing such a tool and conducting long-term evaluations are proposed as future research directions.

Acknowledgment. This research was supported by project "MSCAfellow5_MUNI" (No. CZ.02.01.01/00/22_010/0003229). The authors would like to thank CSIRT-MU for providing access to real-world data.

References

1. Agency, C.I.S.: SamSam Ransomware. https://us-cert.cisa.gov/ncas/alerts/AA18-337A (2018). Accessed 14 Sept 2023
2. Apruzzese, G., Pierazzi, F., Colajanni, M., Marchetti, M.: Detection and threat prioritization of pivoting attacks in large networks. IEEE Trans. Emerg. Top. Comput. **8**(2), 404–415 (2020)
3. Ayala, L.: Active medical device cyber-attacks. In: Cybersecurity for Hospitals and Healthcare Facilities: A Guide to Detection and Prevention, pp. 19–37. Apress, Berkeley, CA (2016)
4. Bai, T., Bian, H., Daya, A.A., Salahuddin, M.A., Limam, N., Boutaba, R.: A machine learning approach for RDP-based lateral movement detection. In: 2019 IEEE 44th Conference on Local Computer Networks (LCN), pp. 242–245. IEEE, New York, NY, USA (2019)
5. Bai, T., Bian, H., Salahuddin, M.A., Abou Daya, A., Limam, N., Boutaba, R.: RDP-based lateral movement detection using machine learning. Comput. Commun. **165**, 9–19 (2021)
6. Bartos, V., Zadnik, M., Habib, S.M., Vasilomanolakis, E.: Network entity characterization and attack prediction. Futur. Gener. Comput. Syst. **97**, 674–686 (2019)
7. Bian, H., Bai, T., Salahuddin, M.A., Limam, N., Daya, A.A., Boutaba, R.: Uncovering lateral movement using authentication logs. IEEE Trans. Netw. Serv. Manage. **18**(1), 1049–1063 (2021)
8. Binde, B., McRee, R., O'Connor, T.: Assessing outbound traffic to uncover advanced persistent threat (2011). SANS Institute
9. Bowman, B., Laprade, C., Ji, Y., Huang, H.H.: Detecting lateral movement in enterprise computer networks with unsupervised graph AI. In: 23rd International Symposium on Research in Attacks, Intrusions and Defenses (RAID 2020), pp. 257–268. USENIX Association, San Sebastian (2020)
10. Dong, C., et al.: Bedim: lateral movement detection in enterprise network through behavior deviation measurement. In: 2021 IEEE 23rd International Conference on

High Performance Computing & Communications; 7th International Conference on Data Science & Systems; 19th International Conference on Smart City; 7th International Conference on Dependability in Sensor, Cloud & Big Data Systems & Application (HPCC/DSS/SmartCity/DependSys), pp. 391–398. IEEE (2021)

11. Dong, C., Yang, J., Liu, S., Wang, Z., Liu, Y., Lu, Z.: C-bedim and s-bedim: lateral movement detection in enterprise network through behavior deviation measurement. Comput. Secur. **130**, 103267 (2023)

12. E-ISAC: Analysis of the cyber attack on the ukrainian power grid (2016). https://media.kasperskycontenthub.com/wp-content/uploads/sites/43/2016/05/20081514/E-ISAC_SANS_Ukraine_DUC_5.pdf

13. González-Manzano, L., de Fuentes, J.M., Lombardi, F., Ramos, C.: A technical characterization of APTs by leveraging public resources. Int. J. Inf. Secur. **22**, 1–18 (2023)

14. Hofstede, R., et al.: Flow monitoring explained: from packet capture to data analysis with NetFlow and IPFIX. Commun. Surv. Tutorials **16**(4), 2037–2064 (2014)

15. Husák, M., Apruzzese, G., Yang, S.J., Werner, G.: Towards an efficient detection of pivoting activity. In: 2021 IFIP/IEEE International Symposium on Integrated Network Management (IM), pp. 980–985. IEEE, New York, NY, USA (2021)

16. Liu, Q., et al.: Latte: large-scale lateral movement detection. In: MILCOM 2018–2018 IEEE Military Communications Conference (MILCOM). IEEE, New York, NY, USA (2018)

17. Los Alamos National Laboratory. https://networkx.org. Accessed 14 Sept 2023

18. Marques, R.S., Al-Khateeb, H., Epiphaniou, G., Maple, C.: Apivads: a novel privacy-preserving pivot attack detection scheme based on statistical pattern recognition. IEEE Trans. Inf. Forensics Secur. **17**, 700–715 (2022)

19. Powell, B.A.: Detecting malicious logins as graph anomalies. J. Inf. Secur. Appl. **54**, 102557 (2020)

20. Powell, B.A.: Role-based lateral movement detection with unsupervised learning. Intell. Syst. Appl. **16**, 200106 (2022)

21. Ramaki, A.A., Rasoolzadegan, A., Bafghi, A.G.: A systematic mapping study on intrusion alert analysis in intrusion detection systems. ACM Comput. Surv. **51**(3), 1–41 (2018)

22. Salema Marques, R., Al Khateeb, H., Epiphaniou, G., Maple, C.: Pivot attack classification for cyber threat intelligence. J. Inf. Secur. Cybercrimes Res. **5**(2), 91–103 (2022)

23. Sarafijanovic-Djukic, N., Pidrkowski, M., Grossglauser, M.: Island hopping: efficient mobility-assisted forwarding in partitioned networks. In: 2006 3rd Annual IEEE Communications Society on Sensor and Ad Hoc Communications and Networks, vol. 1, pp. 226–235. IEEE (2006)

24. Smiliotopoulos, C., Kambourakis, G., Barbatsalou, K.: On the detection of lateral movement through supervised machine learning and an open-source tool to create turnkey datasets from sysmon logs. Int. J. Inf. Secur. **22**, 1893–1919 (2023)

25. Staniford-Chen, S., Heberlein, L.: Holding intruders accountable on the internet. In: Proceedings 1995 IEEE Symposium on Security and Privacy, pp. 39–49 (1995)

26. Storm, D.: MEDJACK: hackers hijacking medical devices to create backdoors in hospital networks. https://www.computerworld.com/article/2932371/medjack-hackers-hijacking-medical-devices-to-create-backdoors-in-hospital-networks.html (2015). Accessed 14 Sept 2023

27. Tankard, C.: Advanced persistent threats and how to monitor and deter them. Netw. Secur. **2011**(8), 16–19 (2011)

28. TrapX   Labs.   https://securityledger.com/wp-content/uploads/2015/06/
    AOA_MEDJACK_LAYOUT_6-0_6-3-2015-1.pdf   (2015).   Accessed   14   Sept
    2023
29. Valeur, F., Vigna, G., Kruegel, C., Kemmerer, R.A.: Comprehensive approach to
    intrusion detection alert correlation. IEEE Trans. Dependable Secure Comput.
    1(3), 146–169 (2004)
30. ViaSat: KA-SAT Network cyber attack overview. https://news.viasat.com/blog/
    corporate/ka-sat-network-cyber-attack-overview (2022). Accessed 14 Sept 2023
31. WikiLeaks: Vault7:   Archimedes   documentation.   https://wikileaks.org/
    vault7/#Archimedes (2017). Accessed 14 Sept 2023
32. Wilkens, F., Haas, S., Kaaser, D., Kling, P., Fischer, M.: Towards efficient recon-
    struction of attacker lateral movement. In: Proceedings of the 14th International
    Conference on Availability, Reliability and Security. ARES 2019, ACM, New York,
    NY, USA (2019)
33. Zhang, Y., Paxson, V.: Detecting stepping stones. In: Proceedings of the 9th Con-
    ference on USENIX Security Symposium, Vol. 9. p. 13. SSYM 2000, USENIX
    Association, USA (2000)

XSS Vulnerability Test Enhancement for Progressive Web Applications

Josep Pegueroles Valles(✉) ⓘD, Sebastien Kanj Bongard,
and Arnau Estebanell Castellví

Universitat Politècnica de Catalunya, Jordi Girona 1-3, 08034 Barcelona, Spain
{josep.pegueroles,sebastien.kanj}@upc.edu

Abstract. Progressive Web Applications produce false negative results when scanned with security vulnerability scanners. In this paper the authors investigate the causes behind vulnerability scanners missing simple vulnerabilities when being used on Progressive Web Applications (PWAs).

Moreover, an analysis of the caveats of only having fully automated vulnerability scans and manual pentests, without a semi-automatic tool covering the gap between the two, will be performed. An explanation of how such tool has been built will be delivered at the end of the paper.

Keywords: Progressive Web Application · security · vulnerability scanners · XSS · sqli · false negatives

1 Introduction

During a penetration test against an ecommerce website, the authors of this paper noticed that Qualys [1], a commercial web application scanning tool which ranks in the first positions of the Gartner ranking [2], had missed the most basic Cross-Site Scripting (XSS) vulnerability. In order to exploit this vulnerability you just needed to use a non-complex XSS payload, inserting '<img src = x onerror = javascript:alert(1) >' in the input field of the search functionality of the main page.

The first idea of the researchers was to rerun the scan. Surprisingly, the scan missed it again. The situation did not change regardless of how many times we repeated the experiment. That was an unauthenticated scan, so there was no reason for Qualys to miss such a simple vulnerability. We tried getting some logs from Qualys in order to figure out what was going on. Unsurprisingly, the logs returned by Qualys were very limited and did not provide enough information to discern what was happening between the web application scanning tool and the Progressive Web Application. Moreover, as this was a scan performed to an external company we did not have access to the machine hosting the application to retrieve the logs directly from the apache2 or nginx log directory.

Lastly, we realized that when thinking about the penetration test as a whole, at that moment he had no semi-automatic way of testing for XSS vulnerabilities. If Qualys was missing one XSS in the main page it was probably missing even more XSS vulnerabilities

S. Goel and P. R. Nunes de Souza (Eds.): ICDF2C 2023, LNICST 571, pp. 152–163, 2024.
https://doi.org/10.1007/978-3-031-56583-0_10

in the rest of the webpage. How could we test all the input fields without spending too much time when Qualys was not working properly?

The need for a semi-automatic tool that could allow the pentester to hunt for XSS vulnerabilities while allowing him to tweak parameters or define payload dictionaries in order to make sure all vulnerabilities were found became a reality.

2 About Progressive Web Applications

Before Progressive Web Apps (PWAs) were a reality, business looking to build a webpage with fast loading times, high performance and deep functionality looked at native apps. PWAs offer the same rich capabilities with additional benefits. Code for PWAs can be written once and deployed across web, Android and iOS platforms, saving teams time and expenditure.

PWAs are web applications that have been designed so they are capable, reliable and installable. These three pillars transform them into an experience that feels like a platform-specific application. Understanding the Service Worker is crucial in understanding how PWAs work. The introduction of the Service Worker by Google in late 2014 is the heart of modern web application architecture that enables a PWA to deliver content to users faster, even offline.

"The JavaScript Service worker runs in the background separate from the web page and operates as the intermediary between the user and content. It hosts the platform's logic and intercepts requests from the user. A PWA's Service Worker functions as "the dispatcher" of the app, deciding whether to respond to the user with cached content or reach out to the internet for current content." [3].

3 The Target

The authors of this paper needed to discover why Qualys had not worked in the first place and then build an alternative tool to use in future pentests where this situation happened again.

The easiest choice was to recreate the scenario that had caused this research to happen. The authors built the same Progressive Web Application found in the pentest (from fingerprinting he knew it was an Open Source solution) and tried to recreate the vulnerable endpoint. The ecommerce website was using the Vue Storefront application [4], which as explained before used a Progressive Web Application architecture.

Their architecture looks like this (Fig. 1):

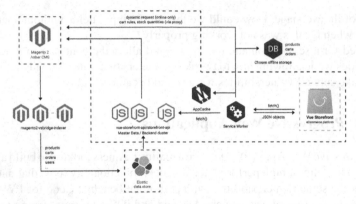

Fig. 1. Architecture of the Vue Storefront application.

As can be seen in the picture, Vue Storefront can use Magento 2 or a variety of CMSs as the back-end, and then uses its own engine as the frontend. Interestingly, the application also uses an Elasticsearch data storage and indexer in order to index content and retrieve it in a faster way, and uses workers to communicate the front-end with the back-end.

4 The Setup

In order to test the application, the authors recreated the same environment in a server under their control. They took a free open-source template for the Vue storefront application and recreated the vulnerable application found during the pentest. The sever was using a Vue Store application which had a search input where the parameter q was vulnerable to a XSS vulnerability (Fig. 2).

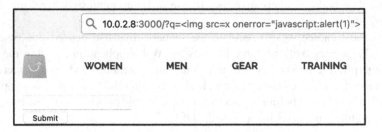

Fig. 2. Search box vulnerable to a XSS injection.

When injected, the browser would produce a reflected XSS vulnerability, as the input was provided as a get parameter and was injected directly to the browser after being processed and returned by the server. The request as can be seen in the server is the following (Fig. 3):

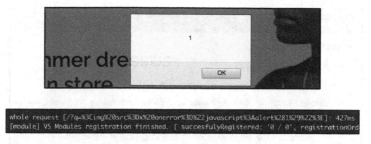

Fig. 3. Execution of the XSS vulnerability and Request as seen in the server.

As can be seen, the q parameter is injected with the beforementioned payload, which inserts an alert(1) popup using javascript code. The interesting part is analysing what Qualys and other web vulnerability scanners do when they find a similar scenario.

Once having the application recreated in a testing environment we prepared a Qualys scan and doublecheck that it was still missing the XSS vulnerability. Although Qualys did rank the webpage with a High Severity and when checking the found vulnerabilities one can see lots of reported XSS vulnerabilities (89) (Fig. 4):

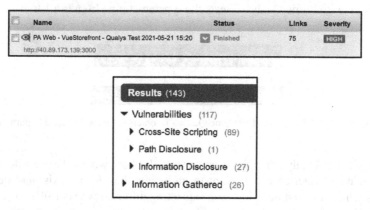

Fig. 4. Qualys scan results and List of vulnerabilities found by Qualys.

The truth is that all of them are false positives, as Qualys mistakes them as an Unencoded Characters vulnerability, which is a vulnerability which means that the input you have inputted to the application does appear in the response but does not produce a valid XSS injection. Surprisingly, Qualys still places them in the Cross-Site Scripting category. Once it had been proved that Qualys was missing the XSS vulnerability we gathered the logs from the vulnerable server and analyzed them in order to see what Qualys was doing (Fig. 5).

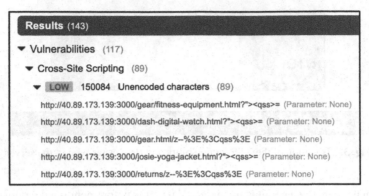

Fig. 5. Detail of the vulnerabilities found by Qualys.

5   Analysing the Logs

When first reviewing the logs it can be seen that Qualys starts analysing the main page at slash ('/'). And then it starts checking for files like crossdomain.xml, random.html files, and after parsing the pages he stars testing the parameters of the same page. In Fig. 6 you can see the first time Qualys detects the q parameter and sends a 1 to it.

```
whole request [/]: 529ms
```

```
whole request [/?q=1]: 455ms
```

Fig. 6. Start of the scan and First time Qualys interacts with the vulnerable parameter.

The next step Qualys does is to enumerate the files within the website, in order to do so it mixes queries which point to endpoints that do not exist and queries to endpoints which do exist but adding or requesting different types of files to enumerate the underlying page in the parameters of the request.

Although not common, during the scan of the application Qualys does find the vulnerable endpoint and tries to inject it in different ways (Fig. 7).

```
1   /?q=
2   /?q=%00%3Cscript%3E_q%3Drandom(X146984300Y1_1Z)%3C%2Fscript%3E
3   /?q=%22%20onEvent%3DX146984300Y1_1Z%20
4   /?q=%22'%3E%3Cqss%20a%3DX146984300Y1_1Z%3E
5   /?q='%20onEvent%3DX146984300Y1_1Z%20
6   /?q=1
```

Fig. 7. Payloads sent to the vulnerable endpoint.

The most interesting thing that can be found is that Qualys does consume the '?q=' endpoint 1873 times in a 7 h scan, but still does not send a valid injection payload and hence it does not find the vulnerability. With this information we started analysing the page's source code to see why Qualys was not finding the vulnerability.

There are two reasons why Qualys might have missed the XSS vulnerability. Probably it is not one of the two but a combination of both. The first reason is that from the analysis of the logs Qualys produced we can confirm that Qualys did not try any payload which was indeed valid for the injectable parameter. It is hard to believe that it just "missed it" or that it does not have any valid payload in its dictionary, so probably the reality is that with its custom intelligence, Qualys was not able to detect the reflection of the payload, and hence stopped trying to inject in that specific parameter.

The second reason is that Vue storefront uses a window backbone dispatcher which is basically in charge of receiving the information from the server and rendering it in the front-end. The window dispatcher looks as follow (Fig. 8):

```
1  <script>
2  window.__INITIAL_STATE__={version:"",__DEMO_MODE__:!1,config:{server:{host:"0.
   0.0.0",port:3e3,protocol:"http",api:"api-search-query",devServiceWorker:!1,
   useHtmlMinifier:!0,htmlMinifierOptions:{minifyJS:!0,minifyCSS:!0},
   useOutputCacheTagging:!1,useOutputCache:!1,outputCacheDefaultTtl:86400,
   availableCacheTags:["attribute","C","category","checkout","compare","error",
   "home","my-account","P","page-not-found","product","taxrule"],
   invalidateCacheKey:"aeSu7aip",invalidateCacheForwarding:!1,
```

Fig. 8. Web dispatcher.

The window dispatcher requests a snapshot of the webpage at the initial request, and based on the user's behaviour and using Javascript, it changes the view of the user only using the client and without the need to request anything from the server.

In our opinion, Qualys just sees the initial response from the server, and as the server is using a dispatcher to render the webpage, and does not initially inject received payloads directly into the HTML code, Qualys does not see the injection happening. Moreover, Qualys probably does not let Javascript from applications run in its testing sandbox, so as the dispatcher is never allowed to render the front page the injection does not actually happen for Qualys.

Moreover, this is totally aligned with the 89 Unencoded characters vulnerability that Qualys has reported. Each time it has tried to inject into the website, the website has returned a response which includes a window dispatcher which in turn includes the injected payload. This is the reason why Qualys sees its input is being reflected in the response, without it confirming a XSS.

It is important to note that this specific behaviour has not only been seen in the firstly analysed webpage, but has also happened in the past in other webpages which were also using dispatchers to render applications.

6 Additional Web Vulnerability Scanners

With the conclusions from the previous section, the question that comes to mind is if this is something which is common across vulnerability scanners or if perhaps is a behaviour that one can only observe in Qualys.

Thus, the test that follows is to run the scan with BurpSuite's Active Scan++ [5], a commercial solution from PortSwigger, and with OWASP's ZAP [6], which is advertised as the "most widely used web app scanner".

We started with BurpSuite, and launched a crawl, a passive scan and an active scan to the webpage. When launching the scan, even if it has not finished yet, we observe a similar behaviour than the one found in Qualys. In the Issue Activity from BurpSuite this can be seen as follows (Figs. 9, 10 and 11):

#	Task	Time	Action	Issue type	Host
87	10	13:51:52 24 May 2021	Issue found	Cross-site scripting (DOM-based)	http://10.0.2.8:3000
86	10	13:51:52 24 May 2021	Issue found	Cross-site scripting (DOM-based)	http://10.0.2.8:3000
85	10	13:51:52 24 May 2021	Issue found	Cross-site scripting (DOM-based)	http://10.0.2.8:3000
84	10	13:51:52 24 May 2021	Issue found	Cross-site scripting (DOM-based)	http://10.0.2.8:3000
83	10	13:51:52 24 May 2021	Issue found	Cross-site scripting (DOM-based)	http://10.0.2.8:3000
82	10	13:51:52 24 May 2021	Issue found	Cross-site scripting (DOM-based)	http://10.0.2.8:3000
81	10	13:51:52 24 May 2021	Issue found	Cross-site scripting (DOM-based)	http://10.0.2.8:3000
80	10	13:51:51 24 May 2021	Issue found	Cross-site scripting (DOM-based)	http://10.0.2.8:3000
79	10	13:51:51 24 May 2021	Issue found	Cross-site scripting (DOM-based)	http://10.0.2.8:3000
78	10	13:51:51 24 May 2021	Issue found	Cross-site scripting (DOM-based)	http://10.0.2.8:3000
77	10	13:51:51 24 May 2021	Issue found	Cross-site scripting (DOM-based)	http://10.0.2.8:3000
76	10	13:51:51 24 May 2021	Issue found	Cross-site scripting (DOM-based)	http://10.0.2.8:3000
75	10	13:51:51 24 May 2021	Issue found	Cross-site scripting (DOM-based)	http://10.0.2.8:3000
74	10	13:51:51 24 May 2021	Issue found	Cross-site scripting (DOM-based)	http://10.0.2.8:3000
73	10	13:51:51 24 May 2021	Issue found	Cross-site scripting (DOM-based)	http://10.0.2.8:3000
72	10	13:51:51 24 May 2021	Issue found	Cross-site scripting (DOM-based)	http://10.0.2.8:3000
71	10	13:51:51 24 May 2021	Issue found	Cross-site scripting (DOM-based)	http://10.0.2.8:3000
70	10	13:51:51 24 May 2021	Issue found	Cross-site scripting (DOM-based)	http://10.0.2.8:3000
69	10	13:51:51 24 May 2021	Issue found	Cross-site scripting (DOM-based)	http://10.0.2.8:3000

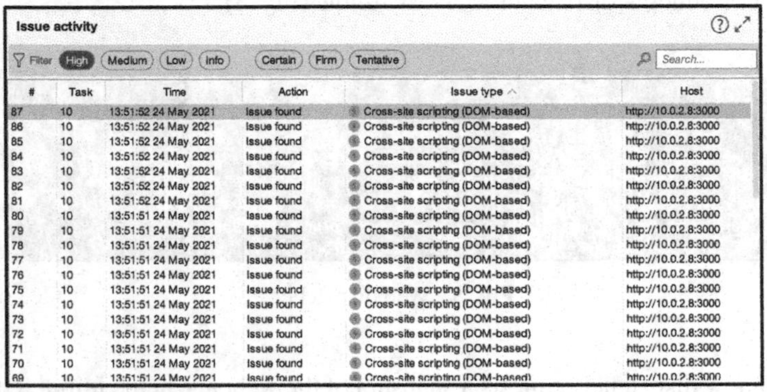

Fig. 9. False positive XSS vulnerabilities found by BurpSuite.

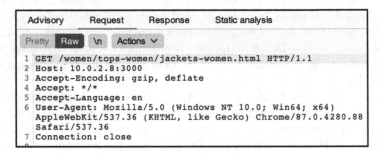

Fig. 10. Request of a false positive XSS vulnerability.

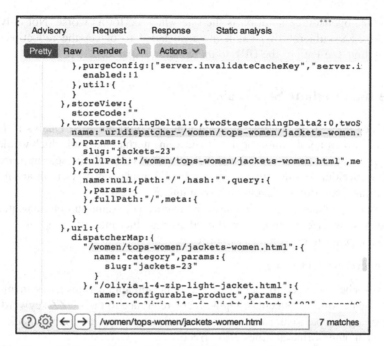

Fig. 11. Response that leads BurpSuite to think it was actually a confirmed vulnerability.

When reviewing the outcome of those vulnerabilities one can easily see they are false positives. As it was happening with Qualys, BurpSuite is mistakenly taking the reflection of the URL path in the window dispatcher as a Cross-site Scripting vulnerability.

As BurpSuite sees this behaviour it understands there are many ways to modify the DOM by reflecting whatever is given as the path and reports it as a XSS vulnerability. Nevertheless, what is actually happening is that the application is properly sanitizing whatever is injected in the path or parameters of the request and hence they all are false positives. Once the scan is finished, it is confirmed that BurpSuite does not find the parameter q to be vulnerable.

The last experiment is to rerun the scan using OWASP's ZAP (Fig. 12).

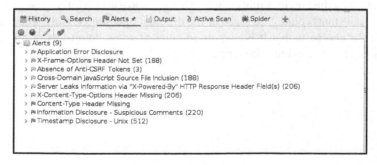

Fig. 12. OWASP's ZAP outcome.

Sadly, the opensource solution is the one which performs worse. Not only it has missed the XSS vulnerability, but it has also failed to detect the reflection that is happening from the Path of the URL to the window dispatcher.

7   The Intermediate Scan Layer

As explained in Sect. 1, once we realised that we could not trust Qualys to find the majority of XSS vulnerabilities, the need to have an intermediate tool which would cover the gap between the manual pentest and the automated vulnerability scan appeared. The approach we decided to follow was to leverage of different opensource tools and integrate them in a single solution to develop our own intermediate tool.

The list of opensource tools that has used to create the semi-automatic pentest suite can be seen below. We assume we will need adding other interesting opensource tools to the suite in order to continuously improve it.

1. Wfuzz – The Web Fuzzer [7]

   Wfuzz has been created to facilitate the task in web applications assessments and it is based on a simple concept: it replaces any reference to the FUZZ keyword by the value of a given payload. In the custom tool Wfuzz is used to double check that the findings of other vulnerabilities are correct.

2. Arjun – HTTP Parameter Discovery Suite [8]

   Arjun is a HTTP discovery tool which parses the response of an initial webpage and crawls it up to the depth that you define while extracting all the parameters that it finds.

3. XSStrike – Advanced XSS Detection Suite [9]

   XSStrike uses Arjun as a parameter finder and then injects different payloads (which you can define) in the parameters that it has found.

4. SQLMap - Automatic SQLInjection and database takeover [10]

   SQLMap is an opensource penetration testing tool that automates the process of detecting and exploiting SQL injection flaws and taking over of database servers.

Besides using the previous tools, it was also agreed to use the GoLang language when coding the suite that would glue together the different opensource tools. The reason for that particular choice is that it is way more efficient when doing lots of requests per second as can be seen in the following graph (Fig. 13):

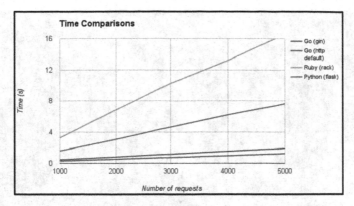

Fig. 13. Time Comparisons of requests between different languages.

As a high-level description, the tool starts using Arjun to crawl and extract parameters from a website, which are later on saved on a txt file. This file is available for the pentester to use in case he needs to test something in all the endpoints using a custom script and needs a dictionary of valid endpoints and parameters.

After the page has been crawled and the parameters have been extracted the next step is to launch first XSStrike to find parameters vulnerable to XSS injections and then to launch SQLMap in the same endpoints and parameters in order to try to find endpoints and parameters vulnerable to SQL injections.

Finally, based on the results from XSStrike and SQLMap, Wfuzz is used to double check that the findings are not false positives, if there is still some doubt the payload is left for the pentester to review. In Fig. 14 you can see a picture of how a scan to a vulnerable endpoint works and how it does find the vulnerable q parameter in the Vue Storefront application.

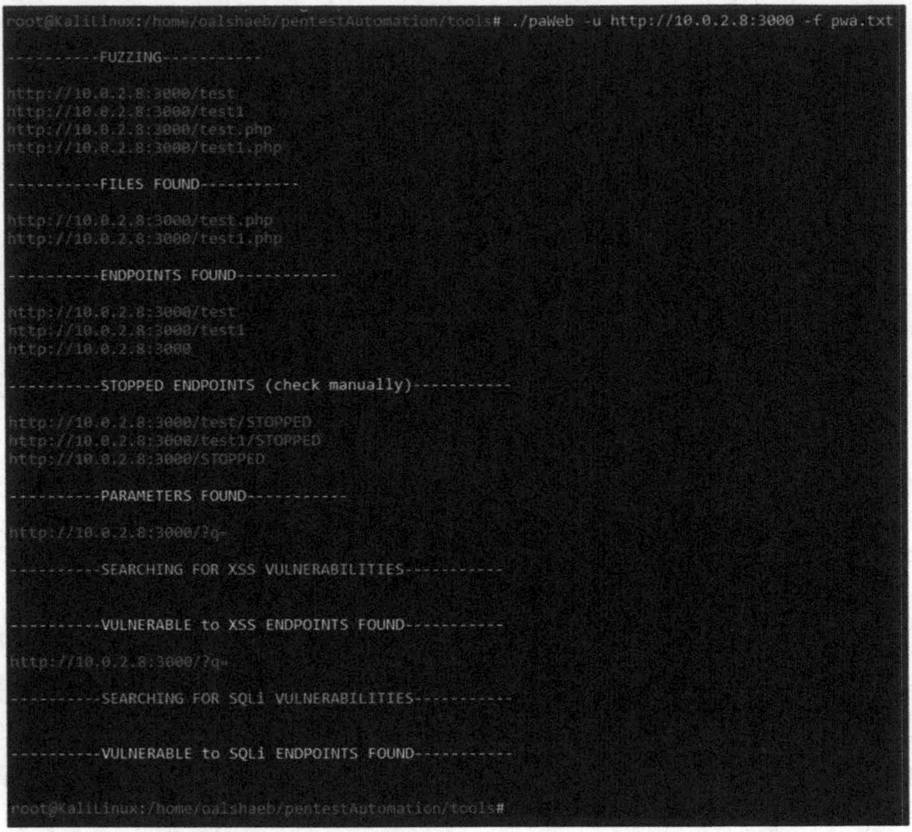

Fig. 14. Example of execution of the developed tool.

8 Conclusions

Penetration testing is rapidly changing. Not only there are new languages and technologies that force pentesters to continuously learn and improve, but also new platforms which need auditing, like IoTs and APIs, which until some years ago were not so widely used as today.

In this paper a problem that was found during a pentest has been depicted, dissected, and analysed in order to find the causes of its behaviour and how to solve it in the future.

After the analysis, it is fair to say that Qualys and other similar web scanners have difficulties when scanning applications that do not use the classic approach of Click -> Request -> Response, but rather when a single request can retrieve enough information for the webpage to continue hours or days without the need of additional requests.

In order to solve this situation, the approach which had more sense and that has been carried out in this research was to build a tool that would allow a pentester to define exactly what he wants to test, keeping a copy of the responses received during the testing in order to clearly differentiate between a false positive and a real vulnerability and also keeping a copy of all the endpoints and parameters tested in case he or she wants to repeat any test manually.

This approach has been proved to be useful when finding this type of vulnerabilities, as the tool that has been developed does detect the q parameter as a vulnerable one. As future work, we propose to enhance and expand the tool and build a process around it to use it in every vulnerability scan or penetration test done.

References

1. Qualys website. https://www.qualys.com/
2. Vulnerability Assessment Gartner Ranking. https://www.gartner.com/reviews/market/vulner ability-assessment
3. Harnessing Modern Web Architecture with Progressive Web Apps. https://mentormate.com/ blog/modern-web-application-architecture/
4. Vue Storefront Headless Ecommerce. https://www.vuestorefront.io/
5. PortSwigger Active Scan++ website. https://portswigger.net/bappstore/3123d5b5f25c412889 4d97ea1acc4976
6. Zed Attack Proxy (ZAP) website. https://www.zaproxy.org/
7. Wfuzz: The Web fuzzer Documentation. https://wfuzz.readthedocs.io/en/latest/
8. Arjunt: HTTP Parameter Discovery Suite Github Project. https://github.com/s0md3v/Arjun
9. XSStrike: Advanced XSS Detection Suite Github Project. https://github.com/s0md3v/XSS trike
10. SQLmap website. https://sqlmap.org/

Detection of Targeted Attacks Using Medium-Interaction Honeypot for Unmanned Aerial Vehicle

Abdul Majid Jamil[1][(✉)], Hassan Jalil Hadi[1], Sifan Li[1], Yue Cao[1],
Naveed Ahmed[2], Faisal Bashir Hussain[3], Chakkaphong Suthaputchakun[4],
and Xinyuan Wang[5]

[1] School of Cyber Science and Engineering, Wuhan University, Wuhan, China
{majidjamil,yue.cao}@whu.edu.cn
[2] Prince Sultan University, Riyadh, Saudi Arabia
nahmed@psu.edu.sa
[3] Bahria University, Islamabad, Pakistan
fbashir.buic@bahria.edu.pk
[4] Bangkok University, Bangkok, Thailand
chakkaphong.s@bu.ac.th
[5] Zhejiang Scientific Research Institute of Transport, Hangzhou, China

Abstract. Over the last two decades, there has been significant growth in the drone industry with the emergence of Unmanned Aerial Vehicles (UAVs). Despite their affordability, the lack of security measures in commercial UAVs has led to numerous threats and vulnerabilities. In addition, software, and hardware complexity in UAVs also trigger privacy and security issues as well as cause critical challenges for government, industry and academia. Meanwhile, malicious activities have increased, including stealing confidential data from UAVs and hijacking UAVs. These attacks are not only illegitimate but also appear to be increasing in frequency and sophistication. In addition, the current defence mechanisms for counterattacks are not sustainable for two reasons: they either demand strict firmware updates for all of the system's devices, or they demand the deployment of a variety of advanced hardware and software. This paper proposes a Medium Interaction Honeypot-Based Intrusion Detection System (MIHIDS) to protect UAVs. Our system assists in detecting active intruders in a specific range (radio frequency) and provides details of attacking technologies to exploit UAVs. Our system is a passive lightweight, signature-based MIHIDS that is simple to integrate into UAV without requiring changes in network configuration or replacement of current hardware or software. The performance assessment demonstrates that in a typical network situation, our proposed framework can identify MitM, Brute-force, and DE-authentication attacks with a maximum detection time of 60 s. Under normal network scenarios, a minimum True Positive Rate (TPR) and performance efficiency is 93% to 95% during a short-distance detector.

Keywords: Unmanned Aerial Vehicle · Medium Interaction Honeypot · Intrusion Detection System

© ICST Institute for Computer Sciences, Social Informatics and Telecommunications Engineering 2024
Published by Springer Nature Switzerland AG 2024. All Rights Reserved
S. Goel and P. R. Nunes de Souza (Eds.): ICDF2C 2023, LNICST 571, pp. 164–185, 2024.
https://doi.org/10.1007/978-3-031-56583-0_11

1   Introduction

Drones, also known as Unmanned Aerial Vehicles (UAVs), have become highly popular in recent years. UAVs are used for commercial and domestic purposes, including surveying agriculture, delivering packages, shooting pictures and films. Aside from that, UAVs are used for even mission-critical tasks, such as pharmaceutical distribution, health and safety monitoring [1,2]. However, these might involve data theft, mission disruption, or stealing and illegally using UAVs.

Attacks on UAVs are becoming more widespread as these devices are computer-controlled and have radio or wireless communication. A system that only serves as a target for attacks, reconnaissance, and compromise is known as a honeypot [3]. Typical uses of honeypots include early warning defence mechanisms, methods for investigating attackers and their approaches, and minimising a monitored network's attack surface.

In addition to the honeypot functions mentioned above, we contend that a UAV honeypot brings further benefits, by exploiting the specific characteristics of UAVs (especially the signal strength quality and the capability to move quickly through an area). Using the UAV's signal strength rather than maintaining visual contact with the target, a UAV attack scenario, in particular, enables the attacker to reap the benefits and control the UAV (e.g., by using a strong-signal antenna). Therefore, we claim that a UAV honeypot-based IDS is capable of detecting a UAV attack as long as (i) it transmits a signal that is stronger than UAVs themselves (done with a suitable antenna), and (ii) it is positioned in a desirable range (radio frequency).

High-interaction honeypots are real systems that highlight specific vulnerabilities and they are monitored closely. More specifically, this system creates nothing but a perception of vulnerability, encouraging adversaries to attack it. It may be low, medium, or high interaction, depending on how much interaction the attacker has with the honeypot. Since maintaining high-interaction honeypots is quite expensive, there is a chance that they could be compromised. Meanwhile, low- and medium-interaction honeypots are easier and simpler to monitor and configure because they emulate protocols. Figure 1 depicts a UAV honeypot overview.

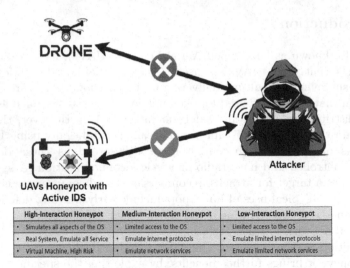

High-Interaction Honeypot	Medium-Interaction Honeypot	Low-Interaction Honeypot
• Simulates all aspects of the OS	• Limited access to the OS	• Limited access to the OS
• Real System, Emulate all Service	• Emulate internet protocols	• Emulate limited internet protocols
• Virtual Machine, High Risk	• Emulate network services	• Emulate limited network services

Fig. 1. UAV Honeypot Overview

This paper proposes a Medium Interaction Honeypot Intrusion Detection System (MIHIDS), a model to gather the most helpful information (attack methods) about the attacker. Our system can help identify active attackers in a specific range (radio frequency), and enlighten on attack methods to compromise UAVs. We evaluate system performance, and accuracy to demonstrate how the honeypot can respond to various realistic attack scenarios. Moreover, our system also detects and generates the logs of each action performed by attackers, and keeps a record of these logs in the MySQL DB for further analysis of these malicious activities. The main contribution of this paper are summarized as follows:

- Provide medium-interaction honeypot for UAV specified and tailored protocols (FTP, SSH, TELNET, and MAVLINK), record as well as analyze malicious activity and distract attackers while reducing the attack surface.
- Experimental analysis of attack traffic and creation of potential attack signatures for MitM, Brute force, and De-Authentication attacks.
- Develop a MIHIDS based on a behavioural rule specification by combining signature-based algorithms. It uses minimal memory, while maximizing detection accuracy by checking for observable behavioural anomalies. An attack event is identified by anomaly detection using a threshold-based approach, which is based on a network traffic profile of attack behaviour.

2   Related Work

Honeypot systems with value lying only in probes are attacked and compromised. Honeypots are of three types, low-interaction, medium-interaction and high-interaction, based on the interaction level they provide to the adversary.

Without real production value, any interaction or communication with the system is thought of as an attack. On the contrary, real systems like Virtual Machines (VM) lie in the class of high-interaction honeypots. High-interaction honeypot systems are keenly monitored and can exhibit specific vulnerabilities. However, these systems are expensive and the risk of being compromised is high. Conversely, low-interaction as well as medium-interaction systems, only emulate protocols. This system has become a priority compared to high-interaction systems for multiple factors [6]. The first factor is low cost and easy maintenance because they can provide detailed and explicit logging along with monitoring functionalities. The second factor is the ease with which these systems can be developed, contained, and secured.

Table 1. Evaluating the Capabilities of Available Honeypots

Reference	Simulated Service	MAVLINK	Level of Interaction	Resource Level	Role
HoneyCloud [16]	SSH,Telnet,HTTP,MySql	No	Physical/Virtual	High	Server
HosTaGe [7]	FTP, SSH, Telnet	No	Virtual	Medium	Server
Heralding [11]	FTP, SSH, Telnet	No	Virtual	Low	Server
Bluepot [10]	L2CAP BT, RFCOMM, OBEX	No	Virtual	Medium	Server
HoneyWRT [13]	Telnet	No	Virtual	Medium	Server
HoneyPy [12]	TCP,UDP	No	Virtual	Medium	Server
Cowrie [14]	SSH, Telnet	No	Virtual	Low	Server
Kojoney2 [15]	SSH	No	Virtual	low	Server

As listed in Table 1, numerous honeypots are capable of monitoring and simulating a variety of general-purpose protocols, including SSH, FTP, and Telnet [3–5,9]. Moreover, the investigation of honeypots in handling the MAVLink protocol for UAVs has not been adequate. Similarly, none of the honeypots can imitate extracted File System (FS) and record all unauthorized modifications of the UAV. Furthermore, most honeypots cannot be configured to impersonate other devices, since they are developed for a single set of use cases. Only a few honeypots have a portability feature to fit a UAV operation or are even directly attached to one [7]. A honeypot must be able to simulate UAV radio interfaces although none of them is designed to do so. Only Bluepot can simulate the rarely used Bluetooth radio [10]. Moreover, the classification of honeypots based on the level of interaction in the above table is the most flexible. Furthermore, the author states that game theory has been used in the past to model security scenarios but has not been applied to the problem of UAV network security [17]. The paper attempts to bridge this gap by proposing a game-theoretic framework for collaborative honeypot defence in UAV networks [18].

3   Proposed MIHIDS

The primary security technologies for UAVs are detection and defence. The system can identify significant attacks from time series using behaviour-based anomaly detection, which can detect attacks at an accurate and consistent stage, also supporting timely early warning. These systems work together to quickly implement the necessary security protections, reducing the probability of an attack.

3.1   Framework Overview

The infrastructure, security protection, application, and user interfaces layers are the four layers that build up the security framework, as depicted in Fig. 2.

The security framework is built on the bottom of the **Infrastructure Layer**. Its purpose is to provide various data and computational resources for different applications. It includes database management, activity logging, and a testbed environment. Databases are used to keep a record of logs and alerts. The testbed environment serves as the interface between the detection and active defence modules. Meanwhile, it is also utilized to carry out various computing operations.

The **Security Protection Layer** serves as the foundation of the security framework, and also performs functions for the defence and detection of all types of security threats. The active defence module is used to protect against attacks, while the detection module is used to identify any unusual intrusions into the system. The two sub-modules of the security layer are described in depth in Sects. 3:3.2 and 3.3.

The **Application Layer** offers different application services for each UAV function, including GPS, UAV flight controller, authentication APP and data collection. Information about users and data from UAVs is collected by using a data collector. The UAV flight controller is used to direct the movement and data transmission of the UAV. The authentication APP can be used for UAV-Server or UAV (client-honeypot) authentication. The GPS is a fundamental component of the UAV flight process, as it provides flight paths and allows the user to track the location of the UAV in real-time.

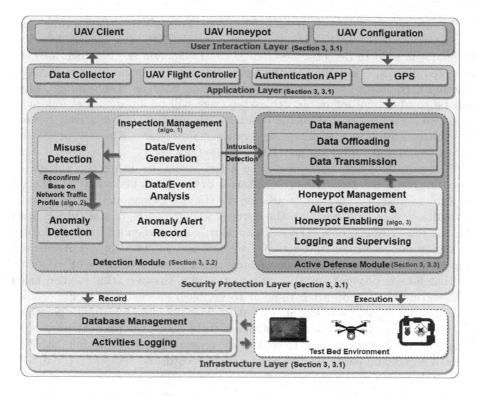

Fig. 2. MIHIDS Framework Overview

The **User Interaction Layer** provides an interactive interface for users that includes the UAV client, UAV honeypot, and UAV configuration.

3.2   Detection Module

Real-time analysis of network traffic is essential for identifying potential intrusions against UAVs while they are in flight. One effective approach is to deploy an intrusion detection system (IDS) that can detect a range of intrusion classes, including signal alteration, routing attacks, malware, and message forging attacks [19,20]. It's also important to develop anomaly detection frameworks that can identify unusual patterns of activity that could indicate malicious behavior. Furthermore, to provide additional protection against hostile actors, the use of honeypots and honeynets in combination with an IDS is recommended. In order to create intelligent devices, it's necessary to provide them with instructions and define rules that govern their behavior, as shown in Algorithm 1. In the case of UAVs, rules are stored in memory (database) and levels of rule acceptance are established. To minimize false-positive predictions, a new IDS has been proposed that is based on rules of behavior.

Misuse detection, detection management and anomaly detection technologies are mainly included in the detection module of MIHIDS. The misuse detection technique is used to detect cyber-attacks. The detection stage, which uses the collected data to compare with the threshold value or signature rule to judge whether it conforms to the rules. If the detection result is "conforming", there will be no abnormal intrusion; otherwise, there will be an abnormal intrusion, as shown in Algorithm 2. This method has high accuracy and relatively mature technology, which is convenient for system maintenance. However, it is very difficult to update and maintain the signature database.

Anomaly detection determines the attack event by using the rule-based matching method based on the rule database of the attack behaviour. It is necessary to establish the "network traffic profile (Device Behaviour)" of the subject normal activities, and compare the current activity status of the subject with the "network traffic profile (Device Behaviour)". Also, when the subject violates its signature-based rules that activity is considered an "invasion". This method can detect intrusions that have never occurred or the type of abuse of authority, and has little dependence on the operating system. However, this method has a high alarm rate. Besides, it is difficult to establish an "network traffic profile" and design a signature-based algorithm. It does not detect normal operations as "intrusion" or ignore the real "intrusion" behaviour. The primary purpose of **Inspection Management** is to control the generating, analyzing, and handling of data events and alerts related to suspicious records.

3.2.1   Signature Development for Intrusion Traffic: By developing signatures of intrusion traffic and utilizing analytics based on an empirical analysis of intrusion and normal traffic, we can efficiently detect various intrusion signatures using a threshold-based technique, which enables us to identify Brute-Force, MitM, and De-Authentication attacks based on network traffic characteristics. Furthermore, we conduct a continuous monitoring of the legitimate client UAV and its specific ports for a probe period of 5 min, followed by the implementation of 4 phases of Brute-Force, MitM, and DE-Authentication attacks lasting for 60–100 seconds.

3.2.1.1 Concurrent Probe or Beacon Response Traffic: Figure 3 describes a network attack record with the concurrent probe or beacon responses on two separate channels with the same BSSID and SSID. Moreover, benign traffic scenarios were examined, but could no concurrent probe response traffic found on different channels in the same frequency range with the same BSSID and SSID.

On the other hand, when they use dual-band frequencies, there may be concurrent beacons if the Server (GCS) broadcasts the same SSID. Since the channels utilised in the 2.4 GHz and 5 GHz bands are different, such concurrent beacons can be clearly differentiated as benign traffic.

In the event of a sudden detection of a large volume of the concurrent probe or beacon response traffic on two different channels with similar BSSID and SSID, the UAV GCS Server can generate traffic analysis warnings, as it may

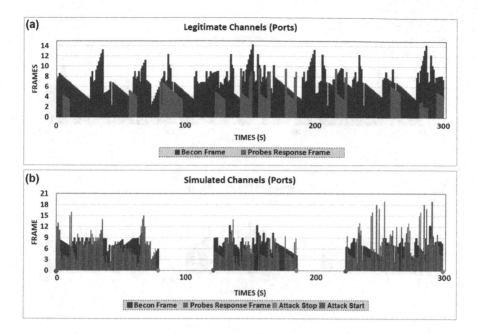

Fig. 3. Network intrusion trace during probe and beacon responses (a) legitimate channel (b) simulated channel

indicate the start of an intrusion. To efficiently detect concurrent probe or beacon response traffic that coincides with attacks, a threshold (TH1) of the beacon or probe response frame is set to 1, allowing for rapid identification during a probe interval. Additionally, the presence of intrusion is validated by examining concurrent traffic in the UAV network.

3.2.1.2 Concurrent Connection Traffic: A network attack trace is shown in Fig. 4 with two channels carrying concurrent authentication frames on the same SSID and BSSID.

A network attack trace is shown in Fig. 5 with simultaneous association requests and response frames originating on 2 different channels with similar BSSID and SSID.

Figures 4 and 5. depict the trace of a network attack, along with concurrent frames on two different channels with identical BSSID and SSID. From these observations, it has been confirmed that concurrent connection traffic can be utilized as an attack signature for the identification of MitM, Brute-force, and DE-Authentication intrusions in a UAV client. When a UAV client is targeted by one of these attacks, two concurrent association frames (request and response) and two concurrent authentication frames (request and response) are captured on both channels, all with similar BSSID and SSID. This is due to the transfer of association and authentication frames between real and simulated channels (ports) by the attacker. To ensure swift detection of concurrent connection traffic containing a Brute-force, MitM, or DE-Authentication intrusion, the threshold (TH2) for association and authentication frames has been set to 1 frame. Setting

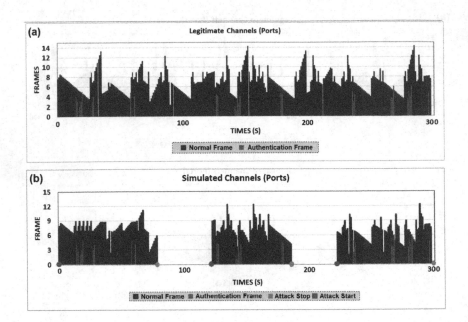

Fig. 4. Network intrusion trace during authentication responses (a) legitimate channel (b) simulated channel

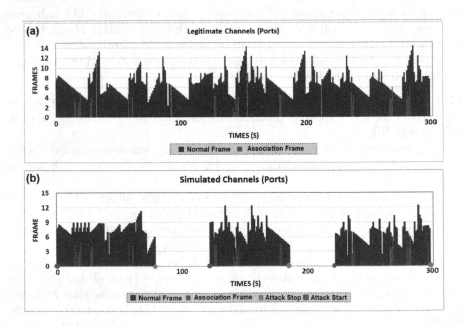

Fig. 5. Network intrusion trace during association responses (a) legitimate channel (b) simulated channel

the threshold value for association and authentication frames to 1 helps to detect and respond quickly to brute-force, MitM, or DE-Authentication intrusions. This is because these attacks are typically automated and fast-paced, with multiple frames being sent in quick succession. A threshold value of 1 helps catch the attack as soon as it starts while minimizing false positives.

Several intrusion signatures are compiled in Table 2 to help identify MitM, Brute-force, and DE-Authentication attempts during a probe interval.

Algorithm 1: Traffic analysis while establishing simultaneous connections. The GCS (UAV-Server) and a specific UAV-Client are monitored in real-time by this method as they establish a connection. This algorithm monitors synchronous communication for association and authentication. Additionally, this algorithm also detects traffic using the source and destination MAC address of the device running in parallel.

Table 2. Several Intrusion Signatures

Intrusion Signature	Statistic Used	Threshold
Concurrent Beacon Traffic	No. of the probe or beacon response	TH1 $\geq$1
Concurrent Connection Traffic	No. of Authentication Frames	TH2 $\geq$1
Concurrent Connection Traffic	No. of Association Frames	TH3 $\geq$1

Algorithm 1: Concurrent UAV Traffic Analysis

Input: UAV Traffic
Output: Number of synchronous frames (AUTHCC and AUTHRC) or (ASSOCC and
     ASSORC), GCS-MAC = MAC ID of the GCS, C-CHANNEL = Current
     channel(port) of the GCS
while *probe-interval* **do**
    Extract SMAC, DMAC, and Channel of the frames;
    if *frame[Dot11].type == 0 and frame[Dot11].subtype == 11* **then**
        while *UAV-Client-MAC in device database* **do**
            if *(smac == GCS-MAC and dmac == UAV-Client-MAC) or (smac ==*
            UAV-Client-MAC and dmac GCS-MAC) and channel == C-CHANNEL
            then
                Count authentication-current-channel(AUTHCC);
            if *(smac == GCS-MAC and dmac == UAV-Client-MAC) or (smac ==*
            UAV-Client-MAC and dmac GCS-MAC) and channel != C-CHANNEL
            then
                Count authentication-rouge-channel(AUTHRC);

    if *frame[Dot11].type == 0 and frame[Dot11].subtype == 1* **then**
        while *UAV-Client-MAC in device database* **do**
            if *(smac == GCS-MAC and dmac == UAV-Client-MAC) or (smac ==*
            UAV-Client-MAC and dmac GCS-MAC) and channel == C-CHANNEL
            then
                Count association-current-channel(ASSOCC);
            if *(smac == GCS-MAC and dmac == UAV-Client-MAC) or (smac ==*
            UAV-Client-MAC and dmac GCS-MAC) and channel != C-CHANNEL
            then
                Count association-rouge-channel(ASSORC);

Algorithm 2: Brute-force, MitM, DE-Authentication attack traffic analyzer: Based on threshold values, this algorithm determines the status of the attack traffic at the completion of each probe interval.

Algorithm 2: Intrusion Traffic Collator

Input: Output of Algorithms 1
Output: Status of Intrusion Traffic
if *(Intrusion-Traffic = True)* **then**
 if *(AUTHCC ≥ TH1 and AUTHRC ≥ TH1 or AOSSCC ≥ TH2 and ASSORC ≥ TH2)* **then**
  CON-Brute-force-Intrusion = True;
 if *(AUTHCC ≥ TH2 and AUTHRC ≥ TH2 or AOSSCC ≥ TH1 and ASSORC ≥ TH1)* **then**
  CON-MitM-Intrusion = True;
 if *(AUTHCC ≥ TH3 and AUTHRC ≥ TH2 or AOSSCC ≥ TH3 and ASSORC ≥ TH1)* **then**
  CON-Credential-Reuse-Intrusion = True;
 if *(CON-Brute-force-Intrusion = True) or (CON-MitM-Intrusion = True) or (CON-Credential-Reuse-Intrusion = True)* **then**
  Intrusion-Traffic = True;
 else
  Intrusion-Traffic = False;

3.3 Active Defence Module

There are mainly two parts of active defence in the MIHIDS security framework including honeypot management and data management. This module uses system-generated defence mechanisms (like control, evasion, deception and detection, etc.) to reach against cyber-attacks. Active defence of decoy technology (Honeypot technology) was primarily studied. The technology is efficient for protecting system security as it deploys vulnerable network services or hosts as bait for deceiving attackers. The data diversion phase of **Data Management**, merges with numerous network protection technologies for the coordination of data collected by the system in the collection, analysis, distribution, firewall and transmission process to make sure safe transmission of data.

Additionally, **Honeypot Management** consists of creation monitoring and logging. It gives administrators a system parameter for managing and configuring user interfaces. In the creation phase, a honeypot is created based on the characteristics of data received from the analysis phase of data management. All events happening in the system are recorded daily with the help of logging and monitoring. The intrusion and detection operations help the system administrator to check the reason of error as well as traces left by attackers. The user identity is authenticated by the authentication APP of the MIHIDS when there is no attack. In this process, numerous operators have data information cooperate for the authentication of user identity. In case of an attack, abnormal behaviour or intrusion is detected by the detection module and the alarm is generated simultaneously, as shown in Algorithm 3. Active defence sets Honeypot for capturing attack behaviour and planning protection measures accordingly.

Algorithm 3: Alert Generation based on the status of attack traffic provided by algorithm 2 predicts the presence of Brute-force, MitM, and DE-Authentication intrusion.

Algorithm 3: Alert Generation

Input: Output of Algorithm 2
Output: Alert Generation and Honeypot Activation
if *(Intrusion-Traffic = False)* **then**
  └ LOG as "No Intrusion Found"
if *(Intrusion-Traffic = True)* **then**
    if *(CON-Brute-force-Intrusion = True and Intrusion-Traffic = True)* **then**
      Alert Generate;
      └ LOG as "Bruteforce"
    if *(CON-MitM-Intrusion = True and Intrusion-Traffic = True)* **then**
      Alert Generate;
      └ LOG as "MitM"
    if *(CON-Credential-Reuse-Intrusion = True and Intrusion-Traffic = True)* **then**
      Alert Generate;
      └ LOG as "Credential-Reuse"
else
    if *(CON-Brute-force-Intrusion = False or CON-MitM-Intrusion = False or CON-Credential-Reuse-Intrusion = False) and Intrusion-Traffic = True)* **then**
      Alert Generation;
      LOG as "Bait Session"

---

4 Deployment

In order to have a real attack model, the implementation is done with a variation of Honeypot Server, Honeypot UAV, Client UAV, and Attacker Machine. The Ubuntu 18.04 virtual machine was used as a testbed. The implementation steps of framework are as follows:

- **Step 1:** Ubuntu VM is used for the deployment and configuration of the MIHIDS server.
- **Step 2:** When the Honeypot server is successfully deployed and configured, prerequisite configurations, such as database installation and SSL certificate generation, are carried out to securely access the Honeypot server dashboard.
- **Step 3:** When the configuration is completed, the MIHIDS server generates a secure, and unique link to establish a connection with the client UAV and honeypot UAV.
- **Step 4:** After that, the client UAV and honeypot UAV are configured on two separate Ubuntu VMs and connected to each other using a unique link generated by the MIHIDS server, thereby establishing a connection between the two VMs.

Figure 6 shows the deployment and working of the proposed system. The workflow of the system is as follows: (1) The server is started successfully, (2) The server finds the already connected devices, (3) If the devices (Client UAV and Honeypot UAV) are not found, it will generate a unique link, (4) The UAV

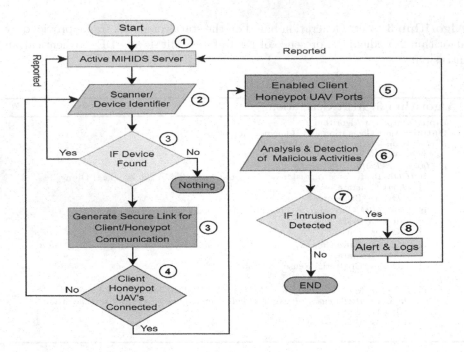

Fig. 6. WorkFlow Diagram

client and UAV honeypot are connected by using the link and reporting to the server, (5) Both devices are configured after connection with the server, (6) The UAV honeypot is activated automatically when the UAV client reports intrusion to the server, (7) The server analyzes the reported traffic, and (8) The server generates logs and alerts against intrusion traffic on the server GUI.

For the connection among UAV, honeypot UAV and honeypot server, we use the WiFi dongle to give the concept of a real-world scenario. When our testbed is configured, we use the Kali Linux VM as an attacker and generate the attack on the client UAV. The honeypot UAV detects the attacks using the IDS set up in our system. Next, the Honeypot server marks this attack as a bait session, activates the honeypot, and transfers all traffic to the Honeypot UAV. Then, all activities are recorded by generating the logs on the honeypot server for further investigation and analysis. Figure 7. is shown the flow of testbed as follows: (1) The Server is run successfully, (2) The UAV client is activated by using the link and reporting to the server, (3) The attacker performs an attack on the UAV client, (4) The UAV honeypot is activated automatically when the UAV client reports intrusion to the server, (5) The server analyzes of the reported traffic, (6) The server generates logs against intrusion traffic on Server GUI.

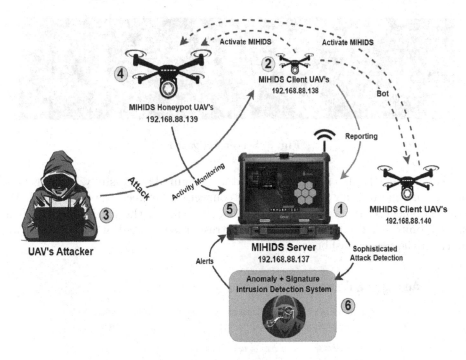

Fig. 7. Testbed Flow Diagram

5 Implementation Result and Analysis

MIHIDS is comprised of several key components, including the MIHIDS Server, MIHIDS Honeypot UAV, MIHIDS Client UAV, Attacker Model, Detection of Attacks, and Alert Generation, Real-Time Monitoring and Attacks Classification.

5.1 MIHIDS Server

The first step is to install the prerequisite libraries: Python 2.7, Flask library, SSL library, and MySQL DB for configuration. The MIHIDS server set-up is installed after the required libraries was installed. After the installation and configuration were completed, the MIHIDS server is activated by executing the script. The server is successfully running at IP address 192.168.88.137 on port 5000. After that, by adding an SSL certificate for the secure server dashboard, the server will generate a unique encrypted password to access the dashboard, as shown in Fig. 8.

```
IP or hostname of server: 192.168.88.137
2022-08-24 00:33:54,691 (root) Cleaned 0 pending sessions on startup
2022-08-24 00:33:55,312 (MIHIDS.server.webapp.app) Created default admin account for the MIHIDS server
*******************************************************************
Password for the admin account is: cfrdambxpjnqgo
*******************************************************************
2022-08-24 00:33:55,312 (root) (MIHIDS.server.server) Starting server listening on port 5000
2022-08-24 00:33:55,313 (root) (MIHIDS.server.server) Server started.
```

Fig. 8. Server Activated

When the MIHIDS server dashboard is configured successfully, it will generate the unique link for establishing the connection between the honeypot UAV and the client UAV, as shown in Fig. 9. Furthermore, the MIHIDS server will start monitoring the client UAV. If an intrusion is detected, it will generate an alert on the server dashboard.

Adding new drone.

The following configuration link will be active for the next 2 minutes. The link needs to be passed as the '--config' parameter to MIHIDS on the machines that you want to act as drones. The link can be used to add several drones to the system.

```
https://192.168.88.137:5000/ws/drone/add/37866ccd-84f9-4c38-8713-369697c4488f
```

Fig. 9. Server Generates a Unique Link

5.2   MIHIDS Client UAV

The second step is to set up the MIHIDS client on the Ubuntu VM. When the configuration and installation was completed, the client UAV establishes a connection with the server using the unique link generated by the MIHIDS server. When the connection is established, the client UAV (IP address 192.168.88.138) is added to the MIHIDS server for monitoring the client UAV network traffic. After that, the client UAV forwards all traffic to the MIHIDS server to monitor UAV intrusions and attacks. Figure 10 shows that the client UAV is configured, and ready for listing network traffic on the specified configured port.

```
2022-08-24 03:29:11,190 (root) (MIHIDS.drones.drones) Waiting for detailed configuration from MIHIDS server.
2022-08-24 03:29:11,401 (root) (MIHIDS.drones.drones) Connected to outgoing socket (tcp://192.168.88.137:5712).
2022-08-24 03:29:11,505 (root) (MIHIDS.drones.drones) Connected to incomming socket (tcp://192.168.88.137:5713).
2022-08-24 03:29:13,712 (root) (MIHIDS.drones.drones) Drone has not been configured, awaiting configuration from MIHIDS server
2022-08-24 03:29:44,462 (root) (MIHIDS.drones.drones) Drone configured and running. (5)
2022-08-24 03:29:44,462 (MIHIDS.drones.client.client) Starting client.
2022-08-24 03:29:44,565 (MIHIDS.drones.client.client) All clients stopped
2022-08-24 03:29:46,569 (root) (MIHIDS.drones.honeypot) Drone configured and running. (5)
2022-08-24 03:29:46,571 (MIHIDS.drones.client.client) Starting client.
2022-08-24 03:29:46,572 (MIHIDS.drones.client.client) Adding ssh bait
2022-08-24 03:29:46,572 (MIHIDS.drones.client.client) Adding http bait
2022-08-24 03:29:46,573 (MIHIDS.drones.client.client) Adding telnet bait
2022-08-24 03:29:46,573 (MIHIDS.drones.client.client) Adding ftp bait
2022-08-24 03:29:46,573 (MIHIDS.drones.client.client) Adding vnc bait
```

Fig. 10. Client UAV Started

5.3   MIHIDS Honeypot UAV

The third step is to set up the MIHIDS honeypot on the Ubuntu VM. When the configuration and installation is completed, the honeypot UAV establishes a connection with the server using the unique link generated by the MIHIDS server. When the connection is established, honeypot configure the required ports (HTTP, MAVLINK, SSH, TELNET, VNC, and FTP). The SSL certificate is added to the MIHIDS honeypot UAV (IP address 192.168.88.139). After that, they can start recording the attacker's activities and lure the attacker. Figure 11 shows that the honeypot UAV is configured, and ready for listing network traffic on the specified configured port.

```
2022-08-24 02:46:24,798 (root) (MIHIDS.drones.honeypot) Drone configured and running. (4)
2022-08-24 02:46:24,800 (root) (MIHIDS.drones.honeypot.honeypot) Started Mavlink capability listening on port 14550
2022-08-24 02:46:24,800 (root) (MIHIDS.drones.honeypot.honeypot) Started SSH capability listening on port 22
2022-08-24 02:46:24,801 (root) (MIHIDS.drones.honeypot.honeypot) Started Http capability listening on port 80
2022-08-24 02:46:24,801 (root) (MIHIDS.drones.honeypot.honeypot) Started Telnet capability listening on port 23
2022-08-24 02:46:24,802 (root) (MIHIDS.drones.honeypot.honeypot) Started ftp capability listening on port 21
2022-08-24 02:46:24,802 (root) (MIHIDS.drones.honeypot.honeypot) Started Vnc capability listening on port 5900
2022-08-24 02:46:24,802 (root) (MIHIDS.drones.honeypot) Honeypot running.
```

Fig. 11. Honeypot Start Listening

5.4   Attacker Model

The Kali Linux VM is used as the attacker model, and the tools used for the attacks are Hydra and Aircrack-ng. Using Kali Linux's Hydra tool, users can brute-force usernames and passwords for various services, including FTP, SSH, TELNET, and MS-SQL. Figure 12 shows that the attacker performed the attack on UAV.

```
┌──(kali㉿kali)-[~]
└─$ hydra -l ubuntu -p ubuntu telnet://192.168.88.138
Hydra v9.1 (c) 2020 by van Hauser/THC & David Maciejak - Please do not use in military
(this is non-binding, these *** ignore laws and ethics anyway).

Hydra (https://github.com/vanhauser-thc/thc-hydra) starting at 2022-08-24 06:56:10
[WARNING] telnet is by its nature unreliable to analyze, if possible better choose FTP,
[WARNING] Restorefile (you have 10 seconds to abort ... (use option -I to skip waiting))
./hydra.restore
[DATA] max 1 task per 1 server, overall 1 task, 1 login try (l:1/p:1), ~1 try per task
[DATA] attacking telnet://192.168.88.138:23/
[23][telnet] host: 192.168.88.138   login: ubuntu   password: ubuntu
1 of 1 target successfully completed, 1 valid password found
Hydra (https://github.com/vanhauser-thc/thc-hydra) finished at 2022-08-24 06:56:37
```

Fig. 12. Aircrack-ng Launch DE-Authentication Attack

Aircrack-ng is used for DE-Authentication attacks. DE-Authentication attacks are a kind of DoS attack that targets communication between a client

UAV and a MIHIDS server. This attack sends disassociated packets to one or more client UAVs currently connected to the access points. Figure 13 shows that the attacker performed the DE-Authentication attack on UAVs.

```
root@kali:~# aireplay-ng --deauth 0 -c 98:5F:D3:4A:B1:31 -a C4:E9:84:3F:26:04
wlan0mon
21:36:31  Waiting for beacon frame (BSSID: C4:E9:84:3F:26:04) on channel 1
21:36:31  Sending 64 directed DeAuth. STMAC: [98:5F:D3:4A:B1:31] [ 1|51 ACKs]
21:36:32  Sending 64 directed DeAuth. STMAC: [98:5F:D3:4A:B1:31] [ 0|52 ACKs]
21:36:32  Sending 64 directed DeAuth. STMAC: [98:5F:D3:4A:B1:31] [ 0|47 ACKs]
21:36:33  Sending 64 directed DeAuth. STMAC: [98:5F:D3:4A:B1:31] [20|49 ACKs]
21:36:33  Sending 64 directed DeAuth. STMAC: [98:5F:D3:4A:B1:31] [24|48 ACKs]
21:36:34  Sending 64 directed DeAuth. STMAC: [98:5F:D3:4A:B1:31] [ 1|52 ACKs]
21:36:34  Sending 64 directed DeAuth. STMAC: [98:5F:D3:4A:B1:31] [ 0|53 ACKs]
21:36:35  Sending 64 directed DeAuth. STMAC: [98:5F:D3:4A:B1:31] [ 1|53 ACKs]
21:36:36  Sending 64 directed DeAuth. STMAC: [98:5F:D3:4A:B1:31] [ 6|48 ACKs]
```

Fig. 13. Aircrack-ng Launch DE-Authentication Attack

5.5   Detection of Attacks

Attacks are detected by IDS and displayed on the MIHIDS server dashboard. Attacks were detected on various enabled ports (HTTP, MAVLINK, SSH, TELNET, VNC, and FTP). There are 3 columns in the attacks recorded table. (i) Capability indicates the ports exploited during attacks, (ii) Attacks indicates the number of attacks detected, and (iii) % indicates the percentage of attacks detected on enabled ports. The results of attack detection shown below are obtained in Fig. 14.

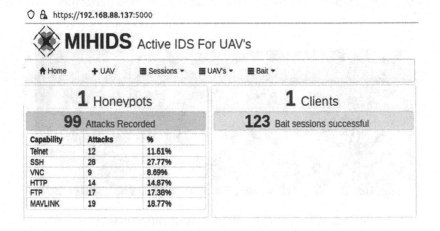

Fig. 14. Server Detect the Attacks

5.6   Alert Generation, Real-Time Monitoring and Attacks Classification

The MIHIDS server generates several distinct attack alerts, including brute force, credential reuse, and MitM attacks on various ports. Our proposed solution also includes a real-time monitoring system and the classification of attacks. The MIHIDS server is used to analyze the attack logs, and monitor the traffic with the help of real-time monitoring on the GUI. Figure 15 depicts the overall logs of real-time monitoring and attack classification. (i) Protocol denotes the exploited protocol during attacks, (ii) Source IP denotes the IP address of the compromised UAV client, (iii) Drone denotes which UAV detected the attacks, and (iv) Classification denotes the types of attacks carried out.

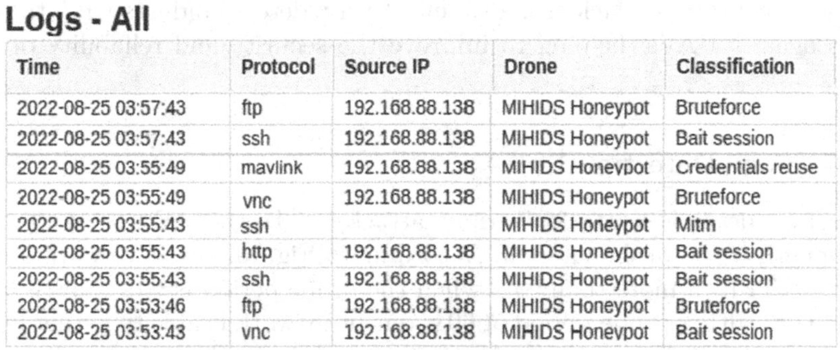

Logs - All

Time	Protocol	Source IP	Drone	Classification
2022-08-25 03:57:43	ftp	192.168.88.138	MIHIDS Honeypot	Bruteforce
2022-08-25 03:57:43	ssh	192.168.88.138	MIHIDS Honeypot	Bait session
2022-08-25 03:55:49	mavlink	192.168.88.138	MIHIDS Honeypot	Credentials reuse
2022-08-25 03:55:49	vnc	192.168.88.138	MIHIDS Honeypot	Bruteforce
2022-08-25 03:55:43	ssh		MIHIDS Honeypot	Mitm
2022-08-25 03:55:43	http	192.168.88.138	MIHIDS Honeypot	Bait session
2022-08-25 03:55:43	ssh	192.168.88.138	MIHIDS Honeypot	Bait session
2022-08-25 03:53:46	ftp	192.168.88.138	MIHIDS Honeypot	Bruteforce
2022-08-25 03:53:43	vnc	192.168.88.138	MIHIDS Honeypot	Bait session

Fig. 15. Real Time Logs and Attacks Classification

6   Results, Discussion and Performance Analysis

The MIHIDS is made to be set up close to real UAV locations and potential attackers. Therefore, it is not required to handle honeypots operating on a large internet scale, but only for attackers within physical or wireless range. We still strive for high efficiency within a low power consumption to run the MIHIDS on low-power or even battery-powered devices (e.g., our system uses limited resources to run on the real device). The ultimate goal is to use real UAVs to carry the MIHIDS or to integrate the MIHIDS into a flight controller for a UAV. To determine this, we measure the CPU usage on an Ubuntu 18.04 system with 2GB of RAM. After successful deployment and implementation, the system is tested to evaluate its performance. Four significant factors were used for the performance analysis of our system. When an attack occurs, the alert is generated, and each prediction outcome of our framework has been classed as a true positive (TP); a true negative (TN), when there is no attack and no alert is generated; a false positive (FP), occurs when an attack is not detected but the alert is generated; a false negative (FN), occurs when there is no attack but no alarm is generated. These factors can be used for finding statistical parameters like accuracy. The accuracy of a model is the number of correct predictions made by the model, and correct predictions indicate higher accuracy. The following equation can be used to calculate accuracy:

$$Accuracy = \frac{Correct\ Predication}{Total\ Cases} * 100 \qquad (1)$$

$$Accuracy = \frac{TP + TN}{TP + TN + FP + FN} * 100 \qquad (2)$$

In our case;

$$Accuracy = \frac{Total\ Attacks\ Detected}{Total\ Attacks\ Performed} * 100 \qquad (3)$$

In general, a UAV honeypot-based IDS with high attack detection efficiency and alert generation efficiency, can effectively detect and respond to cyber attacks against UAVs, helping to improve the security and reliability of these systems.

6.1   Average Detection Rate

The average detection rate for various attacks is shown in Fig. 16 with regard to the length of the probe interval. According to Fig. 16, our framework displays an average TPR of more than 93% when the probe period is 60 s. This is due to the fact that with a probe period of 60 s, our framework is able to gather enough attack frames, or more attack data with the use of several probe intervals, to possibly differentiate between various MitM, Brute-force, and DE-Authentication attacks and their variations. This shows that our algorithm performs more effectively the observation period is more prolonged.

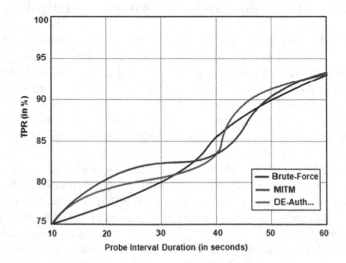

Fig. 16. Average Detection Rate at different distances with various probe interval lengths

6.2   Attacks Detection Efficiency

The attack detection efficiency of the MIHIDS refers to the ability of systems to accurately detect and identify cyber attacks against the UAV. This can be measured by the number of attacks that were successfully detected and identified by the MIHIDS system, as well as the false positive and false negative rates.

Figure 17 demonstrated the attacks detection efficiency of the system. A total 104 attacks were conducted in 4 phases, out of which 99 attacks (MitM, Brute-force, and Credential Reuse) were detected, and the MIHIDS server generated 123 bait sessions. The number of attacks increased in each subsequent phase. The bait sessions also increased according to the number of attacks. (i) In phase 1, a total 13 attacks were performed, and 10 attacks were detected. (ii) In phase 2, a total 21 attacks were performed, and 19 attacks were detected. (iii) In phase 3, a total 30 attacks were performed, and all attacks were detected. (iv) In phase 4, a total 40 attacks were performed, and all attacks were detected. Using the above-mentioned Eq. 3, we determine that the system performance accuracy is 95.19%. A performance percentage indicates that each part is qualified to address the identified issue. This shows that the proposed system is efficient enough to detect targeted attacks on specific ports.

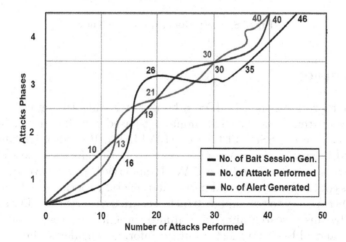

Fig. 17. Attacks Detection Efficiency

6.3   Alerts Generation Efficiency

The alert generation efficiency of the MIHIDS refers to the ability of systems to generate alerts in a timely and effective manner. This can be measured by the speed at which alerts are generated, the alerts accuracy, and the alerts effectiveness in informing relevant parties about the attack.

Figure 18 depicts the alert-generating efficiency of the system. The MIHIDS generates 99 alerts against 104 attacks. Only five alerts are not sent in the case of intrusion detection. The five missed alerts belong to the info category. In the MIHIDS, alert has three categories: critical, medium, and info. The system can't ignore critical and medium alerts, but the info alerts system can ignore them due to false positives.

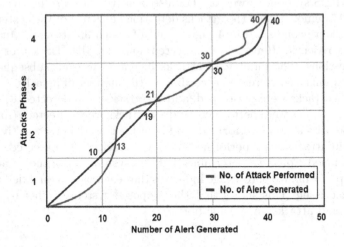

Fig. 18. Alert Generation Efficiency

7   Conclusion

This research proposes the MIHIDS, a honeypot for identifying cyberattacks in the UAV ecosystem. The MIHIDS honeypot-based IDS focuses exclusively on UAV protocols (FTP, SSH, TELNET, MAVLINK). It is also lightweight, so it can be used in small, inexpensive devices and is therefore simple to deploy in various devices (e.g., attached to a UAV, Raspberry Pi). We have examined the effectiveness of the honeypot, and performed several experiments demonstrating the MIHIDS capacity to respond to attack scenarios as close to reality as possible. Additionally, this research aims to evaluate the effectiveness of the honeypot-based IDS, and obtain the most accurate information/alerts about the cyberattacks. Finally, we intend to examine the performance of the honeypot and its capacity for managing numerous connections simultaneously. In terms of future work, we intend to further enhance the MIHIDS by concentrating on enhancing protocol emulation and preventing attacks.

Acknowledgement. The work is supported in part by the Wuhan Knowledge Innovation Program (2022010801010117) and Wuhan AI Innovation Program (2023010402040020) and Major Science and Technology Project of Zhejiang Province - Bilateral Industry Joint R&D Program Project (2021C04007).

References

1. Rodday, N.M., Schmidt, R.D.O., Pras, A.: Exploring security vulnerabilities of unmanned aerial vehicles. In: NOMS 2016–2016 IEEE/IFIP Network Operations and Management Symposium, pp. 993–994 (2016)
2. Pleban, J.-S., Band, R., Creutzburg, R.: Hacking and securing the AR. Drone 2.0 quadcopter: investigations for improving the security of a toy. In: Enabling Technologies, Algorithms, and Applications, Mobile Devices and Multimedia (2014)
3. Nawrocki, M., Wählisch, M., Schmidt, T.C., Keil, C., Schönfelder, J.: A survey on honeypot software and data analysis. arXiv preprint: arXiv:1608.06249 (2016)
4. Pa, Y.M.P., Suzuki, S., Yoshioka, K., Matsumoto, T., Kasama, T., Rossow, C.: IoTPOT: analysing the rise of IoT compromises. In: 9th USENIX Workshop on Offensive Technologies (WOOT 15) (2015)
5. Rist, L., Haslinger, D., Smith, J., Vestergaard, J., Pasquale, A.: Conpot honeypot (2013)
6. Provos, N., Holz, T.: Virtual Honeypots: From Botnet Tracking to Intrusion Detection. Pearson Education, London (2007)
7. Vasilomanolakis, E.: This network is infected: Hostage-a low-interaction honeypot for mobile devices. In: Proceedings of the Third ACM Workshop on Security and Privacy in Smartphones & Mobile Devices (2013)
8. Vasilomanolakis, E., Srinivasa, S., Cordero, C.G., Mühlhäuser, M.: Multi-stage attack detection and signature generation with ICS honeypots. In: NOMS 2016–2016 IEEE/IFIP Network Operations and Management Symposium (2016)
9. Hadi, H.J., Sajjad, S.M., un Nisa, K.: BoDMitM: Botnet detection and mitigation system for home router base on MUD. In: 2019 International Conference on Frontiers of Information Technology (FIT) (2019)
10. Smith, A.: Bluepot: Bluetooth honeypot (2013). https://github.com/andrewmichaelsmith/bluepot
11. johnnykv/heralding: Credentials catching honeypot. https://github.com/johnnykv/heralding
12. foospidy/HoneyPy: A low to medium interaction honeypot. https://github.com/foospidy/HoneyPy
13. CanadianJeff/honeywrt. https://github.com/CanadianJeff/honeywrt
14. Michel Oosterhof. Cowrie honeypot. https://github.com/micheloosterhof/cowrie (2014)
15. Klein, J.C.: Kojoney2 honeypot. https://github.com/madirish/kojoney2
16. Dang, F.: Understanding fileless attacks on Linux-based IoT devices with HoneyCloud. In: Proceedings of the 17th Annual International Conference on Mobile Systems, Applications, and Services (2019)
17. Wang, Y., Su, Z., Benslimane, A., Xu, Q., Dai, M., Li, R.: Collaborative Honeypot defence in UAV networks: a learning-based game approach. arXiv preprint: arXiv:2211 (2022). 01772
18. Su, Z., et al.: Collaborative Honeypot defence in UAV Networks: a learning-based game approach (2022)
19. Hadi, H.J., Cao, Y., Nisa, K.U., Jamil, A.M., Ni, Q.: A comprehensive survey on security, privacy issues and emerging defence technologies for UAVs. J. Netw. Comput. Appl. **213**, 103607 (2023). https://doi.org/10.1016/j.jnca.2023.103607
20. Hadi, H.J., Cao, Y.: Cyber attacks and vulnerabilities assessment for unmanned aerial vehicles communication systems. In: 2022 International Conference on Frontiers of Information Technology (FIT), Islamabad, Pakistan, pp. 213–218 (2022). https://doi.org/10.1109/FIT57066.2022.00047

Power Analysis Attack Based on BS-XGboost Scheme

Yiran Li[✉]

Inner Mongolia University, Hohhot, Inner Mongolia Autonomous Region, China
18910280986@189.cn

Abstract. The power attack is a type of side-channel attack that involves measuring the power consumption of a device to extract secret information. By analyzing power consumption variations, an attacker can deduce the secret key used in the operation. In a class-imbalanced dataset, where the number of samples in one class is much smaller than the other, the power consumption patterns during cryptographic operations may be different for each class. The BorderLine-SMOTE data enhancement scheme was used to generate synthetic samples near the boundaries or at a greater distance from the existing samples, and through these modifications it helps to increase the diversity of the synthetic samples and reduce the risk of overfitting. XGBoost is then used as a classifier to classify the power curves. To evaluate the efficacy of the proposed method, it was applied to the DPA V4 dataset. The results indicated that the original data, when augmented using the Borderline-SMOTE + XGBoost approach, exhibited a substantial improvement in classification precision of up to 34%, outperforming DUAN's method.

Keywords: Borderline-SMOTE · Power Analysis Attack · Data Unbalanced · Data Augmentation Technology

1 Introduction

Side Channel Attack (SCA) is an attack to obtain the secret information of a cryptographic device by analyzing the power, operation time, electromagnetic radiation and other information leaked during the operation of the cryptographic device. The power attack is a type of side-channel attack that involves measuring the power consumption of a device to extract secret information. By analyzing power consumption variations, an attacker can deduce the secret key used in the operation. Power analysis attacks can be divided into two categories, one is non-profiling attacks and the other is profiling attacks.

In non-profiling attacks, the attacker accesses the target device, obtains the power consumption of the target device, and then analyzes the relationship between power consumption and key by statistical analysis. The typical one is a differential power analysis attack [1], in which the attack method is used to obtain sensitive information by obtaining a large number of power curves and dividing the power curves into two groups according to the distinguisher results, and then differencing the two groups of data according to

S. Goel and P. R. Nunes de Souza (Eds.): ICDF2C 2023, LNICST 571, pp. 186–196, 2024.
https://doi.org/10.1007/978-3-031-56583-0_12

the size of the difference value. Correlation Power Analysis (CPA) [2], an attack method to obtain sensitive information by calculating the magnitude of the Pearson Product-moment Correlation Coefficient (Pearson's r) between the power consumption curve and the hypothetical sensitive information. Mutual Information Analysis (MIA) [3], an attack method to obtain sensitive information by calculating the mutual information between the power consumption curve and the hypothetical sensitive information.

Profiling attacks are the most threatening of the power profiling attacks. In this attack, the attacker needs physical access to a pair of identical (similar) devices, which we call the profiling device and the target device. The whole attack consists of two phases (analysis and attack phases). In the first phase, the attacker analyzes the profiling device and uses it to determine the characteristics of the power leak; in the second phase, the attacker uses the model built in the first phase to attack the target device. Typical profiling attacks include Template attacks [4] (TA) and Stochastic models [5]. And in recent years, machine learning is widely used in profiling attacks.

In 2012, HEUSER [6] applied SVM in power analysis attacks and compared SVM with template attacks. 2017, MARTINASEK [7] compared the effectiveness of k-Nearest with other machine learning models such as traditional SVM in attacks and obtained that k-Nearest is a better model choice for power analysis attacks. In 2018, Benadjila [8] introduced a common framework to study and compare the effectiveness of Machine Learning methods against embedded implementations of cryptographic algorithms. In 2020, Perin [9] introduced a power analysis attack based on integrated learning, through which the problem of difficulty in obtaining hyperparameters when using deep learning large models can be solved. 2021, in [10] Lu used end-to-end models, the architecture could directly classify the traces that contain a large number of time samples while whose underlying implementation is protected by masking.

In 2019, Benjamin [11] successfully implemented non-profiling attacks using machine learning instead of Pearson correlation coefficients. 2021, Moos [12] used deep learning to evaluate the leakage of cryptographic devices.

Although many machine learning models have achieved a lot in power analysis attacks, when using machine learning as a classifier for power consumption profiles, the Hamming weight leakage model is usually used (Hamming weight leakage model is the Hamming weight of an intermediate byte when using a cryptographic algorithm run in the target device). However, due to the unbalanced nature of Hamming weight (classes with Hamming weight equal to 4 account for 70/256 of the total data, and classes with Hamming weight equal to 0 and 8 account for only 1/256 of the total data, respectively), this can cause an imbalance in the data. In a data set with class imbalance, the sample size of one class is much smaller than the other, which means that the power consumption pattern during the encryption operation may be different for each class.

To mitigate this risk, it is necessary to balance the classes in the dataset, which in 2020 DUAN [13] makes into a minority oversampling technique (SMOTE) to generate synthetic samples for minority classes.

SMOTE is a popular oversampling technique that generates synthetic samples for classes with a small number of samples by interpolating between existing ones. However, SMOTE is too random, and its principle is to randomly select a sample a from the minority class, find K nearest neighbors, then randomly select a sample b from the nearest neighbors, connect samples a and b, and select a point on the straight line of a and b as the oversampling point, which is easy to generate wrong class samples, and the generated samples go into the majority class, they may not add any new information to the model, and may even lead to overfitting.

1.1 Our Contribution

In order to solve the problem that the generated samples in SMOTE are too similar to existing samples, which do not add new information to the model and may even lead to overfitting, the Borderline-SMOTE (BS) + XGBoost (XGB) scheme is proposed in this paper. The Borderline-SMOTE data enhancement scheme is used to generate synthetic samples near the boundary or at a large distance from existing samples The Borderline-SMOTE data enhancement scheme is used to generate synthetic samples near the boundary or at a large distance from the existing samples, and these modifications help to increase the diversity of synthetic samples and reduce the risk of overfitting. The scheme solves the class repeatability problem in Duan's scheme by using XGBoost as a classifier, which can perform leaf splitting optimization calculation without selecting the specific form of the loss function and relying only on the value of the input data [14], and can effectively improve the classification precision and the model success rate.

1.2 Structure of This Article

This paper is structured as follows. In Sect. 2, analyze the unbalanced feature of the output hamming weight of SBOX, power analysis attack based on machine learning and the imbalance of data class. In Sect. 3, introduce the BS + XGBoost scheme. Section 4 experimental results discussed, analysis and comparison are shown. Section 5 conclusion presented.

2 Background

2.1 Hamming-Weight Model

The Hamming (HM) weight model defines the Hamming weight of a binary data as the number of bits that are compared to 1 in this binary data. In power analysis attacks, the attacker assumes that the power consumption is proportional to the number of bits that are set in the processed data value, so the Hamming weight model is often used to represent the power consumption of the attacked data [13].

2.2 Power Analysis Attack Based on Machine Learning

Power analysis attack based on machine learning can be represented as it constructs a possible template for each possible class $c \in \{1, \ldots, C\}$, where the number of classes C depends on the assumed leakage model. Assume that for each class $c \in \{1, \ldots, C\}$, the attacker obtains a power consumption trace vector $\left\{l_c^i\right\}^{N_c}$, where N_c denotes the number of power consumption trace vectors for class C. Since the template attack relies on a multivariate Gaussian noise model, the power consumption trace vectors are considered to be drawn from a multivariate distribution. Equations (1) and (2) give a more precise expression [14].

$$N(l_c|\mu_c, \Sigma_c) = \frac{1}{(2\Pi)^N 1/2|\Sigma_c|^{1/2}} \exp\left\{-\frac{1}{2}(l_c - \mu_c)^T \Sigma_x^{-1}(l_c - \mu_c)\right\} \quad (1)$$

$$\tilde{\mu}_c = \frac{1}{N_c}\sum_{n_c=1}^{N_c} l_{n_c}, \tilde{\Sigma}_c = \frac{1}{N_c}\sum_{n_c=1}^{N_c} (l_{n_c} - \tilde{\mu}_c)(l_{n_c} - \tilde{\mu}_c)^T \quad (2)$$

These templates are constructed based on the estimation of the expectation $\hat{\mu}_c$ and covariance matrices $\hat{\Sigma}_c$. The secrets recovery in the attack phase is performed using maximum likelihood estimation or the equivalent log-likelihood rule as shown in Eq. (3).

$$\log L_{k^*} \equiv \log \prod_{i=1}^{N_2} P(l_i|c) = \sum_{i=1}^{N_2} \log N(l_i|\mu_c, \Sigma_c) \quad (3)$$

where class C is calculated based on the given secrets guesses k^* and the input leakage model.

A common approach to reduce the computational complexity is to use the Hamming weight leakage model. Using the Hamming weight leakage model, the problem of reducing the computational complexity can be achieved by making assumptions about the entire intermediate values instead of just a few bits of the intermediate values.

2.3 The Imbalance of Data Class

There are two types of imbalances in a dataset. One is class imbalance, which occurs when some classes have more samples than others. The other type is an imbalance within the same class, where there are significantly fewer samples of some subsets than others in the same class. In an unbalanced dataset, the classes with more samples are called majority classes, while classes with fewer samples are called minority classes. Most research in the imbalanced domain focuses on these two classes because multi-class problems can be simplified into two-class problems. Generally, the minority class labels are positive, while the majority class labels are negative. Table 1 shows a confusion matrix for a two-class problem. The first column of the table displays the real class label of the sample, and the first row shows its predicted class label. TP and TN represent the number of correctly classified Positives and Negatives, respectively, whereas FN and FP represent the number of incorrectly classified Positives and Negatives, respectively [14].

Accuracy = (TP + TN)/(TP + FN + FP + TN)
Recall = TP/(TP + FN)
Precision = TP/(TP+FP)

When the data is extremely unbalanced, the samples of the majority class are easier to predict, while the samples of the minority class are less predictable. In situations where the dataset is highly unbalanced, even if the classifier correctly classifies the majority class samples and incorrectly classifies all the minority class samples, the accuracy of the classifier remains high. In this case, the accuracy does not reflect the reliable prediction of the minority class, which leads to a biased model learning.

Table 1. Confusion matrix for two-class problem

	Predicted Positive	Predicted Negative
Positive	TP	FN
Negative	FP	TN

2.4 The Imbalance of Hamming-Weight Value

Since the Hamming weight model is defined as the number of bits 1 in a byte, and a byte has 256 possibilities corresponding to the values 0 to 255, but the Hamming weight is only 0, 1, 2, 3, 4, 5, 6, 7 and 8, which are the nine cases, the distribution of Hamming weight for 256 data is unbalanced, as shown in Table 2. The classification of Hamming weight of 0 and 8 is the smallest, which is only 1/256 of the data respectively, while the Hamming weights of 4 is the most, which is 70/256 of the data.

Table 2. The number of HM weight values in one byte

HM weight	0	1	2	3	4	5	6	7	8
number	1	8	28	56	70	56	28	8	1
P_i	$\frac{1}{256}$	$\frac{8}{256}$	$\frac{28}{256}$	$\frac{56}{256}$	$\frac{70}{256}$	$\frac{56}{256}$	$\frac{28}{256}$	$\frac{8}{256}$	$\frac{1}{256}$

3 BS-XGboost Scheme

In order to solve the problem of model bias caused by data imbalance in the process of using machine learning for power analysis attacks, the authors achieve this through the BS-XGboost Scheme, which improves interpolation and random under-sampling experimental sample rebalancing at the data side and increases the fit using a combined optimization model at the model side.

3.1 Borderline-SMOTE

Borderline-SMOTE is an improvement based on the random sampling algorithm. It fully considers the problem of class repeatability caused by the distribution characteristics of adjacent samples and uses the method of identifying minority class samples to avoid such repeatability. The synthesis principle of boundary samples is illustrated in Fig. 1.

Assuming that S is a sample set, S_{min} is a minority class sample set, $S_{max\,i}$ is an adjacent majority sample set, m is the total number of the adjacent samples, x_i is all attributes of the sample, x_{ii} is all attributes of the adjacent sample, x_n is the adjacent sample, R_{ii} is taken as 0.5 or 1, The steps of the synthesis algorithm are as follows [15]:

1) Assume that $x_i \in S_{min}$, and determine the nearest sample set S_{NN}, and $S_{NN} \subset S$;

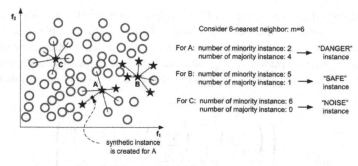

Fig. 1. The synthesis of boundary samples

2) For each sample x_i, determine the number of the nearest sample set that belongs to the majority class, that is $|S_{NN} \cap S_{\max j}|$;
3) Select, $x_i : \frac{m}{2} < |S_{NN} \cap S_{\max j}| < m$, and composite minority class samples. The difference between attribute j of x_i and x_n is recorded as $d_{ij} = x_i - x_{ij}$, so the new synthetic minority sample $h_{ij} = x_i + d_{ij} \times rand(0, R_{ij})$.

3.2 XGBoost

The XGBoost algorithm was proposed by Chen et al. [16] and is widely used in regression and classification problems based on classification and regression powers. The objective function of the XGBoost algorithm consists of two components, the loss function and the regularization, with the expression

$$O_{bj} = \sum_{i=1}^{n} \ell\left(y_i, \hat{y}_i^t\right) + \sum_{i=1}^{l} \Omega(f_i) \tag{4}$$

$$\Omega(f_i) = \gamma T + \frac{1}{2}\lambda \sum_{j=1}^{T} \varpi_j^2 \tag{5}$$

where: $\sum_{i=1}^{n} \ell\left(y_i, \hat{y}_i^t\right)$ forms the loss function of the training sample; $\sum_{i=1}^{t} \Omega(f_i)$ forms the regularization term; γ and λ are the regularization coefficients; the number of leaf nodes is labeled T; ϖ_j is the vector value of the jth node of the decision tree.

The XGBoost objective function is expanded by Taylor's formula to obtain a convex optimization function, so in order to find the ϖ_i that minimizes the objective function, the derivative of ϖ_i and make the derivative function equal to zero can be obtained.

$$\varpi_j = -\frac{\sum_{i \in I_j} g_i}{\sum_{i \in I_j} h_i + \forall \lambda} \tag{6}$$

$$o_{bj}^* = -\frac{1}{2}\sum_{j=1}^{T} \frac{\left(\sum_{i \in S_j} g_i\right)^2}{\sum_{i \in I_j} h_i + \lambda} + yT \tag{7}$$

where: I_i denotes the set of samples of leaf nodes; g_i denotes the number of first-order partial layers of samples contained in leaf node i; h_i denotes the number of second-order braiding derivatives of samples contained in leaf node i; o_{hi} can indicate the superiority of a tree model, and the smaller the o_{hi} value, the better the model. By leading the greedy algorithm and iteratively selecting the optimal structure, the final gain formula is derived as Eq. (8)

$$Gain^* = \frac{1}{2}\left(\frac{\left(\sum_{i\in I_i} g_i\right)^2}{\sum_{i\in I_L} h_i + \lambda} + \frac{\left(\sum_{i\in I_R} g_i\right)^2}{\sum_{i\in I_n} h_i + \lambda} - \frac{\left(\sum_{i\in I_j} g_i\right)^2}{\sum_{i\in I_j} h_i + \lambda}\right) - \gamma \qquad (8)$$

where I_L and I_R denote the set of left and right subtree leaf nodes, respectively.

3.3 BS-XGBoost Scheme

The BS-XGBoost Scheme in this paper is shown in Fig. 2. The whole model consists of two parts.

1. data augmentation of the input data by the Boorderline_SMOTE algorithm;
2. Classification of the augmented data using the XGBoost algorithm as a classifier.

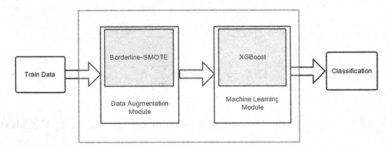

Fig. 2. BX-XGBoost Scheme

4 Experimental Results and Analysis

The data set used in this paper is the DPA Contest v4 data set supplied by the DPA contest. The DPA contest organizes an international academic competition that began in August 2008 and is jointly sponsored by the French National Academy of Sciences and the Paris Institute of Advanced Telecommunications. Its official website is http://www.dpacontest.org [17].

The comparison of the scenarios was evaluated using the classification precision and the model success rate.

4.1 Interesting Points Selection

Due to the high dimensionality of the data in the DPA V4 dataset, with 430,000 dimensions per curve, in order to avoid the problem of high data dimensionality and the model falling into the curse of dimensionality, the correlation analysis between the labels and the data interesting points was performed using the Pearson correlation system [18], calculated as (9)

$$p_{X,Y} = \frac{\text{cov}(X, Y)}{\sigma_X \sigma_Y} = \frac{E[(X - u_X)(Y - u_Y)]}{\sigma_X \sigma_Y} \tag{9}$$

In Eq. (6): cov(X, Y) denotes the difference of agreement between data column X and data column Y samples; σ_X and σ_Y denotes the standard deviation of data column X and data column Y samples, respectively; u_X and u_Y denotes the mean of data column X and data column Y samples, respectively, and E denotes the mean value function.

The 600 dimensions with the largest label-related coefficients are selected as interesting points based on the statistical Pearson's r to achieve the purpose of interesting points selection and avoid the impact of repeated interesting points on machine learning performance, and the calculated Pearson coefficient values are shown in Fig. 3.

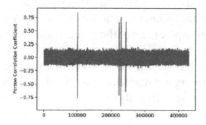

Fig. 3. Pearson's r of traces and labels

4.2 Data Augmentation Based on Borderline-SMOTE

From the DPA V4 dataset, 1000 power consumption curves were selected and the voltage distribution of their different Hamming weight data was viewed through scatter plots. Figure 4-a shows the distribution of the original data, which shows that the data is rather messy and random, and this kind of data is not conducive to machine learning training.

Figure 4-b shows the distribution after SMOTE data enhancement, which can see that the data increased and the distribution has been regular. Since SMOTE is too random, a sample a is randomly selected from the minority class, and after finding K nearest neighbors, a sample b is randomly selected from the nearest neighbors, connecting samples a, b, and choosing a point de on the ab line as the oversampling point. This is easy to generate the wrong class of samples, and the generated samples go into the majority class, as shown in the red figure in Fig. 4-b.

Figure 4-c shows the distribution after Borderline-SMOTE data enhancement. Since Borderline-SMOTE creates synthetic examples only on the decision boundary between two classes, instead of blindly generating new synthetic examples for the minority class, it eliminates the problem of data overlap, as shown by the red circle in Fig. 4-c, where there are no longer generated samples that have gone into the majority class.

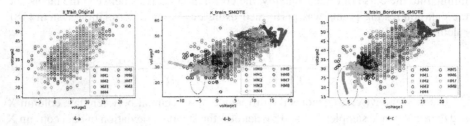

Fig. 4. The Voltage distribution of the HM (original data (4-a), data augmentation by SMOTE (4-b), data augmentation by Borderline-SMOTE (4-c))

4.3 The Classification Precision

From the DPA contest V4 data set, 800 and 1000 traces are randomly selected as the training set, and 600 interesting points are chosen for each trace by Pearson's r introduced in Sect. 4.1. The classification precision of the model is shown in Fig. 5. The classification Precision is shown in Fig. 5. From Fig. 5, we can see that the classification Precision of BS_XGBoost is higher than that of the SMOTE-RF scheme because the problem of the generated samples entering the majority class is solved in Sect. 4.2, the precision of label 1 and label 8 increases significantly.

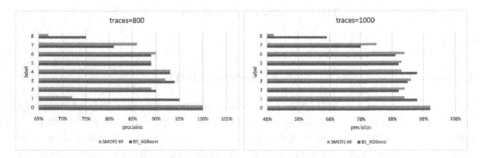

Fig. 5. Classification Precision of the Two Schemes

4.4 Model Success Rate with Different Interesting Points

From the DPA contest V4 data set, 800, 1000, 1500 and 2000 traces were randomly selected as the training set, and 200, 300, 400 and 500 interesting points were selected by Pearson's r as introduced in Sect. 4.1 respectively for each trace. The four sets of data were augmented with Borderline-SMOTE, and the augmented data were substituted into the XGBoost model for training, and then the trained model was tested with another 1000 curves to obtain the the model success rate. As shown in Fig. 6, the BS-XGBoost scheme outperforms the SMOTE-RF scheme for different interesting points and different numbers of original curves.

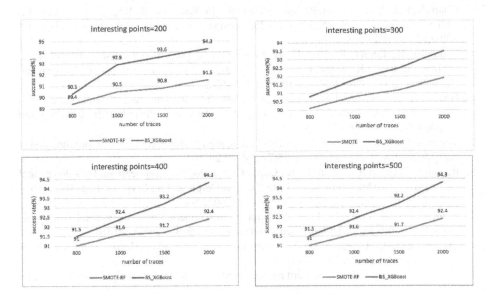

Fig. 6. Model success rate of the two schemes

5 Conclusion

The data in the power analysis attacks may be unbalanced due to classification. In this paper, BS_XGBoost scheme is used to augment the data, which uses the minority class samples on the boundary to synthesize the new samples, so as to improve the class distribution characteristics of samples. The scheme effectively solves the imbalance of data and thus solves the problem of model learning deviation. After the data augmentation of the proposed scheme, the data discrimination between HM = 8 and HM = 7 is significantly augmented. Compared with the scheme in literature [13], using machine learning to carry out model training on the data augmentation of the proposed scheme has significantly improved the classification precision and model success rate not only when the trace number is different (e.g. 800, 1000), but also when the interesting points number is different.

References

1. Kocher, P., Jaffe, J., Jun, B.: Differential power analysis. In: Wiener, M. (ed.) CRYPTO 1999. LNCS, vol. 1666, pp. 388–397. Springer, Heidelberg (1999). https://doi.org/10.1007/3-540-48405-1_25

2. Brier, E., Clavier, C., Olivier, F.: Correlation power analysis with a leakage model. In: Joye, M., Quisquater, J.-J. (eds.) CHES 2004. LNCS, vol. 3156, pp. 16–29. Springer, Heidelberg (2004). https://doi.org/10.1007/978-3-540-28632-5_2

3. Batina, L., Gierlichs, B., Prouff, E., Rivain, M., Standaert, F.-X., Veyrat-Charvillon, N.: Mutual information analysis: a comprehensive study. J. Cryptol.Cryptol. 24(2), 269–291 (2010). https://doi.org/10.1007/s00145-010-9084-8

4. Chari, S., Rao, J.R., Rohatgi, P.: Template attacks. In: Kaliski, B.S., Koç, çK., Paar, C. (eds.) CHES 2002. LNCS, vol. 2523, pp. 13–28. Springer, Heidelberg (2003). https://doi.org/10.1007/3-540-36400-5_3

5. Schindler, W., Lemke, K., Paar, C.: A stochastic model for differential side channel cryptanalysis. In: Rao, J.R., Sunar, B. (eds.) CHES 2005. LNCS, vol. 3659, pp. 30–46. Springer, Heidelberg (2005). https://doi.org/10.1007/11545262_3

6. Heuser, A., Zohner, M.: Intelligent machine homicide. In: Schindler, W., Huss, S.A. (eds.) COSADE 2012. LNCS, vol. 7275, pp. 249–264. Springer, Heidelberg (2012). https://doi.org/10.1007/978-3-642-29912-4_18

7. Martinasek, Z., Zeman, V., Malina, L., et al.: K-nearest neighbors algorithm in profiling power analysis attacks. Radioengineering 25(2), 365–382 (2016)

8. Benadjila, R., Prouff, E., Strullu, R., Cagli, E., Dumas, C.: Deep learning for side-channel analysis and introduction to ASCAD database. J. Cryptogr. Eng.Cryptogr. Eng. 10(2), 163–188 (2019). https://doi.org/10.1007/s13389-019-00220-8

9. Perin, G., Chmielewski, U., Picek, S.: Strength in numbers: improving generalization with ensembles in machine learning-based profiled side-channel analysis (2020)

10. Lu, X., Zhang, C., Cao, P., et al.: Pay attention to raw traces: a deep learning architecture for end-to-end profiling attacks (2021)

11. Timon, B.: Non-profiled deep learning-based side-channel attacks with sensitivity analysis (2019)

12. Moos, T., Wegener, F., Moradi, A.: DL-LA: deep learning leakage assessment: a modern roadmap for SCA evaluations. In: Cryptographic Hardware and Embedded Systems. Universitätsbibliothek der Ruhr-Universität Bochum (2021)

13. Duan, X., Chen, D., Fan, X., et al.: Research and Implementation on power analysis attacks for unbalanced data. Secur. Commun. Netw. 2020(3), 1–10 (2020)

14. Zhou, Z.: Machine Learning, pp. 29–30. Tsinghua Press, Beijing (2016)

15. Han, H., Wang, W.-Y., Mao, B.-H.: Borderline-SMOTE: a new over-sampling method in imbalanced data sets learning. In: Huang, D.-S., Zhang, X.-P., Huang, G.-B. (eds.) ICIC 2005. LNCS, vol. 3644, pp. 878–887. Springer, Heidelberg (2005). https://doi.org/10.1007/11538059_91

16. Chen, T., Gueslrin, G.: XGBoost: a scalable tree boosting system. In: The 22nd ACM SIGKDD International Conference, pp. 758–794. ACM, New York (2016)

17. http://www.dpacontest.org/home/

18. Rodgers, L., Nicewander, W.A.: Thirteen ways to look at the correlation coefficient. Stat 42(1), 59–66 (1988)

Security Analysis of Google Authenticator, Microsoft Authenticator, and Authy

Aleck Nash[1], Hudan Studiawan[2], George Grispos[3],
and Kim-Kwang Raymond Choo[1(✉)]

[1] Department of Information Systems and Cyber Security,
University of Texas at San Antonio,
San Antonio, USA
aleck.nash@my.utsa.edu, raymond.choo@fulbrightmail.org
[2] Department of Informatics, Institut Teknologi Sepuluh Nopember,
Surabaya, Indonesia
hudan@its.ac.id
[3] School of Interdisciplinary Informatics, University of Nebraska-Omaha,
Omaha, USA
ggrispos@unomaha.edu

Abstract. As the use of authenticator applications for two-factor authentication (2FA) has become increasingly common, there is a growing need to assess the security of these applications. In this paper, we present a security analysis of authenticator applications that are widely used on various platforms, such as Google Authenticator, Microsoft Authenticator, and Authy. Our analysis includes an examination of the security features of these applications (e.g., level of protection) as well as the communication protocols used between the applications and the servers. Our results show that these applications have significant vulnerabilities that could compromise the security of the authentication process. Specifically, we found that some authenticator applications store sensitive data, such as secret keys, in plain text, making them vulnerable to attacks. Overall, our findings indicate that there is a need for better security practices in the design and implementation of authenticator applications. We recommend that developers follow best practices for secure coding and use well-established cryptographic algorithms to generate one-time codes.

Keywords: Security analysis · Man-in-the-middle (MITM) attack · Authenticator applications · Authentication protocols

1 Introduction

With the increasing use of digital platforms and services, the security of user accounts has become a critical concern. One way to enhance the security of user

© ICST Institute for Computer Sciences, Social Informatics and Telecommunications Engineering 2024
Published by Springer Nature Switzerland AG 2024. All Rights Reserved
S. Goel and P. R. Nunes de Souza (Eds.): ICDF2C 2023, LNICST 571, pp. 197–206, 2024.
https://doi.org/10.1007/978-3-031-56583-0_13

accounts is by implementing two-factor authentication (2FA), which requires users to provide two forms of authentication, typically a password and a one-time code, to access their accounts. Authenticator applications, which generate one-time codes on users' devices, have become a popular form of 2FA due to their convenience and ease of use [1].

While studies such as [12] identified a number of factors that may lead to poor acceptance of authenticator applications, one cannot deny that authenticator application usage has become more widespread. This reinforces the importance of evaluating the security of these applications since compromised applications can allow attackers to bypass 2FA and gain access to sensitive user data.

Common attacks include man-in-the-middle (MITM), where an MITM attacker seeks to intercept data exchanged between endpoints and consequently compromise the data's confidentiality and integrity [3]. During a MITM attack, a typical situation includes: two endpoints (targets), and an intervening party (the attacker). The attacker gains control over the communication channel connecting the two endpoints and possesses the ability to listen or alter their exchanged messages. This is a common capability considered in many adversary and threat models, such as the Dolev-Yao model and those used in security proofs [5,14,17]. In addition to vulnerabilities in the 2FA protocols, other vulnerabilities (e.g., implementation-related vulnerabilites) may also be exploited [9,15]. For example, SSL vulnerabilities in Android applications can lead to information leakage and the transmission of sensitive data unencrypted. This can put users' personal information at risk, such as login credentials, financial data, and other sensitive information. SSL vulnerabilities can also be exploited by attackers to intercept and manipulate network traffic, leading to potential security breaches. Therefore, it is important for developers to address these vulnerabilities and for users to be aware of the risks associated with using applications that have SSL vulnerabilities [16].

Attacks on SSL/TLS protocols may take many different forms, such as session hijacking, version degradation, Heartbleed, and Berserk [11]. Attacks on the server end and attacks in transit may be divided into two groups. Side channel attacks, manipulation attacks, and certificate manipulation are examples of assaults at the server end. Cipher-based and compression-based attacks are both types of transit attacks. Furthermore, SSL stripping is a frequent attack that takes advantage of the flaw of many open ports for the same application server [11]. A taxonomy for MITM attacks against HTTPS is provided in another study [18], which contains a variety of these attacks' attributes. The capacity to intercept and alter encrypted communication, the application of fake digital certificates to pretend to be trustworthy websites, and the abuse of holes in the SSL/TLS protocols used by HTTPS are some features of MITM attacks against HTTPS that are often seen. However, designing secure 2FA protocols is not an easy feat, as partly demonstrated by the number of 'break-and-fix' attempts [9,19]. For example, the authors of [14] identified weaknesses in another previously proposed 2FA protocol for the Internet of Things (IoT) and proposed a fix to addressing the weaknesses.

In this paper, we present a security analysis of authenticator applications that are widely used in several platforms, namely: Google Authenticator[1], Microsoft Authenticator[2], and Authy[3]. Our analysis aims to identify vulnerabilities and weaknesses in the security features and protocols of these applications and provide recommendations for improving their security. We mainly use the MITM technique to perform the analysis.

The rest of this paper is organized as follows. Section 2 describes the methodology used in our analysis. Section 3 presents the results of our security analysis, including an assessment of the security features and protocols of the authenticator applications. Finally, Sect. 4 concludes the paper.

2   Research Method

As previously discussed, a MITM attacker generally seeks to intercept the communication between two parties, and in our context, an authenticator application (client) and a web application (server). However in this study, we act as a security researcher who can then eavesdrop on the data in the communication, as shown in Fig. 1.

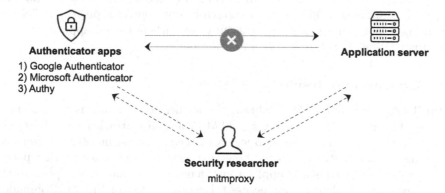

Fig. 1. Methodology to analyze authenticator applications

For the security analysis, we set the three authentication applications as the 2FA method for the service applications shown in Table 1. Then, we simulated a man-in-the-middle (MITM) attack by utilizing a proxy to capture the traffic generated by the authentication app and service applications such as Facebook and Twitch. We used Mitmproxy [4], which is an open-source Java-based SSL proxy that acts as an intermediary between the server and end-users, such as computers, nameservers, and mobile devices. It acts as an HTTP and HTTPS proxy and records the traffic and requests being made.

---

[1] https://support.google.com/accounts/answer/1066447.
[2] https://www.microsoft.com/en-us/security/mobile-authenticator-app.
[3] https://authy.com/.

Mitmproxy was installed and configured on all laptops and mobile devices mentioned in Table 1. We then started the data generation phase by login into each application using Google Authenticator, which was configured as the authentication method across the applications in Table 1. Then the data was obtained from Mitmproxy for security analysis. The experiment was repeated after configuring Microsoft Authenticator and then Authy as the authentication method across the applications.

In analyzing the data, we set the following considerations as guidelines to evaluate the security of these applications and services:

1. What level of protection do these authentication applications offer?
2. What type of standard authorization protocol is implemented by the applications? Are there any weaknesses associated with it?
3. Are sensitive data still appearing in the traffic when performing MITM attacks?
4. How can an attacker use the sensitive data to log in to the server as the user?

3   Results and Analysis

In this section, we present the results of the study and highlight the key findings and their significance. This section showcases our contribution to the field by providing valuable insights into the security of authentication applications and recommendations to address vulnerabilities found.

3.1   Experimental Results

From Table 1, we were able to obtain the authentication tokens for all applications. This means that, during a MITM attack, the attacker can obtain the authentication token and use it to log in to the server as the original user. We are going to demonstrate exactly how that can be done later in this paper. We also observed that some applications, namely Robinhood, use poor methods to exchange credentials for access tokens, as shown in Fig. 2a. Robinhood uses the password grant type, in which the client application collects the user's password and sends it to the authorization server. This method allowed us to obtain the password in plain text, without any encryption. This method is not recommended at all.

In fact, the latest OAuth 2.0 Security Best Current Practice specification recommends against using this grant entirely, and it is also being removed in the OAuth 2.1 update. Although we were able to see that Robinhood uses some good security features, such SHA348 to hash SRI (Subresource Integrity). However, the user password was left without encryption. Contrary to Robinhood, we found that Twitch encrypted the password with RSA-OAEP (Optimal Asymmetric Encryption Padding) as depicted in Fig. 2b. Twitch uses Persisted Query, which is a query string received on the server side with a unique identifier (SHA-256 hash) as shown in Fig. 2c. This identifier can be sent by the client instead of the corresponding query string, thereby reducing the request size dramatically.

```
{
    "al_pk": "7F867EDC-C71B-467F-B0A1-8DCBA5D4D2E3",
    "al_token": "                    ",
    "client_id": "                    ",
    "device_token": "                    ",
    "expires_in": 86400,
    "grant_type": "password",
    "password": "            ",
    "scope": "internal",
    "username": "            "
}
```

(a) Robinhood unencrypted credentials

origin: login_or_register_page
encrypted_password: wrapped_password_RSA-OAEP_

(b) Twitch ecrypted password

```
[
 {
    "operationName": "CoreAuthCurrentUser",
    "variables": {},
    "extensions": {
      "persistedQuery": {
        "version": 1,
        "sha256Hash": "bc444c5b28754cb660ed183236bb5fe0
                      83f2549d1804a304842dad846d51f3ee"
      }
    }
 }
]
```

(c) Twitch query identifier

Fig. 2. Robinhood unencrypted credentials and Twitch encryption

We also observed that both the signature method and the digest method algorithms are based on SHA256 in Outlook, as Microsoft recommends SHA256 or better over weaker algorithms such as SHA1, as shown in Fig. 3a. For Facebook, Slack, and Discord, the authentication passcodes generated by the 2FA app were found in plaintext, which can come in handy for the attacker (Fig. 3b).

For most of the applications, we were able to detect the operating system used, but not the version, as shown in this parameter: *sec-ch-ua-platform: "Windows"*. The traffic from Outlook included user agent information such as the 2FA App and version, and OS type and version, and CFNetwork/Darwin and versions, along with client information such as email address and ePCT (Fig. 3c).

Additionally, we were able to obtain the Client ID, Client Secret, Access Token, and Refresh Token for the Gmail application, as shown in Fig. 4a. This allows not only to log in to the server using the access token but also to use the refresh token to generate new access tokens indefinitely as long as the token is not expired or revoked. For this reason, Gmail seems to be the least secure application when MITM attacks are performed (Fig. 4b).

```
<SignatureMethod Algorithm="http://www.w3.org/2001/04/xmldsig-more#
                            hmac-sha256">
</SignatureMethod>
<Reference URI="#EncPsf">
  <Transforms>
    <Transform Algorithm="http://www.w3.org/2001/10/xml-exc-c14n#">
    </Transform>
  </Transforms>
  <DigestMethod Algorithm="http://www.w3.org/2001/04/xmlenc#sha256">
  </DigestMethod>
  <DigestValue>6vWvweaFM/kJWFVyCka35b+CAoyw5/BzyfCPrUp1QBA=
  </DigestValue>
</Reference>
```

(a) Outlook signature method

```
2fa_magiclogin: z-app-2943702915378-4002966658259-truncated-here
remember: 1
has_remember: true
2fa_code: 485965
2fa_action: submit_primary
```

(b) Slack authentication passcode in plain text

```
client_id: 81feaced-5ddd-41e7-8bef-3e20a2689bb7
redirect_uri: https://account.microsoft.com/auth/complete-signin-oauth
response_type: code
login_hint: authenticateme6@outlook.com
x-client-SKU: MSAL.Desktop
x-client-Ver: 4.45.0.0
uaid: 25c8caf7849b4aa9a3af263e5be12836
issuer: mso
ui_locales: en-US
epct: AQABAAAAAAD--truncated-here
```

(c) Outlook captured information

Fig. 3. Outlook signature method, Slack plain passcode, and Outlook captured information

It is important to mention that the reason we were able to obtain the authentication access tokens for these applications was that certificate pinning was not implemented. Certificate pinning is an online application security technique designed to thwart MITM attacks, by accepting only authorized certificates for the authentication of client-server connections. This technique makes it extremely difficult for cybercriminals to utilize fraudulent certificates to gain access to applications through MITM, compromise certificate authorities, and issue invalid certificates.

If a single certificate is compromised, an attacker can produce a valid certificate for any hostname by signing it with the compromised CA root certificate, which enables the attacker to MITM any TLS connection [10]. To manage these issues, Evans et al. [6] suggested certificate pinning technique which can be implemented in two ways:

1. Leaf certificate (public key): pins the server's specific public key certificate. This is usually achieved by hard coding its fingerprint. An alternative way is to just pin the server's public key.

Table 1. Summary of results

Application	2FA App	Attributes						Potential Risk
		ID	Secret	Auth token	Refresh token	OS	App info	
Facebook	Google	No	No	Yes	No	Yes	Yes	Passcode is in plaintext
	Microsoft	No	No	Yes	No	Yes	Yes	
	Authy	No	No	Yes	No	Yes	Yes	
Twitch	Google	Yes	No	Yes	No	Yes	Yes	The token can be reused;
	Microsoft	Yes	No	Yes	No	Yes	Yes	Passcode is in plaintext
	Authy	Yes	No	Yes	No	Yes	Yes	
Dropbox	Google	No	No	Yes	No	Yes	Yes	The token can be reused
	Microsoft	No	No	Yes	No	Yes	Yes	
	Authy	No	No	Yes	No	Yes	Yes	
Slack	Google	Yes	No	Yes	No	Yes	Yes	Passcode is in plaintext
	Microsoft	Yes	No	Yes	No	Yes	Yes	
	Authy	Yes	No	Yes	No	Yes	Yes	
Discord	Google	No	No	Yes	No	No	No	Passcode is in plaintext
	Microsoft	No	No	Yes	No	No	No	
	Authy	No	No	Yes	No	No	No	
Robinhood	Google	Yes	No	Yes	No	Yes	Yes	Password is in plaintext
	Microsoft	Yes	No	Yes	No	Yes	Yes	
	Authy	Yes	No	Yes	No	Yes	Yes	
Gmail	Google	Yes	Yes	Yes	Yes	Yes	No	The token can be reused; Refresh token can be used to generate new tokens
Outlook	Microsoft	Yes	No	Yes	No	Yes	Yes	The token can be reused

```
scope: https://www.google.com/accounts/OAuthLogin
grant_type: authorization_code
client_id: ███████.apps.googleusercontent.com
client_secret: ██████QcT3lO7GsGZi2G4lIT
code: 4/0AdQt8qh2wmlh3h_bubzy3wvfhdD9-truncated-here
```

(a) Gmail client_id and client_secret are exposed

```
{
    "access_token": "ya29.A0AVA9y1s1y400ZK5U4mV3B1x3-truncated-here",
    "expires_in": 3599,
    "id_token": "eyJhbGciOiJSUzI1NiIsImtpZCI6ImZ-truncated-here",
    "refresh_token": "1//0fh1vLJ-e8dAHCgYIARFAGA8SMwF-truncated-here",
    "scope": "https://www.google.com/accounts/OAuthLogin",
    "token_type": "Bearer"
}
{
    "mfa_required": true,
    "mfa_type": "app"
}
```

(b) Gmail refresh token

Fig. 4. Gmail client_id, client_secret, and refresh token

2. Root certificate (intermediary): pins a specific root CA or intermediary certificate. Then, the server can renew its leaf certificate as needed as long as it is signed by the intermediary certificate or the pinned root [10].

A number of studies show that applications with incorrect application of SSL pinning and certificate pinning are at risk of MITM attacks. For example, Fahl

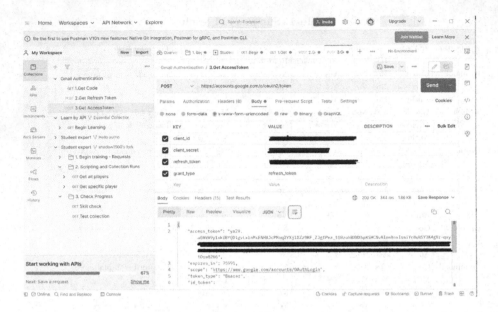

Fig. 5. Login interaction with Postman

et al. [7] performed an investigation of Android applications and found that many of them allowed self-signed certificates, did not validate the hostname, and did not encrypt certain connections at all. According to their analysis, more than 1000 applications out of 13,500 had an incorrect implementation of the validation methods, making them prone to a MITM attack. This also suggests that application developers are unable to sufficiently deal with certificate validation in general and with certificate pinning in particular [13].

Another research showed that the situation is getting worse over time rather than improving [2]. Interviews with application developers with broken validation indicate that developers do not fully completely understand the security consequences of such poor implementation [8]. Developers often ignore MITM attacks as a threat, and they prefer to use self-signed certificates as it is more convenient for them [13]. Certificate pinning stands out as the most recommended protection measure among all available advanced measures. With correct implementation, certificate pinning minimizes the risk of MITM attacks [2].

3.2   Using the Sensitive Data to Log into the Server

To demonstrate the sensitivity of the obtained data, we used Postman[4] to interact with the login servers. Postman is an API platform for developers to build, test, and iterate their APIs. It can be used to automate API calls and API testing. For our purpose, we used the information we obtained from the Gmail

---

[4] https://www.postman.com/.

application through Mitmproxy (such as client ID, client secret, and refresh token) to generate a new access token from gmail.googleapis.com as shown in Fig. 5.

We can see the status 200 OK which means that the request was correct, and the desired response has been sent to the client. We received a new access token which can be regenerated indefinitely unless the token is expired or revoked. The attacker can use the access token to retrieve messages from a specific email, using the GET function request from https://gmail.googleapis.com/gmail/v1/users/{{USER_ID}}/messages. However, the former request is sufficient for our demonstration purposes. We repeated this experiment multiple times, and we were able to obtain a new access token in every request. This means that once the refresh token is captured by an attacker, it can be used to generate new access tokens to maintain access to the victim's account.

4   Conclusion and Future Work

In this paper, we have conducted a thorough security analysis of authenticator applications, specifically Google Authenticator, Microsoft Authenticator, and Authy. We have identified vulnerabilities that can be exploited by attackers to compromise the security of these applications. Our findings reveal that the security of authenticator applications is not foolproof and requires constant attention and updates to prevent attacks. We recommend that developers and users of authenticator applications implement more secure protocols to enhance the security of their applications.

Overall, this paper highlighted the importance of security in authentication applications and the need for continuous research to stay ahead of potential threats. We hope that our analysis will contribute to the development of more secure authenticator applications in the future.

References

1. Aloul, F., Zahidi, S., El-Hajj, W.: Two factor authentication using mobile phones. In: 2009 IEEE/ACS International Conference on Computer Systems and Applications, pp. 641–644 (2009)
2. Buhov, D., Huber, M., Merzdovnik, G., Weippl, E.: Pin it! improving android network security at runtime. In: 2016 IFIP Networking Conference (IFIP Networking) and Workshops, pp. 297–305 (2016)
3. Conti, M., Dragoni, N., Lesyk, V.: A survey of man in the middle attacks. IEEE Commun. Surv. Tutorials 18(3), 2027–2051 (2016)
4. Cortesi, A., Hils, M., Kriechbaumer, T., contributors: mitmproxy: a free and open source interactive HTTPS proxy (2010). https://mitmproxy.org/ [Version 9.0]
5. Do, Q., Martini, B., Choo, K.R.: The role of the adversary model in applied security research. Comput. Secur. 81, 156–181 (2019)
6. Evans, C., Palmer, C., Sleevi, R.: RFC 7469: Public key pinning extension for HTTP (2015)

7. Fahl, S., Harbach, M., Muders, T., Baumgärtner, L., Freisleben, B., Smith, M.: Why eve and mallory love Android: an analysis of Android SSL (in) security. In: Proceedings of the 2012 ACM Conference on Computer and Communications Security, pp. 50–61 (2012)
8. Fahl, S., Harbach, M., Perl, H., Koetter, M., Smith, M.: Rethinking SSL development in an appified world. In: Proceedings of the 2013 ACM SIGSAC Conference on Computer & Communications Security, pp. 49–60 (2013)
9. Gavazzi, A., Williams, R., Kirda, E., Lu, L., King, A., Davis, A., Leek, T.: A study of multi-factor and risk-based authentication availability. In: 32nd USENIX Security Symposium, USENIX Security, pp. 1–18 (2023)
10. Georgiev, M., Iyengar, S., Jana, S., Anubhai, R., Boneh, D., Shmatikov, V.: The most dangerous code in the world: Validating SSL certificates in non-browser software. In: Proceedings of the 2012 ACM Conference on Computer and Communications Security, pp. 38–49 (2012)
11. Keerthi, V.K., et al.: Taxonomy of SSL/TLS attacks. Int. J. Comput. Netw. Inf. Secur. 8(2), 15 (2016)
12. Marky, K., etal.: "nah, it's just annoying!" a deep dive into user perceptions of two-factor authentication. ACM Trans. Comput. Hum. Interact. 29(5), 43:1–43:32 (2022)
13. Merzdovnik, G., Buhov, D., Voyiatzis, A.G., Weippl, E.R.: Notary-assisted certificate pinning for improved security of Android apps. In: 2016 11th International Conference on Availability, Reliability and Security (ARES), pp. 365–371 (2016)
14. Modarres, A.M.A., Sarbishaei, G.: An improved lightweight two-factor authentication protocol for IoT applications. IEEE Trans. Industr. Inf. 19(5), 6588–6598 (2023)
15. Narayanan, A., Lee, K.: Security policy audits: why and how. IEEE Secur. Priv. 21(2), 77–81 (2023)
16. Onwuzurike, L., De Cristofaro, E.: Danger is my middle name: experimenting with SSL vulnerabilities in android apps. In: Proceedings of the 8th ACM Conference on Security & Privacy in Wireless and Mobile Networks, pp. 1–6 (2015)
17. Peeters, C., Patton, C., Munyaka, I.N.S., Olszewski, D., Shrimpton, T., Traynor, P.: SMS OTP security (SOS): hardening SMS-based two factor authentication. In: ASIA CCS: ACM Asia Conference on Computer and Communications Security, pp. 2–16 (2022)
18. Stricot-Tarboton, S., Chaisiri, S., Ko, R.K.: Taxonomy of man-in-the-middle attacks on HTTPS. In: 2016 IEEE Trustcom/BigDataSE/ISPA, pp. 527–534 (2016)
19. Zhou, Z., Han, X., Chen, Z., Nan, Y., Li, J., Gu, D.: Simulation: demystifying (insecure) cellular network based one-tap authentication services. In: 52nd Annual IEEE/IFIP International Conference on Dependable Systems and Networks (DSN), pp. 534–546 (2022)

Cybersecurity and Forensics

APTBert: Abstract Generation and Event Extraction from APT Reports

Chenxin Zhou[1], Cheng Huang[1,2(✉)], Yanghao Wang[1], and Zheng Zuo[3]

[1] School of Cyber Science and Engineering, Sichuan University, Chengdu, China
opcodesec@gmail.com
[2] Anhui Province Key Laboratory of Cyberspace Security Situation Awareness
and Evaluation, Hefei, China
[3] Chengdu University of Information Technology, Chengdu, China

Abstract. Due to the rapid development of information technology in this century, APT attacks(Advanced Persistent Threat) occur more frequently. The best way to combat APT is to quickly extract and integrate the roles of the attack events involved in the report from the APT reports that have been released, and to further perceive, analyze and prevent APT for the relevant security professionals. With the above issues in mind, an event extraction model for APT attack is proposed. This model, which is called APTBert, uses targeted text characterization results from the security filed text generated by the APTBert pre-training model to feed into the multi-head self-attention mechanism neural network for training, improving the accuracy of sequence labelling. At the experiment stage, on the basis of 1300 open source APT attack reports from security vendors and forums, we first pre-trained an APTBert pre-training model. We ended up annotating 600 APT reports with event roles, which were used to train the extraction model and evaluate the effect of event extraction. Experiment results show that the proposed method has better performance in training time and F1(77.4%) as compared to traditional extraction methods like BiLSTM.

Keywords: Advanced Persistent Threat · Event Extraction · Abstract Generation · Pre-training

1 Introduction

Since the 21st century, APT incidents emerge in an infinite number of ways, resulting in enormous impact on individuals, organizations and society. In order to better prevent APTs, relevant security practitioners must first be aware of and understand APTs from prior attack events, analyze and summarize their features and laws, so as to better combat APTs [1]. Given that there are a large number of APT reports available on the Internet (official websites of security vendors, forums, social platforms, etc.), this paper aims to automatically extract attack events from APT reports, so that security practitioners can find the core

© ICST Institute for Computer Sciences, Social Informatics and Telecommunications Engineering 2024
Published by Springer Nature Switzerland AG 2024. All Rights Reserved
S. Goel and P. R. Nunes de Souza (Eds.): ICDF2C 2023, LNICST 571, pp. 209–223, 2024.
https://doi.org/10.1007/978-3-031-56583-0_14

content and key actors of the event more quickly. Furthermore, this topic can also provide a role extraction scheme for constructing a knowledge graph of attack events, and then become the basis for reasoning about downstream knowledge. If a new APT event appears on the open source website, the extraction work can be completed immediately and the elements of the event can be added to the event knowledge graph.

By analyzing existing attack event extraction mining technology for cyber security attack reports, in this paper, we find that the text characterization from most of the extraction methods is not effectively represented. With this in mind, the paper investigates how to perform a more comprehensive characterization of the security text. Furthermore, existing work is not complete for the role definition for APT events. To address the aforementioned issues, this paper proposes a set of event role definition and extraction schemes for APT reports, which can efficiently extract key information in APT reports.

In summary, the main innovation points and contributions of the paper are as follows:

- We introduce a TextRank algorithm based on similarity between sentences to extract important sentences from the APT report in order to generate a abstract, which is convenient for quickly understanding the core content of the report.
- We define 14 types of key event roles in APT attacks, and collect 11,082 sentences from 600 APT reports and annotate them as the training and evaluation dataset of the model.
- We collect 863 texts in the security field for self-supervised pre-training. And we generate the APTBert pre-training model, then perform text characterization based on this model. It enables rare texts in the security field to be effectively represented. And we put forward the event role extraction method based on APTBert and conduct experiments, compared with the traditional extraction model, it performs better in the experiment result.

The remainder of this article is organized as follows. **Section** 2 surveys the relevant work about abstract generation and event extraction. Methods of abstract generation and event extraction are described in **Sect.** 3. Our experiment design and implementation and its result and analysis will be seen in **Sect.** 4. Limitations are presented in **Sect.** 5. Finally, we conclude our contributions and improvements in **Sect.** 6.

2   Related Work

2.1   Abstract Generation

Abstract generation methods are mainly divided into two categories: extraction-based method and abstraction-based method [2]. The typical extraction-based method is TextRank algorithm, which is proposed by Mihalcea [3] et al., it generates sentence weights based on the similarity between words and the frequencies between sentences, and then extracts high-weight sentences for sequential combination so that will be no grammatical problems and the key points of the full text can be grasped. In addition, the typical abstraction-based method is the text topic model LDA [4]. We will only consider whether the next word appears at the same time, without taking into account the order in which the words appear. However, it still requires a lot of extra training time for the encoder and decoder.

2.2 Event Extraction

Event extraction techniques are usually trained with text characterization as the basis for supervised deep learning. In the general field, Malte [5] et al. splice the characterization of the open source knowledge map as the feature input to represent the Bert pre-training model; Dongfang Lou [6] et al., construct a multi-layer two-way network model which is used as an encoder and a decoder; Yubo Chen [7] et al. use a convolution neural network model with multiple pooling layer structures to semantic information relations are extracted. In the security field, researchers often combine excellent models in general fields with text features in the security field to propose event extraction schemes that can perform better on security texts. For example, Semih [8] et al. use CNN [9] as an encoder to encode the result of embedding in a new way, and as the input of the CRF layer, it performed well on short texts containing noise; Ning Luo [10] et al. propose a BiLSTM model with a sliding window to fuse inter-sentence information, and finally proved that the text-level learning model performs better than the sentence-level learning model in the role extraction of most event; Jakub [11] et al. use information open source platforms such as Twitter to collect intelligence related to border security; furthermore, some work focuses on introducing external features to improve the recall and precision of the model. For example, Benjamin [12] et al. use alarm graphs and event feature embedding to detect APT attacks. For sequential data like text, a common learning network structure is RNN [13]. However, the recurrent neural network system is not effective in dealing with long text sequences. Then the LSTM was originally designed and the "forget gate" was introduced [14]. However, the model structure of LSTM itself is relatively complex, there is a bottleneck for LSTM for longer sequence data. A multi-headed self-attention neural network performs better in solving sequence tokens [15]. And the multi-headed self-attention mechanism acts as an integration to prevent overfitting. This model can greatly improve the computational speed and learning ability, and facilitate the performance and processing of very long texts. This enables the text to be processed from sentence level to text level so that the accuracy of prediction can be improved.

3   Methodology

In this section, we first study on combining sentence similarity and sentence centrality to generate an abstract through the TextRank algorithm. Then we present our APTBert pre-training model to extract APT events. The overall design framework of APT report abstract generation and event extraction is shown in Fig. 1. First, the collected dataset is cleaned and then two parallel processes are performed: abstract generation and event extraction. In addition, the abstract generation module, which is mainly relied on TextRank algorithm, takes the whole APT report as input and extract the APT report through APTBert pre-training model.

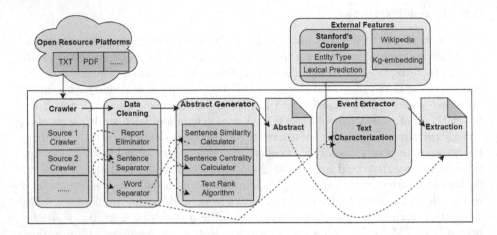

Fig. 1. Overall Framework

3.1   Data Cleaning

This module contains three steps: report elimination, sentence separation, word separation. For report elimination, we eliminate irrelevant or low-quality reports artificially. And then we use scripts, which are programmed in Python, to divide sentences of a report and each sentence is divided into words based on spaces and punctuation marks. Each word and punctuation is treated as a separate token, and the BRAT annotation tool is used to annotate the event roles.

3.2   Abstract Generator

In this section, we present abstract generator method based on TextRank algorithm. First we get word separations from previous stage, and we calculate the sentence similarity according to them. Then we calculate the sentence centrality which is based on the sentence similarity. After that, we set a sentence similarity value as the threshold, if one's sentence similarity is bigger than the threshold, it will be generated as part of the abstract. The TextRank algorithm flow diagram is as follow.

Algorithm 1. TextRank Algorithm

1: $INPUT : Document T$
2: $spilt(T)into[S1, S2, ..., Sm]$
3: $spilt(Si)into[t1, t2, ..., tn]$
4: **for** i in m **do**
5:    **for** j in m **do**
6:       $Similarity(S_i, S_j) = \frac{\sum\limits_{k=1} (t_k \epsilon S_i \wedge t_k \epsilon S_j)}{log^{|S_i|} + log^{|S_j|}}$
7:    **end for**
8:    **for** i in n **do**
9:       $S_i = \sum\limits_{j=1}^{N} Similarity_{i,j}/N$
10:       **if** $Si > threshold$ **then**
11:          $Res.append(Si)$
12:          $Return Res$
13:       **end if**
14:    **end for**
15: **end for**

Sentence Similarity Calculation. For a given piece of text T, it is first divided into sentences according to its content (according to punctuation splits):

$$T = [S_1, S_2, \ldots, S_m] \tag{1}$$

After the clause is completed, go out and deactivate the word and split the word for each clause:

$$S_i = [t_{i,1}, t_{i,2}, \ldots, t_{i,n}] \tag{2}$$

After each sentence has been divided, the similarity can be calculated based on the co-occurrence frequency between the two sentences, and for a given two sentences:

$$Similarity(S_i, S_j) = \frac{\sum\limits_{k=1} (t_k \epsilon S_i \wedge t_k \epsilon S_j)}{log^{|S_i|} + log^{|S_j|}} \tag{3}$$

A higher similarity score of two sentences indicates a stronger association. Sentence similarity is also the basis for calculating the importance of sentences in the text.

Sentence Centrality Calculation. We introduce sentence centrality based on sentence similarity to describe how the sentence is related to other sentences in the full text and thus can quantitatively represent the importance of the sentence. After getting the similarity between sentences then it can be used as the weight between sentences. Let the weight between sentences i and j be Similarity, then the centrality S of sentence i is as below:

$$S_i = \sum_{j=1}^{N} Similarity_{i,j}/N \tag{4}$$

The centrality of a sentence calculates the arithmetic mean of the degree of association of the sentence with other sentences in the full text. If this mean is higher then it indicates that the sentence is of high importance in the full text, then the choice of whether or not to extract the sentence can be made based on this value, and the larger the centrality value the more likely it is that the sentence will be extracted as part of the abstract.

Abstract Generation. We include a sentence as part of the abstract when its importance score is greater than the set threshold. It allows the more important sentences in the text to be filtered out to generate an abstract. We input longer security reports piece by piece for abstract extraction, then we can have an overall grasp of the general meaning of the text.

3.3   Event Extractor

In this section, we first have to know what is needed to be extracted so that we define 14 types of APT attack event roles. And characterizing information as a tensor is the foundation of deep learning. So we propose a pre-training framework similar to Bert, which is called APTBert. And we output the characterization through multi-headed self-attention mechanism. Finally we extract an event through this method.

Role Definition. Based on previous work related to cyber attack event extraction, we define 14 types of roles in attack events (see Table 1 for specific role types and definitions) for which can be extracted automatically, thus helping relevant practitioners to understand the attack event and work further based on it.

Based on the work of Satyapanich [16] et al. the roles of cyber security events are classified into 13 roles of attacker, victim, attack mode, attack tool, loss, number of victims, purpose, location, time, CVE, vulnerability, vulnerable system, and version of vulnerable system. We added five new event role types of victim location, sensitive information, attacker clues, means of defense and related activities. In addition, we merged CVE vulnerabilities and other vulnerabilities (unified as the vulnerabilities exploited by the attack), merged the number of victims into the victim role as well, and merged the version of the vulnerability system into the vulnerability system. This allows for a more comprehensive division of APT events in terms of roles, thus improving the extraction of events.

Text Characterization. According to APTBert pre-training model, the token embedding is generated by first quantizing the tokens in successive sentences using word2vec. Segment embedding is used to distinguish the context and position embedding characterizes the position of a token in a sentence as a tensor, so that the position of each token can be learned by the model. The position of each token can be learned by the model. The position representation formulas are given in formula (1) and formula (2):

Table 1. Attack event role types and definitions

Event Roles	Definition
Attackers	Entities that initiate cyber attacks against other entities in an APT event
Victims	Entities subject to attacker-initiated cyber attacks in APT incidents
Related Activities	Related activities involved in the APT event
Attack Time	The time when the attacker launched the cyber attack
Victim Location	The country or region where the victim is located
Means of Attack	The technical means utilized by the attacker during the cyber attack
Attack Tools	Tools utilized by attackers in the course of a network attack
Sensitive Information	Important data or information about the victim
Purpose of The Attack	The purpose of cyber attacks carried out by attackers
Damage Caused	Financial and reputational damages caused in the APT incident
Vulnerabilities Exploited By The Attack	Software, hardware, protocol or system vulnerabilities exploited by the attacker in the course of a network attack
Vulnerable Systems	The vulnerable system attacked by the attacker
Defensive Tools	Means of defense against cyber attacks used in the APT incident
Attacker Clues	Information exposed by the attacker in the APT incident

$$PE_{(pos,2i)} = \sin(\frac{pos}{10000^{\frac{2i}{d_{model}}}}) \tag{5}$$

$$PE_{(pos,2i+1)} = \cos(\frac{pos}{10000^{\frac{2i}{d_{model}}}}) \tag{6}$$

The three embeddings are stitched together and fed into an encoder module using a 6-layer self-attention mechanism [17] with multiple heads. Each encoder module finally performs a residual splicing and regularization operation on the tensor. The residual [18] unit can be implemented as a layer-hopping connection, where the input of the unit is directly added to the output of the unit and then activated. For the regularization operation, layer normalization [19] is used in the Bert framework, and BN layer in CNN can accelerate the training of the model and prevent the model from overfitting and gradient disappearance. However, there are some problems if the BN layer is directly applied in RNN [20], if a test text is longer than the training text, Batch Normalization will be problematic. In addition, Stanford provides the already trained natural language processing tool corenlp [21]. It includes named entity recognition, which gives the entity type of the token. As well as discriminating the lexical nature of the token. We use corenlp's entity type prediction results and lexical prediction results as two external features. In addition, Wikipedia provides node representation based on knowledge graph. Kg-embedding [22] also applies graph representation algorithm for each node. After completing pre-training, the authors stitch the results of characterization via APTBert with the named entity recognition results provided by corenlp, lexical results and features from graph embedding provided by Wikipedia as the final text characterization results to be input to the event role extraction model.

Event Extraction. Unlike the traditional string recurrent neural networks such as LSTM [23] and GRU [24], we use a multi-headed self-attention mechanism for event extraction. This results for better performance in solving sequence tokens with the following equation:

$$Attention\,(K, Q, V) = softmax(QK^t/\sqrt{d})V \tag{7}$$

The multi-headed self-attention mechanism supports parallel token input, making the computation much faster. And the CRF layer allows adding some constraints to the final constraint labels before output, thus ensuring the validity of the prediction labels. In addition, in the loss function of the CRF [25] layer, there are two types of scores: the first score is the emission score, which is calculated by building an emission matrix to obtain the emission score. At the same time, a transfer score matrix is also obtained, which stores the transition score between all tags transferred to each other. Accordingly, this transfer score matrix can be randomly initialized before training the model, and all random scores in this matrix will be updated during the training process, in other words, the CRF layer can learn these constraints by itself without constructing this matrix artificially. The loss function part of the CRF consists of two parts, the score of the true path and the total score of all paths. The score of the true path should be the highest score of all paths. Building each possible path with a score of Pi and a total of N paths, the total score of the paths is

$$P_{total} = P_1 + P_2 + \ldots + P_N = e^{S_1} + e^{S_2} + \ldots + e^{S_N} \tag{8}$$

In turn, the loss function equation is

$$LossFunction = Precision/(P_1 + P_2 + \ldots + P_N) \tag{9}$$

where S is calculated as

$$S_i = EmissionScore + TransitionScore \tag{10}$$

In the output part, the BIO-event role type is used to implement the sequence token. If the prediction result of a token is B, it means that the token is the first token of the role type; if it is I, it is the other part of the role type (except the beginning part); if it is O, it means that the token does not belong to any role type.

Firstly, the token is input, and the named entity recognition and lexical prediction are performed by corenlp to generate the corresponding encoding; in addition, the token is passed through the already trained APTBert pre-training model to generate the token embedding; then the graph features are introduced by kg-embedding. The four features are stitched together and used as the input of the multi-headed self-attention mechanism; after the self-attention mechanism module containing layer normalization and residual linking is input to the CRF layer to learn the constraints and finally generate the predicted probability distribution.

For the prediction results, the paper uses cross entropy as the loss function.

$$L = (\sum_i L_i)/N = - \sum i \sum_{c=1}^{M} y_{ic} \log(p_{ic}) \tag{11}$$

Among them: M is number of categories; y_{ic} is symbolic function (0 or 1), if the true category of sample i is equal to c take 1, otherwise take 0; p_{ic} is The predicted probability that observation sample i belongs to category c, and the loss is back-propagated to train the model.

4   Experiments

4.1   Datasets

We crawled through a total of 863 open source APT reports on the official websites of security forums and security vendors (e.g. Kaspersky, HP, IBM), each APT report describes the course of an APT incident. And we used 863 APT reports as the self-training corpus of APTBert. Among the 863 APT reports, 600 reports with 11082 sentences were randomly selected for subscripts, and each word, symbol was considered as a token. Then the event role annotation was performed, and the annotation was decided according to the number of votes. As shown in Table 2, the average number of event role types in each report after annotation was counted.

4.2   Evaluation Metrics

In the event extraction class task, three metrics, precision, recall and F1 value, are usually used to evaluate the effectiveness. The extraction of event elements is divided into two categories from two parts, T stands for the actual value is the target category and F stands for the actual value is not the target category. p stands for the predicted value is the target category and N stands for the predicted value is not the target category. Then TP indicates that both actual and predicted values are target categories. And where the precision is used to measure the probability of making a correct prediction which is calculated as:

$$\text{Precision} = \text{TP}/P \tag{12}$$

Table 2. Statistics on the number of roles in the attack

Event Roles	Amount
Attackers	12.93
Victims	8.66
Related Activities	5.34
Attack Time	2.16
Victim Location	3.72
Means of Attack	3.86
Attack Tools	13.73
Sensitive Information	5.45
Purpose of The Attack	3.56
Damage Caused	2.17
Vulnerabilities Exploited By The Attack	2.08
Vulnerable Systems	3.51
Defensive Tools	4.12
Attacker Clues	0.85

Recall is used to measure the proportion of predictions made that cover all elements, and is calculated as:

$$Recall = TP/T \tag{13}$$

Due to the existence of a mutually sacrificial quantitative relationship between precision and recall, the F1 value, which can combine the two, is introduced in order to evaluate the most overall prediction task, where the F1 value is positively correlated with both precision and recall, as calculated by the following formula:

$$F1 = 2 * Recall * Precision/(Recall + Precision) \tag{14}$$

If F1 is higher, it means that the better performance is achieved when for precision and recall importance weights are considered consistent.

4.3   Design and Evaluation

To evaluate the performance of APTBert pre-training model and other methods proposed in this paper, a series of experiments are designed. For our experiments, they can briefly be separated to two parts, abstract generation module and event extraction module, which were presented above in the overall framework.

Abstract Generation Evaluation. The abstract generation module is based on TextRank algorithm. For a piece of APT attack report, after the process of data cleaning, we get the sentence similarity of this report. The mean value of the similarity with all other sentences is used as the score of the importance of the sentence. When the importance score of a sentence exceeds the threshold, the sentence is extracted as part of the abstract and then we get an abstract of this report. For the result evaluation,we select 50 pieces of APT reports to be generated, and we choose to compare the abstract which is generated by TextRank with the one generated by LDA model. And the average number of sentences of an abstract is also our evaluation criteria to show the performance.

Event Extraction Evaluation. We input the separated words to the APTBert pre-training model. In the self-attention mechanism stage, 6 layers of encoder are set for deep encoding, and each encoder section contains residual linking and regularization operations. The vector characterization is generated through the APTBert model and sent to the multi-headed self-attention mechanism module for feature extraction by stitching with the lexical feature encoding corresponding to the token, the Wikipedia graph node feature encoding and the entity type feature encoding finally through the CRF layer. The probability distribution of each token is learned from the constraints, and the loss value is calculated using cross-entropy as the loss function and then back-propagated to optimize the parameters of the multi-headed self-attention mechanism network. Finally, we compare the result with BiLSTM model to show the performance of APTBert model.

4.4   Result and Analysis

Abstract Generation. The following is the result of an abstract generation for a specific APT report. The abstract can be read to get a general idea of the entire report. The abstract generates the main elements of an APT incident that occurred in October 2018, and it can be seen that the main attack-side players and victim-side players can be presented in the abstract. By generating abstracts for 50 texts using the LDA model and the methods of this thesis pair, the results are as follows:

Table 3. The effect of different methods of abstract generation

Abstract Generation Method	Grammar Error Rate	Average Number of Sentences
LDA	27%	17.6
TextRank	0%	14.8

Compared with other abstract generation methods such as LDA, the results of this experiment have the advantage that grammatical correctness can be guaranteed.

Event Extraction. We divided the 600 reports into 500/50/50 as training set/test set/evaluation set for effect evaluation. The experiments show that using the APTBert pre-training model as the base representation, splicing three external features provided by Corenlp tool, entity type, lexicality and knowledge embedding provided by Wikipedia as input, and trained by multi-headed self-attention neural network, the performance is better compared with the traditional scheme. The extraction results of all characters were evaluated together and their F1 values were calculated and reached 77.4%. The specific performance is shown in Table 4.

Table 4. Different methods of attack event extraction effect

Embedding	Extraction Model	Recall	Precision	F1
Word2vec	BiLSTM	0.471	0.794	0.591
Glove	BiLSTM	0.509	0.802	0.623
Bert-base-uncased	BiLSTM	0.643	0.886	0.745
APTBert	**Multi-head Self-Attention**	**0.677**	**0.902**	**0.774**

In addition, Table 5 shows a demonstration of the effect of this APT report extraction.

Table 5. Example of event role extraction results

Event Role	Content
Attackers	Cloud Atlas
Victims	industries and governmental entities
Related Activities	cyber-espionage operations
Attack Time	beginning of 2019 until July
Victim Location	Russia, Central Asia and regions of Ukraine
Means of Attack	spear-phishing, spear-phishing emails
Attack Tools	PowerShell backdoor, malicious remote templates, polymorphic VBS implant, polymorphic HTA
Sensitive Information	context file computed by the HTA
Purpose of The Attack	compromise its targets, compromise high value targets, PowerShell and VBS modules to execute on the local computer
Damage Caused	null
Vulnerabilities Exploited By The Attack	CVE-2017-11882, CVE-2018-0802
Vulnerable Systems	Microsoft
Defensive Tools	IoC-based defence
Attacker Clues	null

We can see that the performance of the APTBert-based attack event extraction model in regards to the task of extracting the event elements. Among the extracted attacker entities are the hacker group Cloud Atlas, the victims are industrial entities and governments, etc., the time of the attack is from July 2019 to launch the attack, using attacks such as phishing emails, and the relevant vulnerabilities exploited are CVE-2017-11882 and CVE-2018-0802.

5   Limitations

The existing problems and possible improvement directions of the paper include the fact that the proposed method of the paper is higher than the traditional methods in terms of recall rate, but still only 67.7%. In order to improve the recall rate, the APTBert pre-training model can be pre-trained on a richer corpus, and the training task of whether it is a contextual sentence can be introduced. In addition, the definition of roles in APT attacks is not comprehensive enough, and more related work can be read to classify the roles of APT events in a more fine-grained way; finally, more external features such as (dependency graphs in corenlp, etc.) can be introduced to do ablation experiments to improve the extraction effect and evaluate the model's relative effectiveness.

6   Conclusion

In this paper, we first investigate and propose an APTBert pre-training model to address the problem that existing work cannot effectively characterize the proprietary vocabulary in the security field. And then we define 14 types of key roles in APT events and identifies two main goals of the APT report-oriented attack event extraction task, abstract generation and event extraction. In addition, we investigate how to generate abstracts from APT reports. And the role of attack events are extracted from APT reports. Finally, in this paper, 863 texts from the security domain were collected for self-supervised pre-training. The APTBert pre-training model is generated and the text is characterized based on this model. It enables the effective characterization of the raw texts in the dedicated domain. And the APTBert-based event extraction method is proposed and experimented, which has better performance in the experimental results compared with the traditional extraction model, reaching 77.4% of F1 value.

Acknowledgment. This work was supported in part by National Key Research and Development Program of China (No.2021YFB3100500), Sichuan Science and Technology Program (No.2023YFG0162), and Open Fund of Anhui Province Key Laboratory of Cyberspace Security Situation Awareness and Evaluation (No.CSSAE-2021-001).

References

1. Moon, D., Im, H., Kim, I., et al.: DTB-IDS: an intrusion detection system based on decision tree using behavior analysis for preventing APT attacks. J. Supercomput. **73**, 2881–2895 (2017). https://doi.org/10.1007/s11227-015-1604-8

2. Rush, A.M., Chopra, S., Weston, J.: A neural attention model for abstractive sentence summarization. In: Conference on Empirical Methods in Natural Language Processing (2015)

3. Mihalcea, R., Tarau, P.: TextRank: bringing order into text. In: Proceedings of the 2004 Conference on Empirical Methods in Natural Language Processing, pp. 404–411 (2004)

4. Blei, D.M., Ng, A.Y., Jordan, M.I.: Latent dirichlet allocation. J. Mach. Learn. Res. **3**(Jan), 993–1022 (2003)

5. Ostendorff, M., et al.: Enriching BERT with knowledge graph embeddings for document classification. arXiv preprint: arXiv:1909.08402 (2019)

6. Lou, D., et al.: MLBiNet: a cross-sentence collective event detection network. arXiv preprint: arXiv:2105.09458 (2021)

7. Chen, Y., et al.: Event extraction via dynamic multi-pooling convolutional neural networks. In: Proceedings of the 53rd Annual Meeting of the Association for Computational Linguistics and the 7th International Joint Conference on Natural Language Processing (Volume 1: Long Papers), pp. 167–176 (2015)

8. Yagcioglu, S., et al.: Detecting cybersecurity events from noisy short text. arXiv preprint: arXiv:1904.05054 (2019)

9. LeCun, Y., Bottou, L., Bengio, Y., et al.: Gradient-based learning applied to document recognition. Proc. IEEE **86**(11), 2278–2324 (1998)

10. Luo, N., et al.: A framework for document-level cybersecurity event extraction from open source data. In: 2021 IEEE 24th International Conference on Computer Supported Cooperative Work in Design (CSCWD), pp. 422–427. IEEE (2021)

11. Piskorski, J., Tanev, H., Balahur, A.: Exploiting twitter for border security-related intelligence gathering. In: 2013 European Intelligence and Security Informatics Conference, pp. 239–246. IEEE (2013)

12. Burr, B., et al.: On the detection of persistent attacks using alert graphs and event feature embeddings. In: NOMS 2020–2020 IEEE/IFIP Network Operations and Management Symposium, pp. 1–4. IEEE (2020)

13. Nguyen, T.H., Cho, K., Grishman, R.: Joint event extraction via recurrent neural networks. In Proceedings of the 2016 Conference of the North American Chapter of the Association for Computational Linguistics: Human Language Technologies, pp. 300–309. Association for Computational Linguistics, San Diego, California (2016)

14. Gers, F.A., Schmidhuber, J., Cummins, F.: Learning to forget: continual prediction with LSTM. Neural Comput. **12**(10), 2451–2471 (2000). https://doi.org/10.1162/089976600300015015

15. Guo, Q., Huang, J., Xiong, N., Wang, P.: MS-pointer network: abstractive text summary based on multi-head self-attention. IEEE Access **7**, 138603–138613 (2019). https://doi.org/10.1109/ACCESS.2019.2941964

16. Satyapanich, T., Ferraro, F., Finin, T.: CASIE: extracting cybersecurity event information from text. In: Proceedings of the AAAI Conference on Artificial Intelligence, vol. 34, no. 05, pp. 8749–8757 (2020)

17. Vaswani, A., et al.: Attention is all you need. In: Advances in Neural Information Processing Systems, vol. 30 (2017)

18. He, K., et al.: Deep residual learning for image recognition. In: Proceedings of the IEEE Conference on Computer Vision and Pattern Recognition, pp. 770–778 (2016)

19. Ba, J.L., Kiros, J.R., Hinton, G.E.: Layer normalization. arXiv preprint: arXiv:1607.06450 (2016)

20. Santurkar, S., et al.: How does batch normalization help optimization? In: Advances in Neural Information Processing Systems, vol. 31 (2018)

21. Manning, C.D., et al.: The Stanford CoreNLP natural language processing toolkit. In: Proceedings of 52nd Annual Meeting of the Association for Computational Linguistics: System Demonstrations, pp. 55–60 (2014)

22. Wang, Q., Mao, Z., Wang, B., et al.: Knowledge graph embedding: a survey of approaches and applications. IEEE Trans. Knowl. Data Eng. **29**(12), 2724–2743 (2017)

23. Hochreiter, S., Schmidhuber, J.: Long short-term memory. Neural Comput. **9**(8), 1735–1780 (1997)

24. Chung, J., et al.: Empirical evaluation of gated recurrent neural networks on sequence modeling. arXiv preprint: arXiv:1412.3555 (2014)

25. Huang, Z., Xu, W., Yu, K.: Bidirectional LSTM-CRF models for sequence tagging. arXiv preprint: arXiv:1508.01991 (2015)

Assessing the Effectiveness of Deception-Based Cyber Defense with CyberBattleSim

Quan Hong[1,2], Jiaqi Li[1,2], Xizhong Guo[1], Pan Xie[3], and Lidong Zhai[2(✉)]

[1] School of Cyber Security, University of Chinese Academy of Sciences, Beijing, China
guoxizhong23@mails.ucas.ac.cn

[2] Institute of Information Engineering, Chinese Academy of Sciences, Beijing, China
{hongquan,lijiaqi,zhailidong}@iie.ac.cn

[3] China United Network Communications Group Co., Ltd., Beijing, China
xiepan@chinaunicom.cn

Abstract. Deception-Based Cyber Defense technology involves deploying various elements within a network to deliberately mislead and deceive potential attackers, enabling the early detection and warning of cyberattacks in their nascent stages. However, there is a lack of systematic research on defensive effectiveness, applicability in different scenarios, and potential synergies with other defense mechanisms of various deception technologies. To address this research gap, this study incorporates negative rewards within the CyberBattleSim platform to simulate the consequences imposed on adversaries when encountering deception techniques. We then assess the efficacy of diverse cyber deception strategies through the cumulative reward trend of attackers. Furthermore, we simulated the combined deployment of different deception technologies and the deployment of deception technology in distinct network scenarios, to evaluate the synergistic impact of deception technologies when coupled with other defensive measures and explore the suitable application scenarios of deception technology. The outcomes of multiple experiments conducted on the CyberBattleSim platform demonstrate that deception technology can impact attackers by delaying or preventing penetration and the combination of distinct deception techniques can yield varying enhancements in defense effectiveness. Additionally, the combination of Shock Trap and honeypot technology can maximize the defense effect.

Keywords: CyberBattleSim · Deception-Based Defense · Cybersecurity · Defense Effect Evaluation · Simulation

1 Introduction

The essence of cyber security lies in offensive and defensive confrontation. However, the current state of affairs indicates an imbalance in terms of time,

S. Goel and P. R. Nunes de Souza (Eds.): ICDF2C 2023, LNICST 571, pp. 224–243, 2024.
https://doi.org/10.1007/978-3-031-56583-0_15

resources, information, and roles between the offensive and defensive sides. Moreover, the attack method determines the direction of cyber-defense technology development, resulting in a persistent lag for defenders. To reverse this imbalance, defenders are constantly exploring novel active defense strategies and technologies, such as moving target defense(MTD) and the honeypot. Among these technologies, we believe that deception-based defense technology holds immense potential to shift the offense-defense balance and enable proactive defense because it can not only enhance the effectiveness of defense methods but also analyze the behavior and techniques of attackers. Cyber deception technology, as denoted by previous research [12], leverages deceptive tactics within the domain of cyber security defense to interfere and mislead attackers by creating false information. This defense strategy can not only delay and consume the attacker's time but also provide early detection and warning of potential cyber threats.

Currently, deception technology has become a critical defense mechanism within the cyber security field, with widely employed technologies including the honeypot and honeynet. However, despite the existence of a variety of classic deception defense techniques, their practical application in real-world environments still faces several intricate evaluation challenges. Firstly, it is difficult to effectively quantify and evaluate the actual effectiveness of deception defense technologies in a network, making it difficult for security teams to make informed choices among divergent deception defense technologies. Secondly, the effects of distinct deception defense technologies in different network scenarios and against different attack methods have not been fully studied, which makes it difficult for defenders to maximize their defense effects when formulating network security defense strategies. Finally, the comprehensive defense effect of the combination of different deception defense technologies lacks sufficient digital evidence support, hampering the provision of clear guidance to defenders when implementing complex multi-layered network security strategies. In summary, due to the lack of comprehensive evaluation of deception defense technologies, it becomes challenging for security teams to select appropriate deception defense technologies in different scenarios. Therefore, this paper aims to explore the defensive effects of employing various deception techniques either individually or in combination across diverse scenarios. Furthermore, the acquired insights regarding defense effectiveness will be utilized to identify suitable application scenarios for the employed defense technologies, thereby providing valuable guidance to cybersecurity professionals in the design and implementation of robust defense systems. The principal contributions of this paper are as follows:

- We leverage the CyberBattleSim platform [19] for our experimentation and research, enabling us to validate and compare the defense effects of three distinct deception technologies: honeypot, decoy, and Shock Trap. We will elaborate on our reasons for choosing these three deception techniques in Sect. 2.
- We pioneer the application of the CyberBattleSim platform as a means to guide defenders by assessing the synergistic effect achieved through the combination of various deception techniques.

- Our study introduces an innovative approach by utilizing the CyberBattleSim platform to identify suitable application scenarios for the newly proposed defense technology. To exemplify this, we employ the novel deception technology called "Shock Trap" [13] as a case study to validate its application scenarios.
- This research provides a solution that enables researchers to quickly verify the defense effects of different deception strategies under a custom network architecture with less resource investment. This provides guidance for enterprises to select and deploy a combination of different deception techniques in a network environment to maximize the effectiveness of their defenses.

The rest of the paper is structured as follows. In Sect. 2, we elaborate on the process of incorporating deception techniques into the CyberBattleSim platform and the reward parameters configured for each specific deception technique. In Sect. 3, we propose three research questions that serve as the focal points of investigation in this paper, and conduct experimental evaluations for each research question, thus providing strong support for our research. Section 4 presents a brief review of related research work. In Sect. 5, we outline and discuss the limitations of our approach, while also delineating potential major research works in the future. Finally, we conclude this paper in Sect. 6.

2   Methodology

In this section, we provide a comprehensive overview of the CyberBattleSim platform [19] and its characteristics. Additionally, we describe the simulation environment we have constructed on this platform to evaluate the defense effects of various deception techniques. While the CyberBattleSim platform does not inherently support the simulation and testing of deception technology, we refer to the approach of introducing negative reward values proposed by Walter et al. [20]. This mechanism enables the attacker to acquire negative rewards upon encountering deception elements, thereby simulating the penalty of deception defense techniques on the attacker. To enhance the precision of defense effect evaluation, we configure the negative reward parameters according to the principles and properties of deception techniques. This study simulates honeypot, decoy, and Shock Trap in CyberBattleSim. The main reasons for choosing these technologies are as follows. Firstly, these technologies are all active defense technologies based on deception strategies. Evaluating the defense effect of active defense technologies can provide substantial help and guidance for enterprises when deploying and applying state-of-the-art defense technologies. Secondly, the honeypot and decoy are well-established and widely used deception defense technologies. In addition, these two technologies exhibit divergent levels of interactivity enabling us to conduct a useful comparative analysis that yields valuable insights. Thirdly, Shock Trap is an emergent deception defense technology in recent years. The simulation of Shock Trap can not only demonstrate the ability of our study to evaluate the efficacy of nascent technologies but also reflect the ability of this research to select applicable scenarios for emerging technologies. Finally, simulations of mature and emerging deception active defense techniques underscore the comprehensiveness and generality of our study. This means that our research methodology is not only applicable to technologies that have been widely used but also to technologies that are emerging, thus providing a comprehensive evaluation and guidance for different types of defense technologies. In Sect. 2.2, we will provide a comprehensive introduction to the fundamental principles of these technologies and explain the procedure of their integration into the CyberBattleSim platform.

2.1 Environment Details

CyberBattleSim. CyberBattleSim is an open-source cyber attack and defense simulation tool released by Microsoft in April 2021. It is an experimental research platform based on reinforcement learning. It can abstract computer network and cyber security concepts at a high level, thereby abstracting the enterprise network environment into a simulation environment in which researchers can study the behavior and strategies of automated attack agents. The simulated environment consists of a network topology and a parameterized set of vulnerabilities, which can be exploited by potential attackers to move laterally in the network provided by the simulated environment. The evaluation of offensive and defensive effectiveness relies on two primary metrics: the number of simulated steps taken to accomplish a specific objective, and the cumulative reward of simulated steps across training epochs [19]. Additionally, CyberBattleSim allows researchers to design and modify simulation environments based on specific research scenarios and requirements. CyberBattleSim uses reinforcement learning algorithms to train automatic agents that are deemed attackers or defenders. These agents interact with the simulation environment to explore the optimal behavior strategy in a simulated cyber scenario. Various algorithms are employed by CyberBattleSim to train automatic agents, including Credential Lookup, Tabular Q-Learning, Deep Q-Learning (DQL), Random Search, epsilon-greedy [19]. These algorithms possess unique advantages and disadvantages, as well as distinct application scenarios, which can be selected according to network topologies and goals.

Simulation Environment. Based on CyberBattleSim, we built an abstract network simulation environment called TinyCTF. It is a modified version of the Toy Capture the Flag (ToyCTF) simulation environment provided by CyberBattleSim. The state space of TinyCTF is shown in Fig. 1. TinyCTF is an abstract representation of an enterprise's internal network topology that simulates various network assets with different security levels and attacker agents.

TinyCTF consists of 10 nodes, with each node representing either a machine or a service running on a machine. The client node serves as the initial node for the attacker to initiate lateral movement within the intranet. The edges within the graph symbolize the various attack methods that an attacker can employ. The attacker can employ three attack methods: local attack, remote attack, and authenticated connection to discover and gain control of nodes in the network. Specifically, performing a local attack can obtain credentials or other sensitive information on the controlled machine, while performing a remote attack can

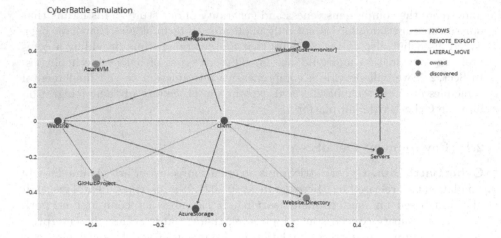

Fig. 1. The state space of TinyCTF.

discover nodes or exploit vulnerabilities on a known machine to acquire credentials. Authenticated connection means using already obtained credentials to log in and control other systems, but certain conditions must be met such as the machine being discovered, valid credentials, and enabled authentication service. The simulation environment is only partially observable for the attacker. As a result, the attacker must take action to incrementally explore the network starting from the nodes it currently possesses.

2.2   Integrating Deception Technology into CyberBattleSim

In recent years, numerous representative deception defense technologies have emerged, including Honeypot, Decoy, Honeytoken, Shock Trap, and Chaff bug [5,12,14,16]. In this section, we first introduce the basic concepts of the three deception-based active defense techniques chosen for simulation and then elaborate on their instantiation within the CyberBattleSim simulation environment. Furthermore, this section will introduce and explain the setting of the corresponding negative reward values.

Deception Defense Techniques to Evaluate. The honeypot is a cybersecurity mechanism that diverts adversaries' attention away from the real target through strategies such as luring and deception, and at the same time detects attacks early and collects attack-related data [21]. The concept of the honeypot was not initially developed for cybersecurity purposes. In 2004, Provos [17] introduced a virtual honeypot framework and demonstrated its application in the security field, which subsequently led to the widespread adoption of the honeypot in the security field. Although the basic concepts of decoy and honeypot are very similar, there exist several differences between them. Firstly, the decoy takes the form of low-fidelity, low-interaction fake systems and is commonly used to detect early attack stages like port scanning and information gathering. The honeypot is generally deployed in the form of high-fidelity, high-interaction fake systems, which can interact more with attackers, thereby revealing more attack behaviors and methods. Secondly, the decoy is easier for administrators to create and manage than the honeypot. Recent research has demonstrated that the decoy can delay and consume an attacker's time even if they are discovered [8]. Shock Trap [13] is a deception defense technology that leverages vulnerabilities as defense resources. Different from defense technologies focused on vulnerability identification and patching, its core idea is to deploy traps based on vulnerabilities in the system and embed corresponding security mechanisms to prevent vulnerabilities from being successfully exploited. When an attacker exploits a vulnerability that builds a trap, the trap will be triggered, and then security mechanisms will detect, deny, and track the attack to deter the attacker.

Based on the principles and deception strategy of the honeypot, decoy, and Shock Trap, we configure varying negative reward values to integrate them into the simulated environment. As the attacker progresses through the exploration and control of nodes, they will inevitably encounter the deception elements established within the simulated environment. Each of the three deception techniques is implemented and characterized differently in the simulated environment.

Decoy. Within the simulated environment, the decoy is represented as virtual nodes that are generated by cloning real nodes. These decoy nodes cannot be connected or controlled by attackers. On other nodes, the attacker will find credentials that connect to the decoy nodes, but any attempt to utilize such credentials will fail. In our experimental setup, the attacker will get a reward value of -100 for the initial connection to the decoy node, and a reward value of -1 for subsequent connecting to the same decoy node.

Honeypot. The honeypot, like the decoy, is also represented as virtual nodes that are generated by cloning real nodes, but they can be connected or controlled by attackers. In our experimental configuration, the initial connection to a honeypot node by the attacker will yield a reward value of -100, and subsequent connecting to the same honeypot node shall incur a diminished penalty, amounting to a reward value of -1. Moreover, the honeypot node also contains a large number of bogus credentials, and when the attacker uses these fake credentials to connect to other nodes, an alert is also generated, which is reflected in our experiment as giving the attacker a reward value of -10.

Shock Trap. Shock Trap is strategically deployed on real nodes in the simulated environment. Since Shock Trap can deploy traps to prevent attackers from exploiting vulnerabilities, we regard the nodes where Shock Trap is deployed as nodes that cannot be controlled. In our experimental configuration, an attacker who exploits a vulnerability on a shock trap deployment node for the first time will receive a reward value of -150, and subsequent exploits of the same vulnerability will result in a reward value of -1. Moreover, as Shock Trap is a new technology, we will assess its defense effect in various scenarios and identify suitable application scenarios for its deployment. Finally, we will explain why we set different negative reward parameters like this in Sect. 2.3.

2.3   Reward Parameters

CyberBattleSim employs two metrics to evaluate the attacking agents: the number of simulation steps required to control the network and the cumulative reward earned by the agent during the attack. A reward value is a floating-point number that reflects the value of the attacker-controlled nodes. In our experimentation, we employed a standardized value of 1000 for all nodes that did not deploy the deception elements. However, it is acknowledged that this approach may not accurately represent real-world scenarios, where systems possess varying levels of value, such as critical infrastructure being more valuable than common systems in practical contexts. Nonetheless, this decision was influenced by several factors. Firstly, it aligns with the default configuration of the CyberBattleSim platform and the node value settings introduced by Walter et al. [20] in their integration of deception elements into the CyberBattleSim. Secondly, the objective of our experiments was to evaluate the defensive effectiveness of deception techniques by examining their impact on cumulative rewards. Therefore, unifying the values of nodes can provide a more general scenario to comprehensively evaluate the defense effect. The cumulative reward serves as an indicator of the attacker's degree of control over the network, with higher values indicating greater occupation. Moreover, it is noteworthy that CyberBattleSim itself only employs positive rewards within its framework. To assess the defense effect of the deception defense technology, we introduced various negative reward mechanisms based on the properties of deception technology, and then we compared and analyzed the impact of various deception defense technologies on cumulative rewards.

We define different negative reward values as illustrated in Table 1. The initial negative reward value assigned to an attacker upon triggering a deception technique for the first time depends on the impact the deception technique has on the attacker. For instance, when an attacker first connects to a honeypot or decoy, they will be penalized with a -100 reward value. Likewise, when an attacker first connects to a node deployed with Shock Trap, they will be penalized with a -150 reward value. The reasons why we chose to configure negative rewards in this way are as follows:

1. At present, regarding the evaluation of the defense effect of deception technology, research mainly focuses on the delay of attack time and the reduction of attack scans after the introduction of deception technologies such as honeypots/decoys. For example, studies by Aggarwal et al. [1] explored the proportion of attacks targeting conventional systems versus honeypot systems after the introduction of the honeypot, while Kocaogullar et al. [15] studied the capture of attack packets in the presence of honeypots. Balogh et al. [6] assessed the delay effect on attackers upon the introduction of honeypots. However, these studies are only limited to the evaluation of some aspects of

the defense effect of deception technology and lack a comprehensive evaluation of the impact of technologies such as honeypots and decoys on attackers. Taking the honeypot as an example, its impact on attackers encompasses three dimensions. Firstly, it delays attacks and provides timely alerts, affording defenders the time required for identifying and responding to attacks. Secondly, it can confuse attackers and redirect attack traffic toward false targets, thereby reducing attacks on real systems. Lastly, it facilitates the collection of data on attacker methods and attack characteristics, supporting the development of more advanced artificial intelligence-based defense technologies. Nonetheless, comprehensive assessments that consider the collective influence of these three aspects on attacks are lacking, and there are no standardized evaluation criteria for deception defense technologies. Consequently, we opt to customize negative reward values based on the distinct defense attributes of deception technologies. While the honeypot and decoy can divert and delay attacks, they cannot entirely prevent attackers from intruding. Their countermeasures against attackers mainly arise from defenders potentially leveraging the data they gather to profile attackers. Consequently, we set the negative reward value for the honeypot and decoy at one-tenth of the real node value, i.e., -100. Compared with technologies such as the honeypot that only detects and delays attacks, Shock Trap not only detects and denies the attack but also traces the attack, potentially exposing the identity and location of the attacker, thereby acting as a deterrent. To better compare and analyze the effect of deception defense technology, we slightly elevate the negative reward value for Shock Trap to reflect its distinct defensive characteristics.

2. Currently, there are relatively few studies evaluating the effectiveness of deception defense technologies using CyberBattleSim. We refer to the parameter settings proposed by Walter et al. [20], whose research has demonstrated that using these values can yield favorable evaluation outcomes.

3. The initial negative reward value after the deception element is triggered depends on the proactive nature of the defense. However, its value fluctuations have minimal impact on the attacker's cumulative reward trend. This is because, in our experimental scenario, only a single deception element is deployed. For automated agents simulating thousands of attacks, the cumulative reward is affected by the initial negative reward value only after the initial triggering of the deception technique. Subsequent cumulative reward trends are primarily influenced by the frequency of repeated triggers of the deception element, which, in turn, is influenced by the specific attributes of the deception element and the algorithm driving the attacker agent. We have also conducted corresponding experimental verification in Sect. 3.1.

In this study, the reward value assigned to the attacker for repetitively triggering deception elements within the simulated environment is set to -1. This determination is not only influenced by the parameter settings established by Walter et al. [20] but also rooted in several considerations. Firstly, during the process of an attacker's attempts to intrude on a network, they often connect with deceptive elements multiple times. If the negative reward value is set too

Table 1. The reward value for the agent's actions

Behavior of the attacking agent	reward value
Wrong credentials/password	−10
Repeated Mistake	−1
Trigger Shock Trap	−150
The exploit works	+50
Connect honeypot or decoy	−100
Control of node	+1000
Control of honeypot	0

high, the attacker's cumulative rewards will drop rapidly, which does not accurately reflect the practical scenario. In our experiments, establishing a reward value of −1 for the attacker's repetitive triggering of deception elements serves to provide a realistic reflection of the current attack and defense situation. Importantly, this configuration yields results that are consistent with the outcomes observed in numerous studies evaluating deception techniques. Further elaboration on this point can be found in Sect. 3. Secondly, the assessment of defense technology's effectiveness primarily focuses on the trend of the attacker's cumulative reward, and the specific size of this negative reward value mainly affects the speed rather than the fundamental direction of the trend change. The key lies in the number of triggers of this negative reward value, which is the core factor in evaluating defense effects. This study also proves this point in Sect. 3.1.

We set the value of the honeypot node to 0 because attackers will not gain any benefit from controlling the honeypot and will only consume their time. Furthermore, within the source code of CyberBattleSim, a negative reward value configuration exists explicitly designed to address situations involving incorrect password entries during the authentication process, with a default reward value set at −10. While this configuration is deactivated by default in CyberBattleSim, it is important to note that the honeypot environment contains a substantial number of fake credentials. Hence, when an attacker attempts to authenticate using these fake credentials and subsequently fails, we treat this behavior as analogous to an incorrect password entry. To account for this, we have enabled the configuration in CyberBattleSim for handling incorrect passwords, resulting in a penalty of −10 reward points for attackers, regardless of whether they employ counterfeit credentials or enter incorrect passwords.

3   Evaluation

Our experiments utilize two distinct algorithms to train the attacking agent, namely Random Search and Deep Q-Learning (DQL). The Random Search algorithm is implemented by having the attacking agent randomly select an action at each step, while the Deep Q-Learning algorithm leverages the Deep Q-Network

(DQN) to learn from previous experiences to achieve the highest possible reward in the fewest steps. The experiment aims to explore and answer the following three research questions:

RQ1. How effective are deception defense technologies such as the Shock Trap, Honeypot, and Decoy in defending against cyber-attacks?

RQ2. Can the combination of defense technologies such as the Shock Trap, Honeypot, and Decoy, effectively enhance the security of information systems? Furthermore, which pairing of two deception techniques yields the highest degree of defense effectiveness?

RQ3. How does the defense effect of the Shock Trap vary across different scenarios? Specifically, which network topology scenarios are most suitable for its deployment? Additionally, what level of protection can the Shock Trap provide to the system within its optimal deployment scenario?

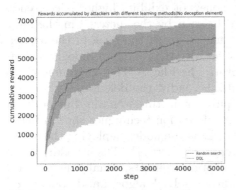

(a) Cumulative rewards plot of the agent without deception elements.

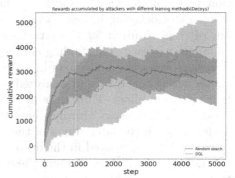

(b) Cumulative reward plot of the agent under decoy deployment.

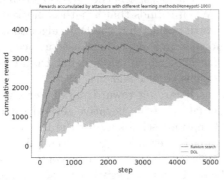

(c) Cumulative reward plot of the agent under honeypot deployment.

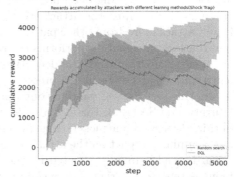

(d) Cumulative reward plot of the agent under Shock Trap deployment.

Fig. 2. The cumulative reward plot of the agent under the non-deception defense technology, decoy, honeypot, and Shock Trap.

3.1   RQ1: Evaluate Different Deception Defense Techniques

To minimize the interference of deceptive element position in the network on defense effectiveness, we deployed the deceptive elements on the same node (GitHubProject) in the TinyCTF environment. Figure 2 illustrates a comparison of the defensive effects of various strategies (no deception elements and decoy, honeypot, and Shock Trap respectively used on the same node) in the TinyCTF scenario. The colored shading in the figures shows the standard deviation from each line.

Based on the experimental results, we observed that all three deception techniques, namely the decoy, honeypot, and Shock Trap, can impede the attacker to some extent in the TinyCTF scenario. This observation aligns with the outcomes of other research endeavors that have assessed deception techniques via real-world deployments [8] and Capture The Flag (CTF) [6]. A comparison of Figs. 2b, 2c, and 2d, revealed the following conclusions. Firstly, in comparison to the decoy and Shock Trap, the honeypot exhibits higher effectiveness in terms of delaying attacks, which can be seen by the increase in the number of steps required for the attacking agent to reach the peak of the average cumulative reward. This finding is consistent with the results of Balogh et al. [6] who deployed some honeypots in a Capture The Flag (CTF) environment and subsequently collected and analyzed data. Secondly, the defense effects of the honeypot and Shock Trap are almost equivalent in this scenario, but both are superior to the decoy. Thirdly, these three deception techniques show a better performance in the later stages of the attack, as the nodes deploying the deception elements are located in the deep layers of the network. The attacking agent is unaffected until it encounters these deception elements. Finally, none of the three deception techniques significantly affect the DQL algorithm-driven attacking agent, particularly Shock Trap. The role of the Shock Trap is to prevent attackers from entering deep nodes for further attacks, but the DQL algorithm can adaptively adjust the attack strategy. When it finds that a path is blocked, it will attack more from other paths. It is worth noting that the DQL algorithm-based attacking agent outperforms the random search algorithm-based attacking agent after incorporating the deceptive elements , which implies that DQL can learn and adapt better in the presence of defensive mechanisms.

In this section, we validate our opinions regarding reward parameter configuration in Sect. 2.3. First of all, the fluctuation of the negative reward value obtained when the attacker triggers the deception technology for the first time has a minimal impact on the attacker's cumulative reward trend. The cumulative reward trend is mainly affected by the frequency with which the deception element is repeatedly triggered. Secondly, the oscillation in negative reward values resulting from repeated activation of the deception technology by the attacker influences the rate of change in cumulative rewards, yet it does not significantly alter the fundamental trend. Furthermore, a high setting of this negative reward value leads to cumulative reward trends that deviate from the authentic attack and defense scenarios.

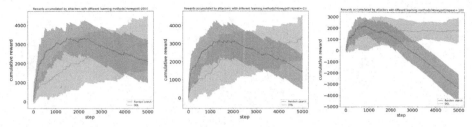

(a) Cumulative reward plot when the negative reward for the first trigger is -200.   (b) Cumulative reward plot when the negative reward for repeated triggers is -2.   (c) Cumulative reward plot when the negative reward for repeated triggers is -10

Fig. 3. The cumulative reward plot of the agent after the honeypot's reward parameters are modified.

We employed the prior assessment of the honeypot defense efficacy as a reference point and modified the negative reward value assigned when the attacker first triggers the deception technology, setting it to -200. All other control conditions remained unaltered, and we subsequently conducted the controlled experiment. Through a comparative analysis between Fig. 2c, and Fig. 3a, we can deduce that the fluctuation in the negative reward value upon the initial activation of the deception technology has a minimal impact on the attacker's cumulative reward trend. It will only slightly affect the cumulative reward obtained by the attacker throughout the intrusion process. To illustrate, following 5000 steps taken by the attacker, the average cumulative reward for the attack agent driven by the random search algorithm decreased from approximately 2150 to about 2050. Similarly, the average cumulative reward for the attack agent driven by the DQL algorithm also decreased by approximately 100.

In addition, we also conducted another set of controlled experiments, adjusting the negative reward values for the attacker to repeatedly trigger the deception technique to -2 and -10 respectively. During this process, all other control conditions remained constant, and subsequent experimental tests were conducted. By comparing the results in Figs. 2c, and 3b, we can draw the conclusion that for negative reward values that repeatedly trigger deception elements, moderate changes will have a certain impact on the rate of change of the cumulative reward, but will not change its basic trend. In comparing Fig. 2c, 3b, and 3c, it becomes evident that when the negative reward value for the repetitive triggering of deception elements is set at a high level, the attacker's cumulative reward will become negative. This outcome is inconsistent with the realities of cyber security. After conducting numerous experimental iterations, we set the negative reward value for repeated triggering of deception elements to -1. Under such a reward parameter configuration, we evaluate and test the honeypot's defense effect. By comparing Fig. 2a, and 2c, it becomes evident that the average cumulative reward of the attack agent driven by the random search algorithm decreased by approximately 50%, while the average cumulative reward of the attack agent

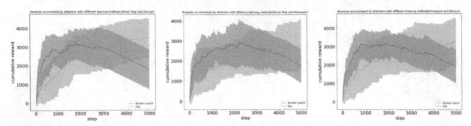

(a) The cumulative reward plot of the agent under the combination of decoy and Shock Trap.

(b) The cumulative reward plot of the agent under the combination of honeypot and Shock Trap.

(c) The cumulative reward plot of the agent under the combination of honeypot and decoy.

Fig. 4. The cumulative reward plot of the agent under the combination of different deception techniques.

driven by the DQL algorithm decreased by roughly one-third. This observation confirms the efficacy of honeypots in diverting and attracting cyber attacks, aligning with the results of other honeypot evaluation studies [1,2,7,18].

3.2 RQ2: The Effect of Combining Different Deception Defense Technologies

A study conducted in 2021 [20] showed that deploying the same defense technology at multiple nodes in CyberBattleSim would affect defense effectiveness. To better evaluate the effect of different combinations of deception defense techniques, we conducted an experiment in the TinyCTF scenario. In the experiment, we combined Shock Trap, honeypot, and decoy deception defense technologies in pairs, and deployed them on the same node (GitHubProject) to eliminate interference from the number of deception elements in the experimental results. Based on the experimental results illustrated in Fig. 4, it can be concluded that employing a combination of deception elements within nodes enhances the overall defense effectiveness compared to their individual deployment. However, it is crucial to note that the degree of improved defensive outcomes varies across different combinations of deception elements. Specifically, the combination of Shock Trap and honeypot exhibits greater efficacy in comparison to the pairing of decoy and honeypot.

The analysis of Figs. 2b,2c, and 4c reveals significant conclusion. When defending against agents driven by a random search algorithm, whether the decoy and honeypot are deployed individually or combined in the same node, they all exhibit similar defensive effects. This similar defensive effect is mainly manifested in the ability to delay the action of the attacking agent and the effect of suppressing the cumulative reward of the attacking agent. By comparing Fig. 2, 4a, and 4b, we can draw the following conclusions. The defense effect can be significantly improved by combining Shock Trap with either the honeypot or decoy, compared to their individual deployment. Particularly, the combined deployment of the Shock Trap and honeypot yields the best effect. When combating agents driven by random search algorithms, the combined deployment of Shock Trap and honeypot can effectively delay their actions and significantly decrease their cumulative reward value. Meanwhile, when dealing with the attacking agent driven by the DQL algorithm, it can restrain the upward trend of the attacking agent's cumulative reward and lower its peak value. The effectiveness of the honeypot in countering the adaptive strategies of DQL complements the limitations of the Shock Trap. Specifically, the honeypot serves as a magnet for attracting attack agents toward the node where Shock Trap is deployed. The Shock Trap, in turn, can prevent attackers from further breaching the node, thereby preventing subsequent attacks. When the attacking agent realizes the futility of launching attacks, it will adaptively adjust its strategy and choose to control the network from alternative paths. However, the coexistence of the honeypot within the Shock Trap-deployed node continues to allure attack agents, leading to a repetitive cycle of attack attempts until the agent eventually ceases its attack. Hence, we conclude that the combination of Shock Trap and honeypot can maximize its defensive effect. This finding also demonstrates the compatibility of the Shock Trap, which can be effectively combined with other deception defense technologies to enhance defense capability. The analysis and comparison of defense effects achieved through different combinations of defense technologies can offer valuable references for cyber defense practitioners in devising effective defense systems.

3.3   RQ3: Shock Trap Applicable Scenarios

To investigate the effectiveness of Shock Trap in different network scenarios and identify the optimal application scenarios, we conducted experiments using three network topologies with varying complexity: TinyCTF, ToyCTF, and StarCTF. The TinyCTF topology, which was introduced in Sect. 2.1, includes two attack paths for potential attackers. ToyCTF is a simulated environment provided by CyberBattleSim, which is very similar to TinyCTF but only contains one attack path. We also introduced a simple scenario, StarCTF, in which a client node can only access subsequent data nodes through a key service node. The three network topologies used are representative. After moderate abstraction and combing, the architecture of most enterprises can be represented by different variants of these network topologies. The effectiveness of Shock Trap in different network scenarios was evaluated by deploying it at the same position in ToyCTF and TinyCTF scenarios and comparing the results. The experimental results are shown in Fig. 2d, and Fig. 5a. It can be seen from the results that Shock Trap was able to effectively prevent attackers from attacking nodes in ToyCTF, where only one attack path was present. However, in TinyCTF, where multiple attack paths existed, Shock Trap had limited defense capabilities as attackers could bypass it through other paths.

To validate our conclusions, we conducted an experiment in which Shock Trap was deployed at the key service nodes of the StarCTF scenario. As shown in Fig. 5b, the results demonstrate that Shock Trap was highly effective in preventing the agent's attack, leaving it unable to obtain any cumulative rewards and only subjected to constant punishment. This outcome differs from the results obtained in the ToyCTF scenario, where the agent was able to gain some accumulated rewards by exploiting other vulnerable nodes before encountering Shock Trap. From these experiments, it was concluded that Shock Trap is suitable for deployment at key facilities such as routers or switches that can connect multiple systems and play a crucial role in the network topology. Moreover, the approach employed in this study provides references for cyber defense personnel in identifying the applicable scope of the technology and expeditiously identifying the optimal application scenario, all while minimizing costs and streamlining environment configuration.

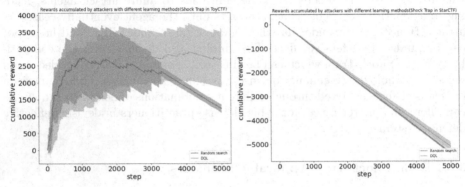

(a) The cumulative reward graph of the agent after deploying Shock Trap in the ToyCTF.

(b) The cumulative reward plot of the agent under Shock Trap deployment in the StarCTF.

Fig. 5. The cumulative reward plot of the agent after deploying Shock Trap in different scenarios.

4   Related Work

With the continuous evolution of offensive and defensive confrontations, novel deception defense technologies are constantly emerging, such as Chaff Bug and Shock Trap. To enhance the effective application of these defense technologies, it becomes imperative to undertake an evaluation of their practical efficacy. This necessitates the utilization of methodologies encompassing game theory, simulation techniques, and real-world scenario deployments. Game theory-based approaches provide a theoretical foundation for comprehending the role of deception technology, but the insights provided are relatively abstract, and the evaluation results may deviate from the actual situation. Aggarwal et al. [2,3] proposed a non-cooperative dynamic deception game. Through experiments and game theory modeling, they deeply studied the proportional impact of the timing and quantity of deception on attack behavior and non-attack behavior. However, this method is still limited to the theoretical level, and difficult to directly map to practical applications. The deployment of deception techniques in real-world scenarios, coupled with data collection, is currently regarded as the most precise evaluation approach. Nonetheless, this strategy presents several drawbacks, including substantial time and resource demands and the difficulty in controlling factors within the assessment environment. Ferguson-Walter et al. [10] analyzed four separate incidents roughly six months apart by tracking a three-person red team on a live operational network to assess the impact on attackers of the presence of decoys and being informed of the decoys. This research can provide insights into actual adversarial behavior but has limitations such as the small number of participants and the absence of control conditions. HAN et al. [11] assessed deception techniques in web applications by quantifying false positives in a production environment and evaluating detection accuracy in a controlled red team experiment involving 150 participants. This approach strikes a balance between real-world environments and controlled experiments but entails substantial manpower and time resources. In 2022, Kocaogullar et al. [15] deployed multiple honeypots within an actual network environment, collecting data over 14 days. Through an analysis of the gathered data, they explored the impact of high-interaction honeypots and low-interaction honeypots on attacks, including the types and proportions of attacks attracted, IP addresses captured, etc. Ferguson-Walter et al. [8,9] designed a network penetration testing experiment involving over 130 professional red team members. Their study analyzed the impact of cyber deception and psychological deception on attackers and evaluated the effectiveness of the decoy. This experimental approach takes into account the complexity of real-world scenarios and provides more specific insights into the evaluation and practical application of deception techniques.

Simulation techniques are an assessment method between theoretical and practical for evaluating deception techniques. This method can obtain relatively accurate assessment results in a short time while conserving substantial time and resources. Aggarwal et al. [1] proposed a simulation tool called "HackIt" to evaluate the effectiveness of honeypot deception timing in mitigating cyber attacks. The results obtained through this simulation approach are consistent with the conclusions obtained through dynamic deception games [2]. Balogh et al. [6] used the Capture The Flag (CTF) game to analyze and evaluate the effectiveness of honeypots in affording defenders additional time for detection and response, as well as their impact on delaying attackers. Compared with real-world scenarios, the utilization of CTF games for evaluating defense effects offers heightened controllability and facilitates more straightforward data collection. Compared to simulation tools such as "HackIt", CTF games provide more realistic datasets and simulations of attacker and defender behavior. In this study, we employ Microsoft's open-source cyber attack and defense simulation tool, CyberBattleSim [19], for a comprehensive evaluation of multiple deception technologies' defense effects. Other research on the CyberBattleSim platform also confirmed the feasibility of using CyberBattleSim to evaluate the efficacy of deception techniques. For example, Amin et al. [4] defined two types of attackers within the CyberBattleSim platform and explored the impact of deploying the decoy on these distinct attacker types.

The most closely related work to our research is a 2021 paper [20]. Their work incorporated multiple deception techniques into CyberBattleSim and investigated their impact on attacking agents driven by different algorithms. Moreover, they examined how the quantity and location of deception elements within the network affect the overall effectiveness of defensive measures. Drawing inspiration from the methods presented by Walter et al. [20], our work has innovated and expanded in many aspects. Firstly, our study goes beyond evaluating and comparing the individual defensive capabilities of different deception technologies. We conduct experiments to assess the defense effects achieved through the combination of various defense techniques. Secondly, we investigate leveraging platforms like CyberBattleSim to streamline the testing and identification of suitable application scenarios for emerging defense technologies. By utilizing such platforms, we can accelerate the evaluation process and help to identify the most promising deployment application scenarios for new defense technologies. Finally, we integrate a novel defense technology known as Shock Trap into the CyberBattleSim platform. Through a comparative analysis, we examine the distinguishing characteristics of the Shock Trap in contrast to other defense technologies like the honeypot and decoy.

5   Discussion

We incorporated deception techniques such as honeypot, decoy, and Shock Trap into the CyberBattleSim platform, and simulated the punishment of deception techniques on attacker behavior by introducing different negative reward mechanisms. We assess the defense effectiveness by comparing the impact of deception defense techniques on the attacker's cumulative reward. The results demonstrate that platforms such as CyberBattleSim can not only provide a rapid verification and testing environment for new defense techniques but also facilitate the identification of optimal defense technique combinations.

This study has made progress in assessing the effectiveness of deception technologies and identifying appropriate scenarios and combinations for defense technologies. However, some limitations and inadequacies need to be acknowledged. Firstly, the study only involves three deception defense technologies and has a small sample size, which limits its representativeness for the broader range of deception technologies. Secondly, there are certain differences between simulated scenarios and actual scenarios. For instance, the efficacy of defense technologies in simulated scenarios may align with theoretical expectations, but in the actual environment, managers' configuration errors may affect the defense effect, leading to differences. Additionally, system values vary in real-world scenarios, whereas simulated environments employ uniform node values, thereby deviating from the complexities of actual situations. Finally, the research is conducted within the CyberBattleSim platform, subject to some inherent constraints and limitations, mainly reflected in the following aspects:

- After turning on negative rewards in CyberBattleSim, the cumulative rewards of attacking agents are difficult to converge, and the introduction of deception elements further exacerbates this problem.
- The evaluation of defense effects primarily relies on a single index, namely the change in cumulative reward for attacking agents, which may not fully reflect the impact of deception elements on attackers.
- CyberBattleSim primarily analyzes the lateral movement cyber attack technology within the intranet, which limits its application scenarios.
- The limitations of the CBS platform prevent it from accurately simulating complex attack methods and vulnerability modes, resulting in a restricted range of simulated attack agents and vulnerability types. Consequently, the platform fails to fully reflect real-world attackers and vulnerabilities.

Given the above problems, future research work will focus on improving and exploring the following aspects. Firstly, evaluating and researching more deception defense technologies and other cyber defense technologies on the Cyber-BattleSim platform, to better understand their defensive effects, strengths and weaknesses, and synergies. Secondly, adopt more evaluation methods and standards. Besides using the cumulative reward as the evaluation index of the attack effect, the number of simulation steps required for an agent to control a network will also be employed. The fewer steps an agent takes, the better its attack strategy. Thirdly, an open challenge currently facing simulation technology is the discrepancy between simulation evaluation results and actual scenario evaluation results. In subsequent work, we will assign different values to different nodes in the simulation environment to reduce this difference, to provide more accurate and comprehensive guidance for the deployment of defense technology in real scenarios. Finally, enhancing the CyberBattleSim platform by abstracting and modeling the real network traffic, will enable simulations of more diverse network scenarios.

6   Conclusions

Based on CyberBattleSim, an open-source simulation tool from Microsoft, this paper introduces and investigates deception technologies such as decoy, honeypot, and Shock Trap in an abstract enterprise network topology environment. The objective is to explore the impact of these deception technologies individually or in combination on attacker agents. In addition, we also designed three different network topologies within the CyberBattleSim platform and deployed Shock Trap in each of them for experiments. The experimental results show the effectiveness of deception defense technologies, including the Shock Trap, honeypot, and decoy, in effectively delaying and preventing attackers. In particular, deploying the Shock Trap in combination with other deception defense technologies such as decoy or honeypot can significantly improve the defense effect. Furthermore, the experiments conducted within the CyberBattleSim platform, involving the deployment of Shock Trap in various network topologies, reveal that it is suitable for deployment in facilities that can connect multiple systems and play an important role in the network topology.

To sum up, enterprises need to invest a lot of manpower and time resources to evaluate and verify the effectiveness of defense technologies, and there are many uncontrollable factors during the evaluation process, that may pose threats to network security. This research presents a method for identifying suitable application scenarios and optimal combinations of defense techniques while minimizing deployment costs and simplifying environment configurations. The research results provide a valuable reference for security teams to design and implement multi-layered defense systems within real-world environments. In addition, based on the results of this study, security teams can systematically deploy and verify defense technologies in actual scenarios, thus yielding substantial time and workload savings. This strategic approach also facilitates the deployment of a defense system harmonious with the current network architecture, thereby maximizing its defense efficacy.

References

1. Aggarwal, P., Gautam, A., Agarwal, V., Gonzalez, C., Dutt, V.: *HackIT*: a human-in-the-loop simulation tool for realistic cyber deception experiments. In: Ahram, T., Karwowski, W. (eds.) AHFE 2019. AISC, vol. 960, pp. 109–121. Springer, Cham (2020). https://doi.org/10.1007/978-3-030-20488-4_11
2. Aggarwal, P., Gonzalez, C., Dutt, V.: Cyber-security: role of deception in cyber-attack detection. In: Nicholson, D. (ed.) AHFE 2016. AISC, vol. 501, pp. 85–96. Springer, Cham (2016). https://doi.org/10.1007/978-3-319-41932-9_8
3. Aggarwal, P., Gonzalez, C., Dutt, V.: Modeling the effects of amount and timing of deception in simulated network scenarios. In: 2017 International Conference on Cyber Situational Awareness, Data Analytics and Assessment (Cyber SA), pp. 1–7. IEEE (2017)
4. Al Amin, M.A.R., Shetty, S., Kamhoua, C.: Cyber deception metrics for interconnected complex systems. In: 2022 Winter Simulation Conference (WSC), pp. 473–483. IEEE (2022)
5. Almeshekah, M.H., Spafford, E.H., Atallah, M.J.: Improving security using deception. Technical report, CERIAS technical report 13. Center for Education and Research Information Assurance and Security, Purdue University (2013)
6. Balogh, Á., Érsok, M., Erdődi, L., Szarvák, A., Kail, E., Bánáti, A.: Honeypot optimization based on CTF game. In: 2022 IEEE 20th Jubilee World Symposium on Applied Machine Intelligence and Informatics (SAMI), pp. 000153–000158. IEEE (2022)
7. Crouse, M., Prosser, B., Fulp, E.W.: Probabilistic performance analysis of moving target and deception reconnaissance defenses. In: Proceedings of the Second ACM Workshop on Moving Target Defense, pp. 21–29 (2015)
8. Ferguson-Walter, K., Major, M., Johnson, C.K., Muhleman, D.H.: Examining the efficacy of decoy-based and psychological cyber deception. In: USENIX Security Symposium, pp. 1127–1144 (2021)
9. Ferguson-Walter, K., et al.: The Tularosa study: an experimental design and implementation to quantify the effectiveness of cyber deception. Technical report, Sandia National Lab. (SNL-NM), Albuquerque, NM, United States (2018)

10. Ferguson-Walter, K., LaFon, D., Shade, T.: Friend or faux: deception for cyber defense. J. Inf. Warfare **16**(2), 28–42 (2017)
11. Han, X., Kheir, N., Balzarotti, D.: Evaluation of deception-based web attacks detection. In: Proceedings of the 2017 Workshop on Moving Target Defense, pp. 65–73 (2017)
12. Han, X., Kheir, N., Balzarotti, D.: Deception techniques in computer security: a research perspective. ACM Comput. Surv. (CSUR) **51**(4), 1–36 (2018)
13. Hong, Q., Zhao, Y., Chang, J., Du, Y., Li, J., Zhai, L.: Shock trap: an active defense architecture based on trap vulnerabilities. In: 2022 7th IEEE International Conference on Data Science in Cyberspace (DSC), pp. 24–31. IEEE (2022)
14. Hu, Z., Hu, Y., Dolan-Gavitt, B.: Towards deceptive defense in software security with chaff bugs. In: Proceedings of the 25th International Symposium on Research in Attacks, Intrusions and Defenses, pp. 43–55 (2022)
15. Kocaogullar, Y., Cetin, O., Arief, B., Brierley, C., Pont, J., Hernandez-Castro, J.C.: Hunting high or low: evaluating the effectiveness of high-interaction and low-interaction honeypots (2022)
16. Lu, Z., Wang, C., Zhao, S.: Cyber deception for computer and network security: survey and challenges. arXiv preprint arXiv:2007.14497 (2020)
17. Provos, N., et al.: A virtual honeypot framework. In: USENIX Security Symposium, vol. 173, pp. 1–14 (2004)
18. Robertson, W.: Using web honeypots to study the attackers behavior. Ph.D. thesis, TELECOM ParisTech (2017)
19. Microsoft Defender Research Team: Cyberbattlesim. https://github.com/microsoft/cyberbattlesim (2021). Created by Christian Seifert, Michael Betser, William Blum, James Bono, Kate Farris, Emily Goren, Justin Grana, Kristian Holsheimer, Brandon Marken, Joshua Neil, Nicole Nichols, Jugal Parikh, Haoran Wei
20. Walter, E., Ferguson-Walter, K., Ridley, A.: Incorporating deception into cyberbattlesim for autonomous defense. arXiv preprint arXiv:2108.13980 (2021)
21. Wikipedia: Honeypot (computing) (2022). https://en.wikipedia.org/wiki/Honeypot_(computing)

DynVMDroid: Android App Protection via Code Disorder and Dynamic Recovery

Weimiao Feng[1], Rui Hu[1,2]([✉]), Cong Zhou[1,2], and Lei Yu[1]

[1] Institute of Information Engineering, Chinese Academy of Sciences, Beijing, China
{fengweimiao,hurui,zhoucong,yulei1993}@iie.ac.cn
[2] School of Cyber Security, University of Chinese Academy of Sciences, Beijing, China

Abstract. To protect Android applications from reverse engineering, more and more adversarial analysis techniques are proposed, such as packing, encryption, obfuscation, etc. As one of the most advanced techniques for obfuscation, code virtualization at the dex bytecode level has evolved from hiding meta information to protect executable instructions. However, previous approaches are proved to have a certain degree of vulnerability at the directive opcode replacement. In this paper, we present DynVMDroid, a reinforcement system based on code virtualization to protect Android applications from reverse engineering. DynVMDroid consists of two components, a reinforcement engine and a custom runtime environment. The reinforcement engine disrupts the inherent structural order and extends the length of the original instructions from key methods, converting them into virtual code in Android applications. The custom runtime environment dynamically recovering the virtual instructions to ensure the protected application work properly. To verify its performance and compatibility, we have applied DynVMDroid to 10 applications. In addition, various attack methods have been adopted on the protected applications to validate their security. Our experimental results show that the applications protected by DynVMDroid perform correctly and effectively against common reverse analysis techniques with acceptable performance losses.

Keywords: Android application reinforcement · Code disorder · Dynamic recovery

1 Introduction

With the popularity of Android, many users take it as their first choice and download various applications from the app store. Unfortunately, some unauthorized reverse engineers crack the applications in order to profit from them. This worrisome phenomenon leads to threats to users' privacy and infringement of developers' intellectual property rights. So far, many solutions to reinforce Android applications rely on mature technologies such as dynamic loading, encryption,

© ICST Institute for Computer Sciences, Social Informatics and Telecommunications Engineering 2024
Published by Springer Nature Switzerland AG 2024. All Rights Reserved
S. Goel and P. R. Nunes de Souza (Eds.): ICDF2C 2023, LNICST 571, pp. 244–257, 2024.
https://doi.org/10.1007/978-3-031-56583-0_16

anti-debugging, etc., which means that some reverse analysts with special purposes also understand these techniques and develop countermeasures. A class of schemes known as code obfuscation [2,4,6–8,11–13,16] makes reverse engineering harder. Among them, code virtualization based on virtual machine (VM) hides real code by converting original instructions into virtual instructions, greatly raising the threshold for reverse engineering. However, recent research [?] shows that an analyst can analyze the virtual codes through the specific instruction format.

In this paper, we propose DynVMDroid, an Android application reinforcement system based on code disorder and dynamic recovery to combat this attack mode. It implements high-intensity protection, preventing Android applications from reverse engineering. Our key insight is that if the Dalvik instruction format is altered, then it will be hard for analysts to analyze the logic of the program based on the inherent structure, and the ordinary attack approach will no longer work. Different from the previous work, which only maps the opcodes of instructions while the arrangement of virtual opcodes and operands still maintain the original format, we disorder the opcode and operand in each instruction and implement a custom interpreter to dynamically recover the instructions. Our carefully designed scheme guarantees the consistency of program operation results although the instructions look different from analysts' perspective. To analyze the applications protected by the DynVMDroid system, they are forced to analyze every single executed instruction, which greatly increases the cost of reverse engineering the code.

We conduct experiments to ensure the applications reinforced by DynVM-Droid is compatible with popular Android platforms without functions change. The security test includes manual attack and universal deobfuscating tool. Besides, we employ the performance test on protected applications. The experimental results show that the applications reinforced by DynVMDroid have certain security and the performance indicators are within an acceptable range.

There are some challenges in our work. First, code virtualization at Java level is not widely used due to efficiency and compatibility problems. Our work needs to ensure the protected applications work correctly with modest cost. Second, the Dalvik interpreter interprets instructions according to specific instruction format while our designed system breaks this rule by changing the original Dalvik instruction format. Therefore, we need to consider the influence of the transformation on instructions when an application runs.

In summary, our main contributions include the following aspects:

- We propose an approach to change the inherent format of Dalvik instructions and dynamically recover the original instructions, improving the protected capability at instruction level and ensuring the applications work properly.
- We present DynVMDroid, a reinforcement system based on code disorder and dynamic recovery to protect Android applications from instruction analysis attacks.
- Our evaluation demonstrates DynVMDroid is more protective than traditional obfuscating methods, increasing the difficulty of the attack as much as

possible. Besides, we also validate that the scheme is effective in protecting real-world software applications.

2   Related Work

2.1   Classic Code Obfuscation Schemes

There are several common types of code obfuscation including data obfuscation, control flow obfuscation and code virtualization.

Data obfuscation focuses on string encryption and identifier renaming [6–8,13]. As the strings and identifiers in a program usually suggest specific and understandable meaning, scanning engines can take advantage of this feature to understand the code. To avoid this, apk obfuscation tools replace the meaningful strings and identifiers with meaningless ones.

Control flow obfuscation hides the control flow diagram of the original application [7,13,16] to prevent from static analysis by making the application's control flow graph look more complex. A representative approach named control flow flattening (CFF) first appears in Chenxi Wang's thesis [2]. CFF uses a *switch* structure instead of using easily identifiable loops and conditional jumps to transfer the control flow to avoid static and dynamic analysis.

Code virtualization is a typical method of code obfuscation. Zhao et al. [11] presented a scheme that translates the dex bytecode into the common LLVM intermediate representations. Shu et al. [4] proposed a protection scheme named opcode permutation. The scheme is shown in Fig. 1. Each Dalvik instruction includes two parts: opcode and operand. The opcode section specifies the handling procedures to be performed. The mechanism generates a randomly sorted number sequence as virtual opcode and implements a linear mapping between Dalvik opcode and virtual opcode. Zhou et al. [12] proposed a similar approach but extended the length of the virtual opcodes. The idea of code virtualization forces an analyst to move from a familiar instruction set (e.g., arm) to an unfamiliar custom virtual instruction set, hoping to increase the time and effort of reverse engineering.

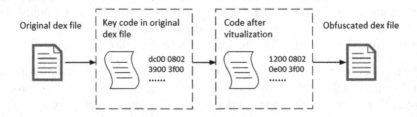

Fig. 1. The classic code virtualization scheme.

2.2   Attack Scheme

With regards to conventional instruction virtualization schemes, the analysts usually perform reverse analysis on the reinforced applications [?] by the following steps. The first step is to locate the entrance to the custom interpreter. As the core module of the virtual execution engine, the interpreter is where the virtual instructions to be executed. Then, it is necessary to find the mapping relationship between each virtual instruction and the handler assigned by the scheduler before execution. Finally, analysts can take advantage of the mapping relationship to recover the original instruction flow of the target code area to obtain the execution logic of the code. For the state-of-art code virtualization scheme mentioned above, when attackers find the opcode mapping table, they can easily restore the original instruction according to the Dalvik instruction structure. In this paper, we call this attack scheme as instruction-intrinsic format analysis.

3   Overview

3.1   Basic Idea

To resist attacks based on instruction-intrinsic format analysis, we break the original structure of instructions by code disorder and dynamically recover the original orders of the opcodes and operands of the instructions. In this way, the attackers cannot recover the original instructions even if they get the opcode mapping table. Detail implementation and algorithms are described in Sect. 4. Figure 2 depicts the architecture of DynVMDroid.

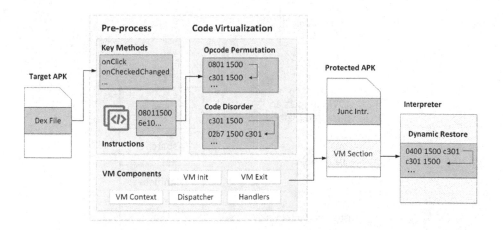

Fig. 2. Overview of the architecture of DynVMDroid. The reinforcement engine is located on the server end that provides reinforcement services for Android applications. The execution part is located on the mobile end where runs the reinforced apk.

DynVMDroid consists of two components, a reinforcement engine and a custom runtime environment. The reinforcement engine mainly disrupts the inherent structural order and extends the length of the original instructions from key methods, converting them into virtual code in Android applications. The custom runtime environment dynamically recovers the virtual instructions to ensure the protected applications work properly. Similar to other VM-based protection scheme, DynVMDroid system should be used to protect the most critical code regions instead of the entire program to minimize run-time overhead.

3.2   Reinforcement Process

The reinforcement engine works as the following steps.

Step 1. Extracting files. The reinforcement system receives an original apk file as input which is unpacked to obtain the dex file and other files such as resource files.

Step 2. Selecting methods. In this step, the dex file is analyzed, while the reinforcement engine selects the key methods to be protected according to the primary rules or specified by the users.

Step 3. Code virtualization. This module first extracts instructions from the method structure. Then, it conduct code permutation and code disorder to generate virtual instructions.

Step 4. Repacking apk. The original instruction stream are cleared from the key methods. Instead, this part are filled with some junk bytecodes. Finally, the processed dex file with other files are repacked in a new apk file.

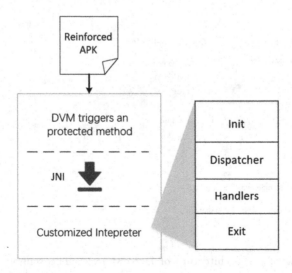

Fig. 3. The execution process

3.3   Execution Process

When the program executes to the protected method, the Dalvik VM calls the corresponding JNI function since the protected method has been changed to the native methods, as shown in Fig. 3. The Dalvik VM transfers execution rights to the custom VM for interpretation and execution. It first initializes the obfuscated codes, decrypting and filling back into the code item field of the method. Then the virtual instructions are executed by the custom interpreter which contains a central loop to schedule, decode, and execute instruction streams. A dispatcher is responsible for identifying each instruction and distributing it to the corresponding handler to execute the virtual instruction. Finally, the custom VM puts back the return value to the Dalvik VM through the JNI interface.

4   Implementation

4.1   Pre-processing Session

Considering the execution efficiency, we select key methods instead of reinforcing all of them. DynVMDroid can protect methods containing sensitive API calls or key algorithms specified by developers. Since we change the original format

---

Algorithm 1. Metadata Collection Algorithm

Input: $Original\_Insns$
Output: New_Insns
  1: $vm\_opcode \leftarrow$ GENRANDOMVMOPCODE()
  2: $index \leftarrow 0$
  3: $extend \leftarrow 0$
  4: **for** $original\_ins$ in $Original\_Insns$ **do**
  5:     $rawOpcode \leftarrow$ GETOPCODE($original\_ins$)
  6:     $pc \leftarrow$ GETOFFSET()
  7:     $tmpIns \leftarrow$ REPLACE($original\_ins, vm\_opcode$)
  8:     **if** $rawOpcode == OP\_GOTO$ **then**
  9:        $tmpIns \leftarrow$ EXTENDTOGOTO32($tmpIns$)
10:        $codeInfo \leftarrow$ INSINFO($pc + extend, index, tmpIns$)
11:        $extend \leftarrow extend + 2$
12:     **else if** $rawOpcode == OP\_GOTO16$ **then**
13:        $tmpIns \leftarrow$ EXTENDTOGOTO32($tmpIns$)
14:        $codeInfo \leftarrow$ INSINFO($pc + extend, index, tmpIns$)
15:        $extend \leftarrow extend + 1$
16:     **else**
17:        $codeInfo \leftarrow$ INSINFO($pc + extend, index, tmpIns$)
18:     **end if**
19:     $code\_info\_dict.push(pc, code\_info)$
20:     Refresh $index$
21: **end for**
22: **return** New_Insns

---

of the instructions, the Dalvik VM cannot correctly interpret them with a non-standard format. Therefore, we label the key methods as native to generate corresponding JNI functions which will soon be interpreted and executed by our custom interpreter.

4.2 Code Disorder

In this section, we describe some critical techniques of code virtualization at instruction level in DynVMDroid system.

Metadata Collection. We collect some metadata from the original instructions before adopting code disorder transformation. Algorithm 1 is the pseudo-code of the metadata collecting algorithm. First, generate 256 numbers (a random sequence from 0 to 255) required for opcode permutation which is described in Sect. 2. Next, traverse all the instructions. For each instruction, extract the original opcode and record the value of *pc* which indicates the offset of the current instruction in the instruction flow. Then, conduct opcode permutation to get an intermediate instruction before extending *goto* and *goto/16* instructions to *goto/32* instructions in case of data overflow. Afterwards, collect the order of the instruction in one instruction flow as *index*, and the total number of words (each word equals to 2 bytes) extended up to the current instruction as *extend*. Finally, a new structure named *codeInfo* is composed with the metadata collected above. We collect all the *codeInfo* and refresh *index*.

Table 1. Special instructions and payload that need modified and their length and descriptions.

Instruction or payload	Description
if-test	Conditional jump instruction whose offset needs modified
goto	Unconditional jump instruction whose offset needs modified.
goto/16	
try-catch	Exception handling instruction whose start address of the try-item statement and the address of the exception catch handler need modified
packed-switch	Switch-like instruction payload whose address of the corresponding opcode needs fixed respectively.
sparse-switch	
fill-array-data	Arrays padding instruction whose operand indicates the address of arrays

Code Disorder. The most crucial aspect in DynVMDroid reinforcement process is code disorder. In this step, we destructure each instruction in the key methods, separating one instruction into two parts, which are a word-long starting with opcode and the rest part. Take the instruction *move-object/from16 v1, v21* as an example, whose corresponding bytecode is *0x08011500*. It is decomposed into *0xc301* and *0x1500* after opcode replacement and destructure. We move the two bytes led by the opcode to the end of the current instruction, and finally add two bytes at the beginning of the instruction. The low-order byte indicates the position of the opcode and the high-order byte is a random number. The final form of *0x08011500* is *0x02b71500c301*.

Fix Offset. Code extension brings about variation of bytecode in some instructions which are characterized by the operand part containing offsets. So when dealing with certain instructions, the offset needs fixed. Table 1 shows the instructions and payload characterized by opcodes. Spacial instructions include *if-test, goto, goto* and *try-catch* whose operands carry offsets needed recalculate and fix. Besides, when the first byte of an instruction is *0x00*, the meaning of the instruction accounts for the second byte whose number might be *0x00, 0x01, 0x02* or *0x03*. *0x00* indicates a *nop* instruction. If the second byte is *0x01* or *0x02*, the instruction represents *packed-switch-payload* and *sparse-switch-payload* respectively. Otherwise, the instruction indicates *fill-array-data* when the second byte is *0x03*.

4.3   Custom Interpreter

To ensure the obfuscated methods run properly, we implement a custom interpreter to interpret and execute virtual instructions. Algorithm 2 is the instructions parsing algorithm. For each instruction in virtual instruction set, fix *pc* first which points to the first byte of the current instruction. Next, fetch *index* indicating the position of the opcode. Through the opcode, we can get the operands and determine which handler interprets and execute the instruction. Finally, the scheduler continues to find the next instruction to execute.

Algorithm 2. Instructions Parsing Algorithm

Input: $Virtual\_Insns$
1: **for** *ins* in $Virtual\_Insns$ **do**
2:      Fix PC
3:      $index \leftarrow$ FETCHINDEX
4:      $opcode \leftarrow$ FETCH($index$)
5:      $operand \leftarrow$ PARSEINS($opcode$)
6:      HANDLE($opcode, operand$)
7: **end for**

---

5   Evaluation

In this paper, we evaluate the reinforcement function in four aspects of functionality, compatibility, security, performance. They are defined as the following concepts.

- Functionality: Whether the function of the application changes after reinforcement.
- Compatibility: Whether the reinforced application can run stably on the Android OS.
- Security: The ability to withstand attacks from reverse engineering.
- Performance: The execution overhead of the reinforced application.

We evaluate DynVMDroid and observe what extent it meets these four criteria.

5.1   Environment Setting

We applied DynVMDroid to 10 different applications without any types of protection in the real world. We were limited to 10 applications because we have to manually verify their correctness and efficiency respectively. Due to the complexity of testing and the limitations of experimental equipments, all cost-related experiments were conducted on Android 10 and Android 12 platforms according to statistics.

5.2   Compatibility and Functional Analysis

First, we installed the applications protected by DynVMDroid on experimental equipments to test the main process, main functions and main interface, observing whether there were any abnormalities on runtime. During the testing process, we did not find that the programs crashed or had any obvious freezes, and the function of the application did not change after the reinforcement.

5.3   Security Analysis

Manual Attack. We manually analyze a method protected by DynVMDroid from the perspective of an analyst. First, we obfuscate a function *onClick* with a statement *Toast* in it and packed it into an apk. Then, we employ reverse engineering on the reinforced apk file with the following steps.

Step 1. Start dynamic debugging via IDA Pro. Since the protected function is extracted, it cannot be obtained only by static analysis. Therefore, we adopt dynamic analysis via the state-of-the-art disassembler IDA pro [5] on the app and find the app using VMP technique to protect onClick function.

Step 2. Find the start address of the protected function. We need to add a breakporint at JNIMethodStart in order to get the start address of the protected JNI function from memory.

Step 3. Recover information of the protected function from memory. In this step, we suppose the analyst find the mapping between the original opcode and the virtual opcode. After recovering the opcodes, we script to dump the corresponding code from the memory to recover the function.

Step 4. Analyze the recovered file. We use IDA pro to disassembly the recovered dex file. As shown in Fig. 4, we can find the comparison from the pseudo-code output result. The left part of Fig. 4 shows the disassembly result of

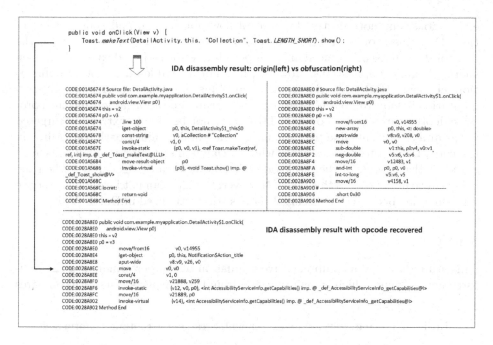

Fig. 4. Comparison of original program and its static decompilation results for IDA pro and disassembly results for opcode recovered

original function. In contrast, the obfuscated instructions are completely different from the original instructions as shown on the right part. The instructions on the bottom of Fig. 4 indicate the results for recovering the opcodes, we still cannot get any information about the original instruction from it.

Deobfuscation Tools. We employ 4 representative deobfuscating tools on Dyn-VMDroid and other obfuscating schemes. The tools include Simplify [3], Deoptfuscator [9], TIRO [10], dexMonitor [17]. Table 2 shows the result of the test. Simplify executes the code to be decompiled through simulating Dalvik VM, learns its function and then simplifies the decompiled code into an understandable form. It is commonly used to parse strings such as key function names and regular

Table 2. Test results with deobfuscation tools

	Identifier Renaming	control flow obfuscation	classic code virtualization	code disorder
Simplify	✓	✗	✗	✗
Deoptfuscator	✗	✓	✗	✗
TIRO	✓	✓	✗	✗
dexMonitor	✓	✓	✓	✗

expressions, but not effective for control flow obfuscation and code virtualization. Deoptfuscator is designed to converted obfuscated applications with the control flow obfuscation mechanism, especially performed by dexGuard on open source Android applications. However, it is not available on the other obfuscation schemes. TIRO targets locations where obfuscation may occur, applies instrumentation to monitor for obfuscation, collects run-time information and then produce deobfuscated code. However, TIRO may not be able to extract all targeted paths and constraints due to static imprecision and complex path constraints in the code. Dexmonitor places hooks where a Dalvik instruction is about to be executed so that a view of the disclosed code and data can be generated when the program counter reaches this point. However, the idea can not be applied on code virtualization because the disclosed code is still virtualized in Dalvik VM.

5.4   Cost

This study provides a comprehensive evaluation of the performance of the reinforcement system, which is mainly tested from three aspects. First, we compares

Table 3. The data set and its experimental results for runtime performance

System	Application	CPU(%)		Memory(MB)		
		Before	After	Before	After	Increase(%)
Android 10	XAPK Install	6.72	4.68	80.78	88.66	9.75
	Auto Click	4.07	6.95	81.72	94.63	15.80
	Skin Tool	18.64	23.19	219.54	195.20	−11.07
	MirrorPlus	15.24	25.20	217.29	219.11	0.84
	RandoChat	9.25	15.78	121.46	127.92	5.32
	Calendar	20.39	15.31	163.13	156.44	−4.10
	Calculator	3.52	3.53	26.01	27.76	6.73
	Diary	3.68	5.68	120.20	141.46	17.69
	Music Player	15.57	16.33	148.72	158.85	6.81
	File Transfer	2.57	4.48	80.42	82.76	2.90
Android 12	XAPK Install	–	–	–	–	–
	Auto Click	7.18	11.15	207.59	211.40	1.84
	Skin Tool	7.51	14.02	242.72	291.58	20.13
	MirrorPlus	15.53	14.06	351.49	339.26	−3.48
	RandoChat	13.12	18.52	311.62	324.81	4.23
	Calendar	38.70	25.90	312.71	403.16	28.92
	Calculator	9.29	8.93	140.07	137.12	−2.11
	Diary	10.63	11.67	240.75	271.92	12.95
	Music Player	26.84	28.78	326.07	389.44	19.43
	File Transfer	–	–	–	–	–

the changes in APK file size of protected applications before and after hardening. Second, we measure the increment of CPU utilization and memory usage when the application is running before and after hardening, so as to evaluate the impact of reinforcement on the runtime performance of the application. Through these tests, the performance of the hardened system can be fully evaluated.

Increment in Size of APKs. The size of the APK file can have an impact on the download, installation, and update speed of the application, as larger APK files take longer to download and install. Larger APK files may cause the device to run out of storage space, making it impossible to install applications or prevent other applications from functioning properly. Therefore, when developing and optimizing applications, we need to consider the size of the APK file and minimize unnecessary resources and code to improve the performance and user experience of the application.

Figure 5 compares the changes in APK file size of protected applications before and after hardening. We can see from Fig. 5 that although some files (such as encrypted virtual instructions and custom interpreter files) are newly generated during the hardening process, the increase in the size of the APK file is still within the normal range and will not have a great impact on user's installation and use. In protected applications, there is a certain correlation between the increment of APK file size and the complexity and function increment of the application before and after hardening. Since each instruction in the protected function body is expanded, the longer the sequence, the larger the increment of the APK file after hardening.

Runtime Overhead. In this experiment, we randomly simulated clicks for each protected application through the Monkey [14] tool, and obtained the CPU resource and memory resource usage at the application runtime with the Mobileperf [15] tool. Finally, we recorded and analyzed the results. Table 3 shows

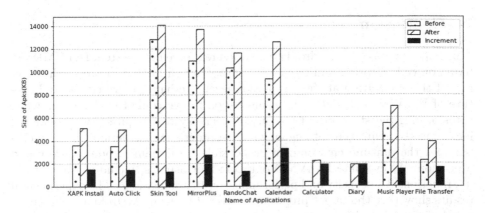

Fig. 5. Comparison of APK file size before and after application obfuscation

the data set and the results for runtime performance, noted that the two original applications of XAPK Install and File Transfer are not competitive on Android 12 platform so we did not record the results.

From Table 3, we can see that the average CPU occupancy of the protected applications tends to be larger than the original applications, mainly derived from the decryption and interactions with the custom interpreter. Nonetheless, the volume of changes are within an acceptable range. After reinforcement, the overall memory usage of hardened applications is slightly higher than that of original applications. This is because when the application runs to a protected method, decryption operations will be performed. At this time, the virtual instruction sequence will be decrypted and loaded into the memory, resulting in an increase in memory usage. However, the runtime memory usage of hardened applications is still within the normal range, and has not caused a major impact on system operation.

6   Discussion

In this section, we discuss the limitations of DynVMDroid, possible solutions and future work. First, analysts can run the obfuscated method by dynamic debugging and observe the register variables to infer the rules of instruction transformation. Although this manual analysis process is very time-consuming and challenging, this intrinsic makes it possible to recover the program bytecode. We can defend this attack by adding anti-debugging mechanism. Besides, the VM may reduce the efficiency of the program's operation not to mention that we employ code virtualization on the application. If the application is heavy and rich in functionality, we can only reinforce a few of the methods and avoid the functions with high time complexity. In future work, we will simplify the interpretation process of instructions to enhance the performance of program execution. In addition, we might as well improve the prototype and compare it with enhanced reinforcement system.

7   Conclusion

This paper proposes an Android application reinforcement system DynVMDroid based on code disorder and dynamic recovery, which further improves the security of the application at the instruction level. We have described the architecture of DynVMDroid and its implementation to overcome the challenges while transforming the structure of instructions. The system requires two assemblies including the reinforcement engine which disorder the instructions in key methods and the runtime environment responsible for dynamic code recovery and execution. We evaluate DynVMDroid from four aspects, including compatibility, functionality, security and performance on 10 applications. The experimental results show that the target programs protected by DynVMDroid are effectively resist manual attacks and the state-of-the-art deobfuscation tools. Besides, it achieves acceptable range of code size, cpu occupancy and memory usage.

References

1. Wang, C., Davidson, J., Hill, J., Knight, J.: Protection of software-based surviv-ability mechanisms. In: 2001 International Conference on Dependable Systems and Networks, pp. 193-202 (2001). https://doi.org/10.1109/DSN.2001.9
2. Simplify. https://github.com/CalebFenton/simplify. Accessed 11 Apr 2022
3. Shu, J., Li, J., Zhang, Y., Gu, D.: Android app protection via interpretation obfus-cation. In: 2014 IEEE 12th International Conference on Dependable, Autonomic and Secure Computing, pp. 63-68 (2014). https://doi.org/10.1109/DASC.2014.20
4. Eagle, C.: The IDA Pro Book. No Starch Press, San Francisco (2011)
5. Tang, Z., Chen, X., Fang, D., Chen, F.: Research on java software protection with the obfuscation in identifier renaming. In: 2009 Fourth International Conference on Innovative Computing, Information and Control (ICICIC), pp. 1067-1071 (2009)
6. dexGuard. https://www.guardsquare.com/dexguard. Accessed 11 Apr 2022
7. Stringer JAVA obfuscator. https://jfxstore.com/stringer. Accessed 11 Apr 2022
8. Deoptfuscator. https://github.com/Gyoonus/deoptfuscator. Accessed 11 Apr 2022
9. Wong, M.Y., Lie, D.: Tackling runtime-based obfuscation in Android with tiro. In: Proceedings of the 27th USENIX Conference on Security Symposium, pp. 1247–1262. SEC'18, USENIX Association, U (2018)
10. Zhao, Y., et al.: Compile-time code virtualization for Android applications. Comput. Secur. **94**, 101821 (2020). https://doi.org/10.1016/j.cose.2020.101821
11. Zhou, W., Wang, Z., Zhou, Y., Jiang, X.: Divilar: Diversifying intermediate language for anti-repackaging on Android platform. In: Proceedings of the 4th ACM Conference on Data and Application Security and Privacy, pp. 199–210. CODASPY '14, Association for Computing Machinery, New York, NY, USA (2014). https://doi.org/10.1145/2557547.2557558
12. Aonzo, S., Georgiu, G.C., Verderame, L., Merlo, A.: Obfuscapk: an open-source black-box obfuscation tool for Android apps. SoftwareX **11**, 100403 (2020). https://doi.org/10.1016/j.softx.2020.100403
13. UI/Application exerciser monkey. https://developer.Android.com/studio/test/monkey. Accessed 15 Mar 2020
14. Mobileperf. https://gitee.com/sanmejie/mobileperf. Accessed 11 Apr 2022
15. Yang, X., Zhang, L., Ma, C., Liu, Z., Peng, P.: Android control flow obfuscation based on dynamic entry points modification. In: 2019 22nd International Conference on Control Systems and Computer Science (CSCS), pp. 296–303 (2019). https://doi.org/10.1109/CSCS.20
16. Cho, H., Yi, J.H., Ahn, G.J.: DexMonitor: dynamically analyzing and monitoring obfuscated Android applications. IEEE Access **6**, 71229–71240 (2018). https://doi.org/10.1109/ACCESS.2018
17. Xue, L., et al.: Parema: an unpacking framework for demystifying VM-based android packers, pp. 152–164. Association for Computing Machinery, New York, NY, USA (2021). https://doi.org/10.1145/3460319

Improvement of an Identity-Based Aggregate Signature Protocol from Lattice

Songshou Dong[1,2,3], Yanqing Yao[1,2,3(✉)], Yihua Zhou[4,5], and Yuguang Yang[4,5]

[1] State Key Laboratory of Software Development Environment, Beihang University,
Beijing 100191, China
yaoyq@buaa.edu.cn
[2] State Key Laboratory of Cryptology, Beijing 100878, China
[3] Key Laboratory of Aerospace Network Security, Ministry of Industry and Information
Technology, School of Cyber Science and Technology, Beihang University, Beijing 100191,
China
[4] Faculty of Information Technology, Beijing University of Technology, Bejing 100124, China
{zhouyh,yangyang7357}@bjut.edu.cn
[5] Beijing Key Laboratory of Trusted Computing, Beijing 100124, China

Abstract. In 2022, Li et al. [1] proposed a quantum secure and non-interactive
identity-based aggregate signature protocol from lattices. In the end of their paper,
they claimed that their scheme has key escrow problem. Based on this fact, we
improve their scheme and propose a lattice-based certificateless aggregate signature protocol (L-CASP). Furthermore, our scheme has same signature size as Li
et al. scheme and can avoid key escrow problem. Finally, we prove that our scheme
is existentially unforgeable against adaptive chosen message attacks (EUF-CMA)
under type I adversary and a type II adversary in the random oracle model (ROM).

Keywords: Lattice · certificateless · key escrow problem · signature · security

1 Introduction

Digital signatures can generally be divided into three categories: certificate-based,
identity-based, certificateless.

For certificate-based signature schemes, public key infrastructure (PKI) is an important mechanism to maintain certificates and spread trust information among users in a
hierarchical manner. As we all know, due to the generation and management of so many
certificates are quite time-consuming, PKI is very expensive to deploy in practice and is
very troublesome to use. Therefore, the introduction of the certification authority (CA)
and PKI into the network coding system and the additional verification of each certificate
will greatly reduce its performance.

For identity-based signature schemes, it can also be easily modified to be used in
network coding to simplify the management of public keys. However, the inherent problem of any identity-based primitive lies in key escrow, which means Key-Generation-
Center (KGC) entity knows the private key of any signer. Therefore, KGC can forge

S. Goel and P. R. Nunes de Souza (Eds.): ICDF2C 2023, LNICST 571, pp. 258–263, 2024.
https://doi.org/10.1007/978-3-031-56583-0_17

any signature of any signer as needed. Furthermore, the network coding system based on identity-based homomorphic signature also encounters the same problem and is only suitable for small private networks with low-security requirements.

For a certificateless signature scheme, it does not require key escrow, can avoid malicious KGC, and can better ensure the security requirements in network communications. In 2022, Li et al. [1] proposed a quantum secure and non-interactive identity-based aggregate signature protocol from lattices. In the end of their paper, they claimed that their scheme has key escrow problem. Based on this fact, we improve their scheme and propose a lattice-based certificateless aggregate signature protocol (L-CASP).

2 System Model, Algorithm Model and Security Model

Different from Li et al.'s scheme [1], our scheme is certificateless which avoids the key escrow problem. The following is the algorithm model and security model of our scheme.

2.1 Algorithm Model

1) Setup: Given a security parameter 1^n, KGC will generate system parameters *params* and secret value *msk*.
2) Generate public key and secret value: Given a signer's identity $ID \in \{0, 1\}^*$, outputs the public key p_{ID} and secret value c_{ID};
3) Generate a partial private key: Given a signer's identity $ID \in \{0, 1\}^*$ and a public key p_{ID}, ID outputs the partial private key s_{ID}.
4) Generate private key: Given the signer's identity $ID \in \{0, 1\}^*$ and the partial private key c_{ID}, the user outputs the private key sk_{ID} and key pk_{ID}.
5) Signature: Given a triple (m_{ID}, ID, sk_{ID}), the user generates a signature $Sig_{ID} = z_{ID}$.
6) Aggregation: Given a triple $(m_i, PK = (pk_{ID_i}), Sig_i (i \in [t]))$, Aggregator outputs the aggregated signature Zag;
7) Aggregate verification: input triplet $(m_i, PK = (pk_{ID_i}), (i \in [t]), Zag)$, if Zag is a valid aggregate signature, verifier output 1, otherwise output 0.

2.2 Security Model

There are two types of adversaries in certificateless cryptosystems: type I and type II (A_1 and A_2). For signer ID, A_1: If you know the secret value c_{ID}, but you don't know the master key B, you can replace the user public key pk_{ID}. A_2: Know the master key B, but cannot replace the user public key pk_{ID}. According to different classifications of adversaries, two types of games are defined as Game I and Game II.

The security requirements of the lattice-based certificateless aggregate signature protocol (L-CASP) for cloud healthcare are as follows:

Definition 1. The L-CASP scheme satisfies unforgeability if the adversary wins in probabilistic polynomial time with a non-negligible advantage in the next two games.

Game I. Challenger C plays an interactive game with type I adversary A_1.

1) *Initialization* : Challenger C runs the setting algorithm to generate secret value *msk* and system parameter *params*, keeps *msk* secret, and sends system parameter params to adversary A_1.

2) *Query* : Adversary A_1 can perform polynomial number of queries. For the signer *ID*, the adversary A_1 performs the following query:

 (1) *PK* − *Query* : Adversary A_1 queries the public key of *ID*, and challenger C outputs the corresponding public key pk_{ID}.

 (2) *Hash* − *Query* : Adversary A_1 can query any hash function value.

 (3) *PK* − *Replace* : Adversary A_1 sends pk'_{ID} to challenger C, and challenger C replaces pk_{ID} with pk'_{ID}.

 (4) *PPK* − *Query* : Adversary A_1 queries the partial private key of *ID*, and the challenger C outputs the partial private key s_{ID}. If the private key sk_{ID} of *ID* is replaced, A_1 will not be able to execute *PPK* − *Query*.

 (5) *SV* − *Query* : Adversary A_1 queries the secret value of *ID*, challenger C returns c_{ID} to adversary A_1. If c_{ID} is replaced, adversary A_1 will not be able to perform secret value lookup.

 (6) *Sign* − *Query* : Adversary A_1 inputs the tuple (m_{ID}, ID, sk_{ID}), and the challenger C outputs the signature $Sig_{ID} = (z_{ID})$.

3) *Forge* : adversary A_1 output tuple $(M = \{m_1, m_2, \cdots m_t\}, P = \{(ID_1, pk_1), (ID_2, pk_2), \cdots (ID_t, pk_t), \}, Zag)$. The opponent wins if the following requirements are met:

 (1) *Sig* is not obtained through *Sign* − *Query*;

 (2) Aggregate verification $(M, P, Zag) = 1$;

 (3) There is at least one identity *ID* for which the adversary A_1 did not perform *PPK* − *Query* or replace the main private key B.

The advantage of adversary A_1 winning is defined as: $Adv_{A_1}^{L-CASP} = \Pr[A_1 wins]$.

Game II. Challenger C and the second type of opponent A_2 start an interactive game.

1) *Initialization* : Challenger C runs the setup algorithm to generate the secret value msk and system parameters params, and then sends them to the adversary A_2.

2) *Query* : Adversary A_2 performs the same polynomial query as in game I.

3) *Forge* : the adversary A_2 output tuple $(M = \{m_1, m_2, \cdots m_t\}, P = \{(ID_1, pk_1), (ID_2, pk_2), \cdots (ID_t, pk_t), \}, Zag)$. The opponent wins if the following requirements are met:

 (1) *Sig* is not obtained through *Sign* − *Query*;

 (2) Aggregate verification $(M, P, Zag) = 1$;

 (3) There is at least one identity *ID* for which the adversary A_2 did not perform *SV* − *Query* or replace the secret value c_{ID}.

The advantage of adversary A_2 winning is defined as: $Adv_{A_2}^{L-CASP} = \Pr[A_2 wins]$.

3   Our Protocol

In this section, we will introduce our L-CASP in detail. In our scheme, we use the *TrapGen* algorithm [2] and the *SamplePre* algorithm [3]. Additionally, all polynomial computations of our protocol are defined on $R_q = Z_q[X]/(X^n + 1)$. The following are details. Figure 1 describes the process of key generation (This is the core step of our improvement, as you can see, the user's private key is generated in two parts).

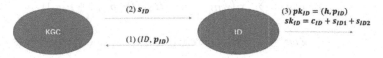

Fig. 1. The process of key extraction

(1) Setup Phase

The Setup Phase is basically the same as the reference [1], except that we add a hash function $H_3 : \{0, 1\}^* \to (B_\beta)^*$, $B_\beta = \{r \in R : \|r\| \le \beta_3\}$.

(2) Key Extraction Phase
1) The user ID selects polynomial $c_{ID}R_q$, calculates $p_{ID} = h * c_{ID}$ and send p_{ID} to KGC;
2) KGC computes $k_{ID} = H_3(ID, p_{ID})$, gets $s_{ID} = (s_{ID1}, s_{ID2})^T$ (which meets $H_3(ID, p_{ID}) = s_{ID1}, + h s_{ID2}$, $\|(s_{ID1}, s_{ID2})\| \le \sigma\sqrt{2n}$) through $SamplePre(h, B, \sigma, (k_{ID}, 0))$ and sends s_{ID} to the user ID;
3) User ID computes the private key $sk_{ID} = c_{ID} + s_{ID1} + s_{ID2}$, lets public key $pk_{ID} = (h, p_{ID})$.
(3) Sign Phase

The user ID can generate a valid signature on any message $m_{ID} \in \{0, 1\}^*$ as follows. ID gets the random polynomial w_{ID} by the seed and the algorithm $GaussFunction$ [1], selects two polynomial $y_{ID,2} \leftarrow D_{R,s}$, $y_{ID,3} \leftarrow D_{R,s}$, computes $y_{ID,1} = w_i - h y_{ID,2} - h y_{ID,3}$, $e_{ID} = H_1(PK, w_{ID}, m_{ID})$ ($PK = (pk_{ID_i})$, $i \in [N]$), $z_{ID,1} = y_{ID,1} + s_{ID,1} e_{ID}$, $z_{ID,2} = y_{ID,2} + s_{ID,2} e_{ID}$, $z_{ID,3} = y_{ID,3} + c_{ID} e_{ID}$ and outputs $z_{ID,1}$ with the probability $\min(\frac{D_{R,\sigma}(z_{ID,1})}{M_1 D_{R,\sigma, s_{ID,1} e_{ID}}(z_{ID,1})}, 1)$ ($M_1 \approx e$), $z_{ID,2}$ with the probability $\min(\frac{D_{R,\sigma}(z_{ID,2})}{M_2 D_{R,\sigma, c_{ID} e_{ID}}(z_{ID,2})}, 1)$ ($M_2 \approx e$), $z_{ID,3}$ with the probability $\min(\frac{D_{R,\sigma}(z_{ID,3})}{M_3 D_{R,\sigma, c_{ID} e_{ID}}(z_{ID,3})}, 1)$ ($M_3 \approx e$). Next ID could generate a signature $z_{ID} = h^{-1} z_{ID,1} + z_{ID,2} + z_{ID,3}$ and sends it to the aggregator.

(4) Sign-Agg Phase

The aggregator get all $w_{ID_i}, i \in [N]$ by the seed and the algorithm $GaussFunction$ [1], the set of public keys $PK = (pk_{ID_i})$, $i \in [N]$, all messages m_{ID_i} and $w_{ID_i}, i \in [N]$, calculates the hash value $(x_1, x_2, ..., x_N) \leftarrow H_2(w_{ID_1}, pk_{ID_1}, m_{ID_1}, \cdots, w_{ID_N}, pk_{ID_N}, m_{ID_N})$, and an aggregate signature $Zag = \sum_{i=1}^{N} x_i z_{ID_i}$.

(5) Verify Phase

Given public keys $PK = (pk_{ID_i})$, $i \in [N]$, the message set $m_{ID_i}, i \in [N]$, and the aggregate signature Zag, the verifier gets all $w_{ID_i}, i \in [N]$ by algorithm $GaussFunction$ with seed, computes $(x_1, x_2, ..., x_N) \leftarrow H_2(w_{ID_1}, pk_{ID_1}, m_{ID_1}, \cdots,$

w_{ID_N}, pk_{ID_N}, m_{ID_N}) and $e_{ID_i}=H_1(PK, w_{ID_i}, m_{ID_i})$, $i \in [N]$, and verifies the correctness of the following conditions:

$$h*Zag = \sum_{i=1}^{N} x_i\left(w_{ID_i} + e_{ID_i}\left(H_3\left(ID_i, p_{ID_i}\right) + p_{ID_i}\right)\right)$$

$$Zag \leq \beta_{ver}\left(\beta_{ver} \geq N\beta_2\left(\sigma\sqrt{n} + 2\right)\left(3\sigma\sqrt{n} + nq\beta_1\right)\right)$$

4 Correctness Analysis

In this section, we analyze the correctness of our scheme. The details are as follows.

$$h * Zag = h \sum_{i=1}^{N} x_i z_{ID_i}$$

$$= h \sum_{i=1}^{N} x_i\left(h^{-1}z_{ID_i,1} + z_{ID_i,2} + z_{ID_i,3}\right)$$

$$= \sum_{i=1}^{N} x_i h\left(h^{-1}z_{ID_i,1} + z_{ID_i,2} + z_{ID_i,3}\right)$$

$$= \sum_{i=1}^{N} x_i\left(z_{ID_i,1} + hz_{ID_i,2} + hz_{ID_i,3}\right)$$

$$= \sum_{i=1}^{N} x_i\left(y_{ID_i,1} + s_{ID_i,1}e_{ID_i} + h\left(y_{ID_i,2} + s_{ID_i,2}e_{ID_i}\right) + h\left(y_{ID_i,3} + c_{ID_i}e_{ID_i}\right)\right)$$

$$= \sum_{i=1}^{N} x_i\left(y_{ID_i,1} + hy_{ID_i,2} + hy_{ID_i,3} + e_{ID_i}\left(s_{ID_i,1} + hs_{ID_i,2} + hc_{ID_i}\right)\right)$$

$$= \sum_{i=1}^{N} x_i\left(w_{ID_i} + e_{ID_i}\left(H\left(ID, p_{ID_i}\right) + p_{ID_i}\right)\right)$$

Firstly, according to the Gaussian sampling [4], $\|y_{ID_i,1}\|$, $\|y_{ID_i,2}\|$, $\|y_{ID_i,3}\| \leq 2\sigma\sqrt{n}$ with overwhelming probability.

Because $\|s_{ID_i,1}\|$, $\|s_{ID_i,2}\|$, $\|c_{ID_i}\| \leq nq$, and $\|e_{ID_i}\| \leq \beta_1$, $\|z_{ID_i,1}\|$, $\|z_{ID_i,2}\|$, $\|z_{ID_i,3}\| \leq 3\sigma\sqrt{n} + nq\beta_1$.

So, the signature $z_{ID_i}, i \in [N]$ satisfies the inequality $\|z_{ID_i}\| \leq (\sigma\sqrt{n} + 2)(3\sigma\sqrt{n} + nq\beta 1)$.

Due to $Zag = \sum_{i=1}^{N} x_i z_{ID_i}$,
$\|Zag\| \leq N\beta_2(\sigma\sqrt{n} + 2)(3\sigma\sqrt{n} + nq\beta 1)$.

5 Existentially Unforgeable Against Adaptive Chosen Message Attacks (EUF-CMA)

Normally, the security of a L-CASP usually needs to be proven from two aspects.

1) Type I attack: Adversary can only replace the signer's public key, but the partial private key of any signer cannot be got;
2) Type II attack: Adversary can only obtain the private key of KGC, but cannot replace the public key of any signer.

The proof method is the same as the proof method in Ref. [5], we will not elaborate here.

6 Conclusion

Through comparison, our scheme has same signature size as Li et al.'s scheme and can avoid key escrow problem. And we prove that our scheme is EUF-CMA under type I adversary and a type II adversary in the random oracle model (ROM).

Acknowledgement. This work is supported by the National Key Research and Development Program of China (No. 2021YFB3100400),the National Natural Science Foundation of China (grant no. 62072023), the Open Project Fund of the State Key Laboratory of Cryptology (grant no. MMK-FKT202120), Beijing Municipal Natural Science Foundation, the Exploratory Optional Project Fund of the State Key Laboratory of Software Development Environment, and the Fundamental Research Funds of Beihang University (grant nos. YWF-20-BJ-J-1040, YWF-21-BJ-J-1041, etc.).

References

1. Li, Q., Luo, M., Hsu, C., et al.: A quantum secure and noninteractive identity-based aggregate signature protocol from lattices. IEEE Syst. J. **16**(3), 4816–4826 (2021)
2. Stehlé, D., Steinfeld, R.: Making NTRU as secure as worst-case problems over ideal lattices. In: Paterson, K.G. (ed.) EUROCRYPT 2011. LNCS, vol. 6632, pp. 27–47. Springer, Heidelberg (2011). https://doi.org/10.1007/978-3-642-20465-4_4
3. Gentry, C., Peikert, C., Vaikuntanathan, V.: Trapdoors for hard lattices and new cryptographic constructions. In: Proceedings of the Fortieth Annual ACM Symposium on Theory of Computing, Victoria, pp. 197–206. ACM (2008)
4. Ducas, L., Durmus, A., Lepoint, T., Lyubashevsky, V.: Lattice signatures and bimodal Gaussians. In: Canetti, R., Garay, J.A. (eds.) CRYPTO 2013. LNCS, vol. 8042, pp. 40–56. Springer, Heidelberg (2013). https://doi.org/10.1007/978-3-642-40041-4_3
5. Dong, S.S., Zhou, Y.H., Yang, Y.G., et al.: A certificateless ring signature scheme based on lattice. Concurr. Comput. Pract. Exp. **34**(28), e7385 (2022)

A Measurement Study on Interprocess Code Propagation of Malicious Software

Thorsten Jenke[✉], Simon Liessem, Elmar Padilla, and Lilli Bruckschen

Fraunhofer FKIE, Zanderstraße 5, 53177 Bonn, Germany
{thorsten.jenke,simon.liessem,elmar.padilla,
lilli.bruckschen}@fkie.fraunhofer.de

Abstract. The propagation of code from one process to another is an important aspect of many malware families and can be achieved, for example, through code injections or the launch of new instances. An in-depth understanding of how and when malware uses interprocess code propagations would be a valuable aid in the analysis of this threat, since many dynamic malware analysis and unpacking schemes rely on finding running instances of malicious code. However, despite the prevalence of such propagations, there is little research on this topic. Therefore, in this work, we aim to extend the state-of-the-art by measuring both the behavior and the prevalence of interprocess code propagations of malicious software. We developed a method based on API-tracing for measuring code propagations in dynamic malware analysis. Subsequently, we implemented this method into a proof-of-concept implementation as a basis for further research. To gain more knowledge on the prevalence of code propagations and the code propagation techniques used, we conducted a study using our implementation on a real-world data set of 4853 malware samples from 1747 families. Our results show that more than a third (38.13%) of the executables use code propagation, which can be further classified into four different topologies and 24 different code propagation techniques. We also provide a list of the most significant representative malware samples for each of these topologies and techniques as a starting point for researchers aiming to develop countermeasures against code propagation.

Keywords: Malware · Code Injections · Code Propagation

1 Introduction

Malware remains a major threat to computer security. 2019 alone saw the release of over 131 million samples [3]. Furthermore, the number of cyber attacks involving ransomware alone almost doubled between 2020 and 2021 [25], with an estimated damage of $20 billion [30]. Developing adequate protection against these threats requires an in-depth analysis of samples. However, malware authors employ various different obfuscation techniques to thwart analysis. During the

S. Goel and P. R. Nunes de Souza (Eds.): ICDF2C 2023, LNICST 571, pp. 264–282, 2024.
https://doi.org/10.1007/978-3-031-56583-0_18

infection phase, malware uses various evasion/obfuscation and deployment techniques, such as packer. A commonly found technique is the propagation of code from one process to another, henceforth referred to as code propagations. Examples include injections into seemingly benign processes to conceal or launch multiple copies to achieve redundancy.

This particular evasion technique has an especially negative impact on dynamic analysis. Most debuggers offer the functionality to follow child processes, but injections are generally harder to follow. API-hooking/observation is another common way to observe malicious functionality. Although it is possible to detect code propagation with system-wide API-hooking, the analyst must be aware that observing the API calls of a singular process may not reveal the entire malicious activity, and observing the activity of all processes will yield too much information to be useful. To garner more granular information about the malware's behavior, virtual machine introspection or full system emulation is used. These methods lead to a similar problem as the system-wide API-hooking. Monitoring the singular launched malware process may not be sufficient due to code propagations, and the information overload of observing the entire system is even more prohibitive in these cases. Therefore, it is imperative to be able to track the malware through new process spawns and code injections in order to filter out the malware's behavior from the entire system's behavior. Alternatively, single-process emulation poses the problem that it must be able to emulate multiple processes to allow the malware to perform its code injections and process creations.

Code propagations have an impact on almost all dynamic analysis techniques. Therefore, the goal of this work is to extend the state of the art by addressing the distribution of malicious code across processes executed by a sample. We believe that this will improve the understanding of the evasive movement of malware and help the community develop tools to address code propagations in dynamic analysis. To gain knowledge about code propagation, we have developed a proof-of-concept implementation consisting of a sandbox part and an analysis part. The methodology of our implementation for detecting code propagations can be incorporated into different dynamic analysis techniques. Using this implementation, we conducted a longitudinal study, using a dataset of real-world malware. We also provide a list of malware samples, representing each class of code propagations found in our study, to allow researchers to immediately test their countermeasures against malicious code propagations.

This paper provides the following contributions:

- A longitudinal study on a representative real-world malware corpus showing the prevalence of code propagation and the variety of used code propagation techniques.
- A method to measure code propagations in dynamic malware analysis.
- A list of malware samples labeled with their respective code propagations.

2 Related Work

Despite the pervasiveness of code propagations and their obstacles, there is little research on this topic.

Barabosch et al. contributed three works [5–7] on process injection based on the analysis of memory dumps and the evaluation of memory regions based on a variety of attributes. They have proposed multiple ways to detect code injections. One technique is based on applying honeypot principles to processes and capturing the injections that way; another is to look for common properties in processes that have been the targets of injections. They have also proposed a taxonomy to describe code injections.

Two works by Korczynski et al. [20,21] propose a framework to capture malware injections and code reuse attacks. They have developed a program called Minerva based on the taint analysis of PANDA [12], aiming to move away from the write-then-execute metric, and propose a different framework based on the flow of information. Other taint analysis approaches include DiskDuster by Bacs et al. [4], API-Chaser by Kawakoya et al. [18], and Panorama by Yin et al. [38] by capturing system-wide information flow.

Ispoglou et al. [14] proposed a malware called malWASH that makes a great use of process injections to hide its functionality from dynamic analysis systems.

Since process injections are also commonly used in packers to thwart analysis, there have also been unpackers focused on tackling them. There has been much research focused on creating several generic unpackers [8,11,13,15–17,19,26,35–37].

Unlike the related work, we do not focus on a single use-case to thwart code propagation. Instead, the purpose of our research is to demonstrate that malware often utilizes code propagation, including the generation of new processes, and to investigate the characteristics of their implementation.

3   Code Propagation

This section covers the basics of code propagation. Since our study will focus on Microsoft Windows, we will use nomenclatures from the Windows ecosystem. However, the concepts presented in this paper should also be applicable to other operating systems.

3.1   Definition

Barabosch et al. [6] propose a definition for host-based code injections. However, their definition does not include other forms of code propagation besides code injections. Therefore, we propose our own definition to broaden the scope of our work.

We define code propagation as an instance of code distribution by a malware M that meets the following criteria:

1. The code is propagated outside of M's currently running process.
2. To propagate, the malware M either uses previously written binaries to spawn new processes or injects code into newly created or already running processes.

3. The code is distributed with the intent of immediately executing it.
4. The distribution does not require any interaction from the user or other processes.

Criterion 1 manifests the idea that the code must leave the currently running process, as our goal is to focus on the movement of malware code across process boundaries.

Criterion 2 defines the way in which malware can propagate its code. This enforces that spawning a process from a binary that was present on the machine before the malware was launched and without injecting any code is not considered a code propagation.

We have added criterion 3 to explicitly exclude persistence techniques, such as using the scheduler or autorun to launch malware after the operating system has been restarted.

Criterion 4 ensures that the code propagation is performed completely autonomously and does not use side effects of other processes.

Code propagations can also be observed in goodware; however, we focus our attention on in-depth malware analysis. Therefore, we do not consider goodware in our research.

3.2   Representation

A set of code propagations conducted by a single malware sample can be described as a tuple consisting of a graph and a weight function that describes the code propagation technique used: Let $G_{mov} = (V, E)$ be a directed graph that describes the movement of malware between processes for a given sample, where V is the set of malware instances and E is the set of code propagations between them.

There are no reflective edges $e \in E$ since code propagations exist only between two different processes.

Additionally, we define the weight function $f : E \to X$ where X is the space of all possible code propagation techniques.

Therefore, the tuple (G_{mov}, f) describes the code propagations for a given malware. G_{mov}, with $|V| > 0$, $|E| \geq 0$, and $|E| \geq |V| - 1$, is called the topology of the code propagations. The weight function will be discussed in the next segment.

3.3   Techniques

This section explains the code propagation techniques by introducing the function $f : E \to X$.

As shown in Fig. 1, the shortest way to propagate code is to spawn a process from a previously written binary or using various injection techniques. The differences between injection techniques can be summarized in the reuse or allocation of resources. For an injection, handles to a **process**, **memory regions**, and **thread** are needed. These steps are also represented in the taxonomy proposed

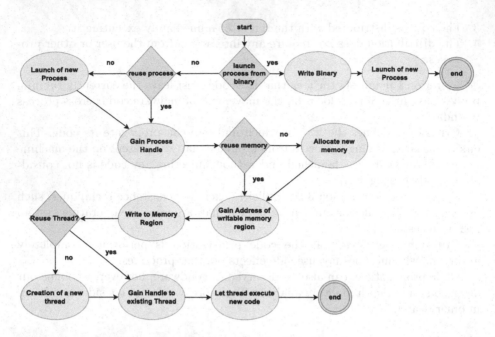

Fig. 1. Decision tree to propagate code in the system. There are two primary paths, one for starting new processes and the other for describing code injections. Code injections differ in their allocation or reuse of resources.

by Barabosch et al. [7]. For each of these resources, it is possible to allocate new ones or reuse existing ones. To ensure general applicability, our proposed method covers methods found in hundreds of different malware families. Many of them have different approaches to implementing code propagations and possibly faulty or broken implementations. There may even be incomplete propagations to subvert analysis or implementations with superfluous steps. As shown in Fig. 1, a code propagation consists of eight steps that must be taken into account. To be able to represent these steps, we have decided that the result of our weight function $f : E \rightarrow X$ should be an unsigned integer of eight bits in length. The advantage of this implementation is that it is the minimal representation possible. Each bit in X represents a trait of the code propagation, so that the eight bits describe every possible interaction between processes. With a bit value of 1 if the stated condition is true and 0 otherwise:

Bit 1: Was a new process spawned?
Bit 2: Was a handle on a process obtained?
Bit 3: Was a new thread spawned?
Bit 4: Was a handle on a thread obtained?
Bit 5: Was new memory allocated?
Bit 6: Was a memory region reused?
Bit 7: Was the data written to the memory region(s)?
Bit 8: Was the thread resumed?

Note that it is possible to generate interprocess interactions with this representation that do not fulfill our definition of code propagations.

4   Measuring Code Propagations

In this section, we describe how to determine the code propagations of a given sample. Code propagation functionality in user mode must be realized through the operating system API. So in order to record this behavior, we must record the functions used to perform the code propagation. Tackling this problem with static analysis is very time-consuming and not feasible due to the multiple possible layers of obfuscation present in modern day malware. Therefore, a dynamic analysis approach was chosen.

Using this approach, each call to a function affecting the eight states described in Subsect. 3.3 was recorded. This recording included the calling process, the parameters passed, the return value, and the values in the relevant out parameters. These recordings contain all the information needed to derive the code propagation topology and techniques used by the malware.

Every code propagation starts with the creation of the handles on a process and a thread. This is done by functions that either spawn a new process or thread or leverage existing processes. Therefore, these functions always initiate a new code propagation. At this point, the process ID (abbr. PID) is known, since the functions for opening or creating processes are directly linked to the PID, except for NtCreateUserProcess, which only returns a handle. In this case, the PID must be derived from the handle, either by using GetProcessId or by parsing the kernel structures. In the next step, the remaining interaction between the currently analyzed process and the target process is examined, e.g., if WriteProcessMemory is used, then the second to last bit is set as described in Subsect. 3.3.

This set of code propagations still includes the process spawns that do not execute code written by the malware. Therefore, the code propagations that do not belong to the family of code injections have to be filtered from the set. So, first, the function used to spawn the process is determined and its parameters are interpreted.

Most functions for spawning processes take an application name parameter and a command line parameter. The main executable used to the spawn the process is checked against a list of files manipulated by the malware and a list of all PE files on the system before the malware has been executed. However, there is a list of binaries that take a special role, like cmd or rundll. These executables are used to spawn other images, which in turn have to be further interpreted. Simply checking for a manipulated image in the command is not sufficient, since, e.g., the del command deletes the file and does not spawn it, so a block list of the shortened commands is used to filter the calls. Also, the DLL run by rundll has to be checked against the previously mentioned manipulated file and allow lists. This leaves only malicious process creations.

The results of the analysis are represented as a graph, with the processes as nodes and the system calls as edges, as described in Sect. 3.2.

4.1   Implementation

The majority of malware is released for Microsoft Windows [3]. Therefore, we focus on malware released for this operating system.

In our search for suitable frameworks to record API calls, we considered two dynamic analysis frameworks, PANDA [12] and Drakvuf [23], as well as Microsoft's hooking framework Detours [27]. PANDA is based on QEMU and provides very fine-grained information to the analyst, such as virtual machine introspection or callbacks at different stages of QEMU's execution. However, it would require a significant amount of additional work to hook arbitrary user land API-functions. Drakvuf is a sandbox based on libvmi that allows introspection into virtual machines. Unfortunately, there seem to be several hurdles when trying to hook user land API-functions [10]. Although both tools are very powerful, they require a significant investment of development time to be able to set the required user land hooks. Since the goal of this work is to explore code propagations and describe how to detect code propagations, we have chosen the most expeditious variant, which is Detours. Detours was developed by Microsoft and offers a very mature and convenient way to construct hooks by handling the installation and overall management of the hooks. However, malware is potentially able to detect the presence of Detours and alter its functionality. Also, Detours is not able to detect code propagations conducted by malware residing in kernel mode.

We have created two hooking libraries for 32-bit and 64-bit, which hook each function that shall be monitored. When a hook is called, an initial log line is created containing the parameters used to call the function. Additionally, the original function is called to preserve the functionality of the program. The return value and the out parameters are used to generate a second log line, and the return value is returned by the hook. This method ensures that every interaction with the monitored function is recorded, while also preserving the functionality of the original. Our hooking libraries are a modified version of traceapi [29]. The logs are generated with a slightly modified version of syelog [28], so that it is capable of writing logs to files.

When deciding on which functions to hook, we have focused on the high-level functions and their often undocumented low-level equivalents. Technically, it would be sufficient to target only the low-level equivalents, but we wanted to gain additional knowledge about the utilization of low-level functions. We have chosen the API functions based on the research of Plohmann et al. [33] and Mitre Att&ck [2]. The full list of hooked functions can be found in the Appendix.

The monitoring libraries are loaded into every process that loads the user32.dll library by using the AppInitDll function found in the registry. Therefore, the hooks are installed before the main image (i.e., the malware) is run.

The logs generated by the hooks are analyzed asynchronously by a Python script, which implements the analysis described above.

5   Code Propagation Study

To gain insight into how code propagations are used in malware, we conducted a longitudinal study.

5.1   Data Set

To conduct this study, we first acquired a data set with a high diversity of families and actors [34].

We have chosen Malpedia[1] [32] as the basis for our data set. It is a strictly manually curated malware corpus, with 7161 samples across 2686 families, and strives for representative coverage of as many malware families as possible by providing a sample for every version of every malware family. For almost every sample, the data set provides an unpacked and dumped version, as well as meta-information, and YARA rules [1]. Since this data set strives to include every version of every family [32], there is no bias towards any particular version of a family. Adding more samples to our data set would not provide any further benefit, as it would only create redundancy and introduce a bias towards a specific version of a family, unless we provide an additional sample for every version of every family. Therefore, we focused our attention on evaluating a single data set.

Since we focus our study on Windows malware, we have filtered the 7161 samples in the data set by excluding every file that is not a PE file or the main representative of the family version. Therefore, we always chose the representative that has been found in the wild. 5758 samples remain after filtering and are therefore our data set.

5.2   Study Setup

We analyzed the Malpedia samples on three Oracle VirtualBox VMs [31], each with 4 GB RAM and 2 CPUs running at 3.20 GHz. To maximize the number of compatible malware with virtual machines, we have chosen Windows 7 as the operating system. The installation includes every service pack and the MS Visual C runtime (MSVCRT) library released by Microsoft for Windows 7. The hardening of the virtual machine was performed as described in [9].

The malware samples are automatically loaded into the VM and launched with a simulated double-click. The double-click ensures that the malware is launched in the most organic way possible, since its parent process is the Explorer. DLL-based malware was run using rundll.exe by calling the DLLmain. The hooks were already installed and the VM was re-booted. The analysis of a sample timed out after 120 s. As shown in [15], most malware finished unpacking after 25 s, and Küchler et al. [22] argue that the majority of samples run for less than two minutes or more than ten minutes. Since we are only interested in the

---

[1] Git commit d366eb0 - Jan 6, 2023.

code propagation of malware, which typically occurs at the very beginning of the execution, we argue that 120 s is sufficient. After the timeout, the logs were collected and sent back to the host for further analysis.

5.3   Results: Topologies

In this section, we discuss the results of our study by analyzing the resulting topologies. We use the graph definition from Sect. 3.2 to describe the code propagations in this section.

Of the entire set of samples, 199 samples (3.5%) failed to create the initial graph and 735 samples (13%) failed the interpretation step. In other words, the malware was never run or the analysis was broken to the point that no start of the interpretation could be found. However, it should be noted that a significant portion of the PE files in Malpedia are not intended to be executed by the user, such as modules. Therefore, it was expected that a significant portion of the samples would fail the interpretation step. These samples were omitted from the statistics. In total, 4853 samples from 1747 families remain, which were successfully analyzed.

There are 1446 DLLs and 3407 executables in the data set. 1351 samples used code propagations. 52 of these samples are DLLs; therefore, 3.6% of the analyzed DLLs use code propagations. 1299 executables (38.13%) have used code propagations. From these numbers, we can see that code propagations play a much larger role for executables than for DLLs. This may be due to the fact that DLLs have a different use case, because DLLs are often loaded by an initial dropper file, so hiding in the system may not be important for them, as this could already have been achieved by the dropper.

Apart from 45 samples (3.33%) that produced circular propagation graphs in our experiments, 1306 (96.67%) samples produced tree structures.

Table 1. 68.24% of the trees have a maximum degree of one. We coin these trees as paths. So, 31.76% of the samples spread their code to two or more processes.

Max Degree	Paths	Star St.	Bran. St.	C. Graphs	$\sum$
1	922	0	0	3	925
2	0	212	36	11	259
3	0	36	6	1	43
4	0	24	5	0	29
5	0	8	5	1	14
6	0	5	2	3	10
7	0	2	1	2	5
8	0	7	1	5	13
9	0	6	2	9	17
>= 10	0	24	2	10	36

Table 2. The longest path in the trees grouped by their topology types. The most common lengths are two and three. The most common length of the longest path for the branching structures is three.

Longest Path	Paths	Star St.	Bran. St.	$\sum$
2	713	203	0	916
3	136	75	36	247
4	44	30	7	81
5	24	9	10	43
6	1	1	2	4
7	1	1	0	2
8	0	1	3	4
9	0	1	0	1
>= 10	3	3	2	8

To further classify the tree structures, we first looked at their maximum degree. We found that 922 (68.25%) of these samples had a maximum degree of one, i.e., they can be categorized as paths (subsequently referred to as path samples), as shown in Table 1. We also found that 713 (77.33%) of all path samples carried out exactly one code propagation, as depicted in Table 2.

To classify the remaining trees, we looked at how many nodes had a degree greater than one. As shown in Fig. 2, 324 (23.98%) trees meet this condition. Due to their similarity to starlike trees [24], we named this class star structures[2].

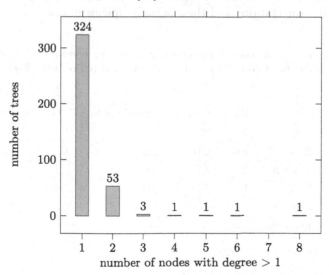

Fig. 2. This graph illustrates the number of trees with the number of nodes with a degree greater than one. There are 324 trees with exactly one node with a degree greater than one.

---

[2] Our definition differs from the definition for starlike trees in that the vertex with degree greater than 1 does not need to be the root.

The highest degree of a tree in Table 1 provides insight into how widely malware of this class spreads in the system. 212 (65.43%) of the samples in this group distribute their code to two processes, and the remaining 112 (34.58%) spread it to more than two processes.

In Fig. 2, the third largest group is 60 (4.44%) trees with two or more nodes with a degree greater than one. Curiously, we found that trees with exactly two nodes with degrees greater than one are caterpillar trees, i.e., trees in which removing all pendant nodes results in a cordless path. The remaining seven trees are more complexly branched than the caterpillar trees. Therefore, we refer to this group as branching structures, as samples of this type have the most intricate structure of all trees. No tree with a branching structure has a shorter longest path than three, as can be seen in Table 2.

In total, we have identified four different topological classes: **Circular Graphs**, **Paths** with a degree of one, **Star Structures** that have only one node with a degree greater than one, **Branching Structures** that have more than one node with degree greater than one.

The vast majority of 922 samples belong to the path topology. The second largest group, with 324 samples, belongs to the star structures. The branching structures and the circular graphs are the least important topology classes with 60 and 45 samples, respectively.

5.4   Results: Propagation Techniques

In this section, we will discuss the code propagation methods by first analyzing the number of propagations and their actual implementation.

Table 3. The number of code propagations per sample. The branching structure and graphs perform the most code propagations, and paths perform the fewest code propagations.

	Paths	Star St.	Branching St.	C. Graphs
min	1	2	4	2
25%	1.0	2.0	4.0	5.0
median	1.0	3.0	6.0	11.0
75%	1.0	5.0	9.0	12.0
average	1.50	8.55	10.30	28.73
maximum	131	357	161	892

First, we provide an overview of the number of code propagations used by the samples in their respective topology types. We hypothesize that path samples use the least number of propagations since they are of the simplest type.

The results are displayed in Table 3. It can be seen that path samples mostly use only one code propagation. However, as indicated by the discrepancy between

Table 4. Occurrence of code propagation techniques in topology types. Each propagation is counted once per sample. The most important code propagation techniques are the spawn of new processes, technique 217 (injection using a newly created process into new memory allocation and executed by a reused thread), and technique 129 (launch of a new process and thread resume). The explanation for the binary codes can be found in Sect. 3.3.

Code Propagation		Paths	Star Str.	Branching Str.	C. Graphs	$\sum$
Propagation	**Binary Code**	–	–	–	–	–
1	00000001	613	270	57	40	980
217	11011001	147	59	17	9	232
129	10000001	106	57	10	4	177
225	11100001	52	13	11	3	79
86	01010110	14	24	8	31	77
209	11010001	50	17	1	4	72
85	01010101	19	10	16	6	51
249	11111001	13	7	1	0	21
241	11110001	9	3	0	1	13
81	01010001	5	3	2	0	10
233	11101001	8	1	0	0	9
137	10001001	5	2	1	0	8
117	01110101	2	2	3	1	8
97	01100001	6	0	0	0	6
118	01110110	2	1	0	3	6
113	01110001	4	0	0	1	5
214	11010110	0	0	0	4	4
221	11011101	0	2	0	1	3
229	11100101	3	0	0	0	3
145	10010001	1	0	0	0	1
161	10100001	1	0	0	0	1
237	11101101	0	1	0	0	1
245	11110101	0	0	1	0	1
253	11111101	1	0	0	0	1

the third quartile and the average, there are a small number of samples that perform significantly more propagations. Star structures use many more code propagations, about nine on average. The branching structures use about 8 and the circular graphs even use almost 29 code propagations on average. By comparing the data, it is evident that the number of code propagations for all types except paths increases greatly.

Subsequently, we focus on the different code propagations as they are used by the samples in their respective types. To represent the code propagation

Table 5. Functions, their number of usages, and the number of samples using the respective functions.

Function	Total Usage	#Samples
WriteProcessMemory	20449	461
VirtualAllocEx	9007	445
CreateProcessW	3309	808
ResumeThread	1838	511
CreateProcessA	1668	423
VirtualProtectEx	959	93
NtWriteVirtualMemory	763	140
SetThreadContext	600	260
CreateRemoteThread	556	139
OpenProcess	446	83
ShellExecuteA	168	102
ShellExecuteExW	145	93
ShellExecuteW	124	77
NtResumeThread	103	67
CreateProcessInternalW	86	73
WinExec	85	65
VirtualQueryEx	65	5
CreateProcessInternalA	31	15
QueueUserAPC	6	6
ShellExecuteExA	3	3

techniques, we interpret the eight bits as described in Subsect. 3.3 as the value of an unsigned integer and use the resulting value for easier reference. The bit representation of the code propagation technique is shown in parentheses next to the unsigned integer. Table 4 shows the total number of code propagations used in the data set. We have chosen to narrow down on fully realized code propagations and, therefore, omit failed code propagations.

In our data set, 24 code propagation techniques are used. The vast majority of samples use the technique of simply spawning a malicious process 1 (00000001). This technique is used in 980 samples, with the majority being in path and star structures at 631 and 270 respectively. The second most widely used propagation technique, 217 (11011001), is an injection into a newly created process with new memory allocation and a thread reuse. Technique 129 (10000001) launches a new process and resumes the main thread. The fourth most common technique is 225 (11100001), which is the spawn of a new process and the reuse of threads and memory.

These findings emphasize the notion that malware uses many ways to distribute its code throughout the system. Consequently, a dynamic analysis machine must be able to keep track of a variety of different code propagation techniques. Failure to do so will result in the inability to properly detect all code propagations.

The next segment focuses on the actual implementation of the code propagations. For this purpose, we look at the usage of functions. The numbers in Table 5 represent the total usage of functions in code propagations in the data set and the number of samples that use the respective functions. We only count the number of calls made directly by the malware. For example, a call to CreateProcessInternalA made by CreateProcessA is not counted. However, a call to CreateProcessInternalA made directly by the malware is counted.

The four most used functions are WriteProcessMemory, VirtualAllocEx, CreateProcessW, and ResumeThread. The function by most individual samples is CreateProcessW. Taking into account Fig. 1, there are two bottlenecks in the graph. There is either the path of starting a new process or the path of injections. In the injection route, the step of writing data to memory (WriteProcessMemory) is the bottleneck, while spawning a process (CreateProcess-Family) is the bottleneck on the other side. Therefore, these functions are essential for code propagations. Thus, they are the topmost used functions in Table 5.

6   Recommended Samples

As a result of our experiments, we want to provide a list of recommended samples that researchers can use to evaluate their countermeasures against code propagations. In this way, researchers do not have to rely solely on theoretical analysis to assess their approaches. First, we provide samples of malware families that belong to the **Path Topology**:

- **Laziok**[3] performs code propagation techniques **85** and **1**.
- **Bfbot**[4] uses code propagation techniques **217** and **86**.
- **Emotet**[5] performs the code propagation technique **225**.
- **Zloader**[6] uses the code propagation technique **249**.
- **Shylock**[7] covers the code propagation technique **209**.
- **Kins**[8] uses the code propagation technique **229**.
- **Ramnit**[9] uses the code propagation technique **253**.
- **Dridex**[10] uses the code propagation technique **97**.
- **Solarbot**[11] uses the code propagation technique **113**.

---

[3] 6adecfaec434b41ecce9911f00b48e4e8ae6e3e8b9081d59e1b46480e9f7dbfc.
[4] f19ce795b4b2421a82ff71a3f3a271032578c80cadd0cc44b1714848b5bb81c0.
[5] f9ef36da6a3786dd672e049aa4028d12d0cd33a4f4771ec70309c89f8f482930.
[6] bd882e2eefd0145ff169d868c1815df272f84a5ad1e501cfa5c3336839774171.
[7] a7a29da4c53d424e1997ff8f2702aea6b76e9f5b60d704f306c353e01cea4d76.
[8] 520ae48364d7e5fe6bdb0a59c9cd1370dee5b26e648677fa84f1f601f727d280.
[9] 89b138eaaade5a1ec36e2d1422ae38059f138e81b722301e713b65a74de521c7.
[10] f24354e54e4b59f6c327b1f7e144092647e726505acde5595a8386e7c2c6fa8a.
[11] 40fa0ae6c2f73af93c304b3e12d22ee38100ac0e18798f2e96b1db37abbca8e8.

- **gameover_dga**[12] uses the code propagation techniques **214** and **86**.
- **Lokipws**[13] uses the code propagation technique **145**.
- **ngioweb**[14] uses the code propagation technique **161**.

For the **Star Structure Topology**, we recommend the following samples:

- **Gozi**[15] uses the code propagation technique **118**.
- **Gootkit**[16] covers the code propagation technique **241**.
- **Cutwail**[17] uses the code propagation technique **221**.
- **Lethic**[18] uses the code propagation technique **233**.
- **Xsplus**[19] uses the code propagation technique **137**.
- **Shifu**[20] uses the code propagation technique **237**.

For the **Branching Structure Topology**, we suggest the following samples:

- **Qakbot**[21] uses the code propagation techniques **225**, **86**, and **1**.
- **Ramnit**[22] covers the code propagation technique **117**.
- **Opghoul**[23] covers code propagation techniques **129** and **81**.

At last, for the **Circular Graph Structure Topology**, we recommend:

- **Gameover DGA**[24] uses code propagation techniques **86** and **217**.
- **Snifula**[25] uses the code propagation technique **245**.

7   Discussion and Conclusion

In this paper, we set out to study the movement of malicious code through the system. We presented a definition for code propagations and a systematized representation of code propagation topologies and techniques. Also, we proposed a methodology for the detection and measurement of code propagations of malicious software.

Consequently, we have used our proof-of-concept implementation to conduct a study on a diverse real-world data set called Malpedia [32]. Our study shows that code propagations are widely used in malware. More than a third of the

---

[12] 072cdcf66b81772724648da4c0ca2429a39504599e07ccfca2ba8af73ec24adc.
[13] 97a614c078ca4302c31a8af24cf19317d76507c5fee17b4df10149157127b19b.
[14] df70581c5a712e2eda57922114534704166f93dc2158c302c58d61a487330546.
[15] be65dc1c2d2cb1ddbb7b08780e608eb0d9cabc706491f5bd7657326018c0c518.
[16] e7fa2707166283e1f0e7422546ee387aae01b5ee5c255a62909da0a3b6cb19c0.
[17] 92c0cc5879215255478b3325bee34353090e08337aa61a92506f0498f7907500.
[18] 92bb2efeea875eb5e8779f13cc50d1a831b3c538eb73e15384f8748266be8ff1.
[19] bff06d770eec594c363a217effbe2ea4e8a618b7ef95da1100e5aef9c847403f.
[20] b2c6c7e9d8bb6f75865324788cf311a5a951e2d4e69137937ecfb0879ebae1ce.
[21] d7489e3f876cb41d61b08bb1f91ed9a9f862761416954649c4ee2c26b5c3c199.
[22] 80823b2e354ed28badde4e8a7525113be5fc61b4a48f64a5f33da9491d2d2aa9.
[23] d22f9035ac8c69bb391bd478b01305c00bef0cb7b1b0b2ea716ad31a3fcc07cb.
[24] 3ff49706e78067613aa1dcf0174968963b17f15e9a6bc54396a9f233d382d0e6.
[25] 104428ccf005b36edfb62d110203a43bdbb417052b31eb4646395309645c9944.

executable samples in our data set use code propagations. We derived typical malware code propagation behavior from a representative data set by investigating the movement of code through the system as well as determining the type of propagation technique used. We have identified four types of code propagation topologies and a set of 24 code propagation techniques. Our study focuses on Windows malware. An analogous study focusing on Android malware may be beneficial due to the increasing popularity of mobile malware.

Lastly, we have provided a list of samples for each code propagation technique and topology. In subsequent work, this list can be used to generate mitigation strategies addressing the various code propagation topologies and techniques.

8 Appendix

8.1 Hooked Functions

The functions that focus on process(-handle) creation on Microsoft Windows are:

– OpenProcess & NtOpenProcess & CreateProcessW & CreateProcessA & WinExec
– CreateProcessInternalA & CreateProcessInternalW & NtCreateUserProcess
– ShellExecuteExW & ShellExecuteExA & ShellExecuteA & ShellExecuteW

The hooked functions that are used to create threads and thread handles on Microsoft Windows are:

– OpenThread & SetThreadContext & NtSetContextThread & NtOpenThread
– ResumeThread & NtResumeThread & CreateRemoteThread & QueueUser-APC

The functions that allocate new memory regions on Microsoft Windows are:

– VirtualAllocEx & VirtualAllocExNuma
– WriteProcessMemory & NtWriteVirtualMemory & VirtualQueryEx

However, we decided not to hook NtAllocateVirtualMemory because a hook on this function makes the virtual machine unresponsive.

8.2 Example for Log Analysis

```
479024d: 2072: +CreateProcessW(<NULL>,C:\Windows\SysWOW64\upnpcont.exe,0,0,0,0,0,<NULL>,18ff04,18ff50)
47b824f: 2072: -CreateProcessW(,,,,,,,,) -> 1 (proc:2168/f0, thrd:2172/ec
47b828e: 2072: +OpenProcess(1f0fff,0,pid=2168)
47b8339: 2072: -OpenProcess(,,) -> f8
47b838c: 2072: +VirtualAllocEx(f8,0,9a4a,1000,40)
47b83c7: 2072: -VirtualAllocEx(,,,,) -> 100000
47b841a: 2072: +WriteProcessMemory(f8,@100000..109a49,27bea0,0)
47b8515: 2072: -WriteProcessMemory(,,,,) -> 1
47b8573: 2072: +CreateRemoteThread(f8,0,0,100000,0,0,18ff6c)
47b87d5: 2072: -CreateRemoteThread(,,,,,,) -> f4 (2176
488e0fa: 2072: +ExitProcess(0)
```

Fig. 3. This log file snippet is taken from the original malware process, launched by the Explorer. The sample belongs to the Laziok family. It is heavily truncated for readability and shows an injection into a new process.

Figure 3 shows a snippet of a log file for a sample of the Laziok family[26]. In the first two lines, the malware launches a process from the upnpcont.exe binary with CreateProcessW. Afterwards, the malware opens the process with OpenProcess to gain a handle, even though CreateProcessW also returns a handle to the new process. The handle f8 is used to allocate new memory in the new process to which the code is written. This memory is executed by a new thread that is spawned at the address where the data were previously written. The process then terminates. At the end of the sandboxing, this new process is still running.

References

1. Alvarez, V.M.: YARA: the pattern matching swiss knife for malware researchers (and everyone else). http://virustotal.github.io/yara/. Accessed 16 Aug 2023
2. ATT&CK, M.: Mitre att&ck (2021). https://attack.mitre.org
3. AVTest: security report 2019/2020. https://www.av-test.org/fileadmin/pdf/security_report/AV-TEST_Security_Report_2019-2020.pdf. Accessed 16 Aug 2023
4. Bacs, A., Vermeulen, R., Slowinska, A., Bos, H.: System-level support for intrusion recovery. In: Flegel, U., Markatos, E., Robertson, W. (eds.) Detection of Intrusions and Malware, and Vulnerability Assessment. Lecture Notes in Computer Science, vol. 7591, pp. 144–163. Springer, Berlin (2012). https://doi.org/10.1007/978-3-642-37300-8_9
5. Barabosch, T., Bergmann, N., Dombeck, A., Padilla, E.: Quincy: Detecting host-based code injection attacks in memory dumps. In: Proceedings of the 14th International Conference on Detection of Intrusions and Malware, and Vulnerability Assessment (DIMVA), Bonn, Germany (2017)
6. Barabosch, T., Eschweiler, S., Gerhards-Padilla, E.: Bee master: detecting host-based code injection attacks. In: Proceedings of the 11th International Conference on Detection of Intrusions and Malware, and Vulnerability Assessment (DIMVA), London, UK (2014)

---

[26] 6adecfaec434b41ecce9911f00b48e4e8ae6e3e8b9081d59e1b46480e9f7dbfc.

7. Barabosch, T., Gerhards-Padilla, E.: Host-based code injection attacks: a popular technique used by malware. In: 2014 9th International Conference on Malicious and Unwanted Software: The Americas (MALWARE), pp. 8–17. IEEE (2014)
8. Bohne, L., Holz, T.: Pandora's Bochs: automated malware unpacking. Master's thesis, RWTH Aachen University (2008)
9. ByteAtlas: Knowledge fragment: Hardening win7 x64 on virtualbox for malware analysis. http://byte-atlas.blogspot.com/2017/02/hardening-vbox-win7x64.html. Accessed 16 Aug 2023
10. D'Elia, D.C., Nicchi, S., Mariani, M., Marini, M., Palmaro, F.: Designing robust API monitoring solutions. IEEE Trans. Dependable Secure Comput. 01, 1–1 (2021)
11. Dinaburg, A., Royal, P., Sharif, M., Lee, W.: Ether: malware analysis via hardware virtualization extensions. In: Proceedings of the 15th ACM Conference On Computer and Communications Security, pp. 51–62. ACM (2008)
12. Dolan-Gavitt, B., Hodosh, J., Hulin, P., Leek, T., Whelan, R.: Repeatable reverse engineering with panda. In: Proceedings of the 5th Program Protection and Reverse Engineering Workshop, pp. 1–11 (2015)
13. Isawa, R., Morii, M., Inoue, D.: Comparing malware samples for unpacking: a feasibility study. In: 2016 11th Asia Joint Conference on Information Security (Asia-JCIS), pp. 155–160. IEEE (2016)
14. Ispoglou, K.K., Payer, M.: malWASH: washing malware to evade dynamic analysis. In: 10th USENIX Workshop on Offensive Technologies (WOOT 16). USENIX Association, Austin, TX (2016). https://www.usenix.org/conference/woot16/workshop-program/presentation/ispoglou
15. Jenke, T., Plohmann, D., Padilla, E.: RoAMer: the robust automated malware unpacker. In: 14th International Conference on Malicious and Unwanted Software (MALWARE), Nantucket, MA, USA, 2019, pp. 67–74 (2019)
16. Jeong, G., Choo, E., Lee, J., Bat-Erdene, M., Lee, H.: Generic unpacking using entropy analysis. In: 2010 5th International Conference on Malicious and Unwanted Software, pp. 98–105. IEEE (2010)
17. Kang, M.G., Poosankam, P., Yin, H.: Renovo: a hidden code extractor for packed executables. In: Proceedings of the 2007 ACM Workshop on Recurring Malcode, pp. 46–53. ACM (2007)
18. Kawakoya, Y., Shioji, E., Iwamura, M., Miyoshi, J.: API chaser: taint-assisted sandbox for evasive malware analysis. J. Inf. Proc. 27, 297–314 (2019)
19. Korczynski, D.: RePEconstruct: reconstructing binaries with self-modifying code and import address table destruction. In: 2016 11th International Conference on Malicious and Unwanted Software (MALWARE), pp. 1–8. IEEE (2016)
20. Korczynski, D.: Precise system-wide concatic malware unpacking. arXiv preprint: arXiv:1908.09204 (2019)
21. Korczynski, D., Yin, H.: Capturing malware propagations with code injections and code-reuse attacks. In: Proceedings of the 2017 ACM SIGSAC Conference on Computer and Communications Security, pp. 1691–1708 (2017)
22. Küchler, A., Mantovani, A., Han, Y., Bilge, L., Balzarotti, D.: Does every second count? time-based evolution of malware behavior in sandboxes. In: Proceedings of the Network and Distributed System Security Symposium, NDSS. The Internet Society (2021)
23. Lengyel, T.K., Maresca, S., Payne, B.D., Webster, G.D., Vogl, S., Kiayias, A.: Scalability, fidelity and stealth in the DRAKVUF dynamic malware analysis system. In: Proceedings of the 30th Annual Computer Security Applications Conference, pp. 386–395 (2014)

24. Lepović, M., Gutman, I.: No starlike trees are cospectral. Discret. Math. **242**(1–3), 291–295 (2002)
25. Magazine, S.: Ransomware attacks nearly doubled in 2021 (2022)
26. Martignoni, L., Christodorescu, M., Jha, S.: OmniUnpack: fast, generic, and safe unpacking of malware. In: Computer Security Applications Conference, 2007. ACSAC 2007. Twenty-Third Annual, pp. 431–441. IEEE (2007)
27. Microsoft: Microsoft detours. https://github.com/microsoft/Detours. Accessed 16 Aug 2023
28. Microsoft: Samples: Syelog. https://documentation.help/Detours/Sam_Syelog. htm. Accessed 16 Aug 2023
29. Microsoft: Samples: Traceapi. https://documentation.help/Detours/Sam_ Traceapi.htm. Accessed 16 Aug 2023
30. Mohammad, A.H.: Ransomware evolution, growth and recommendation for detection. Mod. Appl. Sci. **14**(3), 68 (2020)
31. Oracle: Oracle virtualbox. https://www.virtualbox.org/. Accessed 16 Aug 2023
32. Plohmann, D., Clauss, M., Enders, S., Padilla, E.: Malpedia: a collaborative effort to inventorize the malware landscape. In: Proceedings of the Botconf (2017)
33. Plohmann, D., Enders, S., Padilla, E.: ApiScout: robust windows API usage recovery for malware characterization and similarity analysis. J Cybercrime Digit. Invest. **4**, 1–6 (2018)
34. Rossow, C., et al.: Prudent practices for designing malware experiments: status quo and outlook. In: Proceedings of the 33rd IEEE Symposium on Security and Privacy (S&P), San Francisco, CA (2012)
35. Royal, P., Halpin, M., Dagon, D.: PolyUnpack: automating the hidden-code extraction of unpack-executing malware. In: ACSAC, pp 289–300 (2006)
36. Sharif, M., Yegneswaran, V., Saidi, H., Porras, P., Lee, W.: Eureka: a framework for enabling static malware analysis. In: Jajodia, S., Lopez, J. (eds.) Computer Security - ESORICS 2008. Lecture Notes in Computer Science, vol. 5283, pp. 481–500. Springer, Berlin (2008). https://doi.org/10.1007/978-3-540-88313-5_31
37. Ugarte-Pedrero, X., Balzarotti, D., Santos, I., Bringas, P.G.: RAMBO: run-time packer analysis with multiple branch observation. In: Caballero, J., Zurutuza, U., Rodriguez, R. (eds.) Detection of Intrusions and Malware, and Vulnerability Assessment. Lecture Notes in Computer Science(), vol. 9721, pp. 186–206. Springer, Cham (2016). https://doi.org/10.1007/978-3-319-40667-1_10
38. Yin, H., Song, D., Egele, M., Kruegel, C., Kirda, E.: Panorama: capturing system-wide information flow for malware detection and analysis. In: Proceedings of the 14th ACM Conference on Computer and Communications Security, pp. 116–127 (2007)

An Android Malware Detection Method Based on Optimized Feature Extraction Using Graph Convolutional Network

Zhiqiang Wang[1,2]([⊠]), Zhuoyue Wang[1], and Ying Zhang[1]

[1] Beijing Electronic Science and Technology Institute, Beijing 100070, China
wangzq@besti.edu.cn
[2] State Information Center, Beijing 100045, China

Abstract. With the development of the mobile Internet, mobile devices have been extensively promoted and popularized. Android, as the current popular mobile intelligent operating system, has encountered problems such as the explosive growth of Android malware while bringing convenience to users. The traditional Android malware detection methods have some problems, such as low detection accuracy and difficulty in detecting unknown malware. This paper proposes an Android malware detection method named Android malware detection method based on graph convolutional neural network (AGCN) based on the graph convolutional network (GCN) to solve the above problems. Firstly, we divide the Android software datasets according to family and software features and construct a directed network topology graph. At the same time, the permission features of APK files are extracted and vectorized. Then, we use GCN to learn the features of Android APK files... Finally, we compare AGCN with a multilayer perceptron (MLP), long and short-term memory (LSTM) neural network, bi-directional long and short-term memory (bi-LSTM) neural network, and deep confidence neural network (DCNN) for experiments. Experimental results show that the model has an accuracy of 98.55% for malware detection, demonstrating the detection method's effectiveness.

Keywords: Android Malware · Graph Convolutional Networks · Static Analysis · Graph Features

1 Introduction

As the development of the mobile Internet and the Internet of Things (IoT), smartphones represented by Android phones have rapidly applicated to every aspect of people's lives. Since smartphones contain many sensitive information, more and more attackers are using mobile smart terminals as the primary attack targets. As a result, mobile malwares, such as privacy theft, spam advertisements, and malicious chargebacks, are growing explosively. In the first half of 2021, a total of about 3.85 million new malicious samples were intercepted by 360 Mobile Guard on the mobile terminal, an increase of 267.2%

S. Goel and P. R. Nunes de Souza (Eds.): ICDF2C 2023, LNICST 571, pp. 283–299, 2024.
https://doi.org/10.1007/978-3-031-56583-0_19

compared with the first half of 2020 (1.048 million), and about 2.1 new mobile malicious samples per day on average are intercepted. In the first half of 2022, about 4.23 billion malicious attacks are blocked by 360 Mobile Guard for smartphone users in China, with an average of about 23.386 million malicious attacks per day [1].

The detection of Android malware based on the logical graph is an important research method and hotspot. However, there are problems in the current related work. For example, the feature extraction of logical graph structure is not comprehensive enough, resulting in lower detection accuracy. Moreover, the traditional machine learning algorithm is restricted to the processing of complex functions, and its accuracy is low, so it is difficult to adapt to new samples. Hence, it is a highly extensive research area to explore effective techniques for feature extraction from Android software and enhancing detection efficiency.

This paper conducts research on the detection of Android malware and proposes AGCN based on a graph convolutional neural network. The main innovations and contributions of this paper are as follows:

Design an Android application feature extraction and conversion logic graph algorithm and batch extract the permission features of each application into the corresponding text file (apkpermission.txt). In this technical process, the permission feature document generated by the feature extraction method is used to extract all features. The extracted features are then traversed based on the permission features to generate a permission feature library (Permission Set). Use one-hot encoding to generate feature vectors for determining topology node features. Then, the polar association relationship is constructed, and the directed network topology is formed. And use the topology map structure as an adjacency matrix to transform Android Apply features.

(1) An Android malware detection method based on a graph convolutional network is proposed. Based on the conversion of Android software into logic graphs, an Android malware detection method is designed to improve the traditional deep learning method and detection performance. Through comparison experiments of different neural network architectures and different parameter comparison experiments, the optimal parameter combination of neural network architectures of deep learning model is determined.

(2) Based on a large number of normal and malicious Android software samples, comparative experiments were carried out with four neural network models to verify and evaluate AGCN. The performance of the system is tested according to the performance metrics. Experimental comparisons show that this method has improved accuracy, precision, recall, and F1-score compared with LSTM, MLP, Bi-LSTM, and DBN.

The other sections of this paper are as follows: Sect. 2 introduces related work; Sect. 3 introduces the key technologies and algorithms of the detection method; Sect. 4 introduces the experimental design and result analysis; Sect. 5 summarizes this paper and proposes the following work.

2 Related Work

2.1 Research Status at Home and Abroad

Early analysis methods cannot effectively detect new malicious applications. Using traditional machine learning techniques (such as support vector machines, decision trees, random forests, and Bayesian networks) for Android malicious application detection is more effective than earlier methods. At the same time, the detection effect achieved by using deep learning technology is better than traditional machine learning methods. Abdelmonim Naway et al. [2] identified the deep learning method to detect malicious Android applications. In most of these methods, deep learning is combined with static analysis, while only a few are combined with dynamic analysis and hybrid analysis. Zhiqiang Wang et al. [3] combed through the methods of applying deep learning to Android malicious applications detection. The deep learning models are mainly Convolutional Neural Networks (CNN) and Deep Belief Networks (DBN). The extracted features mainly consist of API call features, permission features, and system call features, while component features, intent features, data flow features, and opcode sequence features are also involved to some extent. TaeGuen Kim et al. [4] proposed a multi-modal deep learning method as a malware detection model. To achieve effective feature representation in malware detection, multiple feature types are extracted to reflect the attributes of an Android application from various aspects. The feature extraction method based on existence or similarity is used to improve these features. A total of 7 static features are extracted, including permissions, components, environments, strings, Dalvik opcode sequences, API call sequences, and shared library function opcode features. Each feature type is used to train its corresponding deep neural network's initial network. The training results of the initial network are then used to train the final network.

In addition to the above methods of combining multiple features and using deep learning models for detecting malicious Android applications, a few researchers have used deep learning models to extract and abstract features from images automatically. Peter Zegzhda et al. [5] built a control flow graph through small files to obtain the features of API call sequence, mapped corresponding protection levels according to permissions required for API call, and then converted API call sequence and protection level into pixels of RGB images. The detection model based on a convolutional neural network was used for detection. A classification accuracy of 93.64% is achieved on a dataset consisting of 7192 normal samples and 24461 malicious samples. Luo Shiqi et al. [6] proposed a texture fingerprinting-based method to extract features of malware content. This method uses information from texture images extracted from the sample application code, which is mapped to uncompressed grayscale values according to the texture image-based method. Combined with API call features, a deep belief network is used to classify Android malware. Zhiqiang Wang et al. [7] proposed an Android malware detection framework based on Convolutional Neural Network (CNN). They used static analysis tools and python scripts to automatically extract 1003 static features, and transformed the features of each sample into a two-dimensional matrix as input to the CNN model. Ganesh et al. [8] used static analysis to extract 138 permission features of four categories, and converted the permission features into 12×12 PNG images. They used convolutional neural networks for model training and detection, including 2000 malicious samples and 500 benign samples. The model achieved a detection accuracy of 93% in a total of 2,500 Android applications. Huang et al. [9] converted.dex-like bytecodes to RGB color codes and converted them to fixed-size color images. These color images are input into a convolutional neural network for automatic feature extraction and training. The experimental data set was collected from January 2017 to August 2017. About 2 million benign and malicious Android applications were collected. The experimental results show that the detection accuracy is 98.4225%.

This paper also analyzes the detection of Android malware based on permission characteristics. Wu et al. [10] used static analysis to detect Android malware and considered some static information, including permissions, component deployment, android intent, and application programming interface (API) calls, to describe the behavior of Android applications. After extracting the application features of malware, the K-means algorithm is used to enhance the modeling ability of malware. In the low-rank approximation, singular value decomposition (SVD) is used to determine the number of clusters. Finally, this system uses the KNN algorithm to classify the application as benign or malicious.

Wang et al. [11] explored the risks systematically caused by permissions in Android applications from three perspectives. They analyzed the risks of individual permissions and a set of collaborative permissions and used three feature ranking methods (mutual information, correlation coefficient, and T-test) to rank Android individual permissions. Risky subsets of permissions were identified by using sequential forward selection and principal component analysis. Second, they evaluate the effectiveness of risk permissions for malicious app detection using support vector machines, decision trees, and random forests to deeply analyze the detection results. Finally, they discussed the feasibility and limitations of malicious application detection based on permission requests. KA Talha et al. [12] proposed a permission-based Android malware detection system named APK Auditor, including a signature database, an Android client, and a central server, which uses static analysis to characterize and classify Android applications. Finally, the performance of the system is tested, yielding an accuracy rate of 88%. Qiao et al. [13] proposed a novel machine-learning approach for malware detection by analyzing Android app usage permissions and API function call patterns. They extract binary and numerical features from the source code and resource files of the apps through static analysis, which are then used for qualitative and quantitative evaluation. Finally, various machine learning methods, such as support vector machines, random forest, and neural networks, are employed for classification. Experimental results show that the proposed method can accurately detect Android malware, and the proposed method can help improve users' awareness of potential risks and mitigate malware threats on Android devices.

2.2 Graph Convolutional Neural Networks

Graph Convolutional Network (GCN) was first proposed by Kipf et al., in 2017 [14]. Based on convolutional operations, Kipf et al. have proposed A neural network model f (A, X) for semi-supervised learning of vertices, in which A is the adjacency matrix of the graph, and X is the input data. Adjusting f(·) on the adjacency matrix of the graph will allow the model to allocate gradient information from the supervised loss L0, and enable it to learn the representation of all nodes. It is a neural network model for processing graph data. The graph convolutional network is a model evolved from the spectral convolutional neural network and the Chebyshev network [15]. The basic structure of the graph convolutional network is shown in Fig. 1.

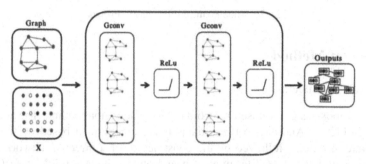

Fig. 1. The basic structure of a convolutional neural network.

The graph convolutional network is similar to the convolutional neural network. The convolution operator is defined on the graph structure, which can continuously expand the node information contained in the node embedding vector during the iterative process [16]. As shown in Fig. 2, a1–a4, the four nodes represent four APK files, and each APK file corresponds to its feature vector p1–p4. The process of graph embedding in graph convolutional neural networks is the process of continuous information propagation, aggregation, and re-propagation among nodes. Each node will get neighbor node information and update itself. Graph data often has a wide range of neighborhood structures near a single node, and the relationship between data is also complex. While CNN is limited to regular data, graph convolutional network has a wider range of applications. GCN can process more structured data, such as social networks and knowledge maps, and extract the spatial characteristics of structured data. GCN directly constructs the learning process on the graph data and provides an end-to-end framework for learning. It has obvious advantages in learning graph data and has better adaptability to learning tasks. GCN puts node representation learning and downstream task learning in the model for end-to-end learning. In order to achieve better adaptability between node feature representation and downstream tasks, GCN supervisory signals guide the parameter updating of task layer and GCN layer. In addition, the structure information and attribute information of the graph are complementary. For the graph with a sparse structure, the addition of attribute information can improve the quality of node representation learning. GCN puts these two kinds of information into the same network layer for simultaneous learning so that the two can synergistically affect the representation of the final node.

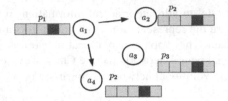

Fig. 2. Node Feature Propagation Process.

3 Detection Method

3.1 Overall Architecture

This paper proposes a GCN-based Android malware detection method. The architecture is shown in Fig. 3. Android software datasets are categorized based on their family and software functions, followed by the construction of a directed network topology graph. Decompile the APK file, unpack it and obtain the AndroidManifest.xml and class.dex files. Then extract the permission features by parsing the XML tree node <uses-permission> of the manifest file and traverse the feature documents of all applications in the feature extraction module. Organize all the permission features as the permission library, and finally compare the features of each APK file with the permission library to determine the node features of the topology map, to train and test the detection model.

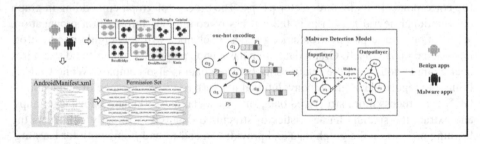

Fig. 3. Detection method architecture.

3.2 Feature Extraction and Processing

This article divides Android APK installation packages according to family and function classification. For example, hackers can remotely access infected mobile devices through DroidKungFu trojans while using the vulnerability root system to disguise themselves. In this paper, we utilize the original information extracted from APK files of each family member to establish a cascade relationship and subsequently construct a directed network topology. Then the topology structure is processed in the form of an adjacency matrix.

In this study, the permission information is selected as the feature attribute of the topology map node. The permission feature can reflect the behavior of Android software in some aspects. The <uses-permission> tag describes the hardware and software features that Android depends on. Table 1 lists several typical Android malware permission characteristics and attack behavior descriptions [5]. The original APK file in binary format cannot be used as the input of the graph convolutional network model for training directly. To obtain the corresponding feature data, they need to be preprocessed and feature extracted.

Table 1. Permission characteristics and attack behavior description of Android malware.

Malware family	Important Sensitive Permissions	Describe
ADRD	INTERNET, ACCESS_NETWORK_STATE, RECEIVE_BOOT_COMPLETED	worm virus
BaseBridge	NATIVE_CODE	root escalation using a Trojan horse
Bgserv	INTERNET, RECEIVE_SMS, SEND_SMS	worm virus
DroidDreamLight	INTERNET, READ_PHONE_STATE	Information Stealing Trojans
Genimi	INTERNET,SEND_SMS	worm virus
jSMSHider	INSTALL_PACKAGES	Destroy system firmware Trojans
Pjapps	INTERNET,RECEIVE_SMS	worm virus
Zsone	INTERNET, RECEIVE_SMS, SEND_SMS	Malicious sending SMS Trojan horse
zHash	CHANGE_WIFI_STATE	root escalation using a Trojan horse

This article uses APKTool and other decompilation tools to reverse-process Android APK files. After processing, a folder containing AndroidManifest.xml is generated. By parsing the XML tree node <uses-permission> of the manifest file, the permission characteristics can be extracted. The specific steps are designed as follows.

Step 1. Decompile the Android APK file. Use the APKTool to decompile APK files in batches to obtain the folder containing AndroidManifest.xml (Table 2);

Table 2. Partial pseudo-code for permission feature extraction.

Permission feature extraction
Input : APK t apklist R* AndroidManifest.xml c
Output : apkpermission.txt Q*
1.for t in R* do /*Iterate through all apk files*/
2.   if t =.apk then
3.   change ".apk" to ".zip"
4.   (name of ZIP) =(name of APK)
5.   for ZIP in R* do /*Iterate through all zip files*/
6.   if ZIP is .apk then
7.   xmlfile = read(c)
8.   create new txtfile with Q*

Step 2. Extracts permission features to form an attribute set. By parsing the XML tree node <uses-permission> of AndroidManifest.xml decompiled in step 1, permission features can be extracted, and the obtained permission features can be store in permission.txt (Table 3);

Table 3. Partial pseudo-code for the feature permission library generation algorithm.

Feature permission library generation algorithm
Input : UpdatePermList.txt t DefaultPermList.txt s
Output: permissionset.txt
1.updatedata ← t
2.for t in list do
3.   updateList ← updatedata.split('\n')
4. State defaultdata ← s
5.   for s in list do
6.   defaultList ← defaultdata.split('\n')
7.   newList ← defaultList+list(set(updateList) - set(defaultList))

Step 3. Generate a permission library. Traverse the permission feature file permission.txt generated by all APK files in step 2, sort out all the permission features that have appeared as the permission library permission set;

Step 4. Generate feature vectors. Compare the permission.txt with the Permission Set generated in step 3, and use one-hot encoding to generate feature vectors. 1 means that the feature exists 0 means that the feature does not exist, and finally, generate node features (Table 4);

Step 5. Build connection relationships. For each APK file, edges are established between all positions of 1 in its permission feature vector and the corresponding positions of 1 in other permission feature vectors to construct the outgoing edge set for this application.;

Table 4. Partial pseudo-code for feature vector generation algorithm.

Feature vector generation algorithm

Input : apkpermission s permissionset t

Output: csvasterdict a csvrowdata b

/*Function to create a .csv file to store the data in the supplied license list*/

1.function CSVFormatter():

2.　　testfile ← open(UpdatedPermList.txt)

3.　　permlist ← data.split('\n')

4.　　b.append(NAME)

5.　　/*ADD NAME COLUMN*/

6.　　b ← permlist + b

7.　　b.append(CLASS)

8.　　/*ADD PERMISSION COLUMN*/

9. end funtion

10./*Ability to create datasets from existing .csv files and provided APK file folders*/

11.function Bagger(datastoredir):

12.　　if datastoredir is "./MalwareAPK then

13.　　　TYPE ← 1

14.　　else

15.　　　TYPE ← 0

16.　　end If

17.　　if len(ApkNameList)≠0 then

18.　　　for ApkName in ApkNameList do

19.　　　　permissions ← root.findall("uses-permission")

20.　　　　a ← dict.fromkeys(fieldnames,0)

21.　　　　a[NAME] ← ApkName

22.　　　　a[CLASS] ← TYPE

23.　　　　for perm in permissions do

24.　　　　　for att in perm.attrib do

25.　　　　　　permelement ← perm.attrib[att]

26.　　　　　　a[permelement] ← 1

27.　　　return result

Step 6. Build network topology maps. Summarize the edge set constructed in step 5 to form the entire network topology;

Step 7. Generate adjacency matrixes. The network topology structure is represented by an adjacency matrix in step 6, with each node's eigenvector stored as a node attribute and its outgoing edge set recorded in the matrix. In this way, the entire topology graph can be efficiently represented and computed through the adjacency matrix.

Figure 4 shows the process of converting Android software into a logic diagram.

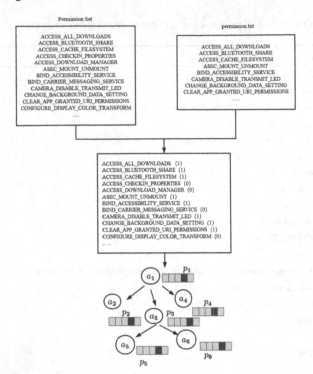

Fig. 4. Schematic diagram of converting Android software into a logic diagram

3.3 Detection Classification

This paper proposes a malware detection method based on a graph convolutional network. In the PyTorch-based Android malware detection system, Fig. 5 illustrates the graph convolutional network structure. The method uses convolutional graph layers, pooling layers, and fully connected layers to implement the detection function. The first layer of the method is the embedding layer, whose role is to convert the discrete input data into a continuous vector representation. Then, multiple parallel operations are performed on the input matrix, such as convolution operations, batch normalization, and max pooling. The parameter of the graph convolution layer is a convolution kernel, which performs convolution operations on the graph structure. During training, these convolution kernels are continuously adjusted to minimize the loss function of the meshes. The convolution kernels mainly obtain the characteristics of the current and adjacent nodes. They obtain local features through aggregation functions. Then shallow learning training is performed to obtain high-dimensional features for classification tasks. Next, the pooling layer concatenates the outputs generated by the convolutional layers into a fixed-length feature vector. Finally, the fully connected layer sends the concatenated vectors to the Softmax classifier for classification and uses regularization technology Dropout to prevent overfitting. The advantage of this method is that it can handle graph-structured data and has certain flexibility and scalability. Therefore, the method has better applicability and scalability in Android malware detection.

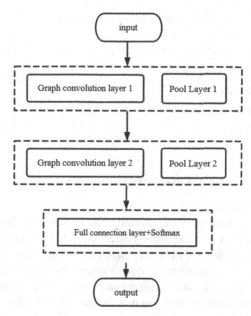

Fig. 5. Neural Network Architecture

The detection and classification part of this paper includes two modules of training and testing. The specific process of the training module is to input the topological graph and node feature vector generated by the feature extraction and processing module into the graph convolutional network. The trained and learned model is used as the final detection model. The test module inputs the test set into the detection model, obtains the final classification result, and calculates evaluation indices to assess the model's classification performance. For the defined model evaluation index, see Sect. 4.

4 Experimental Test and Result Analysis

4.1 Dataset and Experimental Environment

The experimental data set in this paper comes from Drebin [17] and CICDataset, which contains 4202 benign samples, 4679 malicious samples, and 16 malicious application families. Some malicious families and the number of samples are shown in Table 5. In this paper, it is randomly divided into training set, verification set, and test set according to the ratio of 6:2:2. The running and testing of the model are based on the Ubuntu 16.04 operating system, the CPU used is AMD-5800X, and the memory is 32G.

Table 5. Partial malware family datasets.

Serial number	Malware family	Number of samples	Training set	Validation set	Test set
1	FakeInstaller	1127	676	200	251
2	DroidKungFu	968	580	180	208
3	Plankton	882	529	170	183
4	BaseBridge	727	436	130	161

4.2 Determination of Model Parameters

1) Different learning rates

In neural network models, the learning rate is a difficult hyperparameter to set [18]. This is because its size can greatly affect the detection ability of the model. The learning rate controls the speed or step size of error allocation when the weight is updated each time. A higher learning rate can speed up model learning but may result in sub-optimal weights. A lower learning rate can improve the model's weight optimization, including global optima, but may increase training time. Therefore, in order to achieve better performance, the learning rate needs to be gradually reduced during training. By optimizing the learning rate, the model's performance can be improved, and better results can be achieved in experiments. In the comparison experiment, a learning rate value of 0.1 achieved the best detection result with 99.49% accuracy. The results of the comparative experiment are shown in Table 6, and the changing trend of the accuracy rate is shown in Fig. 6.

Table 6. Comparison of experimental results with different learning rates.

Iterations	Learning rate	Accuracy
Epoch = 200	0.1	99.49%
	0.05	98.55%
	0.01	97.50%
	0.005	75.58%
	0.001	68.50%
	0.0001	48.36%

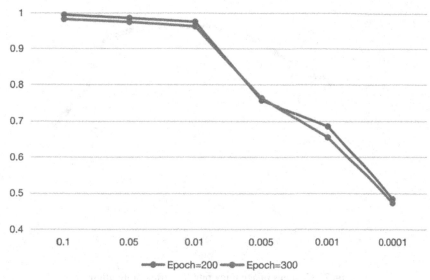

Fig. 6. Changes in accuracy at different learning rates

2) Different iterations

Epoch means to conduct a complete training of the neural network model by using all the sample data in the training set. The number of iterations is the value of Epoch, namely the number of complete training [19]. After multiple rounds of training, the model updates its weights and parameters on the same set to gradually approach the minimum loss function space, improving accuracy and reducing loss. At the same time, methods such as regularization techniques and pruning can also be used to avoid over-fitting problems. The comparison experiment shows that when the number of iterations is 200, the model achieves 99.49%, which is the best detection result of the comparison experiment. The results of the comparative experiment are shown in Table 7, and the changing trend of the accuracy rate is shown in Fig. 7.

Table 7. Comparison of experimental results with different iterations.

Learning rate	Iterations	Accuracy
lr = 0.1	100	92.2%
	150	96.82%
	200	99.49%
	250	98.57%
	300	98.25%
	350	87.24%
	400	75.47%

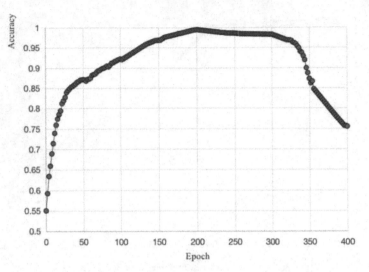

Fig. 7. Changes in accuracy rate for different iterations

4.3 Model Evaluation Metrics

Android malicious application detection is a binary classification problem. There are four possible prediction results. TN indicates that benign samples are predicted to be benign, FN indicates that malicious samples are predicted to be benign, FP indicates that benign samples are predicted to be malicious, and TP indicates that malicious samples are predicted to be malicious. We use the four parameters of accuracy, precision, recall, and F1-score to evaluate the detection model. The parameters and calculation methods are as follows.

The accuracy rate indicates the ratio of the number of correct judgments to the number of all judgments. The higher the accuracy rate, the better the classifier.

$$Accuracy = \frac{TP + TN}{TP + TN + FP + FN}$$

Accuracy rate is a measure of accuracy that represents the ratio of the number of correctly judged positive examples to the number of all judged positive examples.

$$Precision = \frac{TP}{TP + FP}$$

The recall rate is a measure of coverage, which measures how many positive cases are classified as positive cases.

$$Recall = \frac{TP}{TP + FN}$$

F1-score represents the harmonic average evaluation index of precision and recall.

$$F1 - score = \frac{2Precision \times Recall}{Precision + Recall}$$

4.4   Comparative Experiment

In order to verify the effectiveness of the GCN-based Android malware detection model, this paper selects four machine learning algorithms, namely, MLP, LSTM, Bi-LSTM, and DBN, to compare model detection performance. This paper defines a two-layer GCN. The permission database generated by the feature extraction module has 3669 permission features. Therefore, the dimension of the model input is 3669, the dimension of the hidden layer is set to 16, and the output dimension of the last layer of GCN is set to 2 categories. Using ReLU as the activation function, multiple sets of features are extracted and finally classified by the softmax classifier. We randomly use 60% of the dataset as a training set, 20% as a validation set, and 20% as a test set.

4.5   Experimental Results and Analysis

We conduct an evaluation experiment on the Android malware detection method. The core experimental process in this experiment is divided into two stages: training and detection. The test set in this paper consists of 20% malicious and 20% benign samples. The test set contains 641 malicious samples and 1056 benign samples.

Through experiments, the detection method in this paper detected nine malicious applications and 1047 benign applications among the benign test applications, 625 malicious applications, and 16 benign applications among the malicious test applications. The evaluation criteria in this paper include accuracy, precision, recall, and F1-score. Compared with the multilayer perceptron model, long-term, short-term neural memory network model, bidirectional long-term, short-term memory neural network model, and deep confidence neural network model, the experimental results of different deep learning models are shown in Table 8. The experimental results prove the designed effectiveness of Android malware detection methods (Fig. 8).

Table 8. Comparison of experimental results of different deep learning models.

deep learning model	Accuracy	Precision	Recall	F1-score
AGCN	**99.490%**	**99.148%**	**98.495%**	**98.820%**
MLP	98.370%	98.374%	98.371%	98.371%
LSTM	98.460%	98.465%	98.466%	98.466%
Bi-LSTM	97.320%	97.343%	97.328%	97.325%
DBN	93.380%	93.378%	93.377%	93.377%

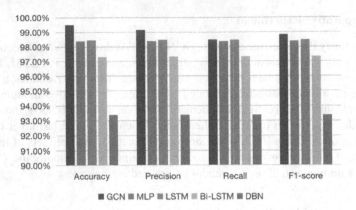

Fig. 8. Comparison of experimental results of different deep learning models

5 Conclusion

This paper conducts thorough research and analysis on Android malware detection technology. Based on the function and family classification of Android software, the construction method of the topology graph is designed. The feature extraction method is designed based on the permission characteristics of Android software. The processed Android softwares are trained and tested, and the deep learning method used is compared with the multilayer perceptron, long-term, short-term memory neural network, bidirectional long-term, short-term memory neural network, and deep confidence neural network. By comparing multiple evaluation indicators, It is verified that the proposed model has a certain degree of advancement compared with the traditional model.

The Android malware detection method based on the graph convolutional network proposed in this paper still has some areas to be improved: 1) It only extracts and analyzes static features, and the detection effect of dynamic features needs to be verified and analyzed experimentally. 2) Currently, The deep learning model for Android malware detection is vulnerable to adversarial attacks. In the future, the adversarial samples automatically generated by the generative adversarial network can be used to retrain deep learning classifiers for adversarial training. The abstraction of the deep learning model can be modified through adversarial training.

References:

1. Data source. https://pop.shouji.360.cn/safe_report/Mobile-Security-Report-202106.pdf
2. Naway, A., Li, Y.: A review on the use of deep learning in Android malware detection (2018)
3. Wang, Z., Liu, Q., Chi, Y.: Review of Android malware detection based on deep learning. IEEE Access **8**, 181102–181126 (2020)
4. Guen, K.T., Kang, B.J., Mina, R., et al.: A multi-modal deep learning method for Android malware detection using various features. IEEE Trans. Inf. Forensics Secur.Secur. **14**(3), 773–788 (2018)
5. Zegzhda, P., Zegzhda, D., Pavlenko, E., et al.: Applying deep learning techniques for Android malware detection, pp. 1–8 (2018)

6. Shiqi, L., Shengwei, T., Long, Y., et al.: Android malicious code classification using deep belief network. KSII Trans. Internet Inf. Syst. **12**(1), 454–475 (2018)
7. Wang, Z., Li, G., Chi, Y.: Multi-classification of Android applications based on convolutional neural networks. In: 2020 International Conference on Computer Science and Application Engineering, Sanya, Hainan, P.R.China (2020)
8. Ganesh, M., Pednekar, P., Prabhuswamy, P., Nair, D.S., Park, Y., Jeon, H.: CNN-based Android malware detection. In: Proceedings of the International Conference on Software Security and Assurance (ICSSA), pp. 60–65 (2017)
9. Huang, T.H.-D., Kao, H.-Y.: R2-D2.: color-inspired convolutional neural network (CNN)-based Android malware detections. In: Proceedings of the IEEE International Conference on Big Data (Big Data), Dec. 2018, pp. 2633–2642
10. Wu, D.-J., Mao, C.-H., Wei, T.-E., Lee, H.-M., Wu, K.-P.: DroidMat: Android malware detection through manifest and API calls tracing. In: 2012 Seventh Asia Joint Conference on Information Security, Tokyo, Japan, pp. 62–69 (2012). https://doi.org/10.1109/AsiaJCIS.2012.18
11. Wang, W., Wang, X., Feng, D., Liu, J., Han, Z., Zhang, X.: Exploring permission-induced risk in Android applications for malicious application detection. IEEE Trans. Inf. Forensics Secur.Secur. **9**(11), 1869–1882 (2014). https://doi.org/10.1109/TIFS.2014.2353996
12. Talha, K.A., Alper, D.I., Aydin, C.: APK Auditor: permission-based Android malware detection system. Digit. Invest. **13**, 1–14 (2015)
13. Qiao, M., Sung, A.H., Liu, Q.: Merging permission and API features for Android malware detection. In: 2016 5th IIAI International Congress on Advanced Applied Informatics (IIAI-AAI), Kumamoto, Japan, pp. 566–571 (2016). https://doi.org/10.1109/IIAI-AAI.2016.237
14. Tan, Y.: A survey of text classification methods based on graph convolutional neural network
15. Gao, H., Cheng, S., Zhang, W.: GDroid: Android malware detection and classification with graph convolutional network. Comput. Secur.. Secur. **106**, 102264 (2021)
16. Feng, P., Ma, J., Li, T., et al.: Android malware detection via graph representation learning. Mob. Inf. Syst. **2021**, 5538841 (2021)
17. Arp, D., Spreitzenbarth, M., Hubner, M., et al.: Drebin: effective and explainable detection of Android malware in your pocket. In: NDSS 2014, vol. 14, pp. 23–26 (2014)
18. Pan, Y., Ge, X., Fang, C., et al.: A systematic literature review of android malware detection using static analysis. IEEE Access **8**, 116363–116379 (2020)
19. Chiang, W.L., Liu, X., Si, S., et al.: Cluster-GCN: an efficient algorithm for training deep and large graph convolutional networks. In: Proceedings of the 25th ACM SIGKDD International Conference On Knowledge Discovery & Data Mining, pp. 257–266 (2019)

ForensiQ: A Knowledge Graph Question Answering System for IoT Forensics

Ruipeng Zhang and Mengjun Xie(✉)

University of Tennessee at Chattanooga, Chattanooga, TN 37403, USA
ruipeng-zhang@mocs.utc.edu, mengjun-xie@utc.edu

Abstract. The increasing number of attacks against the Internet of Things (IoT) has made IoT forensics critically important for reporting and mitigating cyber incidents and crimes. However, the heterogeneity of IoT environments and the complexity and volume of IoT data present significant challenges to forensic practitioners. The advent of question answering (QA) systems and large language models (LLM) offers a potential solution to accessing sophisticated IoT forensic knowledge and data. In light of this, we propose ForensiQ, a framework based on knowledge graph question answering (KGQA), to help investigators navigate complex IoT forensic artifacts and cybersecurity knowledge. Our framework integrates knowledge graphs (KG) into the IoT forensic workflow to better organize and analyze forensic artifacts. We also have developed a novel KGQA model that serves as a natural-language user interface to the IoT forensic KG. Our evaluation results show that, compared to existing KGQA models, ForensiQ demonstrates higher accuracy in answering natural language questions when applied to our experimental IoT forensic KG.

Keywords: Internet of Things · Digital Forensics · Knowledge Graph · Ontology Design · Question Answering

1 Introduction

The rapid adoption of Internet of Things (IoT) not only has resulted in exciting transformation in many sectors, e.g., industry 4.0, smart cities, and smart health, but also has introduced significant challenges in terms of IoT cybersecurity. Recent years have witnessed a quickly growing interest in IoT forensics, as the involvement of IoT in cyber criminal activities becomes increasingly popular. However, the heterogeneous nature of IoT devices and the enormous volume of data they generate make it nearly impossible for IoT forensic investigators, especially those in their early career phases, to possess extensive expertise and up-to-date knowledge in the forensic techniques required for IoT forensics. A recent survey [33] emphasizes the pressing challenges faced by cybersecurity

This work was supported in part by the National Science Foundation (award no. 1663105) and National Security Agency (award no. H98230-20-1-0408).

S. Goel and P. R. Nunes de Souza (Eds.): ICDF2C 2023, LNICST 571, pp. 300–314, 2024.
https://doi.org/10.1007/978-3-031-56583-0_20

practitioners, including the need for technical training, software, and education in IoT digital forensics. There is a strong and critical demand for a more effective framework to support IoT forensic practitioners especially those inexperienced investigators in investigating and promptly responding to IoT-related crimes and security incidents.

Knowledge graph question answering (KGQA) offers a new perspective and approach to facilitate IoT forensic investigation process, assist forensic investigators, and lower the overheads associated with IoT forensics (e.g., learning and searching). Knowledge graphs (KGs) provide a structured representation of real-world objects and their relationships, forming the graphs (often sparse) that can be processed and analyzed using graph algorithms. KGQA systems can leverage Natural Language Processing (NLP) to interpret user intents and reason over KGs. Moreover, KGQA models are capable of answering complex, domain-specific questions. Recent studies show that they can outperform large language models (LLMs) such as GPT-3 and ChatGPT [23,31].

In this paper, we propose ForensiQ, an IoT forensics framework based on KGQA, to address those challenges faced by forensic investigators in IoT forensic investigations. ForensiQ is aimed to simplify and facilitate the access to and analysis of forensic artifacts and cybersecurity knowledge. In ForensiQ, complex forensic artifacts collected from crime scenes are first transformed into structured KGs and then enriched with cybersecurity knowledge. To answer case specific natural language questions, ForensiQ employs a combination of the LLM and graph neural network (GNN) based KGQA model, utilizing the KG as the data source. Leveraging ForensiQ, a variety of overheads such as learning and searching associated with IoT forensics can be significantly reduced, and the analysis of forensic artifacts can be expedited.

Our main contributions are summarized as follows:

1. We have designed a knowledge graph ontology specifically for IoT forensic data analysis. This ontology serves as a standardized vocabulary for organizing case related data and guiding the construction of the IoT forensic knowledge graph.
2. We have curated a comprehensive dataset for IoT forensic KGQA by collecting data from multiple sources. This dataset serves as a valuable resource for evaluating IoT forensic KGQA systems and enables future research in the field of IoT KGQA.
3. We have developed a novel KGQA model for IoT forensics that combines a large language model and a graph neural network. Our experiments demonstrate the effectiveness of the new model in accurately answering natural language questions about the IoT forensic knowledge graph.

The rest of this paper is organized as follows: We provide a brief background and related work on IoT forensics and KGQA in Sect. 2. We then detail our proposed framework in Sect. 3 and present the experimental setup and results in Sect. 4. Finally, we conclude this paper in Sect. 5.

2   Background and Related Work

Digital forensics in IoT can be broadly divided into three categories based on the scope of operation: device forensics, network forensics, and cloud forensics [15]. In device forensics, the investigator acquires the target IoT device from the crime scene and collects evidence directly from the device. This approach focuses on data extracted from the device, such as multimedia files (image, audio, video), local databases, and log files. For example, Alabdulsalam et al. examined the Apple Watch Series 2 and manually extracted messages, pictures, and emails [1], while Li et al. conducted a digital forensic operation simulation on an Amazon Echo using the Alexa Pi and dumped the device's firmware to an image file [21].

As IoT devices are usually connected to a network, network forensics is crucial for identifying cyber attacks in an IoT environment and collecting evidence for subsequent analysis and incident response. This aspect of IoT forensics often employs networking tools such as packet sniffers and analyzers to monitor abnormal activities at the network level. For instance, Rizal et al. proposed a network forensics model to detect flooding attacks on IoT devices, using WireShark to capture and examine network traffic [25]. Koroniotis et al. developed the Particle Deep Framework (PDF) for IoT network forensics, which integrates a deep neural network based on particle swarm optimization algorithms to detect and trace abnormal events in IoT networks [18].

Many IoT devices transmit personal data to cloud providers for functionality and analysis. The involvement of cloud-based processing and storage introduces new challenges to IoT forensics. Cloud forensics is a new approach to tackling digital forensics for cloud-enabled IoT environments. One major issue with cloud forensics is trust, as cloud providers may collude with malicious parties to conceal illegal activities. To address this issue, the Open Cloud Forensics (OCF) model has been proposed to help cloud architects build a forensics-aware cloud infrastructure that supports trustworthy cloud forensic investigations [35]. Another primary challenge for cloud forensics is legal regulation. Data territoriality, cloud content ownership, user authentication, and data preservation are among the main issues that must be considered in cloud forensic investigation [16].

The popularity of deep learning powered natural language processing has sparked extensive research in the field of natural language QA. KGQA, in particular, utilizes structured multi-relational data from a knowledge graph to deliver accurate and reliable results for QA tasks. A KG or knowledge base (KB) is a structured graph representation of facts. It is formally defined as

$$\mathcal{G} = \{(s,p,o)|s,o \in \mathcal{E}, p \in \mathcal{R}\}, \tag{1}$$

where each (s,p,o) is a triple or fact, with s as the subject entity, p as the predicate, and o as the object entity. The entity set is denoted as $\mathcal{E}$ and the relation set as $\mathcal{R}$. In KGQA, the objective is to predict a set of answers $\mathcal{A}_q$ for a given natural language question q, based on a knowledge graph $\mathcal{G}$. For simple questions, the answers can be directly retrieved from the entity set $\mathcal{E}$ ($\mathcal{A}_q \subseteq \mathcal{E}$).

However, for more complex questions, especially those involving numerical or aggregation operations, the answer may need to be derived from the information contained within the knowledge graph.

A KG ontology serves as a framework for understanding domain knowledge and acts as a blueprint for KGs. It promotes the sharing and reuse of domain knowledge by importing concepts from other ontologies or extending its coverage to subdomains. Standard ontologies have been established for IoT, including the Semantic Sensor Network (SSN) Ontology [11], the Smart Applications REFerence (SAREF) ontology [6], and the oneM2M base ontology [24]. In the field of digital forensics, Dosis et al. proposed an innovative approach to representing and integrating digital evidence from various sources using ontologies [8]. Ellison et al. developed an ontology for reactive digital forensics techniques, organizing them based on their purposes and providing a formalized framework [10]. Regarding digital forensics analysis, Sikos et al. outlined four types of knowledge that can be utilized: technical knowledge, investigation process knowledge, cybersecurity knowledge, and case-specific knowledge [30].

Research on integration of IoT and KGQA has increased significantly due to KGQA's capability of providing an intuitive interface for complex domain knowledge. Li et al. developed a KGQA system specifically for smart care of elderly individuals with chronic diseases, improving access to relevant knowledge for primary care staff [19]. In the smart grid sector, Yun et al. designed a fault operation and maintenance KG, along with a QA system for diagnosing faults in electric information collection systems [34]. Tan et al. utilized KG to model concepts in the electric power customer service business and introduced a QA application architecture to enhance customer service intelligence [32]. Chen et al. demonstrated AgriKG, a KG-based agricultural information system that extracts agricultural knowledge from unstructured text and enables QA through subgraph matching [4].

3 Proposed Approach

A high level overview of the ForensiQ framework is shown in Fig. 1. This framework integrates KG ontology design, KG construction, and KGQA into the six phases of the IoT forensic investigation process, which are evidence identification, device acquisition, data extraction, data analysis, evidence examination, and reporting [2]. The investigation begins by identifying forensic artifacts crucial for establishing the crime. Once the relevant evidence is identified, the investigator can utilize ontologies to define the core concepts and attributes related to the specific artifacts under examination. Forensic artifacts, such as log files and network traces, are transformed into structured KGs. This transformation can be achieved through either rule-based or heuristic parsers. The resulting KGs are then intricately linked with common cybersecurity KGs, forming a comprehensive forensic KG through the KG fusion process. Finally, to answer the investigator's natural language questions regarding the case, a KGQA model is trained using the forensic KG and a set of generated questions.

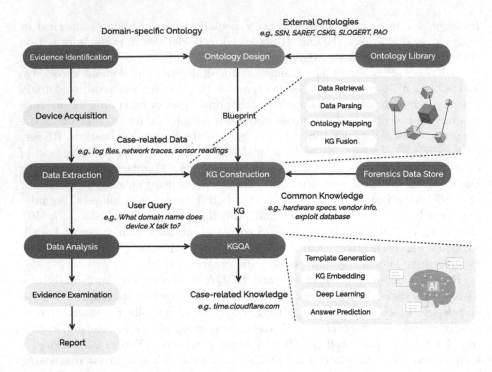

Fig. 1. The ForensiQ IoT forensics framework

3.1   Ontology Design

The proposed IoT forensics ontology is visually presented in Fig. 2. Building upon the SAREF ontology, which defines the properties, functions, and measurements of IoT devices, our ontology extends it further. It incorporates additional concepts to describe ownership, locality, and connectivity of IoT devices. To capture a comprehensive representation of IoT devices, we introduce concepts such as organization, hardware and software information, location, and networking capabilities. These concepts establish connections with well-defined external ontologies that model crucial artifacts generated within IoT environments. Notably, we incorporate the Semantic LOG ExtRaction Templating (SLOGERT) [9] for representing log events and templates, and the Packet Analysis Ontology (PAO) [29] for handling network captures. Furthermore, the inclusion of the SEPSES Cybersecurity KG [17] enriches the ontology by providing valuable resources for identifying vulnerabilities and weaknesses in IoT hardware and software. This assists investigators in identifying potentially compromised IoT devices.

3.2   KG Construction

To create an IoT forensic KG for investigation, we begin by collecting case-related artifacts from the crime scene using forensic data extraction tools. Meanwhile,

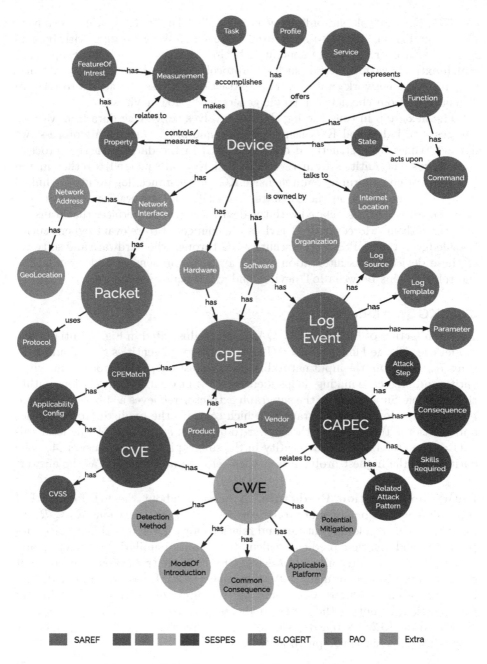

Fig. 2. High-level overview of the proposed ontology

we gather auxiliary cybersecurity knowledge from official sources, including vulnerability databases and vendor information, which can be valuable for the case. Then, we employ data parsing tools to process the unstructured data and build the KG. For example, an online log parser called Drain [12] is used to convert plain-text IoT log files into structured log events. When dealing with binary-formatted network captures generated by IoT devices, we rely on Scapy [26], which extracts various details such as protocol, host, and other packet information from the network captures. This extraction process enables us to retrieve crucial data from the network traffic generated by IoT devices.

The next step in constructing the KG involves converting data from various sources into individual KGs using ontology mapping. During this process, we extract triples from structured data generated in the data extraction process. Afterwards, the entities from the individual KGs are merged together in the KG fusion step to form a comprehensive KG. For instance, log events are linked to IoT devices based on the software responsible for generating the logs, and network packets are associated with the device's network interfaces that transmit or receive them. Moreover, IoT devices are connected to relevant cybersecurity knowledge in the SEPSES cybersecurity KG through the hardware and software of these devices. This integration allows for a comprehensive understanding of the relationships between IoT devices and cybersecurity standards.

3.3 KGQA Model

The architecture of ForensiQ's KGQA model is illustrated in Fig. 3. Initially, the model uses a large language mode (LLM) to infer topic entities $\mathcal{E}_q \subseteq \mathcal{E}$ and relations $\mathcal{R}_q \subseteq \mathcal{R}$ from the input natural language question q. This process, known as entity and predicate linking, helps identify relevant entities and relations within the question. Subsequently, the subgraph extractor retrieves a subgraph $\mathcal{G}_q$ from the IoT forensic knowledge graph $\mathcal{G}$, which contains the predicted topic entities and relations. To determine the answer to question q, the answer predictor calculates the probability of each entity in the subgraph being the answer $\mathcal{A}_q$. The entity with the highest probability is then selected and returned as the answer.

Entity and Relation Predictors. A question about the IoT forensic KG typically contains one or more topic entities $\mathcal{E}_q \subseteq \mathcal{E}$ and relations $\mathcal{R}_q \subseteq \mathcal{R}$. To identify the most relevant entities and relations for a given question q, the entity predictor and relation predictor calculate semantic similarity between q and every entity $e \in \mathcal{E}$. Pretrained LLMs like BERT [7] are trained on extensive text data and are effective for many natural language tasks. Hence, we employ BERT-based models in predictors to measure the proximity of entities and relations to the question. Denoting the entity predictor as $f_e(\cdot)$, the relation predictor as $f_r(\cdot)$, and the LLM as $f_{\text{LLM}}(\cdot)$, the semantic similarity between q and an entity e or relation r can be computed as follows:

$$f_e(q, e) = f_{\text{LLM}}([q; \text{SEP}; e]), \tag{2}$$

$$f_r(q, r) = f_{\text{LLM}}([q; \text{SEP}; r]). \tag{3}$$

Here, $[a; b]$ represents string concatenation of a and b, and SEP denotes BERT's sentence separation token. The entities and relations with the highest similarities are selected as $\mathcal{E}_q$ and $\mathcal{R}_q$.

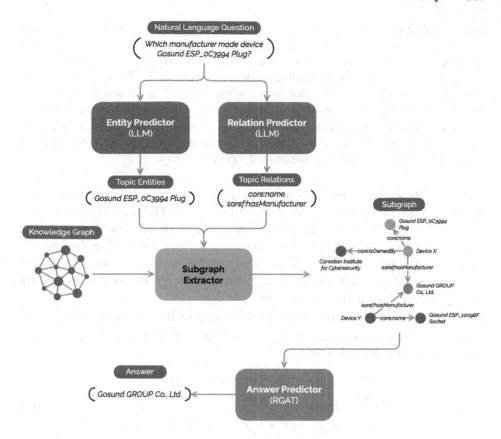

Fig. 3. Overview of the KGQA model architecture

The entity and relation predictors are trained using margin ranking loss to effectively distinguish true topic entities (positive samples) from others (negative samples). Negative sampling is employed during training, which randomly selects only a small number of negative samples for each question. This approach enhances training efficiency and creates a more balanced dataset, considering that the number of positive samples in the original KG is several magnitudes smaller than that of negative samples. Given the similarity f_e of a positive entity and $f_{e'}$ of a negative entity, the loss function for the entity predictor is defined as follows:

$$\mathcal{L}_e = \sum_{e,e' \in \mathcal{E}} \max(0, m - (f_{e'} - f_e)), \tag{4}$$

where m represents the desired maximum distance between f_e and $f_{e'}$. Similarly, the loss function for the relation predictor is defined as:

$$\mathcal{L}_r = \sum_{r,r' \in \mathcal{R}} \max(0, m - (f_{r'} - f_r)). \tag{5}$$

Subgraph Extractor. Utilizing the entity and relation predictors' predictions, the subgraph extractor retrieves the subgraph $\hat{\mathcal{G}}$ from the original KG, representing the question and its answer. This extraction process significantly narrows down the search space by excluding irrelevant KG entities. To construct $\hat{\mathcal{G}}$ containing $\mathcal{E}_q$ and $\mathcal{R}_q$, the extractor first retrieves the k-hop closed neighborhood of all nodes in $\mathcal{E}_q$. Next, edges not present in $\mathcal{R}_q$ are removed, along with any orphan nodes. In addition, inverse edges are incorporated into $\hat{\mathcal{G}}$ to account for reverse relations in q. To enhance the robustness of the answer predictor, a fixed number of random edges are introduced into $\hat{\mathcal{G}}$ as noise.

Answer Predictor. The answer predictor employs a variant of GNN called Relational Graph Attention Network (RGAT) [3]. The predictor comprises a learnable entity embedding module $f_{\text{EMB}}(\cdot)$, L RGAT convolution layers $f_{\text{RGAT}}(\cdot)$, and a linear output layer $f_{\text{OUT}}(\cdot)$. It takes all entities $\mathcal{E}_{\hat{\mathcal{G}}}$ and the edge features of all edges in $\hat{\mathcal{G}}$ as input and generates an array of scores $S_q = \{s_1, s_2, \ldots, s_N\}$, where $N = |\mathcal{E}_{\hat{\mathcal{G}}}|$. Each score represents the probability of an entity in $\hat{\mathcal{G}}$ being the answer entity.

Denote the edge features from the ith entity to the jth entity as $e_{i,j}^{(r)}$, and the hidden state of all entities in $\mathcal{E}_{\hat{\mathcal{G}}}$ at the lth RGAT layer as $\boldsymbol{H}^{(l)}$. The answer predictor can be defined as follows:

$$\boldsymbol{E} = \{e_{i,j}^{(r)}\} \in \mathbb{R}^{C \times B}, r \in \mathcal{R}, (i, r, j) \in \hat{\mathcal{G}}, \tag{6}$$

$$\boldsymbol{H}^{(0)} = f_{\text{EMB}}(\mathcal{E}_{\hat{\mathcal{G}}}) \in \mathbb{R}^{N \times F}, \tag{7}$$

$$\boldsymbol{H}^{(l)} = f_{\text{RGAT}}(\boldsymbol{H}^{(l-1)}, \boldsymbol{E}) \in \mathbb{R}^{N \times F'}, 1 \leq l \leq L, \tag{8}$$

$$S_q = \text{Sigmoid}(f_{\text{OUT}}(\boldsymbol{H}^{(L)})) \in \mathbb{R}^N. \tag{9}$$

Here, $C = |\hat{\mathcal{G}}|$ represents the number of edges in $\hat{\mathcal{G}}$, B is the dimension of the edge features, F is the dimension of the entity features, and F' is the dimension of the entity's hidden state. During inference, the scores S_q are ranked from highest to lowest, and answers with the highest scores are returned since there may be multiple correct answers to a question. The model is trained using binary cross-entropy loss:

$$\mathcal{L}_a = \sum_{i=1}^{N} (y_i \log s_i + (1 - y_i) \log(1 - s_i)), \tag{10}$$

where y_i is either 1 or 0, indicating if the ith entity is the answer entity or not.

4   Experimental Details

4.1   Dataset

To construct the IoT forensic KG for the KGQA evaluation, we curated 43 devices from the CIC IoT dataset [5] and generated four synthetic devices. These devices were enriched with annotations including manufacturer, model, software, hardware, and geolocation information. Manufacturer and model details were obtained using FingerBank[1], a hardware fingerprinting service. The SEPSES Cybersecurity KGs were generated using data from the NIST NVD and MITRE, up until January 2023. The PAO KG was created using network captures from the CIC dataset on January 3, 2022. Additionally, we incorporated log files from Loghub [13] since the CIC IoT dataset lacks IoT device log files.

The KG obtained consists of over 6 million unique subject entities and approximately 45 million triples. Over 80% of the triples originate from the SEPSES Cybersecurity KGs, while PAO triples make up around 14.2% of the total. Triples from other sources such as SAREF and SLOGERT represent only a small portion. To reduce the dataset size and improve relevance to forensic investigation, we removed less relevant triples. Additionally, we balanced the number of triples across all the KGs by randomly sampling from SEPSES, PAO, and SLOGERT KGs. As a result, the reduced KG contains only 0.4% of the triples from the original full KG.

The QA dataset was created using a template-based approach. We manually crafted over 100 question templates and their corresponding SparQL templates based on the ontology design. By inserting randomly selected subject entities into the question templates and utilizing the SparQL templates, we generated over 10,000 synthetic questions. The dataset was then split into training, validation, and testing datasets with an 8:1:1 ratio. Regarding question complexity, the majority of the dataset (69.7%) consists of simple one-hop questions, while two-hop questions account for 23.6% of the total. The number of hops in a question indicates the minimum steps required to reach the answer entities from the subject entity in the KG, with more hops indicating greater complexity.

4.2   Baselines

Fine-tuned LLM. We fine-tuned the RoBERTa [22], a BERT-based model, on our dataset to evaluate its effectiveness in answering IoT forensic questions. A fully-connected linear layer was added as a multi-class classifier for answer entities.

KEQA [14]. KEQA utilizes pretrained KG embeddings (KGE) and employs head entity and predicate embeddings learning, head entity token detection, and joint search to locate the answer entity within the KG.

EmbedKGQA [27]. EmbedKGQA learns a question embedding that captures the relations between the head entity and the answer entity mentioned in the question. It predicts the answer by scoring and ranking entities in the KG using KGE and a scoring function.

TransferNet [28]. TransferNet employs a multi-step approach for KGQA, allowing the model to "jump" from the topic entity to the answer entity. At

---

[1] https://www.fingerbank.org.

each step, the model attends to edges differently by considering the input question.

SSKGQA [20]. SSKGQA predicts the semantic structure of a question and retrieves query graphs based on the predicted structure. It ranks candidate query paths and answer entities using a graph ranking model.

It is important to note that EmbedKGQA, TransferNet, and SSKGQA assume the topic or head entity has already been identified prior to inference. In contrast, the fine-tuned LLM, KEQA, and our model do not make this assumption.

4.3   KGQA Results

We evaluate the accuracy of KGQA models using Hits@k, defined as follows:

$$\text{Hits@k} = \frac{1}{|\mathcal{Q}'|} \sum_{q \in \mathcal{Q}'} \left(\mathbb{1}\big(\exists \text{rank}(a|q) \leq k, a \in \mathcal{A}_q\big) \right). \tag{11}$$

Here, $\mathcal{Q}'$ represents the test question set, $\text{rank}(a|q)$ is the rank of the correct answer a to question q among all answer predictions generated by the model, and $\mathcal{A}_q$ is the set of correct answers for question q. The function $\mathbb{1}(cond)$ equals 1 when $cond$ is true, and 0 otherwise.

Table 1. KGQA Performance of Evaluated Models on the IoT Forensic QA Dataset

Model	Hits@1				Hits@3				Hits@10			
	1-hop	2-hop	3-hop+	Overall	1-hop	2-hop	3-hop+	Overall	1-hop	2-hop	3-hop+	Overall
RoBERTa	36.02%	50.19%	14.06%	38.17%	42.56%	62.65%	25.00%	46.44%	48.40%	73.15%	48.44%	54.52%
KEQA	49.10%	0.39%	1.56%	34.13%	70.93%	0.39%	1.56%	49.23%	96.24%	7.78%	1.56%	68.56%
Ours	**87.76%**	**77.82%**	**59.38%**	**83.56%**	**89.57%**	**82.88%**	**60.94%**	**86.15%**	89.71%	**87.94%**	62.50%	**87.60%**
EmbedKGQA	88.73%	72.37%	**60.94%**	82.98%	89.85%	82.10%	**65.63%**	86.44%	90.26%	86.38%	**68.75%**	87.98%
TransferNet	90.68%	72.76%	39.06%	83.08%	91.10%	73.93%	42.19%	83.85%	91.10%	73.93%	42.19%	83.85%
SSKGQA	**91.10%**	65.76%	48.44%	82.21%	**93.32%**	71.21%	48.44%	85.10%	**97.22%**	80.54%	53.13%	**90.38%**
Ours (w/o EP)	89.43%	**82.88%**	**60.94%**	**86.06%**	89.71%	**85.60%**	60.94%	**86.92%**	89.71%	**89.49%**	60.94%	87.88%

The performance of the KGQA models on questions of varying complexities is summarized in Table 1. Our proposed model achieves an overall Hits@1 of 83.56% on the testing QA dataset. For simple 1-hop and 2-hop questions, our model achieves Hits@1 ranging from 77% to 87%, while for more complex questions, it achieves around 60% Hits@1. Compared to the models such as RoBERTa and KEQA that do not require topic entities as input, our model shows a significant improvement in Hits@k (ranging from 19% to 45%) for questions of all complexities.

To ensure a fair comparison with the models that require topic entities as input, we conducted a benchmark by replacing the entity predictor (EP) with ground truth topic entities as input to the subgraph extractor. The corresponding Hits@k results are presented in the lower section of Table 1. The results demonstrate that our model outperforms previous works in making accurate predictions on the IoT forensic QA dataset, especially for 2-hop questions, as indicated by the Hits@1 and Hits@3 scores. Furthermore, our model achieves an overall Hits@1 result (83.56%) that is comparable to state-of-the-art KGQA models (83.08%) when utilizing the entity predictor.

Table 2. Hits@1 of Evaluated Models on Each Category

Model	SAREF	SEPSES	PAO	SLOGERT	Extra
RoBERTa	22.22%	38.94%	33.89%	6.38%	71.43%
KEQA	15.56%	43.43%	42.78%	0.00%	8.40%
Ours	**97.78%**	**81.20%**	**90.56%**	**87.23%**	**76.47%**
EmbedKGQA	75.56%	81.20%	97.22%	69.15%	84.03%
TransferNet	57.78%	82.36%	**100.00%**	**100.00%**	57.14%
SSKGQA	88.89%	82.20%	**100.00%**	74.47%	58.82%
Ours (w/o EP)	**100.00%**	**83.69%**	90.56%	87.23%	**84.87%**

Table 2 provides the Hits@1 results categorized by the answer categories of the KGQA models. Our approach outperforms the other methods in answering questions related to SAREF, SEPSES, and Extra categories, which predominantly consist of 2-hop and 3-hop+ questions. However, our method struggles with 1-hop questions in the PAO and SLOGERT categories. In these cases, TransferNet and SSKGQA achieve perfect Hits@1 scores of 100%.

We also conducted an ablation study to examine the impact of the entity predictor (EP) and relation predictor (RP) on the accuracy of our model. Table 3 presents the Hits@1 results for our model when EP and/or RP are replaced by ground truth topic entities and relations. Compared to using only the answer predictor with ground truth inputs, incorporating EP and RP results in a 4% decrease in accuracy. EP has a slightly larger impact, causing a 2.50% decrease, compared to RP with a 2.34% decrease, across questions of all complexities. However, for complex questions with three or more hops, RP has a more pronounced effect on the overall prediction accuracy compared to EP.

Table 3. Hits@1 of Proposed Model without Entity Predictor (EP) and/or Relation Predictor (RP)

Model	1-hop	2-hop	3-hop+	Overall
Ours	87.76%	77.82%	59.38%	83.56%
Ours (w/o EP)	89.43%	82.88%	60.94%	86.06% (+2.50%)
Ours (w/o RP)	87.76%	80.93%	68.75%	84.90% (+2.34%)
Ours (w/o EP & RP)	89.43%	85.99%	71.88%	87.50% (+3.94%)

5   Conclusions

We have presented ForensiQ, a framework powered by KGQA for IoT forensics, in this paper. ForensiQ transforms unstructured forensic data into comprehensible KGs. Moreover, it allows users to perform natural language queries for intricate forensic artifacts. To achieve this, we have designed an ontology specifically for IoT forensics by integrating well established ontologies in the field. Utilizing this ontology, we have constructed an experimental KG dataset for IoT forensics. Furthermore, we have developed a KGQA model based on LLM and GNN techniques, which can effectively respond to natural language questions related to the KG. The evaluation results demonstrate the superior performance of our KGQA model compared to several existing models when it comes to answering complex questions.

References

1. Alabdulsalam, S., Schaefer, K., Kechadi, T., Le-Khac, N.-A.: Internet of things forensics – challenges and a case study. In: DigitalForensics 2018. IAICT, vol. 532, pp. 35–48. Springer, Cham (2018). https://doi.org/10.1007/978-3-319-99277-8_3
2. Atlam, H.F., Hemdan, E.E.D., Alenezi, A., Alassafi, M.O., Wills, G.B.: Internet of things forensics: a review. Internet Things **11**, 100220 (2020)
3. Busbridge, D., Sherburn, D., Cavallo, P., Hammerla, N.Y.: Relational graph attention networks. arXiv preprint arXiv:1904.05811 (2019)
4. Chen, Y., Kuang, J., Cheng, D., Zheng, J., Gao, M., Zhou, A.: AgriKG: an agricultural knowledge graph and its applications. In: Database Systems for Advanced Applications, pp. 533–537 (2019)
5. Dadkhah, S., Mahdikhani, H., Danso, P.K., Zohourian, A., Truong, K.A., Ghorbani, A.A.: Towards the development of a realistic multidimensional IoT profiling dataset. In: 2022 19th Annual International Conference on Privacy, Security & Trust (PST), pp. 1–11 (2022)
6. Daniele, L., den Hartog, F., Roes, J.: Created in close interaction with the industry: the smart appliances REFerence (SAREF) ontology. In: Formal Ontologies Meet Industry, pp. 100–112 (2015)
7. Devlin, J., Chang, M.W., Lee, K., Toutanova, K.: BERT: pre-training of deep bidirectional transformers for language understanding. In: Proceedings of the 2019 Conference of the North American Chapter of the Association for Computational Linguistics: Human Language Technologies, Volume 1 (Long and Short Papers), pp. 4171–4186 (2019)
8. Dosis, S., Homem, I., Popov, O.: Semantic representation and integration of digital evidence. Procedia Comput. Sci. **22**, 1266–1275 (2013). https://doi.org/10.1016/j.procs.2013.09.214
9. Ekelhart, A., Ekaputra, F.J., Kiesling, E.: The SLOGERT framework for automated log knowledge graph construction. In: The Semantic Web, pp. 631–646 (2021)
10. Ellison, D., Ikuesan, R.A., Venter, H.S.: Ontology for reactive techniques in digital forensics. In: 2019 IEEE Conference on Application, Information and Network Security (AINS), pp. 83–88 (2019)

11. Haller, A., Janowicz, K., Cox, S., Phuoc, D.L., Taylor, K., LefrançSois, M.: Semantic sensor network ontology. W3c recommendation, W3C (2017)
12. He, P., Zhu, J., Zheng, Z., Lyu, M.R.: Drain: an online log parsing approach with fixed depth tree. In: 2017 IEEE International Conference on Web Services (ICWS), pp. 33–40 (2017)
13. He, S., Zhu, J., He, P., Lyu, M.R.: Loghub: a large collection of system log datasets towards automated log analytics. arXiv preprint arXiv:2008.06448 (2020)
14. Huang, X., Zhang, J., Li, D., Li, P.: Knowledge graph embedding based question answering. In: Proceedings of the Twelfth ACM International Conference on Web Search and Data Mining, pp. 105–113 (2019)
15. Janarthanan, T., Bagheri, M., Zargari, S.: IoT forensics: an overview of the current issues and challenges. In: Montasari, R., Jahankhani, H., Hill, R., Parkinson, S. (eds.) Digital Forensic Investigation of Internet of Things (IoT) Devices. ASTSA, pp. 223–254. Springer, Cham (2021). https://doi.org/10.1007/978-3-030-60425-7_10
16. Karagiannis, C., Vergidis, K.: Digital evidence and cloud forensics: contemporary legal challenges and the power of disposal. Information **12**(5), 181 (2021)
17. Kiesling, E., Ekelhart, A., Kurniawan, K., Ekaputra, F.: The SEPSES knowledge graph: an integrated resource for cybersecurity. In: The Semantic Web – ISWC 2019, pp. 198–214 (2019)
18. Koroniotis, N., Moustafa, N., Sitnikova, E.: A new network forensic framework based on deep learning for internet of things networks: a particle deep framework. Futur. Gener. Comput. Syst. **110**, 91–106 (2020)
19. Li, A., Wei, Q., Han, C., Xing, X.: Research on the construction of smart care question answering system based on knowledge graph. Procedia Comput. Sci. **214**, 1595–1602 (2022)
20. Li, M., Ji, S.: Semantic structure based query graph prediction for question answering over knowledge graph. In: Proceedings of the 29th International Conference on Computational Linguistics, pp. 1569–1579 (2022)
21. Li, S., Choo, K.K.R., Sun, Q., Buchanan, W.J., Cao, J.: IoT forensics: amazon echo as a use case. IEEE Internet Things J. **6**(4), 6487–6497 (2019)
22. Liu, Y., et al.: RoBERTa: a robustly optimized BERT pretraining approach. arXiv preprint arXiv:1907.11692 (2019)
23. Omar, R., Mangukiya, O., Kalnis, P., Mansour, E.: ChatGPT versus traditional question answering for knowledge graphs: current status and future directions towards knowledge graph Chatbots. arXiv preprint arXiv:2302.06466 (2023)
24. oneM2M: oneM2M Technical Specification TS-0012-V3.7.3. onem2m technical specification, oneM2M (2021)
25. Rizal, R., Riadi, I., Prayudi, Y.: Network forensics for detecting flooding attack on internet of things (IoT) device. Int. J. Cyber-Secur. Digit. Forensics **7**(4), 382–390 (2018)
26. Rohith, R., et al.: SCAPY- a powerful interactive packet manipulation program. In: 2018 International Conference on Networking, Embedded and Wireless Systems (ICNEWS), pp. 1–5 (2018)
27. Saxena, A., Tripathi, A., Talukdar, P.: Improving multi-hop question answering over knowledge graphs using knowledge base embeddings. In: Proceedings of the 58th Annual Meeting of the Association for Computational Linguistics, pp. 4498–4507 (2020)
28. Shi, J., Cao, S., Hou, L., Li, J., Zhang, H.: TransferNet: an effective and transparent framework for multi-hop question answering over relation graph. In: Proceedings

of the 2021 Conference on Empirical Methods in Natural Language Processing, pp. 4149–4158 (11 2021)

29. Sikos, L.F.: Knowledge representation to support partially automated honeypot analysis based on wireshark packet capture Files. In: Intelligent Decision Technologies 2019, pp. 345–351 (2020)

30. Sikos, L.F.: AI in digital forensics: ontology engineering for cybercrime investigations. Wiley Interdisc. Rev. Forensic Sci. **3**(3), e1394 (2021)

31. Tan, Y., et al.: Evaluation of ChatGPT as a question answering system for answering complex questions. arXiv preprint arXiv:2303.07992 (2023)

32. Tan, Y., et al.: Research on knowledge driven intelligent question answering system for electric power customer service. Procedia Comput. Sci. **187**, 347–352 (2021)

33. Wu, T., Breitinger, F., Baggili, I.: IoT ignorance is digital forensics research bliss: a survey to understand IoT forensics definitions, challenges and future research directions. In: Proceedings of the 14th International Conference on Availability, Reliability and Security (2019). https://doi.org/10.1145/3339252.3340504

34. Yun, F., Feng, Z., Baofeng, L., Yongfeng, C.: Research on intelligent fault diagnosis of power acquisition based on knowledge graph. In: 2019 3rd International Conference on Electronic Information Technology and Computer Engineering (EITCE), pp. 1737–1740 (2019)

35. Zawoad, S., Hasan, R., Skjellum, A.: OCF: an open cloud forensics model for reliable digital forensics. In: 2015 IEEE 8th International Conference on Cloud Computing, pp. 437–444. IEEE (2015)

I've Got You, Under My Skin: Biohacking Augmentation Implant Forensics

Steven Seiden[1,2]([✉]), Ibrahim Baggili[1,2], and Aisha Ali-Gombe[2]

[1] Baggil(i) Truth (BiT) Lab, Center of Computation & Technology,
Baton Rouge, LA, USA
[2] Division of Computer Science & Engineering, Louisiana State University,
Baton Rouge, LA, USA
sseide3@lsu.edu

Abstract. Recently, people have become interested in embedding technology in their bodies to augment themselves with new abilities. For example, a person may embed a chip in their hand to wirelessly lock and unlock a door. Subdermal augmentation implants, the implant technology that can add these new abilities to a user, are increasing in popularity. With this new technology comes a variety of new forensics and security challenges. In our work, we conceive a modified forensics approach for augmentation implants, which includes device discovery and its associated forensic acquisition and memory analysis. First, we explore three device discovery methods: implant chip reading, X-Ray detection and the use of metal detectors. We then share a case study by implementing an augmentation implant authentication system, acquiring and analyzing its memory. Our results show that when an implant is installed in raw chicken meat, that X-Ray scanners are capable of not only unveiling it, but revealing the exact type of implant to a trained analyst. In the case of metal detectors, only one of the implants were detected, and our results indicate deeply installed implants (1.5 cm or more below the skin) are undetectable. In the case of using RFID and NFC scanners to read compatible chips, we found we could detect the implants up to 1.6 cm and 1.0 cm respectively. We also examined the potential legal and ethical issues surrounding augmentation implant forensics, highlighting cases in which surgical removal could potentially be legally mandated.

Keywords: Biohacking · Implants · Forensics · Ethics

1 Introduction

Due to advancements of modern technology, biohacking, or the act of modifying one's body with the goal of adding an ability, is becoming popular. One of the more common ways that people are biohacking themselves is through subdermal implants. Currently, the most common types of subdermal implants are storage devices that employ one of two wireless technologies: Near Field

S. Goel and P. R. Nunes de Souza (Eds.): ICDF2C 2023, LNICST 571, pp. 315–332, 2024.
https://doi.org/10.1007/978-3-031-56583-0_21

Communication (NFC) and Radio Frequency Identification (RFID) (Matthews 2015). Surveys have shown that as biohacking technology becomes easily accessible, more people would consider it (Michael 2016). Reports showed that 13% of worldwide consumers are "extremely interested" in utilizing a subdermal implant as a form of payment, and 51% of European consumers would consider getting a subdermal implant (Shipper 2021, Marqueta 2021).

This paper examines the use of digital forensics techniques on subdermal implants. As these devices are implanted within a human's body, the process of discovering and potentially extracting them during an investigation can present unique challenges. Additionally, there may be legal, ethical, and procedural considerations that affect the validity of any evidence obtained through this process. To the best of our knowledge, no academic research has yet examined the impact of biohacking on the digital forensics field. We provide the following contributions:

- This is the primary study to explore the forensics of augmentation subdermal implants.
- We explore various device detection techniques on consumer available products using device scanners, metal detectors, and X-Ray technologies
- We explore the viability of memory forensics on an augmentation implant authentication system

To accomplish the aforementioned contributions, we tested the following hypotheses:

Hypothesis H_0 (Scanner Hypothesis). We can discover augmentation implants using an NFC or RFID scanner.

Hypothesis H_1 (Metal Detector Hypothesis). We can discover augmentation implants using metal detectors.

Hypothesis H_2 (X-Ray Hypothesis). We can discover augmentation implants using X-Rays.

Hypothesis H_3 (Verification System Hypothesis). We can retrieve meaningful data from an augmentation implant verification system.

The remainder of this paper is organized as follows: the overview of biohacking via subdermal implants, including a survey of the emerging market, itemizing usage, acceptability, risk, and potential discovery and data retrieval is provided in Sect. 2. Section 3.1 describes the experimental setup, methodology, and tools required for subdermal forensic analysis. This section also dives into the modified forensics process we have conceived for augmentation implants. We then illustrate a forensics investigation involving a subdermal implant based on an authentication system case study in Sect. 4. This is followed by the discussion of our findings and the review of biohacking impacts in Sect. 5. Section 6 describes the related works on subdermal implants and similar products and the novelty of our research contribution. Section 7 describes our future plans, and Sect. 8 concludes the paper.

2 Background

Table 1. A List of the Current Retailers Offering Augmentation Implants for Humans.

Seller	Purpose
Bioteq	General Purpose NFC/RFID
Dangerous Things	General Purpose NFC/RFID
Dsruptive	Medical
I Am Robot	General Purpose NFC/RFID
VeriChip	Medical & Identification
VivoKey	Identification
WalletMor	Payment

Publicly Disclosed Occurrences of People Biohacking Themselves With Subdermal Implants

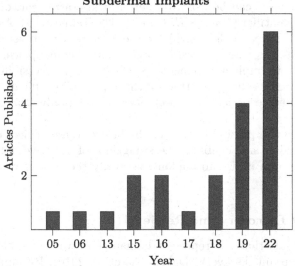

Fig. 1. The Number of Online Articles Describing an Individual Biohacking Themselves With Subdermal per Year Surveyed, Starting With 2005.

2.1 Implants in Practice

To understand how biohacking has emerged over the past few decades, we surveyed online documented cases of people utilizing biohacking on themselves. We found that these cases are growing, as shown in Fig. 1. A major part of today's biohacking involves employing subdermal implants – electronic devices embedded within one's skin that emit a wireless signal. These implants have a variety of uses, such as unlocking doors, storing medical information, and acting as payment methods. While medical implants have existed for some time, the implants used for biohacking differ greatly in that they add additional features to the human body, rather than aiding or correcting existing ones. Thus, to make this distinction clear, we will be referring to these subdermal implants as *augmentation implants*. Amal Graafsta has made these augmentation implants much more attractive to the general population. Graafsta first implanted himself in 2006 with an RFID implant designed for pets, one of the first known cases in which an implant of this kind was installed in a human (TEDx 2013).

Today, several retailers sell augmentation implants designed for human implantation. As seen in Table 1, different companies produce implants for a wide variety of purposes. Some implants are designed for a specific purpose, such as storing medical information or payment methods, where as others exist for those who want to utilize the popular NFC and RFID however they chose.

2.2 Utilizing Implants in an Attack

Augmentation implants today are often used as an identification method. For example, an implant can be used to open a lock, start a car, or store another type of unique identifier (*Red XSIID bundle* 2022, Tanne 2004). As demonstrated by (Patel et al. 2018), it is possible to clone certain portions of the memory on these devices. As this practice becomes more commonplace, the risk of an attacker cloning an implant also increases. Due to the inaccessibility of surgically implanted devices, resolving an attack of this type can be difficult once the attack has been executed, especially for implants with read-only storage (Halamka et al. 2006).

There is also the possibility that in the future, these devices can store more than simple credentials, enabling the smuggling of sensitive data. To discover how an attacker can utilize an implant, we study the various ways a device can be discovered.

2.3 Implant Discovery and Retrieval

Utilizing materials that can represent human skin, we first explore the various methods for implant discovery (Dąbrowska et al. 2016). By implanting several augmentation implants into these materials, we are able to create a realistic implantation scenario. From here, we are able to test different means of implant discovery, such as through an RFID/NFC scanner, X-Ray or metal detector.

Once an augmentation device has been discovered, the data will need to be retrieved. Due to the nature of surgical augmentation implants, this step in the forensic analysis process can prove to be difficult. While current implants feature wireless protocols such as NFC and RFID, direct access to the device via surgical removal may be required for an in-depth analysis in the future. This introduces a new dimension of legal issues over whether or not a surgical removal can be forced upon someone with an augmentation implant, which we will discuss further in Sect. 5.

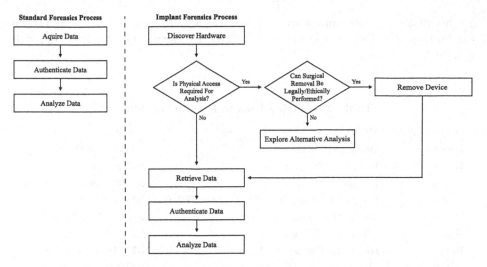

Fig. 2. Comparing Typical Forensics to That of Augmentation Implants.

3   Methodology and Tools

3.1   Augmentation Implants Forensics Process

To perform forensic analysis of augmentation implants, we first needed to devise our approach. A typical forensics process includes:

- The acquisition of hardware and data for analysis
- The authentication of the extracted digital data
- The analysis of the acquired data

With augmentation implants, the forensics process becomes convoluted. Therefore, to conduct a thorough forensics investigation, we devised a revised methodology. A comparison between the traditional forensics process and our modified implant forensic process is shown in Fig. 2. As shown in our modified process, the major setback will occur in the device discovery phase, as well as the physical extraction of the device through surgical removal. These additional steps add a new set of dimensions to the forensics process. We explore both of these challenges in detail in our studies.

In our work, we physically inspect several augmentation implants currently available on the market. After inspecting the implants, we performed our case study. This involves attempting to apply our modified forensics process (Sect. 3.1) to the implants. The first step of this process involves device discovery. We explore different detection methods and the use case scenarios of the discovery methods are determined. Next we study the process of device removal for the cases where this may be necessary, focusing on the process to legally and ethically do so. After this, we explore the methods of data retrieval from the implants. This allows us to perform data authentication and analysis. Our methodology can be summarized as follows: 3.2) Materials Used 3.3) Device Implanting 3.4) Device Detection 3.5) Data Retrieval and Analysis and 3.6) Device Removal.

Table 2. Materials Used to Perform Our Study.

Device Type	Model	Usage
Implant	DangerousThings xSIID	NFC Implant
Implant	DangerousThings xEM	RFID Implant
Implant	DangerousThings flexEM	RFID-emulation Implant
Implant	DangerousThings flexDF2 DESFire EV2 8kB	NFC Implant
Writer	DangerousThings Proxmark	RFID Sniffer/Writer
X-Ray	Triumph II SPECT/CT	Device Detection
Reader	DangerousThings KBR1	NFC Device Reading
Reader	FlipperZero	RFID Device Reading
Metal Detector	Ranseners HTY1	Device Detection
Metal Detector	Garrett Pro-Pointer II	Device Detection

3.2   Materials Used

We used a variety of augmentation implants from implant retailer *DangerousThings*, as outlined in Table 2. The augmentation implants utilized either NFC or RFID technologies. The xSIID and xEM devices take one of the most common forms for augmentation implants, encasing the technology in a bioglass cylinder (*Red XSIID bundle* 2022) (See Fig. 3). The flexDF2 and flexEM (See Fig. 3) implants, on the other hand, are encased in a thin flexible sheet of body-safe plastic. Both forms of implants were used during our studies.

3.3   Implant Installation

To conduct an augmentation implant detection study, we began with device injection. As human testing was impractical for this study, we simulated a real scenario by implanting the devices into synthetic, silicone skin, as well as raw chicken meat bought from a store. We employed both regular and boneless raw chicken legs. We follow the standard procedure for product installation, injecting the implants into the different mediums. This installation process can be seen in Fig. 4, in which a needle is used to inject an implant underneath synthetic skin.

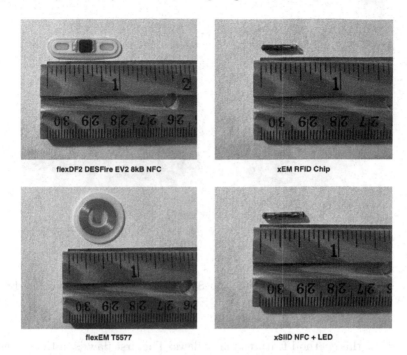

Fig. 3. Examples of Augmentation Implants.

3.4 Implant Detection

A major concern of ours is the detection of augmentation implants. Due to the nature of subdermal implants, the technology can be easily smuggled in a person's body, undetectable by visual analysis. If an adversary is utilizing one of these implants, it first needs to be discovered before it can be examined. Therefore, we introduce several methods in which subdermal implants can be detected. Many of these implants use NFC and/or RFID technologies, which means using an NFC or RFID scanner should allow an examiner to easily detect a device embedded in one's skin. This can be demonstrated in Fig. 4, in which an xSIID implant inserted below synthetic skin is responding to an NFC scanner.

Table 3. The Various Ways to Discover and Locate Implants in the Human Body.

	Pros	Cons	Use Case
Ultrasound	No Radiation Implant Easy to Identify	Needs Physical Contact Limited Scanning Area Scans Are Slow	Searching Single Individual High Accuracy Needed
X-Ray	Scans Are Fast Broad Scanning Area	Radiation Dosage Implant Harder to Identify	Searching Many People Medium Accuracy Needed
Terahertz Scanner	No Radiation Scans Are Fast	Implant Not Always Identifiable	Searching Many People Low Accuracy Needed
Metal Detector	No Radiation Scans Are Unobtrusive	Very Low Detection Rate	Searching Most People Lowest Accuracy Needed

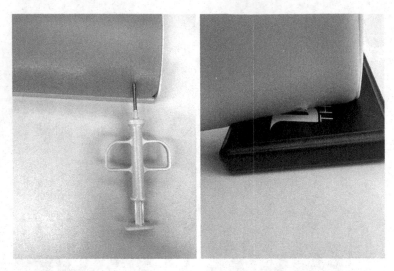

Fig. 4. Injecting the xSSID Implant Into Synthetic Skin and Scanning the Implant From Within the Skin.

However, this method features many flaws. The first flaw is in the extremely limited range of NFC and RFID technologies, in which a scanner has to be within a few centimeters of a chip in order to receive a signal from an implant. The second flaw is that these scanners can only pick up on NFC or RFID signals if the implant is located close to the surface of the skin. Thus, if an attacker wanted to employ this type of implant to smuggle data, they could merely implant the device deeply enough as to not be able to read data without removal. To combat these concerns, we surveyed several technologies that can aid in implant discovery.

The first issue we tackled was finding alternative means of detecting subdermal implants. Matthews (2022) discussed how ultrasound technology could be used in scenarios in which an individual has been identified as a suspect of smuggling an implant. X-Ray technology could be used for searching a large group of people, in potentially more secure environments where accuracy is more important. Terahertz technology could also be applied in searching through large groups, though it may have more trouble detecting deeply implanted devices than the first two methods. Table 3 summarizes each of these technologies and the benefits and drawbacks to each.

3.5   Data Retrieval and Analysis

The next step in forensic analysis is data retrieval. We employed several augmentation implants to study the process of retrieving data from said devices. There are two primary ways to access the data from these devices. The first method is using a scanner such as the Proxmark (See Table 2). The Proxmark scanner supports reading a wide variety of wireless technology and can be used to read data from many augmentation implants on the market today. Once the data is read, it can be either used for analysis or written to another chip in order to impersonate an individual. The same copying approach may be used in future digital forensics investigations to preserve a copy of the evidence.

The second method of acquiring data from augmentation implants is through their companion applications. Implants with specific features for health monitoring or payment can come with a companion smartphone application *(Walletmor* 2021, Dsruptive 2021). These smartphone applications can be used to read data from the implants, as well as write data to them. Other, more generic augmentation implants are meant to work with authentication systems. These systems read data from the augmentation implants to verify if a user is authorized for a specific action like unlocking a door. By analyzing the data read by these authentication systems, we can reveal data stored on the implants, as discussed further in Sect. 4.4.

3.6 Device Removal

During the digital forensics process, physical access to hardware is often critical as it allows for data to be acquired, authenticated and analyzed. However, this requirement can be challenging when attempting to pull data directly from implantable devices because physical access requires surgical removal.

Current augmentation implants can be analyzed by simply reading their data wirelessly. In the future, however, this is likely to change with the advancement of augmentation implant technology. Thus, in the future, a scenario in which one's augmentation implant will need to be removed is increasingly likely.

This brings into question many ethical and legal questions. We can examine existing laws and rulings to infer how augmentation implants will be treated in the future. When someone is defending themselves in court in the United States, they are given certain ethical rights. For example, the rights to medical privacy are granted unless a warrant is provided (Ramirez 2020). People also have protection from unreasonable search and seizure (Team 2022). These protections disallow general body searches, which would encompass searching for an augmentation implant. However, once a warrant is generated, these protections are no longer in effect.

At the same time, however, there are laws in place that allow for a full investigation to ensue unimpeded. In the future, the same rights could be applied towards subdermal augmentation implant removal. This could mean that not only removing the devices, but searching for them entirely, could be disallowed. In past rulings it has been decided that if deemed necessary a defendant could be mandated to take medication to properly represent themselves in court. Therefore, the same could potentially be applied to the removal of biohacking devices (Lieberman 2006).

4 Studies and Results

Our case study included discovering and performing a forensic analysis on augmentation implants available at the time of writing. Our work included two studies. The first was experimenting with three major ways of discovering augmentation implants. The second a proof-of-concept memory analysis of an NFC authentication system that employs the DangerousThings KBR1 alongside a simple authentication program to verify the identifier of scanned augmentation devices.

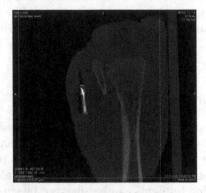

Fig. 5. An X-Ray of an xSIID Implant Within a Bone-in Chicken Thigh.

Fig. 6. An X-Ray of an xEM Implant Within a Boneless Chicken Thigh.

Fig. 7. Testing The flexEM T5577 Implant Being Embedded at Different Depths.

4.1   NFC/RFID Reader Analysis

Table 4. Results of Scanning for the flexEM T5577 Implant using the FlipperZero RFID Reader (left) and Scanning for the flexDF2 DESFire Implant using the DangerousThings KBR1 NFC Reader (right)

0.5 cm	Detected		0.3 cm	Detected
1.0 cm	Detected		0.5 cm	Detected
1.3 cm	Detected		0.7 cm	Detected
1.4 cm	Detected		1.0 cm	Detected
1.5 cm	Detected		1.3 cm	Undetected
1.7 cm	Undetected		1.4 cm	Undetected

To test hypothesis H_0, we embedded various implants into the synthetic silicone skin and attempted to detect them with the DangerousThings KBR1 RFID and FlipperZero NFC readers. All of these implants became undetectable by their respective readers once they were embedded below a certain depth beneath the skin. For this experiment we tested embedding two implants, the flexEM T5577 RFID implant and the flexDF2 DESFire NFC Implant. As seen in Table 4, the flexEM T5577 and flexDF2 DESFire were detectable (meaning no pressure of the metal detector on the skin was required) until embedded at 1.7 cm and 1.3 cm, respectively.

4.2   Metal Detector Analysis

Table 5. Results of Scanning for the flexEM T5577 Implant Using the Garrett Pro-pointer II.

0.5 cm	Detected
1.0 cm	Detected
1.2 cm	Detected
1.4 cm	Detected
1.5 cm	Undetected
1.8 cm	Undetected

To test hypothesis H_1, we performed device discovery using a similar method to our scanner detection, but with the Garrett Pro-Pointer II and Ranseners

HTY1 handheld metal detectors, as shown in Fig. 7. Discovery via metal detectors proved difficult. The Ranseners HTY1 failed to detect all of the implants, even before they were implanted into a medium. The Garrett Pro-Pointer II failed to detect all but the flexEM T5577 implant. The flexEM T5577 augmentation implant was detectable when implanted under the synthetic silicone skin up to about 1.4 cm below the surface, as shown in Table 5.

4.3   X-Ray Analysis

To test hypothesis H_2, we employed a three dimensional X-Ray computed tomography imaging system as one method of device detection. Analyzing the images produced by this system clearly revealed that an implant existed within the meat (See Sect. 3.3), regardless of whether or not bones were present. This is shown in Figs. 5 and 6 and a trained analyst may be able to distinguish between the different types of implants based on the X-Ray. Therefore, it can be presumed that X-Ray technology is feasible to reveal augmentation implants when needed.

4.4   Forensic Case Study

To date, one of the most common applications for augmentation implants is controlling door access. In such a system, an NFC or RFID reader is present. This reader reads data from an implant and verifies whether or not the implant's unique ID is present within an allow-list stored on a server that the scanner communicates with. If the ID is determined to be valid, the user will be successfully authenticated; otherwise, the user will be rejected by the system.

Additionally, certain high-security access points control access through smart cards with NFC and EMV technology. Certain implant retailers, such as DangerousThings, offer to convert EMV cards into implants. Due to the inability to clone EMV chips, these retailers must outfit the original chip to create an implant (Madhoun et al.(2018), *Making payments with an implant* (2017)). This inability to clone these chips is significant because it means that an EMV implant is guaranteed to be the original implant, and not a clone, if successfully verified. Because authentication systems verify the unique augmentation implant ID, this system has the ability to reveal at what time an individual was attempting to authenticate. A forensic analysis of this data may be vital for an investigation, which is what we study below.

To test hypothesis H_3, we constructed an implant authentication system simulating standard door access control. An overview of this system is shown in Fig. 8 with the high-level code in Listing 1.1. For the implementation, we utilized the flexDF2 implant. This system also used the KBR1 NFC reader to read the ID from the implant. By creating a Python program, we built an access controller that reads the device ID from the implant and uses this to authenticate a user. To proceed with a forensics study of this scenario, we ran the program in a VMware VM, and connected the KBR1 NFC reader to the VM. We then presented the implant to the reader, asking the program to authenticate the device. An example of this program running is shown in Fig. 9. After the program had successfully authenticated the device, we analyzed the memory dump of the machine. In Fig. 10, the device ID for the flexDF2 implant can be found in the memory of the machine. Therefore, if one has an implant, especially one that is guaranteed to be an original, such as an implant with EMV technology, it can be shown at what time a specific person was present at a reader. Because of the difficulty in removing and implanting these devices, it is highly unlikely that the physical implant has been stolen or traded. This shows the feasibility of being able to acquire forensically relevant data from these systems and augmentation implants in real-world scenarios.

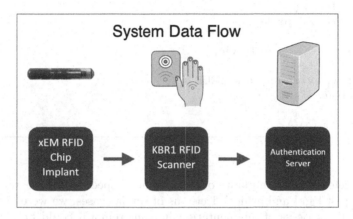

Fig. 8. An Overview of Our Implant Verification System.

```
@research-vm:~$ python3 auth.py
Ready to scan device.
04561F1ABE5B80
Access granted to key 04561F1ABE5B80 at 18:46:59 04/19/23
Ready to scan device.
```

Fig. 9. An Example of a Program Used to Authenticate NFC Chips Being Run.

5   Discussion

By devising our augmentation implant forensics process, we were able to successfully apply the digital forensics process to the emerging field of augmentation implants. This process first involves determining several methods of device discovery. We then created a realistic scenario in which we could approach device discovery through x-rays and metal detectors. Utilizing x-ray technology successfully revealed that an implant existed, illustrating the feasibility of a method that could be used to discover a device. Utilizing metal detectors largely failed and most likely could only detect larger augmentation implants embedded closer to the surface of the skin.

```
p4g...   . g...   .-.. ..|.4g...    g...
                               .hU...  poe...  p.a...
j...  pUb... ...       ..      ...    p..
Access granted to key 04561F1ABE5B80 at 18:46:59 04/19/23 .#> 43
..HM.FA- .     K..R2Q G. (.. =D?.  .*.% .. J& $. ... . 01<../ C..
8 .; .!PE).   '7I9.N .T. , ..+ ....0.... ...Y .e 0.j...  ..f...
```

Fig. 10. The Memory Dump From a Virtual Machine Running the NFC Authentication Program. The ID of the Scanned Implant Is Highlighted.

Listing 1.1 . Authentication System Code

```
1  waitForInput()
2  // Device is presented
3
4  allowDevice = scanDevice()
5
6  if allowDevice equals TRUE
7      authenticate()
8  else
9      restrict()
```

After detecting an implant, one important aspect is device removal. By reviewing past legal and ethical decisions of similar cases, we were able to estimate how the process of augmentation implant removal could be treated. We found that while suspects are often granted the right to medical privacy, this can be navigated around if deemed necessary to conduct a criminal investigation. For example, blood can be tested without requiring a warrant (*Mitchell v. Wisconsin* 2019). Of course, surgical removal is much more invasive than simply drawing blood. We can examine one case in which surgical removal occurred; in a case in New Orleans, Louisiana, a suspect had been shot by a store clerk in self-defense. The injury was non life-threatening, leading the bullet to stay lodged within the suspect. A judge had decided that the bullet would provide meaningful evidence, issuing a warrant mandate surgical removal of the bullet (*Hughes v. United States* 1981). Thus, we can assume that there is a good possibility that one may need to have an augmentation implant surgically removed if it is deemed that the implant can provide meaningful evidence and is not dangerous to remove.

We then evaluated the various means of data retrieval. The amount of data available to be retrieved is currently limited by the technology available with today's augmentation implants. In the future, we expect this technology to become more advanced, meaning that a physical analysis will become much more important. Therefore, rather than attempting to physically gather data from a device, we focused instead on gathering data from a typical implant verification system. In our forensic analysis we were able to reconstruct the ID of an implant, from a computer's memory, when a user presents their implant to a reader for authentication. This would also reveal the date and time a user attempted to authenticate. This information is forensically relevant, and is just one example of the data that can be pulled from state of the art augmentation implants.

6   Related Work

Previous research on these subdermal implants by (Kiourti 2018) primarily focused on studying the feasibility of incorporating NFC and RFID in internal medical devices. Previous research has also covered other types of medical implants, such as the VeriChip, which solely exists to store a serial number linking doctors to peoples' medical data (Tanne 2004). Another device, made by Dsruptive, can store patient information directly on the device (Dsruptive 2021). Research on these devices has explored the privacy and human rights violations that could come along with these implants (Foster & Jaeger 2007), (Sharpe 2008). As biohacking technology improves, the potential for abuse of said technology increases. In this paper, however, we study how this technology can be leveraged by an attacker, the process of discovering biohacking devices and acquiring data for a forensics investigation, analysis of the recovered data, and how these devices may change in the future.

6.1   Forensics of Related Devices

Past work has achieved forensic analysis on a wide variety of mobile devices and applications (Al Mutawa et al. 2012, Bader & Baggili 2010, Hassenfeldt et al. 2019, Husain et al. 2011). Many smart devices can be exploited for forensic analysis through their companion application (Moffett 2019, Awasthi et al. 2018). Certain implants, such as the Walletmor, utilize a companion application of their own (*Walletmor* 2021). Like other devices, forensic analysis can be applied to these companion applications to reveal important data.

Forensic analysis has also been applied to various medical devices, including medical implants (Schmitt 2022). (Grispos et al. 2019) demonstrates the ability to apply forensic analysis to implantable medical devices that communicate with smartphones. While this differs from our study of augmentation implants, the idea of applying forensics to wireless implants is similar.

The forensics process has also been applied to more uncommon electronics, such as mobile phone SIM cards and wireless carkeys (Savoldi & Gubian 2010, Bates 2019). Forensic Analysis has also been applied to the NFC recievers on mobile phones (Lakshmanan & Nagoor Meeran 2017) and wearable devices (Baggili et al. 2015). Forensic analysis has even been applied to Java Card applets a technology that certain implants utilize (Lanet et al. 2014, *VivoKey Apex* 2022).

However, no prior work has focused on biohacking. In our work, we performed forensic analysis on subdermal augmentation implants that people have biohacked into themselves. We evaluated how this analysis differs from that of other devices, and demonstrate how this analysis would take place in a realistic scenario.

7   Future Work

The augmentation implant field is rapidly changing as technology improves. Therefore, the forensic process applied to these implants will need to continuously improve to stay applicable. Future work should evaluate the changes within augmentation implants over time and the security impact that these changes make. For example, as these devices gain more computing power, physical analysis is expected to become more important. If these implants gain sophisticated computing power, wireless analysis of a device could only reveal some of the data required to conduct a thorough forensic analysis. Future work should also study other means of augmentation implant discovery. Our work primarily focused on device discovery through wireless scanners, X-Rays and metal detectors.

Lastly, since our work was limited to the analysis of memory, future work should explore other forensic sources such as companion devices, network, storage and cloud artifacts that may be applicable to augmentation implants.

8   Conclusion

As an emerging field, augmentation implants have the potential to make a major impact on the cybersecurity field, and may create new challenges for digital forensics. A major aspect of these devices is the possibility to be used to smuggle data. This is due to the hidden nature of the devices. We demonstrate the methodology for not only discovering these devices but acquiring data from both the devices themselves and systems that integrate them. In doing so, we are able to streamline a forensics process that will allow for the forensic analysis of augmentation devices.

References

Al Mutawa, N., Baggili, I., Marrington, A.: Forensic analysis of social networking applications on mobile devices. Digit. Investig. **9**, S24–S33 (2012)

Awasthi, A., Read, H.O., Xynos, K., Sutherland, I.: Welcome Pwn: almond smart home hub forensics. Digit. Investig. **26**, S38–S46 (2018)

Bader, M. Baggili, I.: iphone 3GS forensics: logical analysis using apple iTunes backup utility (2010)

Baggili, I., Oduro, J., Anthony, K., Breitinger, F. McGee, G.: Watch what you wear: Preliminary forensic analysis of smart watches. In: 2015 10th International Conference on Availability, Reliability and Security, pp. 303–311 (2015)

Bates, E.A.: Digital vehicle forensics (2019). https://abforensics.com/wp-content/uploads/2019/02/INTERPOL-4N6-PULSE-IssueIV-BATES.pdf

Dsruptive: Using implants for storing COVID vaccine certificates (2021). https://dsruptive.com/using-implants-for-storing-covid-vaccine-certificates/

Dąbrowska, A., et al.: Materials used to simulate physical properties of human skin. Skin Res. Technol. **22**(1), 3–14 (2016)

Foster, K.R., Jaeger, J.: RFID inside. IEEE Spectr. **44**(3), 24–29 (2007)

Grispos, G., Glisson, W.B., Cooper, P.: A bleeding digital heart: identifying residual data generation from smartphone applications interacting with medical devices. arXiv preprint arXiv:1901.03724 (2019)

Halamka, J., Juels, A., Stubblefield, A., Westhues, J.: The security implications of VeriChip cloning. J. Am. Med. Inform. Assoc. **13**(6), 601–607 (2006)

Hassenfeldt, C., Baig, S., Baggili, I., Zhang, X.: Map my murder: a digital forensic study of mobile health and fitness applications. In: Proceedings of the 14th International Conference on Availability, Reliability and Security, pp. 1–12 (2019)

Hughes v. United States (1981)

Husain, M.I., Baggili, I., Sridhar, R.: A simple cost-effective framework for iPhone forensic analysis. In: Baggili, I. (ed.) ICDF2C 2010. LNICST, vol. 53, pp. 27–37. Springer, Heidelberg (2011). https://doi.org/10.1007/978-3-642-19513-6_3

Kiourti, A.: RFID antennas for body-area applications: from wearables to implants. IEEE Antennas Propag. Mag. **60**(5), 14–25 (2018)

Lakshmanan, D., Nagoor Meeran, A.R.: NFC logging mechanism—forensic analysis of NFC artefacts on android devices. In: Dash, S.S., Vijayakumar, K., Panigrahi, B.K., Das, S. (eds.) Artificial Intelligence and Evolutionary Computations in Engineering Systems. AISC, vol. 517, pp. 93–101. Springer, Singapore (2017). https://doi.org/10.1007/978-981-10-3174-8_9

Lanet, J.-L., et al.: Memory forensics of a Java card dump. In: Joye, M., Moradi, A. (eds.) CARDIS 2014. LNCS, vol. 8968, pp. 3–17. Springer, Cham (2015). https://doi.org/10.1007/978-3-319-16763-3_1

Lieberman, E.C.: Forced medication and the need to protect the rights of the mentally ill criminal defendant. Cardozo Pub. L. Pol'y Ethics J. **5**, 479 (2006)

Madhoun, N.E., Bertin, E., Pujolle, G.: An overview of the emv protocol and its security vulnerabilities. In: 2018 Fourth International Conference on Mobile and Secure Services (MobiSecServ), pp. 1–5 (2018)

Making payments with an implant (2017). https://forum.dangerousthings.com/t/making-payments-with-an-implant/643

Marqeta: The European payments landscape in 2030 (2021). https://resources.marqeta.com/c/report-european-payments-landscape?x=hj28Ub&submissionGuid=95961be5-2b0b-4858-9459-d312087827a0

Matthews, D.: I got a computer chip implanted into my hand. Here's how it went.. (2015). https://www.vox.com/2015/9/11/9307991/biohacking-grinders-rfid-implant

Matthews, K.L.: Personal communication. Email correspondence (2022)

Michael, K.: RFID/NFC implants for bitcoin transactions. IEEE Consum. Electron. Mag. **5**(3), 103–106 (2016)

Mitchell v. Wisconsin (2019)

Moffett, O.: The digital forensics of internet-of-things devices, PhD thesis, Utica College (2019)

Patel, J., Das, M.L., Nandi, S.: On the security of remote key less entry for vehicles. In: 2018 IEEE International Conference on Advanced Networks and Telecommunications Systems (ANTS), IEEE, pp. 1–6 (2018)

Ramirez, A. (2020). https://www.aclu.org/news/privacy-technology/police-need-a-warrant-to-collect-dna-we-inevitably-leave-behind

Red XSIID bundle (2022). https://dangerousthings.com/product/red-xsiid-bundle/

Savoldi, A., Gubian, P.: Embedded forensics: An ongoing research about sim/usim cards. In: Handbook of Research on Computational Forensics, Digital Crime, and Investigation: Methods and Solutions, IGI Global, pp. 396–423 (2010)

Schmitt, V.: Medical device forensics. IEEE Secur. Priv. **20**(1), 96–100 (2022)

Sharpe, V.A.: Ethics and indemnification regarding the verichip. Am. J. Bioeth. **8**(8), 49–50 (2008)

Shipper, D.: Beyond cards and mobile phones: Payment form factors of the future (2021). https://aite-novarica.com/report/beyond-cards-and-mobile-phones-payment-form-factors-future

Tanne, J.H.: FDA approves implantable chip to access medical records. BMJ **329**(7474), 1064 (2004)

Team, W.D.: Unreasonable search and seizure (2022). http://law.cornell.edu/wex/unreasonable_search_and_seizure

TEDx: Biohacking - the forefront of a new kind of human evolution: amal graafstra at tedxsfu (2013). https://www.youtube.com/watch?v=7DxVWhFLI6E

VivoKey Apex (2022). https://www.vivokey.com/apex

Walletmor (2021). https://us.walletmor.com/pages/how-it-works-us

Quantum Computing Challenges and Impact on Cyber Security

Hassan Jalil Hadi[1], Yue Cao[1(✉)], Mohammed Ali Alshara[2], Naveed Ahmad[2], Muhammad Saqib Riaz[2], and Jun Li[3]

[1] School of Cyber Science and Engineering, Wuhan University, Wuhan, China
Yue.cao@whu.edu.cn
[2] College of Computer and Information Science, Prince Sultan University, Riyadh, Saudi Arabia
{malshara,nahmed,yjaved}@psu.edu.sa
[3] Datang Internet Technology (Wuhan) Co., Ltd and Hubei Engineering Research Center of Industrial Internet Integration Technology, Wuhan, China
jun_li@bjdv.com

Abstract. Quantum computers pose a significant danger to cyber security. If major fault-tolerant, quantum computers are built, the most extensively used cryptography techniques would fail. The present level of analysis, in terms of quantum technologies and applications, is still in its infancy. The researchers have a hazy view of how to prepare for future quantum computing breakthroughs, particularly in cyber security. The powerful quantum computers capable of breaching current cryptography protections are yet a decade or more away. History has demonstrated that transitioning to quantum-resistant techniques for classical cryptography will most likely take a quantifiable amount of time. In this paper, a comparative analysis of modern cryptographic algorithms concerning quantum computing is performed and its impact on cyber security has been reviewed.

Keywords: Quantum Computing · Quantum Cryptography · Cyber Security · AES · Quantum Key Distribution (QKD)

1 Introduction

Quantum computing (QC) is grounded in quantum mechanics. Quantum mechanics is the theory that regulates how nature operates at the atomic level. This technology can calculate in all four states at the same time, and this scales exponentially. Traditional computers will not be sped up by quantum computing (QC). Instead, it will give an exponential advantage for some sorts of operations, such as factoring very large numbers, with substantial implications for cyber security. Quantum computing (QC) has the potential to revolutionize cyber security in several ways. Cryptography depends heavily on the generation of random quantum numbers. The random generator techniques used by conventional random number generators are frequently manipulated since they are not

© ICST Institute for Computer Sciences, Social Informatics and Telecommunications Engineering 2024
Published by Springer Nature Switzerland AG 2024. All Rights Reserved
S. Goel and P. R. Nunes de Souza (Eds.): ICDF2C 2023, LNICST 571, pp. 333–343, 2024.
https://doi.org/10.1007/978-3-031-56583-0_22

truly random. High-tech companies are creating quantum random number generators (QRNG), which employ quantum optics to produce true unpredictability [1]. The foundation of QuantumSecure Communications (QKD) is the sharing of cryptographic keys between two or more entities, enabling them to secretly exchange information. This secure communication method makes use of quantum physics for entirely private exchanges of keys and can even detect the existence of an eavesdropper.

The potential of quantum computing to decrypt public-key encryption, notably the RSA algorithm, is its most contentious use in cyber security. The RSA encryption algorithm is the core of the almost \$4 trillion e-commerce industry [2]. Conventional computers would take billions of years to crack the RSA encryption algorithm on the other hand QC with around 4,000 error-free qubits potentially overcome RSA in seconds. Yet, this would take around 1 million noisy qubits being used today. Today's highly sensitive economic and national security information could be at high risk once a sufficiently strong QC becomes accessible. The threat of quantum computers to public-key cryptography has prompted the creation of quantum-resistant algorithms. Machine learning (ML) has similarly altered information security, enabling the discovery and avoidance of new threats. The cost of training deep ML models rises dramatically as the amount of data and complexity grows. Quantum machine learning (QML) is a novel arena that claims to improve ML algorithms tenfold faster, extra energy efficient, and more time efficient. Consequently, very effective procedures for recognizing and combating novel assault strategies might develop.

Cryptology is a phenomenon that means to deceive a message. The basic purpose of cryptology is to achieve the security principles i.e., confidentiality, integrity, and availability. Quantum computers can affect the existing techniques in both ways i.e., negatively, and positively. The negative side is that existing techniques could be broken up by quantum computers [4]. Scientists and researchers should be aware of these challenges and proper planning is required to overcome these challenges with timelines when quantum computers will become a reality [5]. Cryptographic techniques based on quantum computing will be more secure than existing cryptographic techniques. Symmetric cryptography is using a single key to encrypt and decrypt the message. Keeping that key secure is a great challenge, especially over public networks [3]. AES and DES is an important symmetric technique. Asymmetric cryptography has the advantage over symmetric cryptography in that it uses two keys instead of one. Encryption is done with one key, the public key, while decryption is done with the other key, the private key [5,7]. RCA and ECC are the two important asymmetric techniques. Quantum computing (QC) has the prospective to overhaul cyber security, but there are momentous difficulties to overwhelm and fundamental inventions to achieve.

A survey conducted in 2022 revealed that nearly half (47%) of the participants worldwide expressed significant worry about security risks associated with quantum computing. Out of all the countries, Australians were the most apprehensive, with 58% expressing concern. Quantum computing, based on the principles of quantum mechanics, has the potential to perform virtual experiments and solve intricate problems that are currently beyond the capabilities of conventional computers. However, cybersecurity experts are alarmed that this technology could potentially breach most modern cryptographic systems, making it a major security threat as shown in Fig. 1.

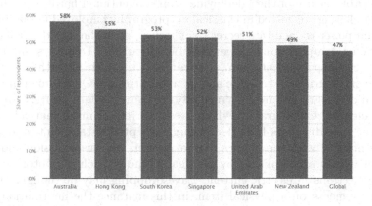

Fig. 1. Concerns about security threats of quantum computing worldwide in 2022

2   Motivation

Massive quantum computers will significantly upsurge computing volume, opening new possibilities for cyber defense. Defense in the nuclear age will have the aptitude to recognize and avert quantum-era threats before they cause any harm [4,6]. Though, QC might be a double-edged sword, meanwhile it may depict new vulnerabilities, such as the capability to rapidly respond to complex arithmetic problems, which are the groundwork of numerous types of encryptions. Industries and organizations may begin preparing now, while post-quantum cryptography ethics are still being determined. That's our motivation to endorse the capabilities and threats of quantum computing toward cyber security.

3   Research Contribution

– Quantum Computing is a new technology and research area that can become a danger to existing cybersecurity algorithms.
– According to the existing research materials, we have identified the challenges and dangers that could be faced by existing cryptographic algorithms.
– The possible solutions to safeguard the classical crypto algorithms have also been taken into consideration and analyzed.

4   Literature Review

Quantum cryptography is the very latest area with plenty of possibilities for advancement. There is a lot of work to be done, and so many issues remain unresolved. The Post Quantum cryptographic solutions are complex due to the unpredictable nature of their deployment on conventional hardware. The classical secret sharing suggested in classical cryptography employed traditional computational power to facilitate secret key sharing. With the introduction of quantum systems, computational power may be overturned. To understand the post-quantum cryptographic situation, it is required to go through the conventional or classic cryptographic structure and its applications in Quantum cryptography. Quantum cryptography provides new ways to communicate securely. Unlike traditional classical cryptography, which uses a variety of mathematical strategies to prevent eavesdroppers from decrypting encrypted data, quantum cryptography is concerned with the physics of information. The transmission and storage of data is always accomplished by physical methods, such as photons in optical fibers or electrons in electric current. Eavesdropping may be thought of as taking measurements on a physical item, in this instance the information carrier. The principles of physics dictate what the eavesdropper can measure and how he can measure it. We can develop and construct a communication system that can always detect eavesdropping using quantum processes. This is because investigations on the quantum transporter of information perturb it, leaving traces behind. From classical to quantum ciphers, here's a quick rundown of the hunt for unbreakable ciphers.

First, Richard Feynman gives the idea of quantum computing in 1982 which works on the principles of quantum mechanics. However, the first two-bit quantum computer was physically developed in 1998 [1]. These computers are very fast and have great computational capability as compared to traditional computers being used today. Quantum computers are a danger to current cryptosystems public key cryptosystems and private key cryptosystems used for data security [5]. Hash-based encryption is also in threat [4].

4.1   Public Key/Asymmetric Cryptography Affected

All of the current public key cryptography methods are based on the factorization of two big prime integers (RSA) and the computation of discrete (DSA and ECC) logarithms [3]. Asymmetric encryption now in use is at risk because of Shor's technique, which is based on huge prime integer factorization. Shor's algorithm's operation will be illustrated with the aid of an example. Let's say we're trying to determine the prime factors that make up the number 15.

This will need to be calculated using a 4-qubit register. Consider the 4-qubit register as a conventional computer's 4-bit register. Since 15 is represented by the binary number 1111, it is simple to determine the prime factors of 15 using a 4-qubit register. operations for every value (0–15) stored in the register can be performed which is the needed step required to perform on a quantum computer. The steps of the algorithm are described below (Table 1):-

Table 1. Qubit registers with remainders

Ref No	Type	Technique	Advantages	Limitation
[1–4]	Public key	RSA	– Dual Keys are involved. – Large Key length up to 2048 bits	– Slow Processing. – Shores algorithm can break it.
[1–3]	Public key	ECC	– Fast generation of keys. – Less computing power is required.	– Smaller Keys are needed. – Smaller quantum computers could break it.
[1–3]	Symmetric Key	AES	– Uses various length keys w.r.t application requirements. – Become more secure if the key length is twice. – Only method of attack is brute force	– Too simple algebraic structure. – Every block is encrypted similarly. – Grover's algorithm is dangerous.
[3]	Hash Function	SHA Family	– Secure from quantum computers	– Grover's algorithm is danger.
[1–4]	Public key	Shore's Algorithm	– It can break public key algorithms. – It is fast as compared to Grover's algorithm. – Polynomial time factorization	– It can factor short prime number only. – Thousands of qubits are required to break long keys.
[1,2,4]	Symmetric	Grover's Algorithm	– It can break symmetric cryptography. – Perfectly carry out algorithm scanning	– Its speed is slow

- Quantum Let $n = 15$, is the number whose factorization is required.
- $x = a$ random number will be selected such that $1 < x < n - 1$.
- x power is raised to every value available in the register and divided by n. The remainder of this operation will be stored in the second 4-qubit register which is the superposition results. Let's select $x = 2$ which is greater than 1 and smaller than 14.
- Received remainders as given in Fig. 1. If the x power is increased to every value in a 4-qubit register, which is a maximum value of 15, and then divided by 15. In the sequence of four numbers, we see that we receive remainders (1, 2, 4, and 8). We may deduce from these results that f = 4 is the sequence for $x = 2$ and $n = 15$. With the above equation, the value of f may be utilized to compute a potential factor. Factors to consider:

$$P = xf/2 - 1 \tag{1}$$

- If a result that isn't a prime number is produced, the process is repeated with alternative f values [3] (Fig. 2).

Register 1	0	1	2	3	4	5	6	7	8	9	10	11	12	13	14	15
Register 2	1	2	4	8	1	2	4	8	1	2	4	8	1	2	4	8

Fig. 2. 4 Qubit registers with remainders

4.2 Symmetric Cryptography Affected

Symmetric cryptography is based on one key called a private key which is used to encrypt the data and its inverse is used to decrypt the data [3]. Grover's created an algorithm that is used by quantum computers to break symmetric cryptography. It works on square root speed-up instead of the classical brute force algorithm. For example, for a $n - bit$ cipher quantum computer will take $2n/2$ time. It searches unsorted databases. This algorithm can search N entries in unsorted database in $\sqrt{N}$ searches. 56-bit DES can be decrypted in only 185 searches [3]. Its limitation is that it is slower than Shor's algorithm.

4.3 Hash-Based Cryptography/Key-Less Cryptography Affected

Hash-based cryptography is also facing the same danger from quantum computers as asymmetric and symmetric cryptography [3,4]. They contain fixed length cipher which is easily breakable by Grover's algorithm. Additionally, it is also tested that Grover's algorithm can be used in combination with the birthday paradox to break hash cryptography [3] (Table 2).

Table 2. Qubit registers with remainders

Ref No	Type	Technique	Advantages	Limitation
[10]	Quantum Communication	Implementation of multipolarities quantum communication network (QCN) By employing the cluster sate-based concept	– Used in distributed quantum computing. – Design for next generation of cyber security system (NGCCS)	– The PQC based on unproven assumptions. – Might be broken In future by developing more sophisticated quantum algorithm.
[11]	QKD for Security protocol	QPC protocol based on multi-particle enabled states (Bell State & 5- qubit state)	– Use of multi-particle entangled states design QPC protocols	– Security Analysis concern: It shows the attacks from outside eavesdroppers, and the attacks from participant and TP are all invalid to under testing protocol.
[12]	QKD for Security protocol	QKD protocol (BB84) deployment with practical implantation on IBM QX	– Using the BB84 protocol the existence of a third-party eavesdropper can be detected. – Observed that with a greater number of qubits that are sniffed by eavesdroppers, the detection will be higher	– Dedicated exercise on BB84 protocol only.
[13]	QKD for Security protocol	Use of protocol dependent on inherent secure nature of quantum cryptography	– Secure against internal and external eavesdropping, masquerading, and brute-force attacks	– Proposed Protocol is vulnerable to super Dense coding of quantum states
[14]	Quantum Security Scheme	A quantum security scheme (QSC)	– Simple Random (No Computation cost). – Intruder-Eve can be detected even on qubit	– Only for RSA based security protocols

4.4   Challenges to Quantum Computers

Several challenges are preventing quantum computers to become a reality [2]. These are probabilistic which means that quantum computers can generate thousands of other solutions besides the correct one. Qubits are not error-free, they can be affected by noise, heat, stray magnetic coupling. Qubits can be affected with bit-flips and phase errors. Coherence is another issue faced by qubits which means that qubits cannot maintain their state for a longer period [2,3].

4.5   Alternate Methods for Secure Communication

Different alternate methods are proposed for secure communication which is based on mathematical problems under the umbrella of post-quantum cryptography which are lattice-based cryptography, code-based cryptography, hash-based signatures, and Multivariate-based cryptography. Quantum cryptography is another proposed method which is based on quantum computing principles i.e., quantum key distribution (QKD) [5].

5   Discussion and Evaluation

RSA is the most important and widely used public key technique which exploits the difficulty of factorizing the product of two large prime numbers [8] Shore's algorithm is a real threat to RSA-2048 because it can factor prime numbers in polynomial time rather than exponential times [1]. It is tested in 2001 and successfully factored the prime number 15 using 7 qubits [2]. A Quantum computer with thousands of qubits is required to factorize the RSA-2048. It is the limitation of Shore's algorithm. It is not a permanent solution to increase the key size for securing the algorithms. There is a chance that RSA-2048 has the $1/7$ probability to break by 2026 and $\frac{1}{2}$ until 2031. ECC is another public key algorithm that is using the elliptic curve technique to encrypt the data. It has shorter keys to encrypt data which is the disadvantage of this algorithm [1,2]. A modified form of Shore's algorithm can break ECC easily [3,4].

Symmetric cryptography is based on one key called a private key which is used to encrypt the data and its inverse are used to decrypt the data [9]. It is more secure than public cryptography because no public key is involved in it. It can be broken by brute force attack which is not easy to break even by quantum computers because quantum computers must check each key combination to match. For a 128-bit cipher, it would take 6 months to check each possibility [10]. If the key size of symmetric algorithms is increased twice then they will provide the same level of security as quantum computers [11,12]. Hash functions also suffer the same threat from quantum computers as asymmetric and symmetric cryptography. To secure hash functions against Grover's algorithm, a hash function must provide 3-bit output for a b-bit security level. If the output size of the hash function is doubled then it will become quantum resistant. SHA-2 and SHA-3 with longer key outputs are safe against quantum computers [14].

6   Impact on Cyber Security

The technique of managing the risk associated with cyber security has become more reliable thanks to theories about quantum computing. Current risk management techniques rely on traditional probability methodologies since current cyber security risk management models are built around the behavior of cyber security [15]. Instead of employing human intellect, which is inadequate, these techniques combine Hilbert space with quantum cognition. From the perspective of cyber security, a risk is defined as the likelihood that threats to or assaults on cyber security assets may result in negative outcomes [16]. Although the foundations of classical probability theories serve as the basis for quantum cognitions, they can be substituted by the axioms of Hilbert space. It might create brand-new, highly efficient mental models by utilizing quantum cognition.

The technique of managing the risk associated with cyber security has become more reliable due to theories about quantum computing. Current risk management techniques rely on traditional probability methodologies since current cyber security risk management models are built around the behavior of cyber security. Instead of employing human intellect, which is inadequate, these techniques combine Hilbert space with quantum cognition. From the perspective of cyber security, a risk is defined as the likelihood that threats to or assaults on cyber security assets may result in negative outcomes. Although the foundations of traditional probability theories serve as the basis for quantum cognitions, they can be substituted by axioms of Hilbert space. It may create brand-new, highly efficient mental models by using quantum cognition. To better decision-making, it will aid in the understanding of the object, the detection of enemies, and the capabilities. Quantum cognition aids in the capacity to recognize superpositions of likely states that are hard to identify using conventional probability theories. In certain circumstances, the probability assets can depend on a single state instead of putting in just one perspective of a problem [17].

As a result of all these factors, quantum computing poses a major threat to our planet. And every nation competing for the top spot is paying close attention to this issue. The main issue with quantum computing is its capability to break practically every type of encryption now in use. Additionally, because of the state details, unauthorized parties may import information. The confidential data of other countries would be in jeopardy if state-sponsored hackers, who are being used in many battles, got their hands on quantum computers. Because, according to experts, the strength of quantum computers may easily break current encryption techniques like RSA, AES, DSA, and ECDSA [18]. Additionally, it will lead to a rise in uncertainty among nations, and they will all begin to doubt one another. This will provide the framework for spatial interactions that will be discouraging. After then, a conflict may even break out. If an unauthorized party manages to get their hands on a machine like this, not only state data but also the data of everyone else is at risk.

Another danger is that even if it is not spoken on the ground, combining a quantum computer with artificial intelligence would be disastrous. While an AI system might suggest a course of action, it is unable to analyze vast amounts of data and select the best option, as quantum computers can [19]. Therefore, the biggest threat to machines and artificial intelligence would be eliminated if those two fields ever united. Unfortunately, the largest threat to robots and the environment is people, therefore with power as previously described, quantum technology and AI might eliminate the whole human species without even removing the possibility to comprehend problems .

7   Conclusion and Future Direction

Quantum computing (QC) has the prospective to overhaul cyber security, but there are momentous difficulties to overwhelmed and fundamental inventions to achieve. Cryptographic techniques based on quantum computing will be more secure than existing cryptographic techniques. Several alternative approaches (under the umbrella of post-quantum cryptography) for secure communication-based on mathematical issues are presented. In the future, Mistrustful Quantum Cryptography (MQC), Position-based quantum cryptography and Device-independent quantum cryptography roles in quantum communication network would be analyzed.

Acknowledgement. The authors would like to thanks Prince Sultan University for the support by paying the registration fees of this article. This work is supported in part by the Wuhan AI Innovation Program (Grant No. 2023010402040020) and the Hubei Province Key Research and Development Program (Grant No. 2021AAA007).

References

1. Vaishnavi, A., Pillai, S.: Cybersecurity in the quantum era-a study of perceived risks in conventional cryptography and discussion on post quantum methods. J. Phys: Conf. Ser. **1964**, 042002 (2021). https://doi.org/10.1088/1742-6596/1964/4/042002
2. Kirsch, Z.J., Ming, C.: Quantum computing: the risk to existing encryption methods (2015)
3. Mavroeidis, V., et al.: The impact of quantum computing on present cryptography. arXiv preprint arXiv:1804.00200 (2018)
4. Arslan, B., et al.: A study on the use of quantum computers, risk assessment, and security problems. In: 2018 6th International Symposium on Digital Forensic and Security (ISDFS). IEEE (2018)
5. Mosca, M.: Cybersecurity in an era with quantum computers: will we be ready? IEEE Secur. Priv. **16**(5), 38–41 (2018)
6. Wallden, P., Kashefi, E.: Cyber security in the quantum era. Commun. ACM **62**(4), 120–120 (2019)
7. Nafis, N.M.: Quantum computing era in perspective of cyber security. No. 4012. EasyChair (2020). Wang, Lidong, and Cheryl Ann
8. Alexander. Cyber security during the COVID-19 pandemic. AIMS Electron. Electr. Eng. **5**(2), 146–157 (2021)
9. Kania, E.B., Costello, J.K.: Quantum technologies, US-China strategic competition, and future dynamics of cyber stability. In: 2017 International Conference on Cyber Conflict (CyCon US). IEEE (2017)

10. Riedel, M.F., Binosi, D., Thew, R., Calarco, T.: The European quantum technologies flagship program. Quantum Sci. Technol. **2**(3), 030501 (2017)
11. Djordjevic, I.B.: Cluster states-based quantum networks. In: IEEE Photonics Conference (IPC), vol. 2020, pp. 1–2 (2020). https://doi.org/10.1109/IPC47351.2020. 9252479
12. Ji, Z., Zhang, H., Wang, H.: Quantum private comparison protocols with several multi-particle entangled states. IEEE Access **7**, 44613–44621 (2019). https://doi. org/10.1109/ACCESS.2019.2906687
13. AL-Mubayedh, D., AL-Khalis, M., AL-Azman, G., AL-Abdali, M., Al Fosail, M., Nagy, N.: Quantum cryptography on IBM QX. In: 2019 2nd International Conference on Computer Applications & Information Security (ICCAIS), pp. 1–6 (2019). https://doi.org/10.1109/CAIS.2019.8769567
14. Ul Ain, N.: A novel approach for secure multi-party secret sharing scheme via quantum cryptography. In: 2017 International Conference on Communication, Computing and Digital Systems (C-CODE), pp. 112–116 (2017). https://doi.org/10.1109/ C-CODE.2017.7918912
15. Ford, P.: The quantum cybersecurity threat may arrive sooner than you think. Computer **56**(2), 134–136 (2023). https://doi.org/10.1109/MC.2022.3227657
16. Lakshmi, D., Nagpal, N., Chandrasekaran, S.: A quantum-based approach for offensive security against cyber attacks in electrical infrastructure. Appl. Soft Comput. **136**, 110071 (2023)
17. Dwivedi, A., Saini, G.K., Musa, U.I., Kunal.: Cybersecurity and prevention in the quantum era. In: 2023 2nd International Conference for Innovation in Technology (INOCON), pp. 1–6. Bangalore (2023). https://doi.org/10.1109/INOCON57975. 2023.10101186.
18. Csenkey, K., Bindel, N.: Post-quantum cryptographic assemblages and the governance of the quantum threat. J. Cybersecur. **9**(1), tyad001 (2023)
19. Fernández Pérez, I., Prieta, F.D.L., Rodríguez-González, S., Corchado, J.M., Prieto, J.: Quantum AI: achievements and challenges in the interplay of quantum computing and artificial intelligence. In: Julián, V., Carneiro, J., Alonso, R.S., Chamoso, P., Novais, P. (eds.) ISAmI 2022. LNNS, vol. 603, pp. 155–166. Springer, Cham (2023). https://doi.org/10.1007/978-3-031-22356-3_15

Correction to: Unraveling Network-Based Pivoting Maneuvers: Empirical Insights and Challenges

Martin Husák⬤, Shanchieh Jay Yang⬤, Joseph Khoury⬤, Đorđe Klisura⬤, and Elias Bou-Harb⬤

Correction to:
Chapter 9 in: S. Goel and P. R. Nunes de Souza (Eds.): *Digital Forensics and Cyber Crime*, **LNICST 571,** **https://doi.org/10.1007/978-3-031-56583-0_9**

The original published version of this chapter, abstract was incomplete. This now has been added.

The updated version of this chapter can be found at
https://doi.org/10.1007/978-3-031-56583-0_9

© ICST Institute for Computer Sciences, Social Informatics and Telecommunications Engineering 2024
Published by Springer Nature Switzerland AG 2024. All Rights Reserved
S. Goel and P. R. Nunes de Souza (Eds.): ICDF2C 2023, LNICST 571, p. C1, 2024.
https://doi.org/10.1007/978-3-031-56583-0_23

Author Index

Printed in the United States
by Baker & Taylor Publisher Services